O.D

OR DREAM

sters Detective Company

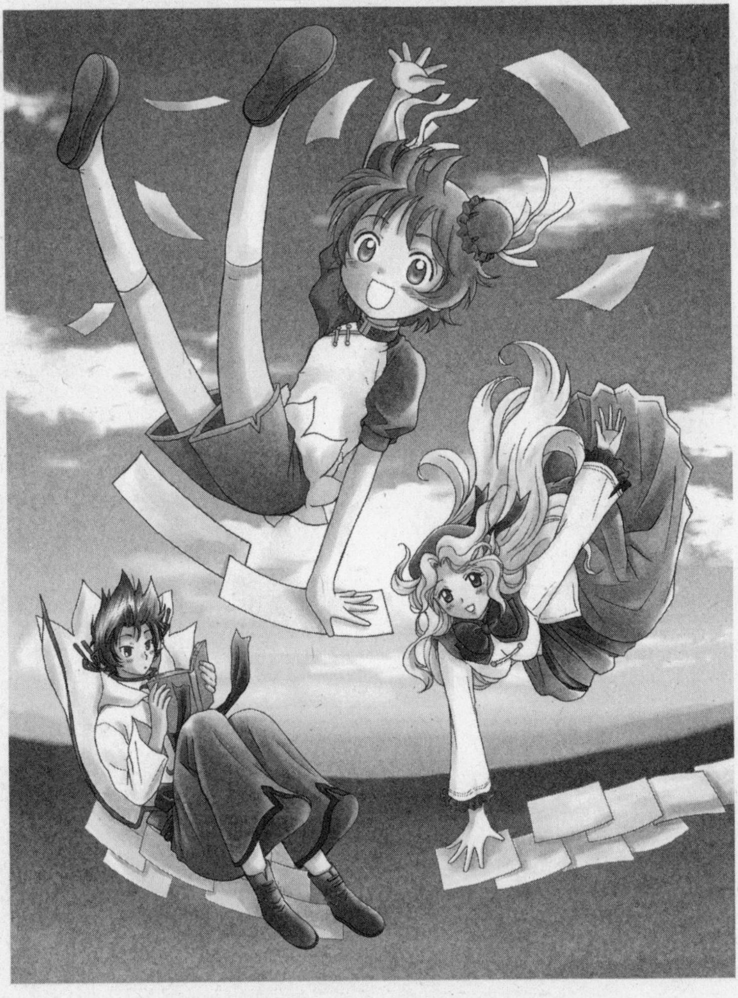

Story by Hideyuki Kurata

Art by Ran Ayanaga

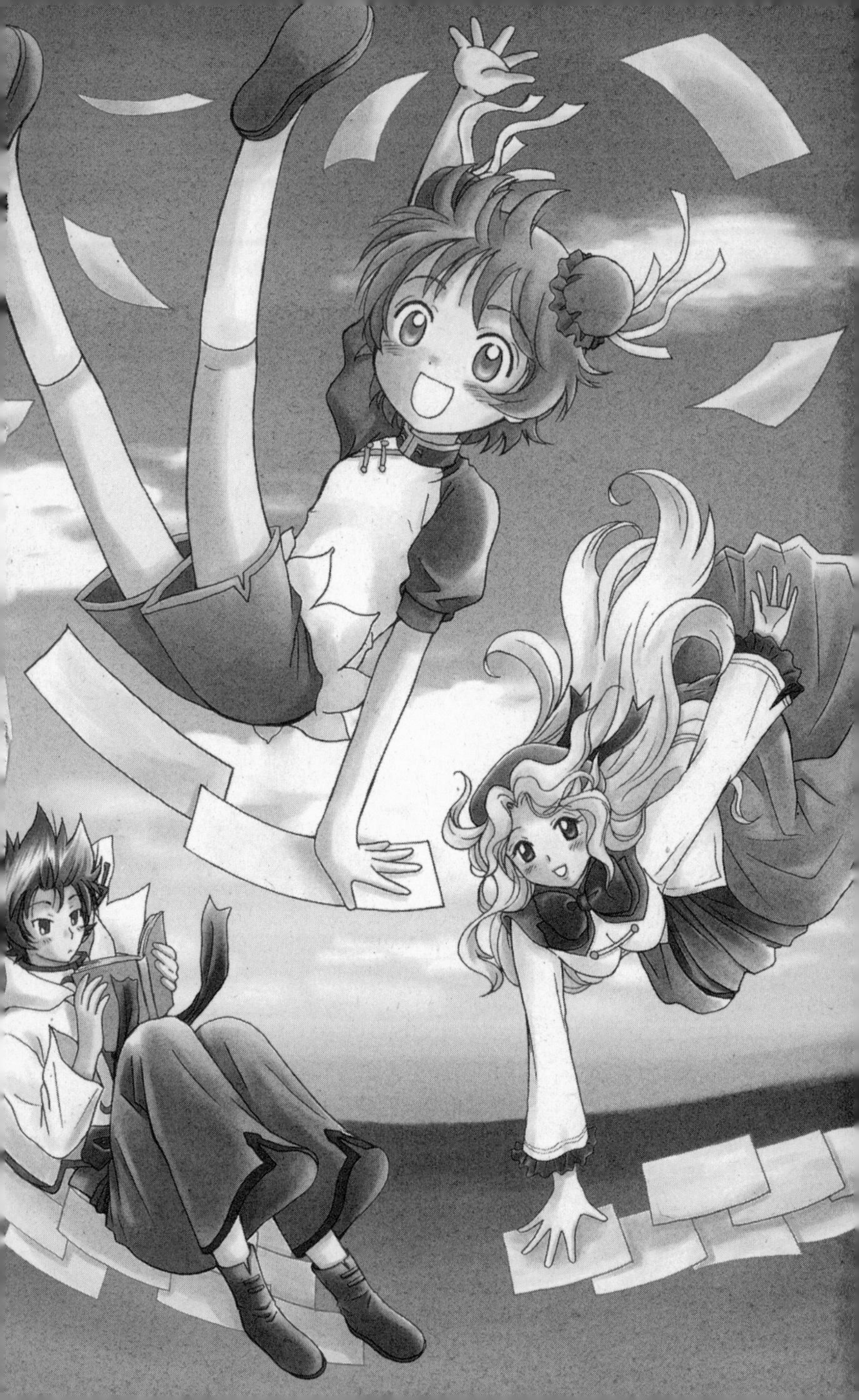

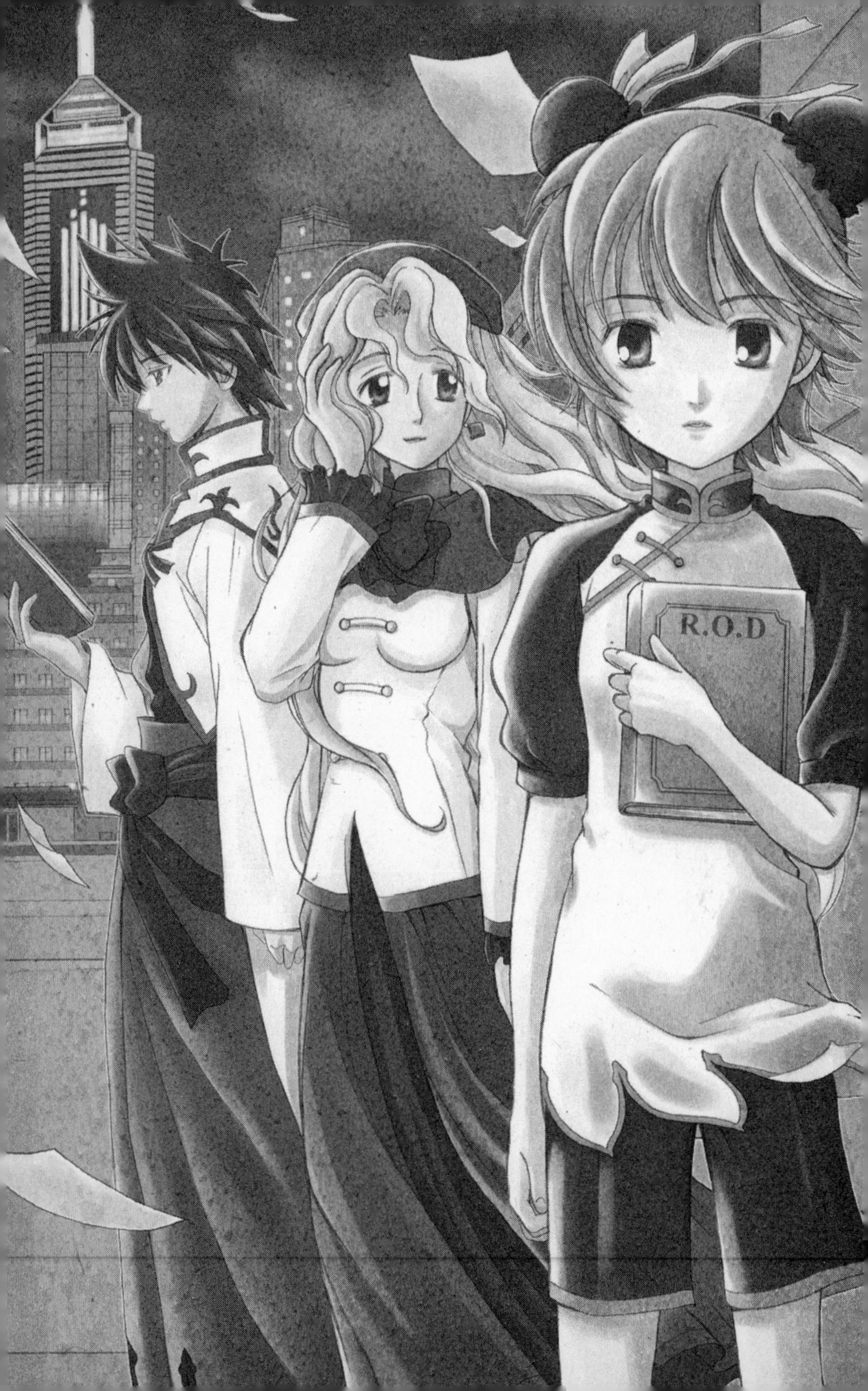
R.O.D

R.O.D

READ OR DREAM

We are Paper Sisters Detective Company

CONTENTS

CHAPTER 1

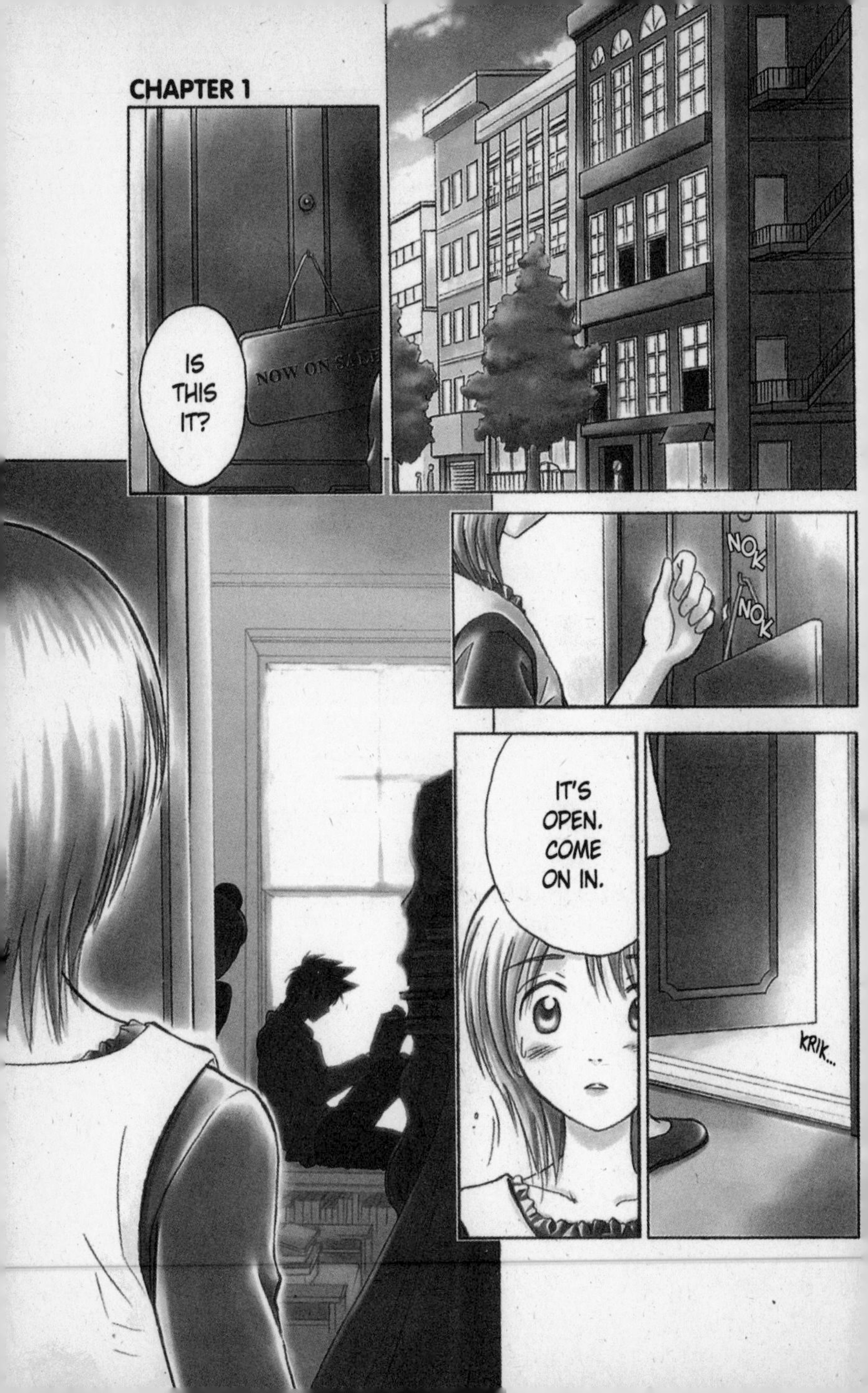
NOW ON SALE
IS THIS IT?
NOK
NOK
IT'S OPEN. COME ON IN.
KRIK...

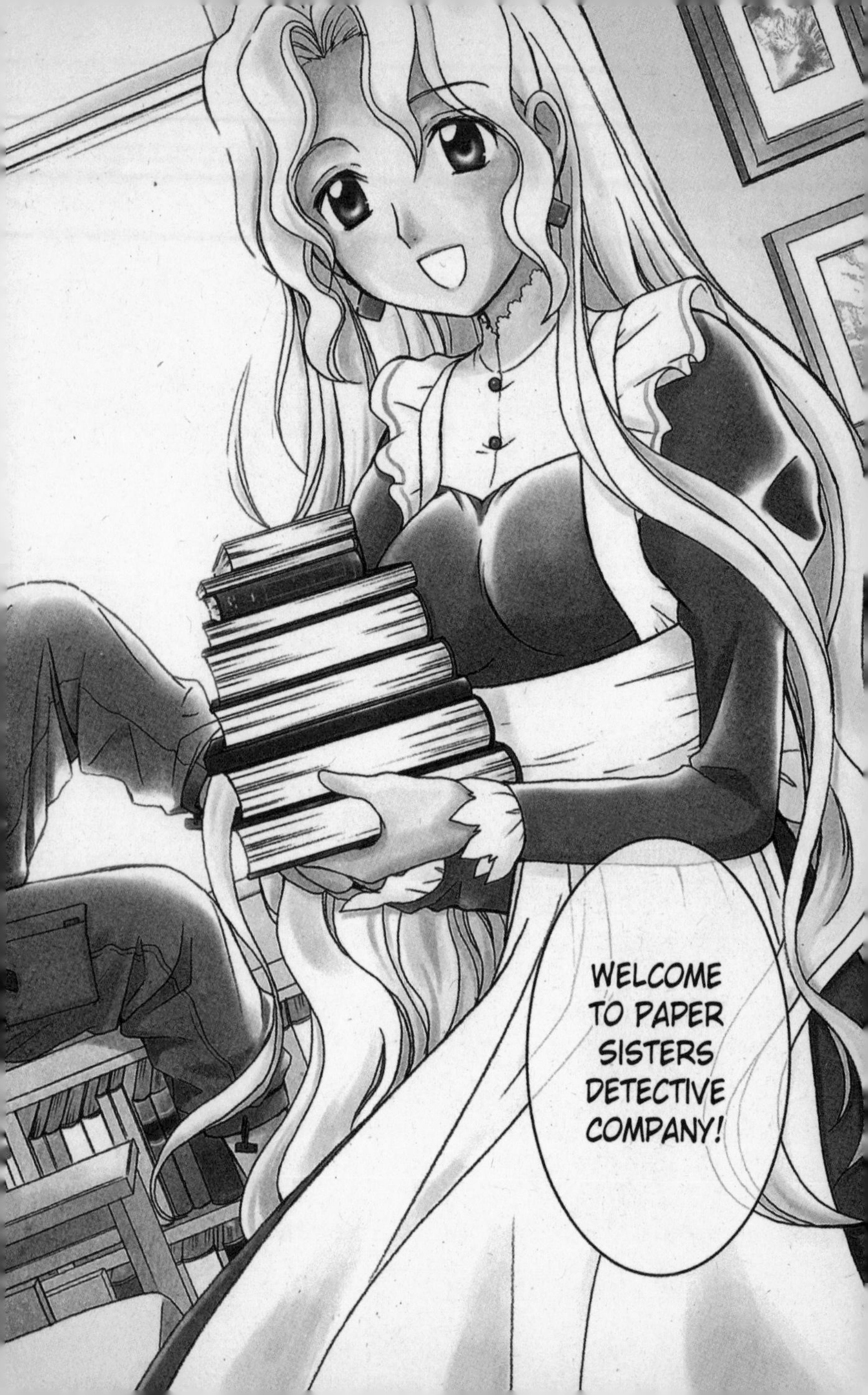
WELCOME TO PAPER SISTERS DETECTIVE COMPANY!

CHAPTER 1

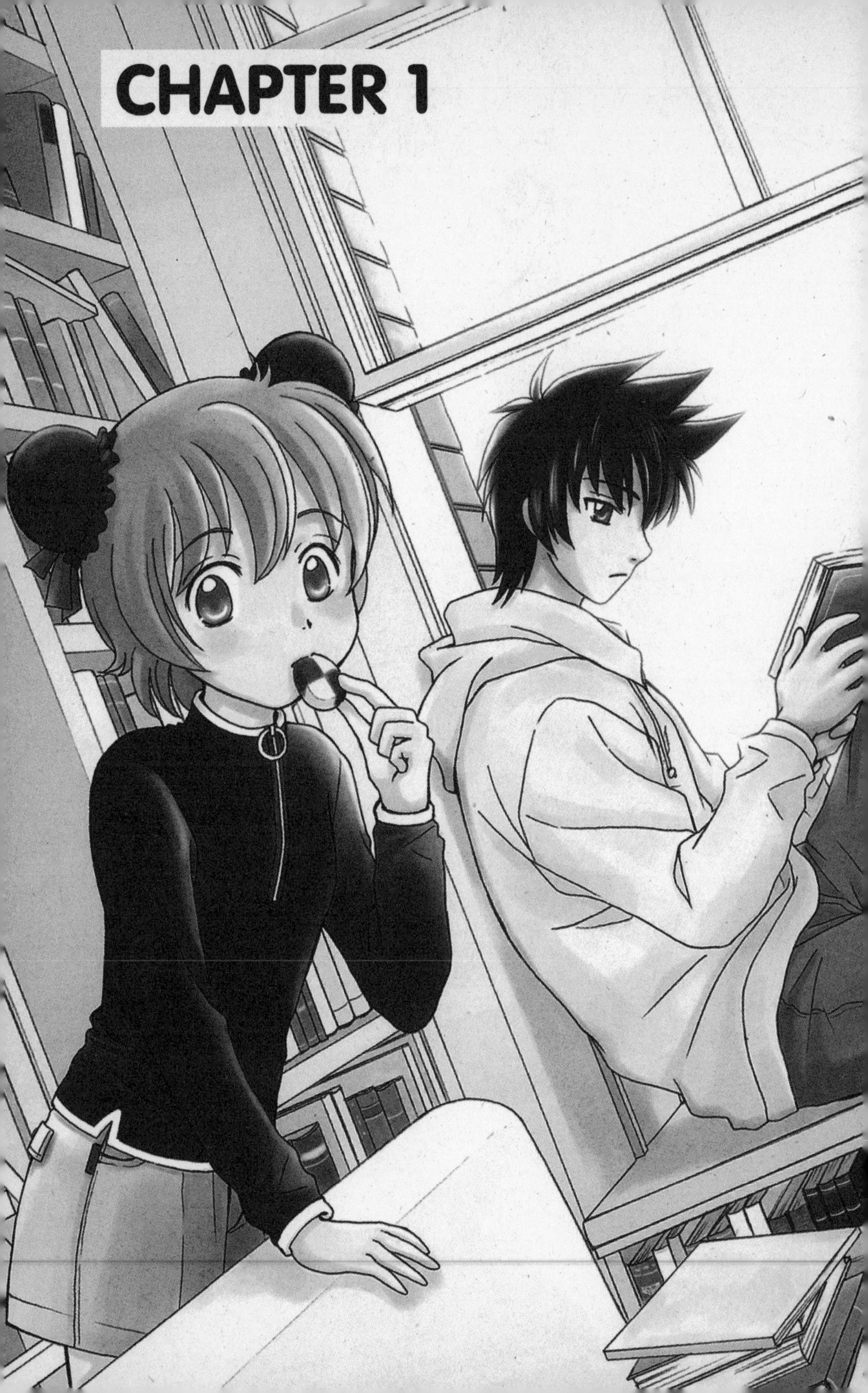

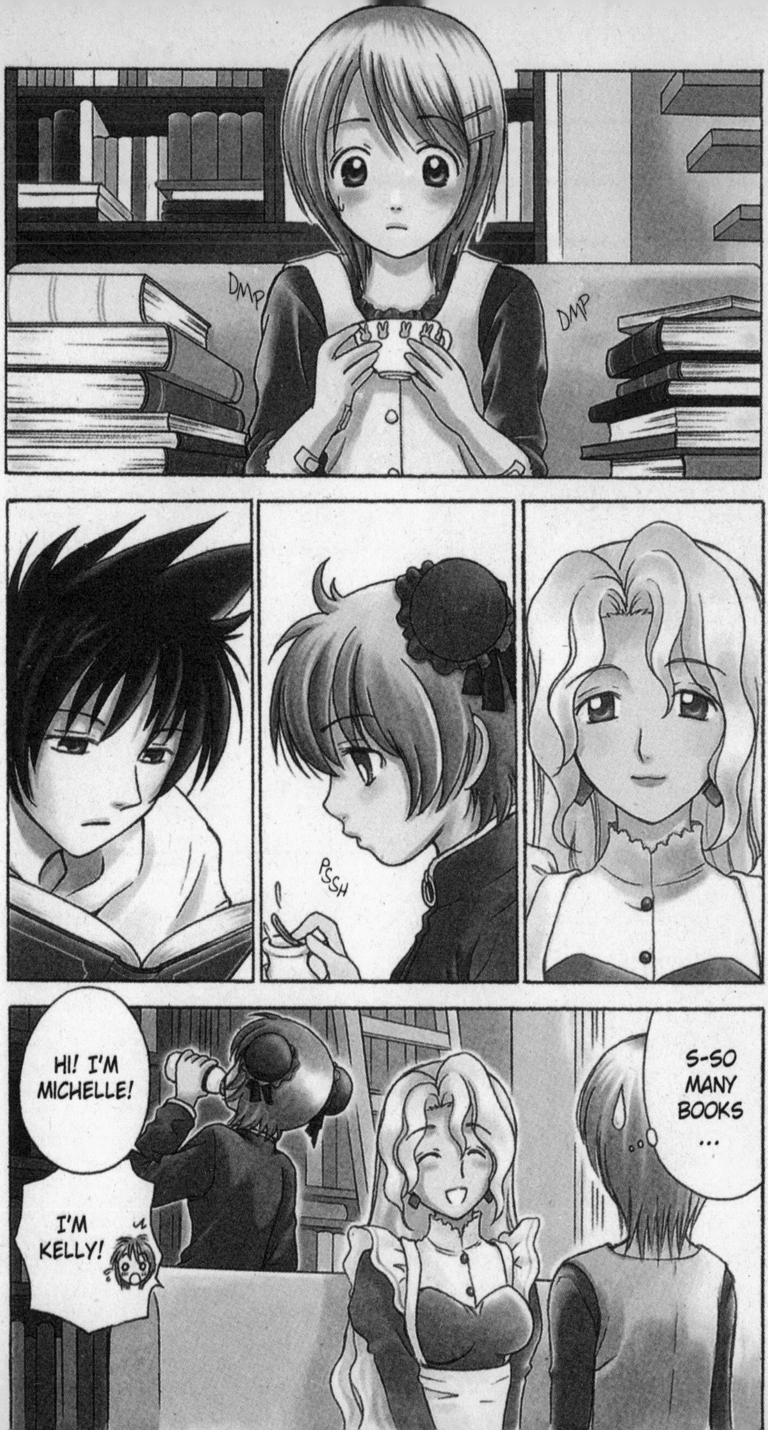
DMP
DMP
PSSH
S-SO MANY BOOKS ...
HI! I'M MICHELLE!
I'M KELLY!

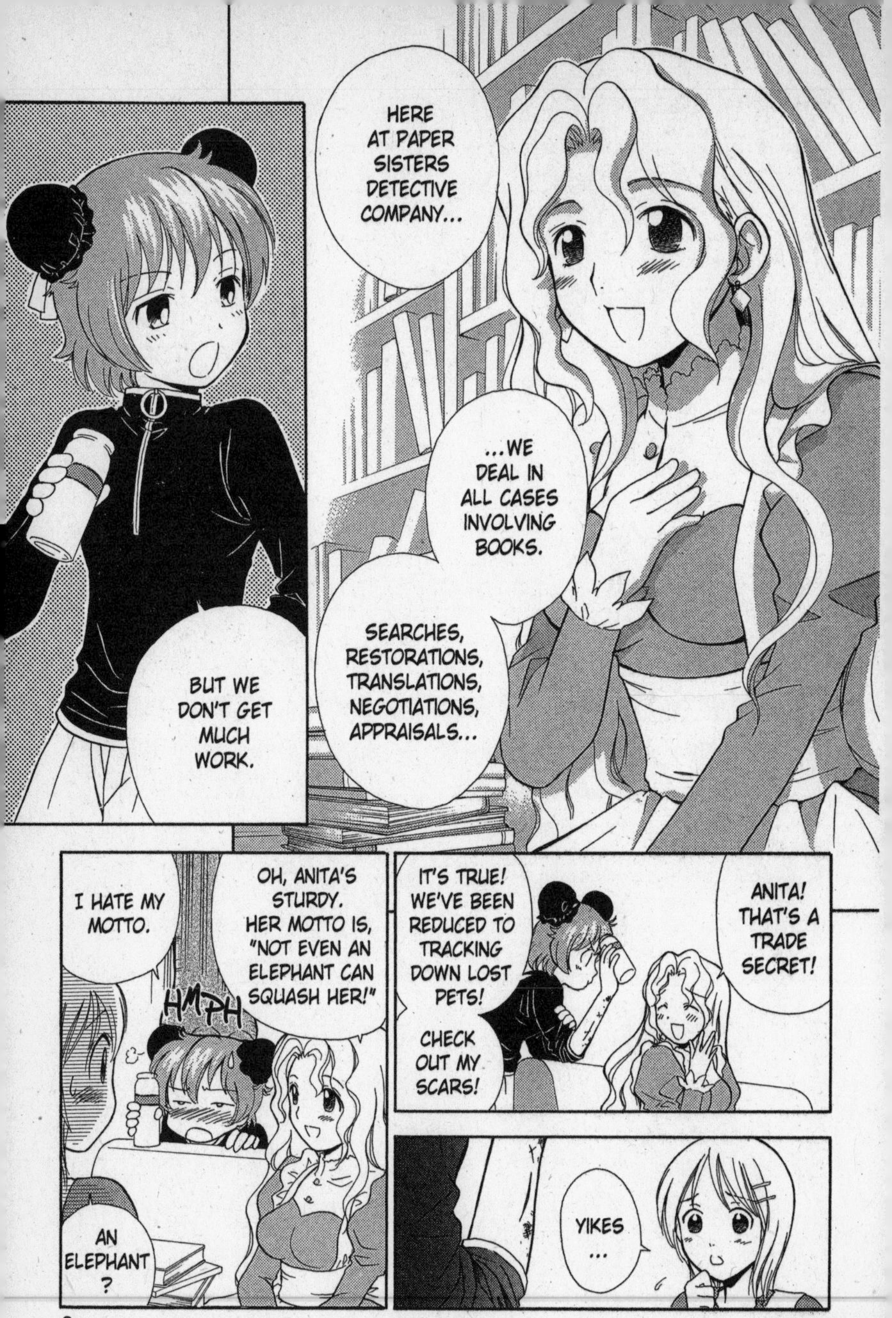
HERE AT PAPER SISTERS DETECTIVE COMPANY...
...WE DEAL IN ALL CASES INVOLVING BOOKS.
SEARCHES, RESTORATIONS, TRANSLATIONS, NEGOTIATIONS, APPRAISALS...
BUT WE DON'T GET MUCH WORK.
ANITA! THAT'S A TRADE SECRET!
IT'S TRUE! WE'VE BEEN REDUCED TO TRACKING DOWN LOST PETS!
CHECK OUT MY SCARS!
YIKES ...
OH, ANITA'S STURDY. HER MOTTO IS, "NOT EVEN AN ELEPHANT CAN SQUASH HER!"
I HATE MY MOTTO.
HMPH
AN ELEPHANT ?

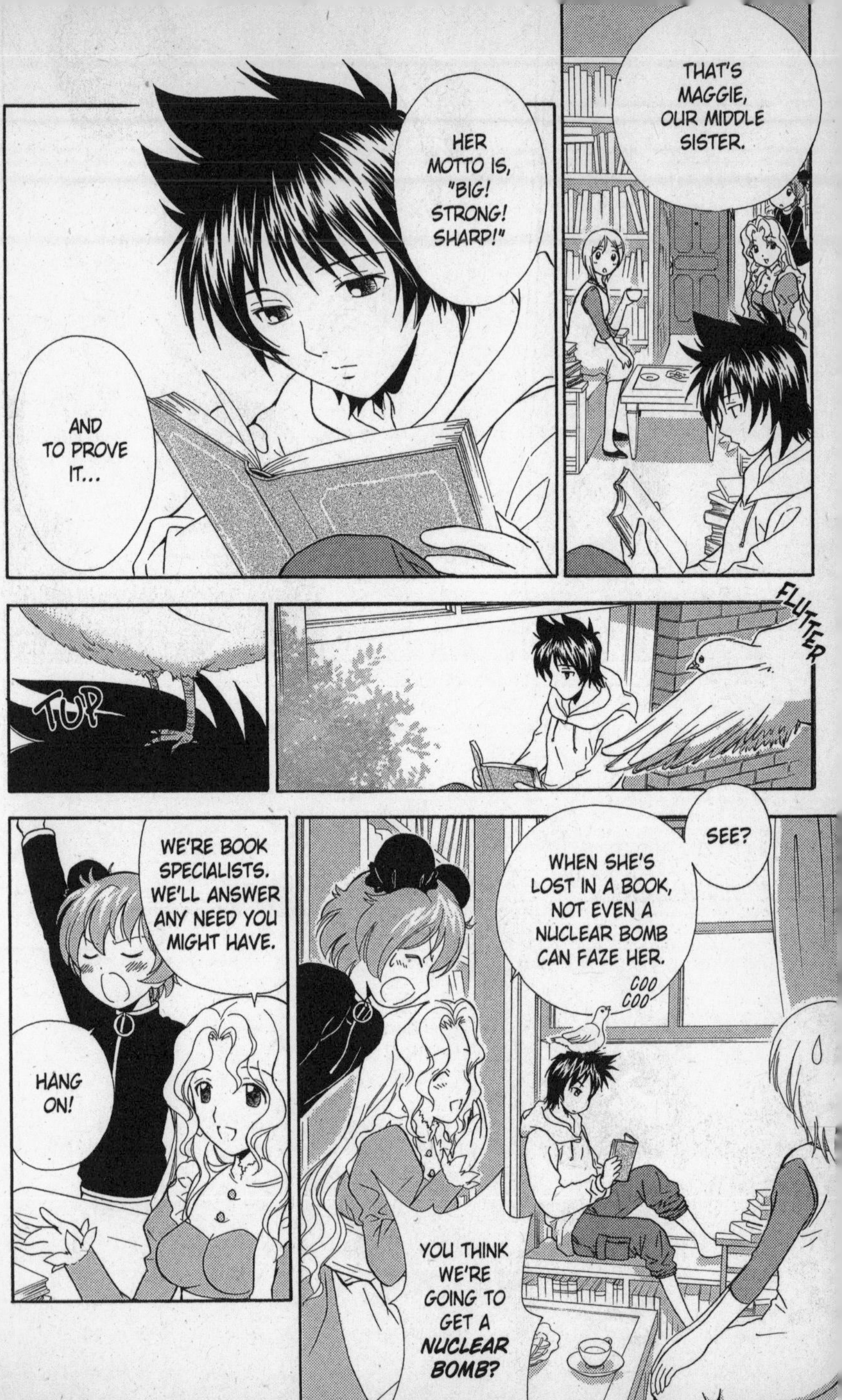
THAT'S MAGGIE, OUR MIDDLE SISTER.
HER MOTTO IS, "BIG! STRONG! SHARP!"
AND TO PROVE IT...
FLUTTER
TUP
SEE?
WHEN SHE'S LOST IN A BOOK, NOT EVEN A NUCLEAR BOMB CAN FAZE HER.
COO COO
YOU THINK WE'RE GOING TO GET A ***NUCLEAR BOMB***?
WE'RE BOOK SPECIALISTS. WE'LL ANSWER ANY NEED YOU MIGHT HAVE.
HANG ON!

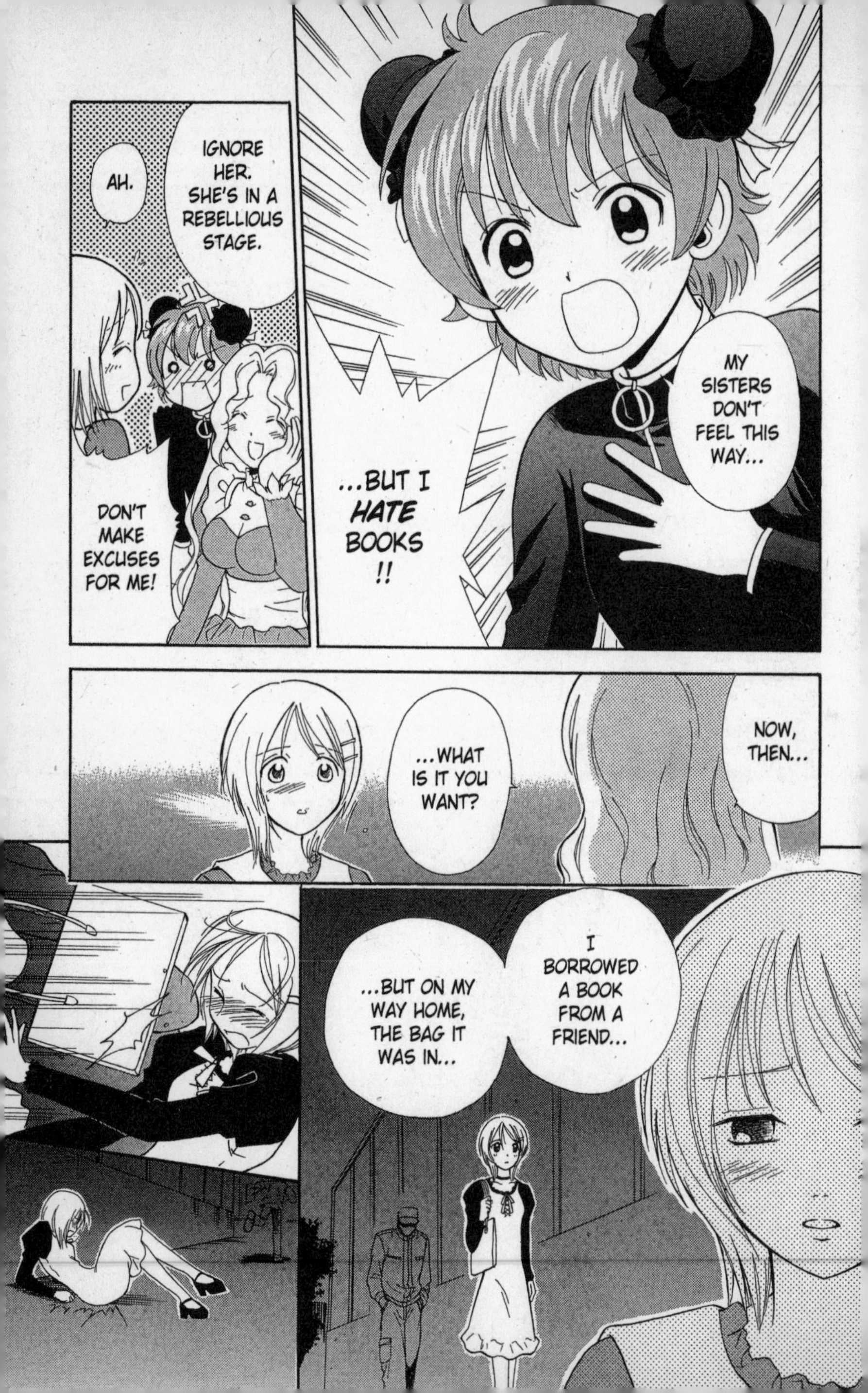
MY SISTERS DON'T FEEL THIS WAY...
...BUT I *HATE* BOOKS !!
IGNORE HER. SHE'S IN A REBELLIOUS STAGE.
AH.
DON'T MAKE EXCUSES FOR ME!
NOW, THEN...
...WHAT IS IT YOU WANT?
I BORROWED A BOOK FROM A FRIEND...
...BUT ON MY WAY HOME, THE BAG IT WAS IN...

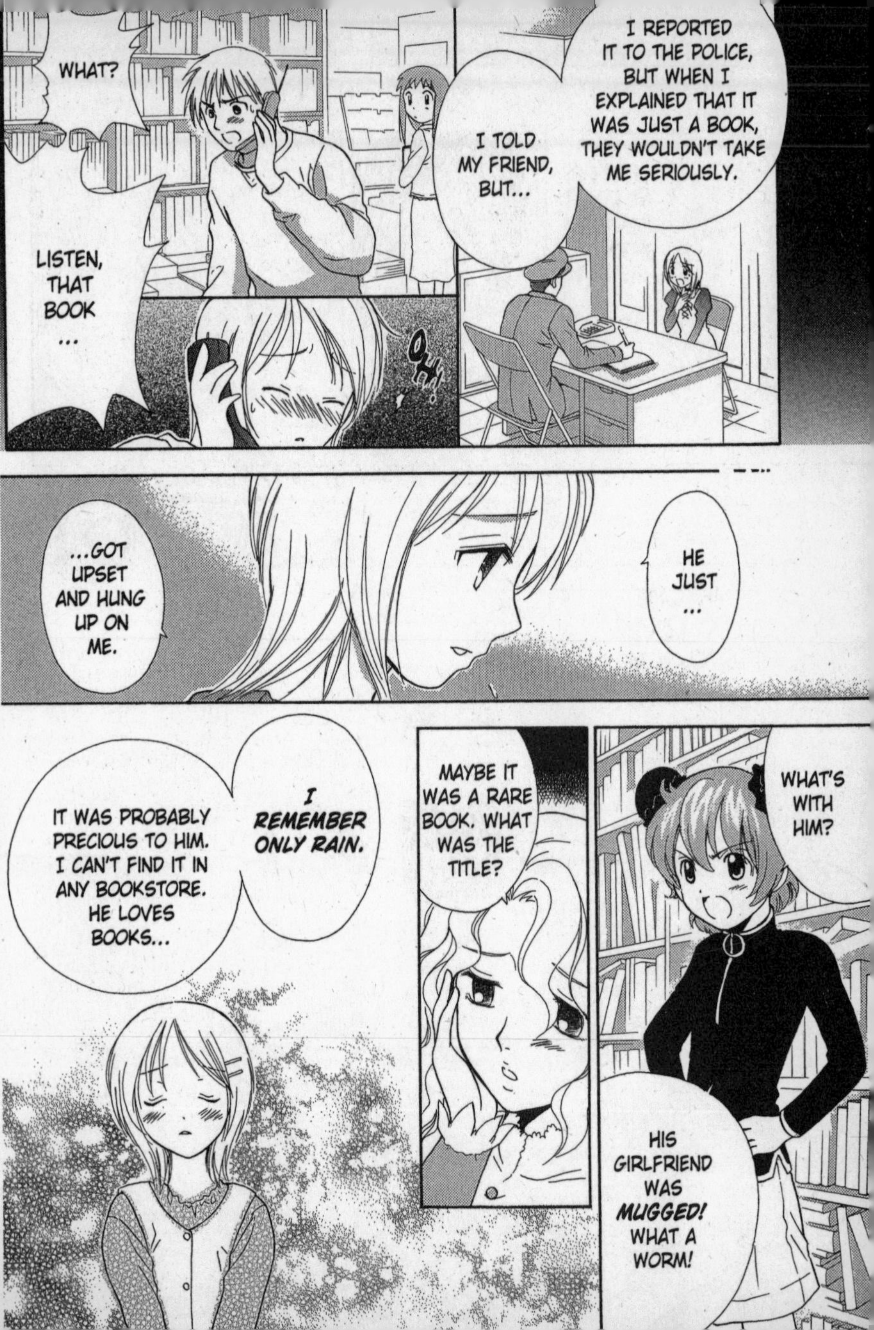
I REPORTED IT TO THE POLICE, BUT WHEN I EXPLAINED THAT IT WAS JUST A BOOK, THEY WOULDN'T TAKE ME SERIOUSLY.
I TOLD MY FRIEND, BUT...
WHAT?
LISTEN, THAT BOOK ...
HE JUST ...
...GOT UPSET AND HUNG UP ON ME.
WHAT'S WITH HIM?
HIS GIRLFRIEND WAS MUGGED! WHAT A WORM!
MAYBE IT WAS A RARE BOOK. WHAT WAS THE TITLE?
I REMEMBER ONLY RAIN.
IT WAS PROBABLY PRECIOUS TO HIM. I CAN'T FIND IT IN ANY BOOKSTORE. HE LOVES BOOKS...

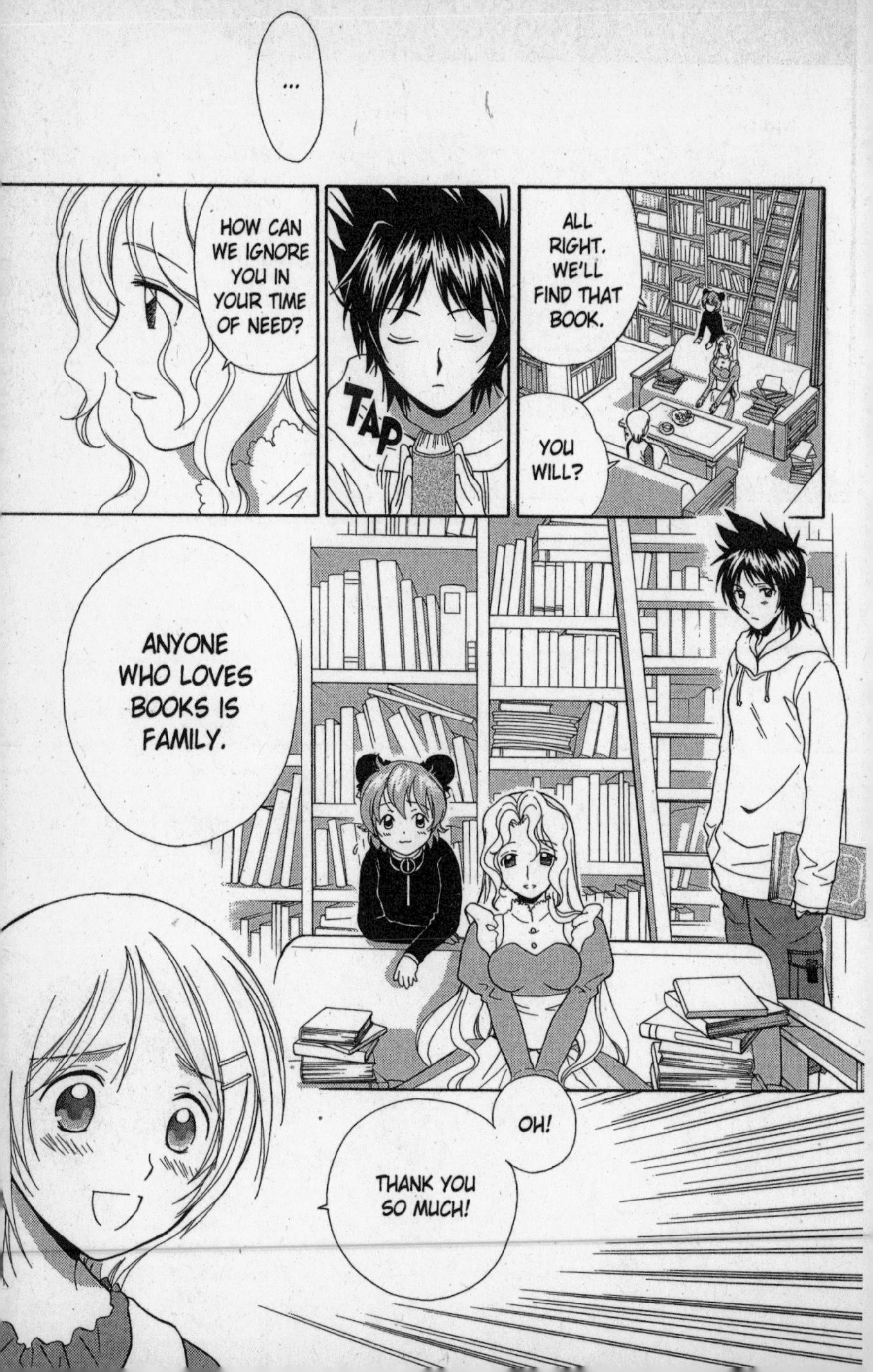
...
ALL RIGHT. WE'LL FIND THAT BOOK.
YOU WILL?
TAP
HOW CAN WE IGNORE YOU IN YOUR TIME OF NEED?
ANYONE WHO LOVES BOOKS IS FAMILY.
OH!
THANK YOU SO MUCH!

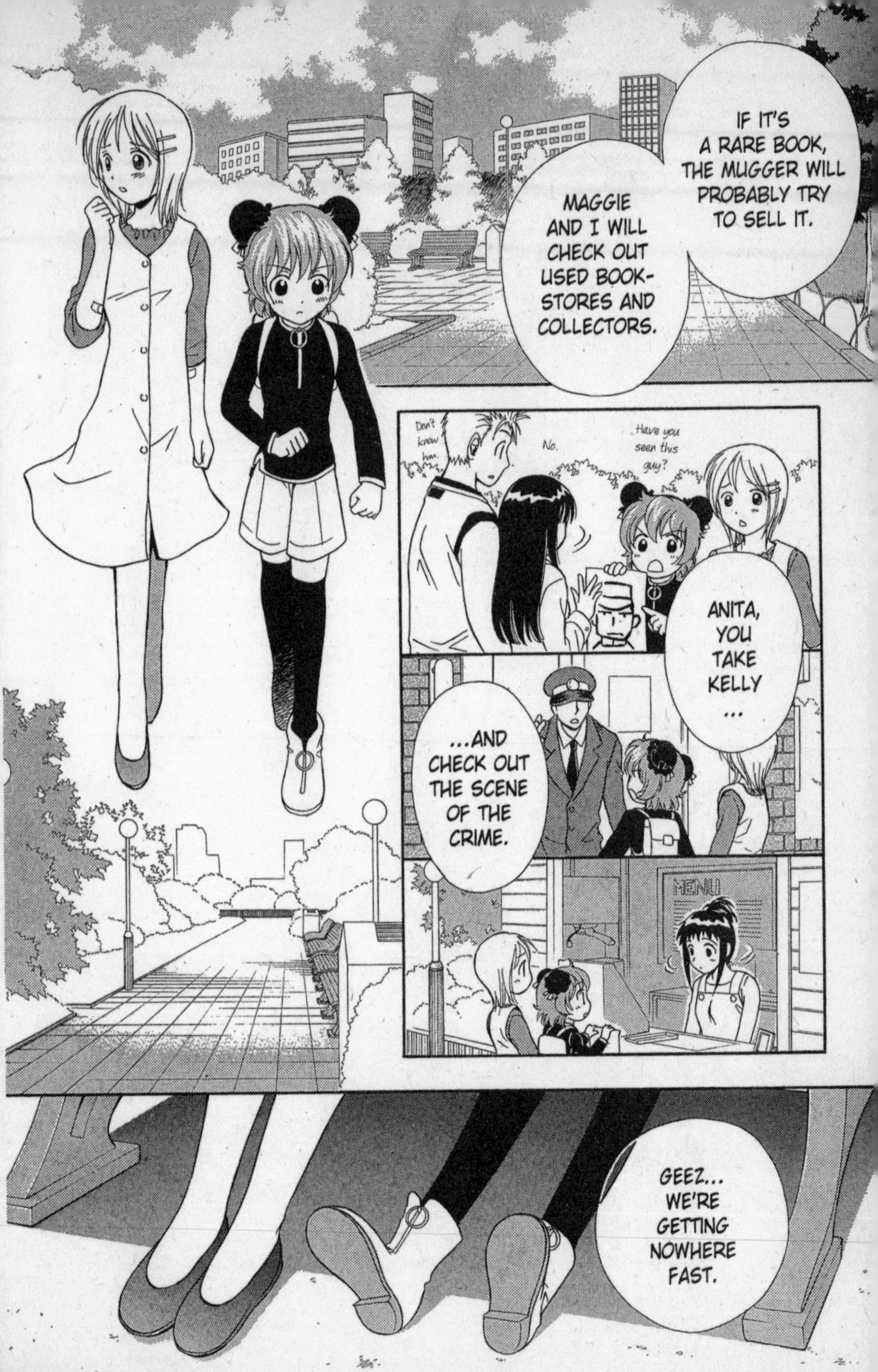
IF IT'S A RARE BOOK, THE MUGGER WILL PROBABLY TRY TO SELL IT.
MAGGIE AND I WILL CHECK OUT USED BOOK-STORES AND COLLECTORS.
Have you seen this guy?
No.
Don't know him.
ANITA, YOU TAKE KELLY...
...AND CHECK OUT THE SCENE OF THE CRIME.
MENU
GEEZ... WE'RE GETTING NOWHERE FAST.

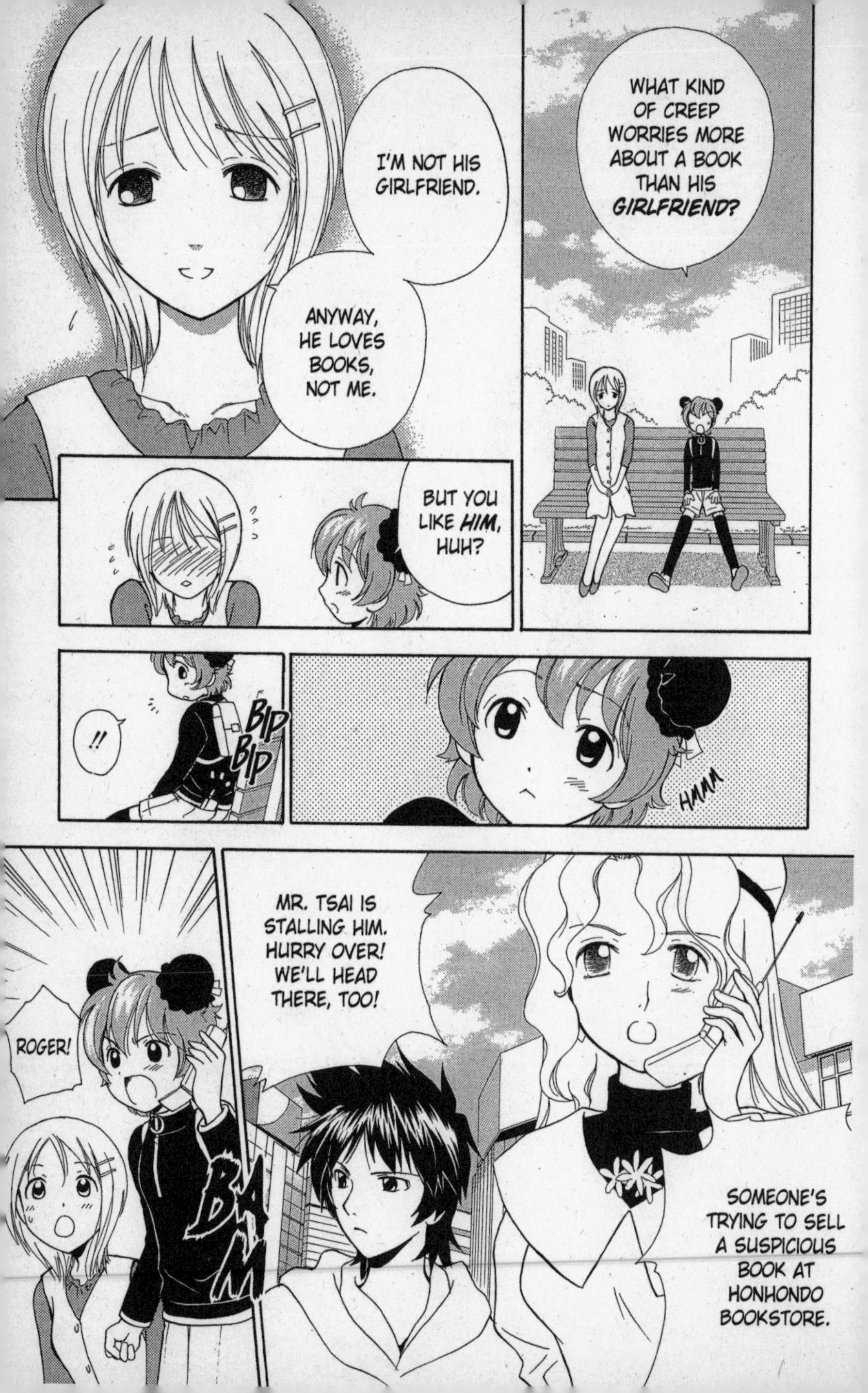
WHAT KIND OF CREEP WORRIES MORE ABOUT A BOOK THAN HIS *GIRLFRIEND?*
I'M NOT HIS GIRLFRIEND.
ANYWAY, HE LOVES BOOKS, NOT ME.
BUT YOU LIKE *HIM*, HUH?
HMMM
BIP BIP
!!
SOMEONE'S TRYING TO SELL A SUSPICIOUS BOOK AT HONHONDO BOOKSTORE.
MR. TSAI IS STALLING HIM. HURRY OVER! WE'LL HEAD THERE, TOO!
ROGER!
BAM

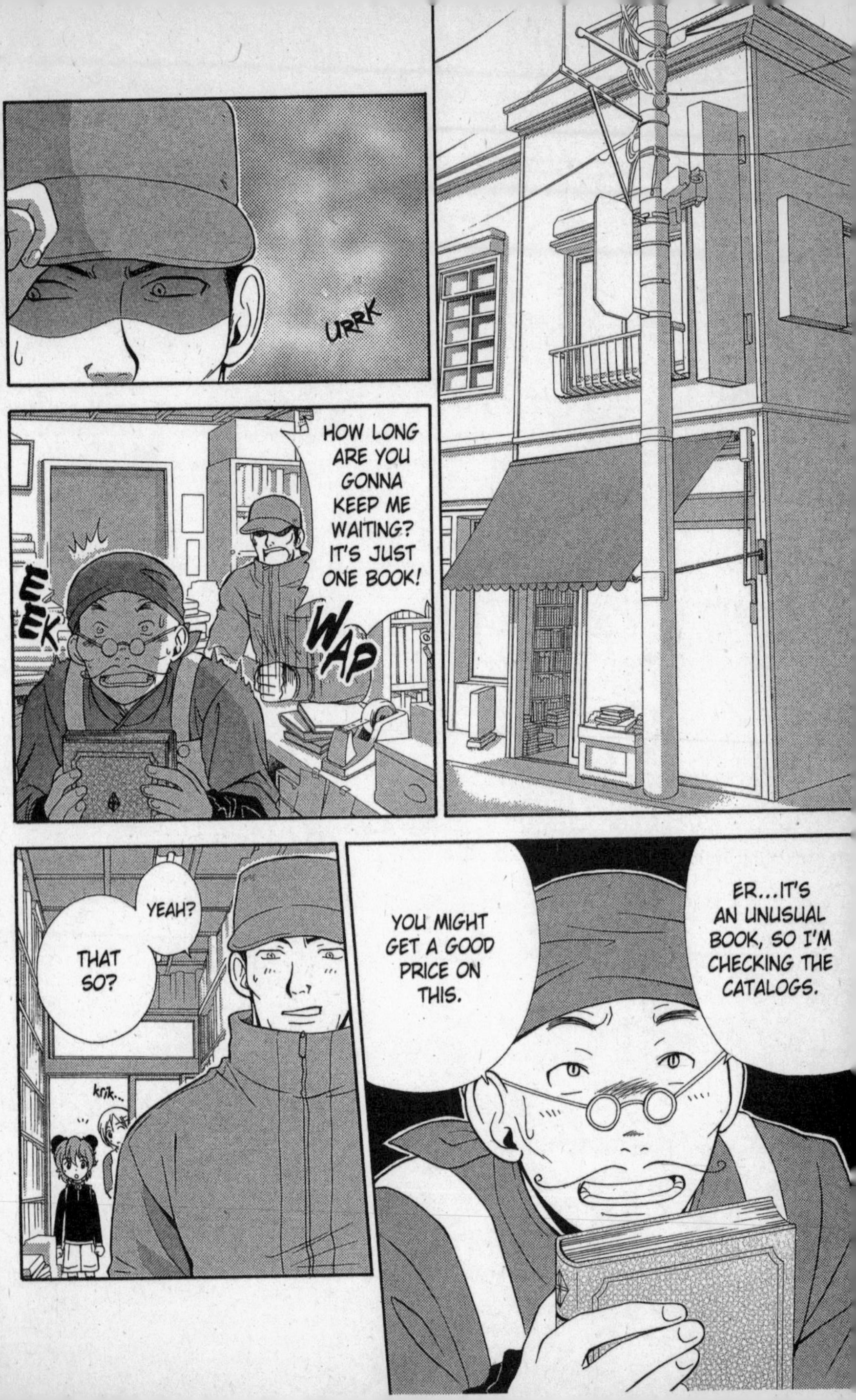
URRK
HOW LONG ARE YOU GONNA KEEP ME WAITING? IT'S JUST ONE BOOK!
EEK
WAP
ER...IT'S AN UNUSUAL BOOK, SO I'M CHECKING THE CATALOGS.
YOU MIGHT GET A GOOD PRICE ON THIS.
YEAH?
THAT SO?
krik...

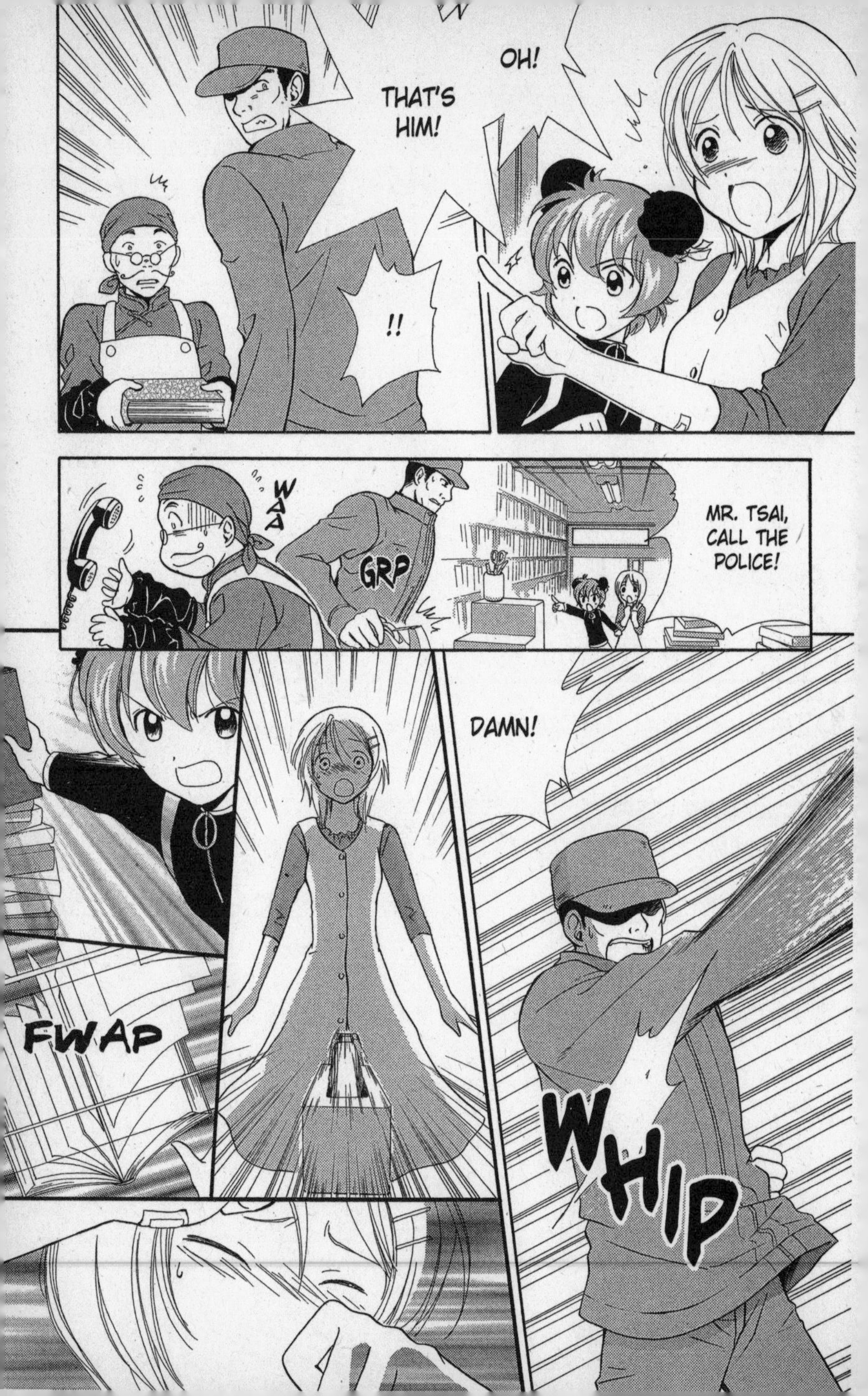
OH!
THAT'S HIM!
!!
MR. TSAI, CALL THE POLICE!
GRP
WAA
DAMN!
WHIP
FWAP

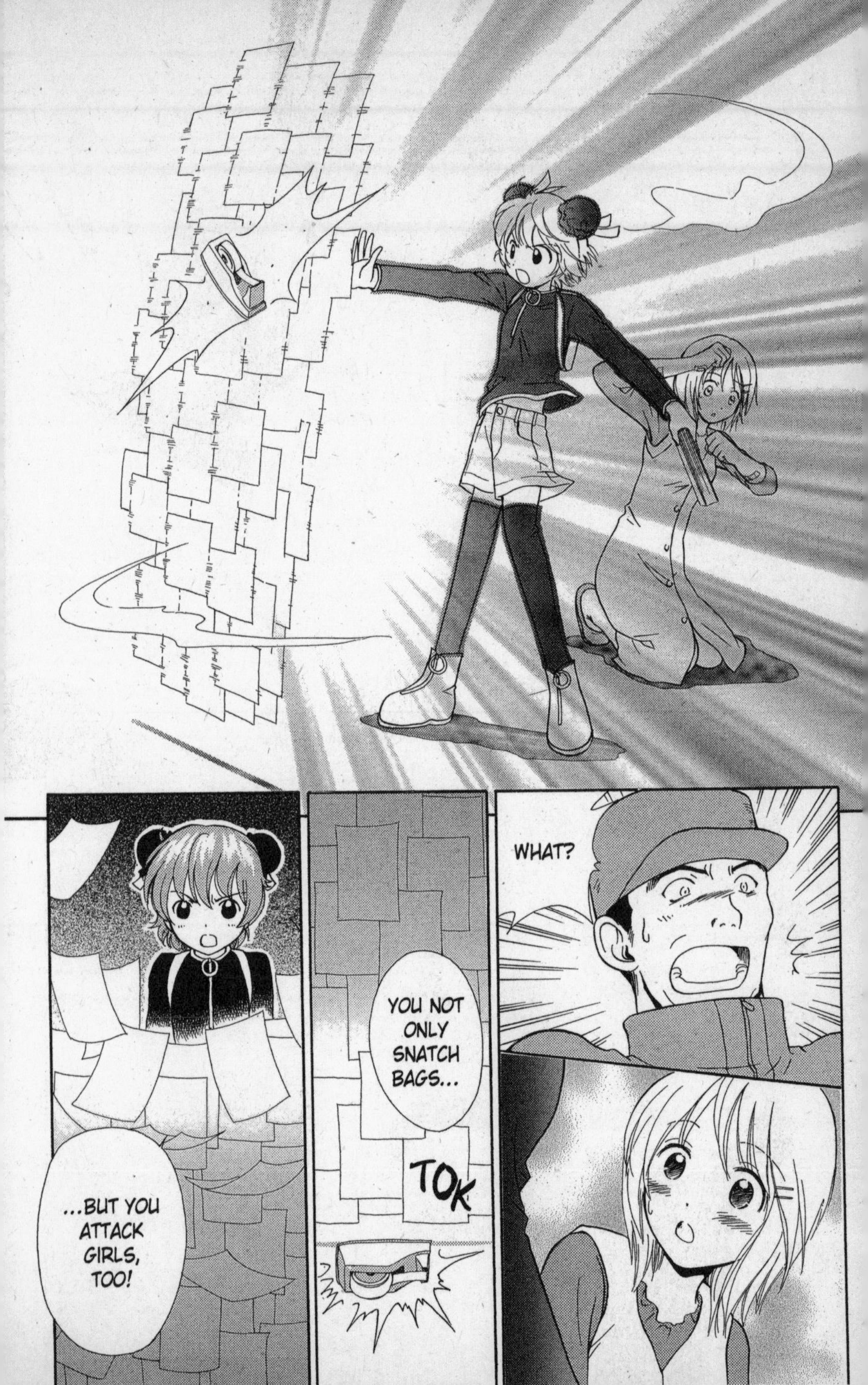
WHAT?
YOU NOT ONLY SNATCH BAGS...
TOK
...BUT YOU ATTACK GIRLS, TOO!

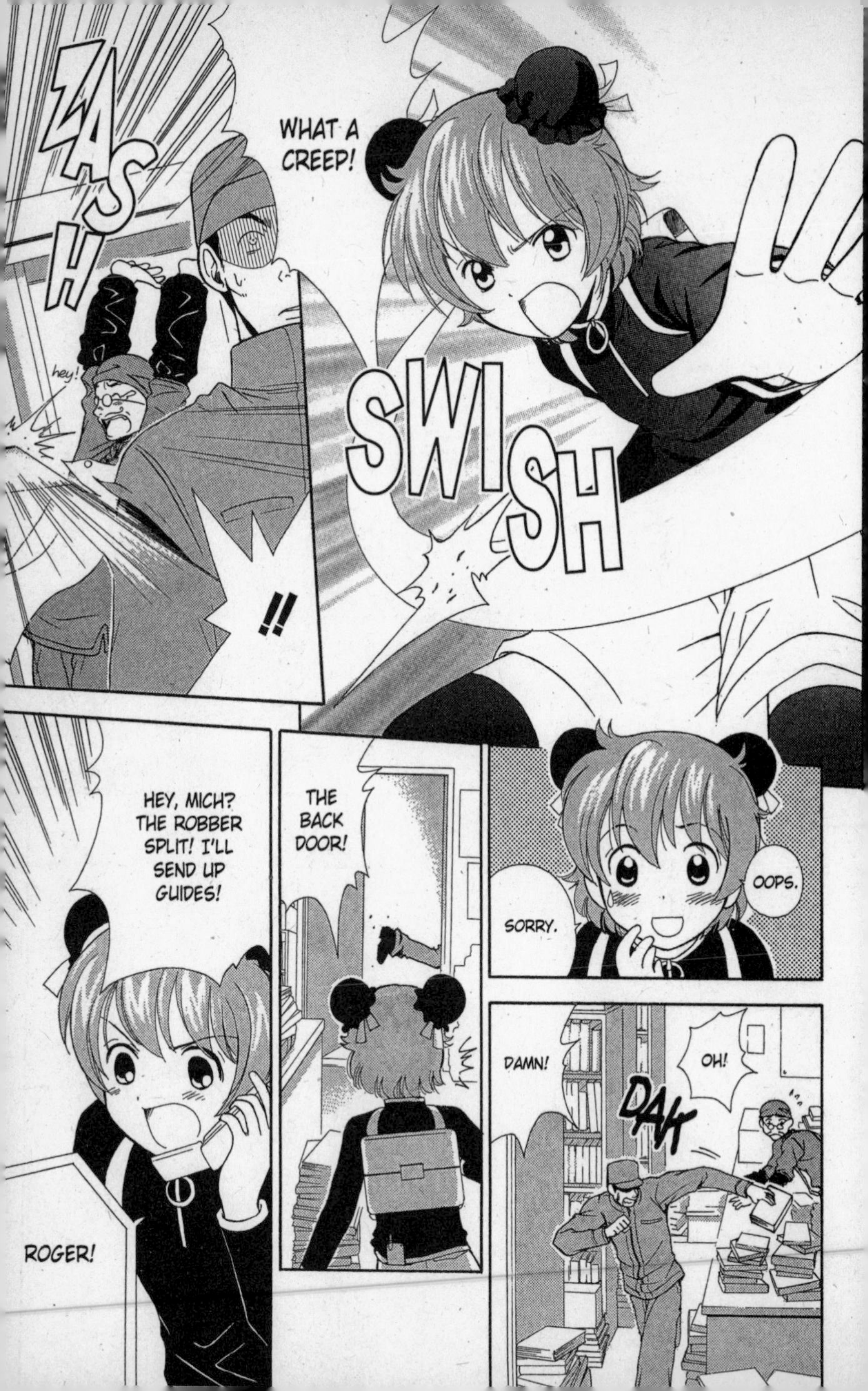
WHAT A CREEP!
SWISH
ZASH
hey!
!!
OOPS.
SORRY.
OH!
DAMN!
DAK
THE BACK DOOR!
HEY, MICH? THE ROBBER SPLIT! I'LL SEND UP GUIDES!
ROGER!

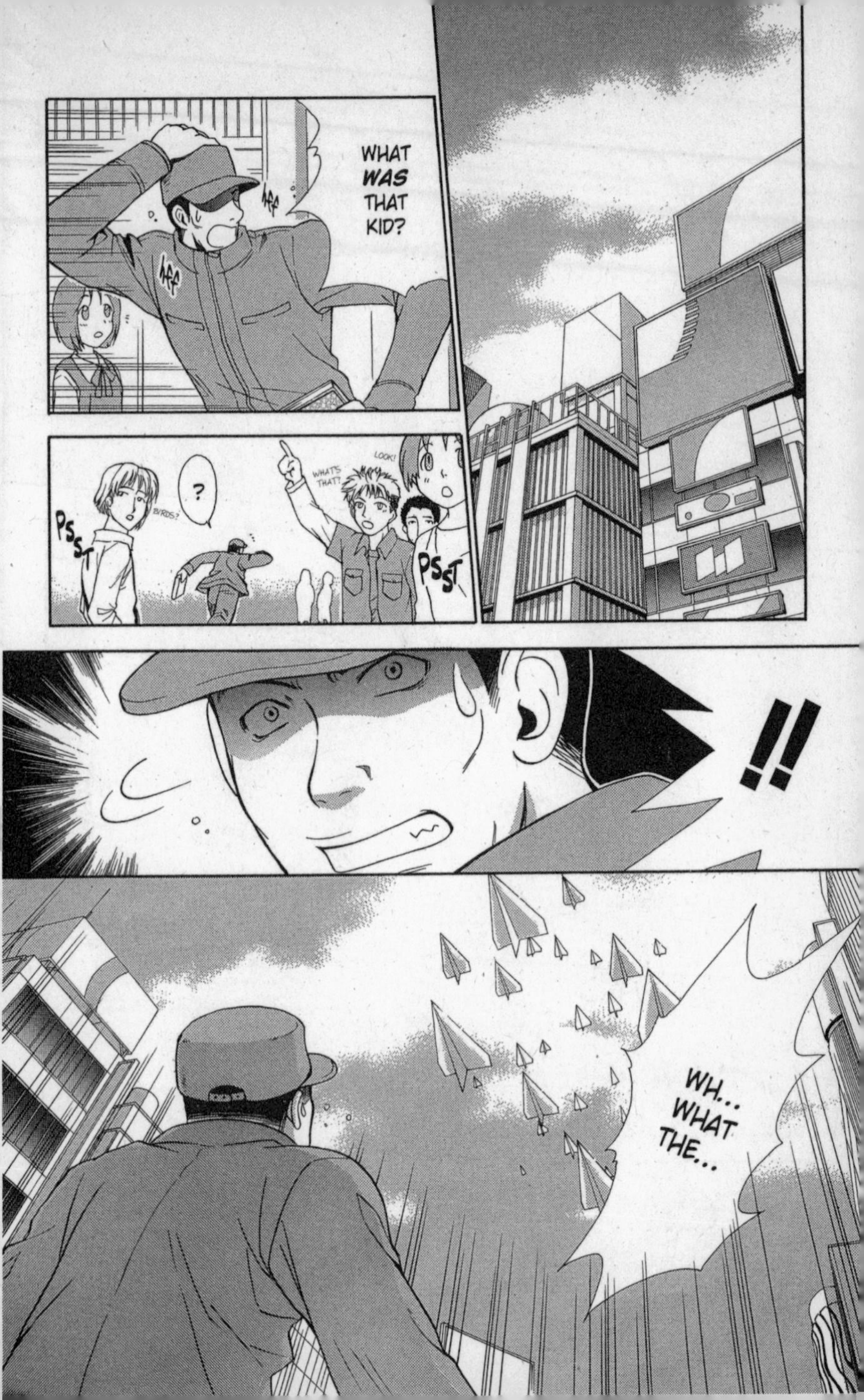
WHAT WAS THAT KID?
hff
hff
LOOK!
WHATS THAT?
PSST
?
BIRDS?
PSST
!!
WH... WHAT THE...

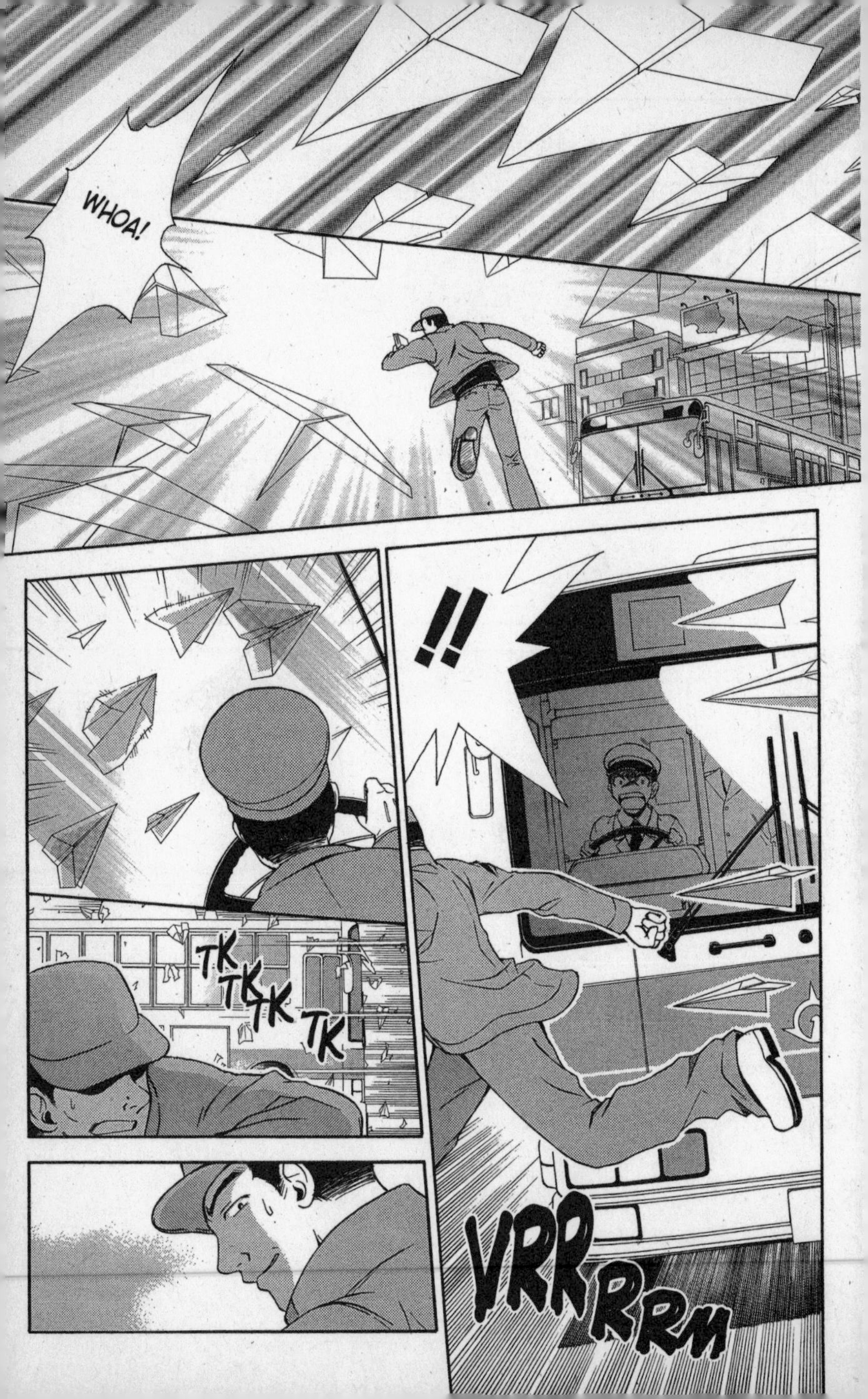
WHOA!
!!
VRRRRM
TK TK TK TK

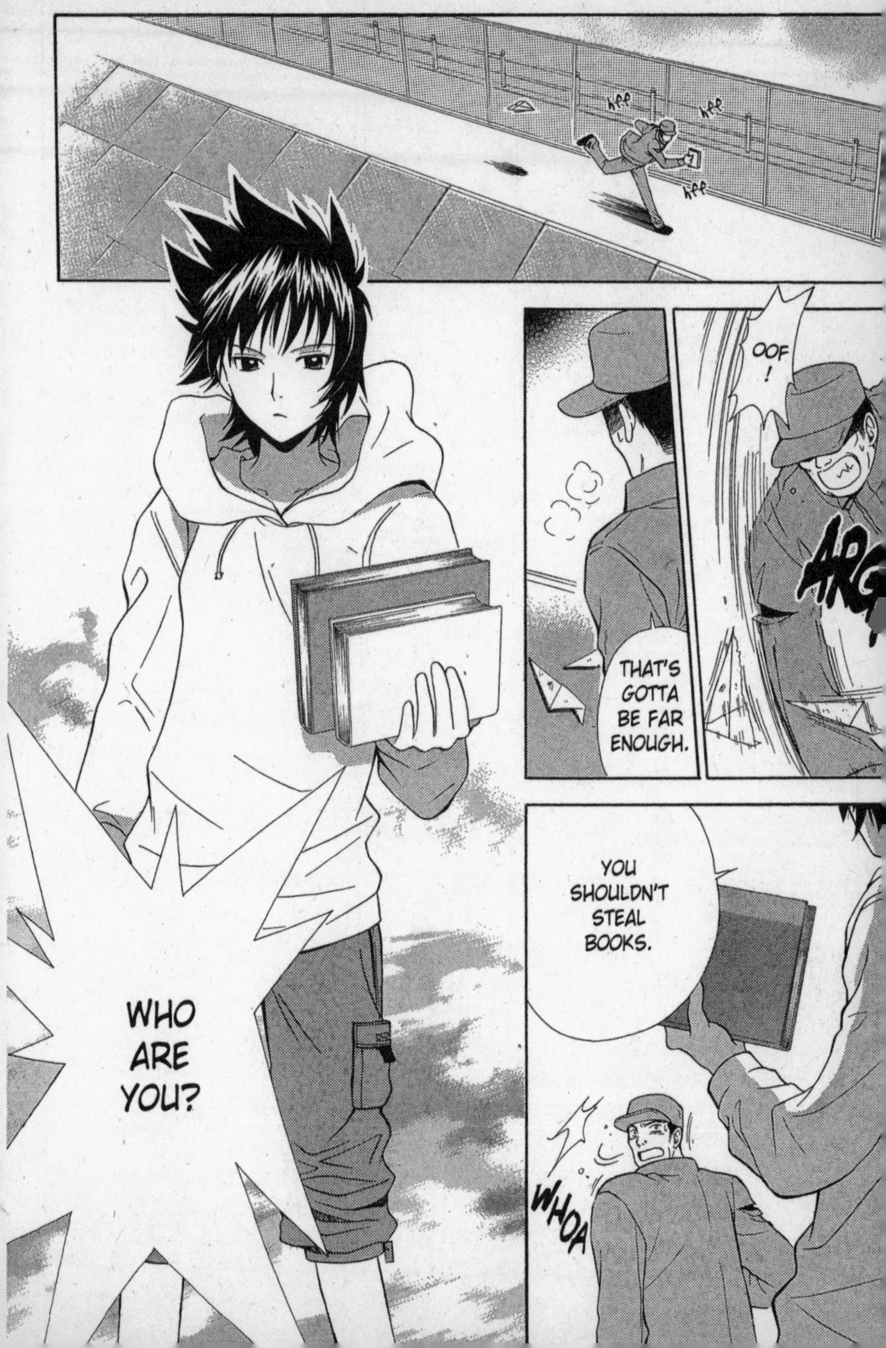
hff
hff
hff
OOF!
ARG
THAT'S GOTTA BE FAR ENOUGH.
YOU SHOULDN'T STEAL BOOKS.
WHOA
WHO ARE YOU?

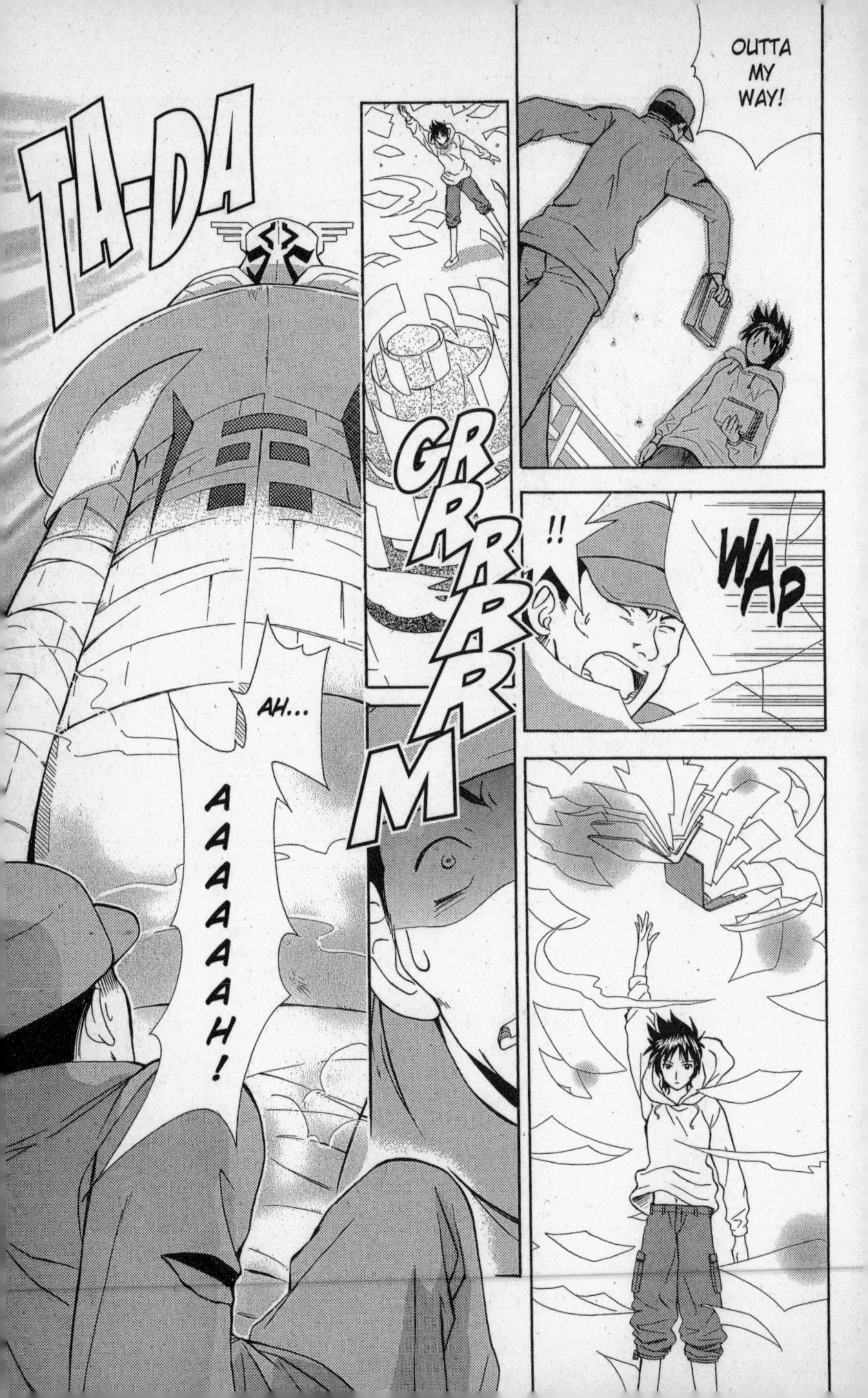
OUTTA MY WAY!
!!
WAP
GRRRRRM
TA-DA
AH...
AAAAAAAH!

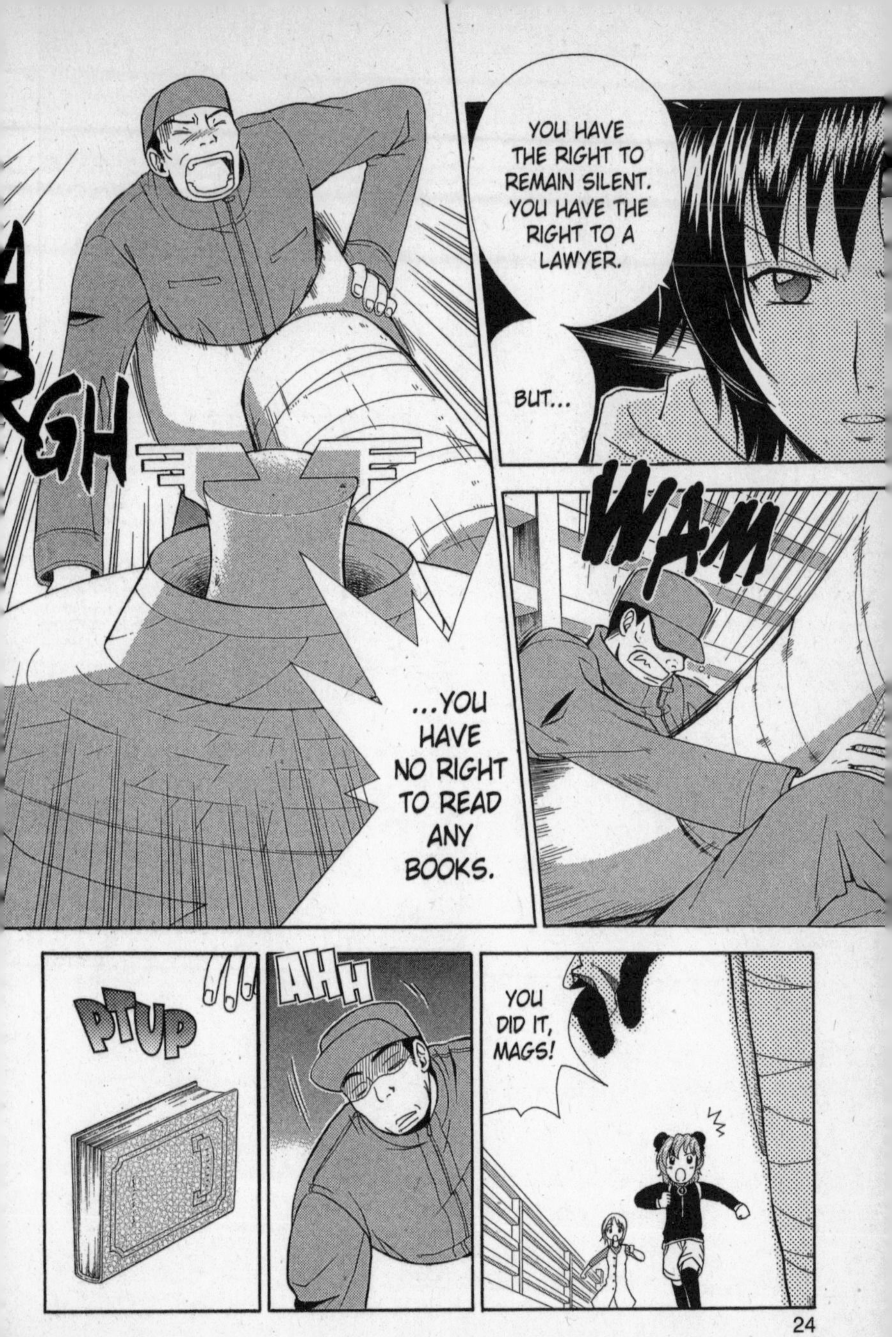
YOU HAVE THE RIGHT TO REMAIN SILENT. YOU HAVE THE RIGHT TO A LAWYER.
BUT...
WAM
GH
...YOU HAVE NO RIGHT TO READ ANY BOOKS.
YOU DID IT, MAGS!
AHH
PTUP

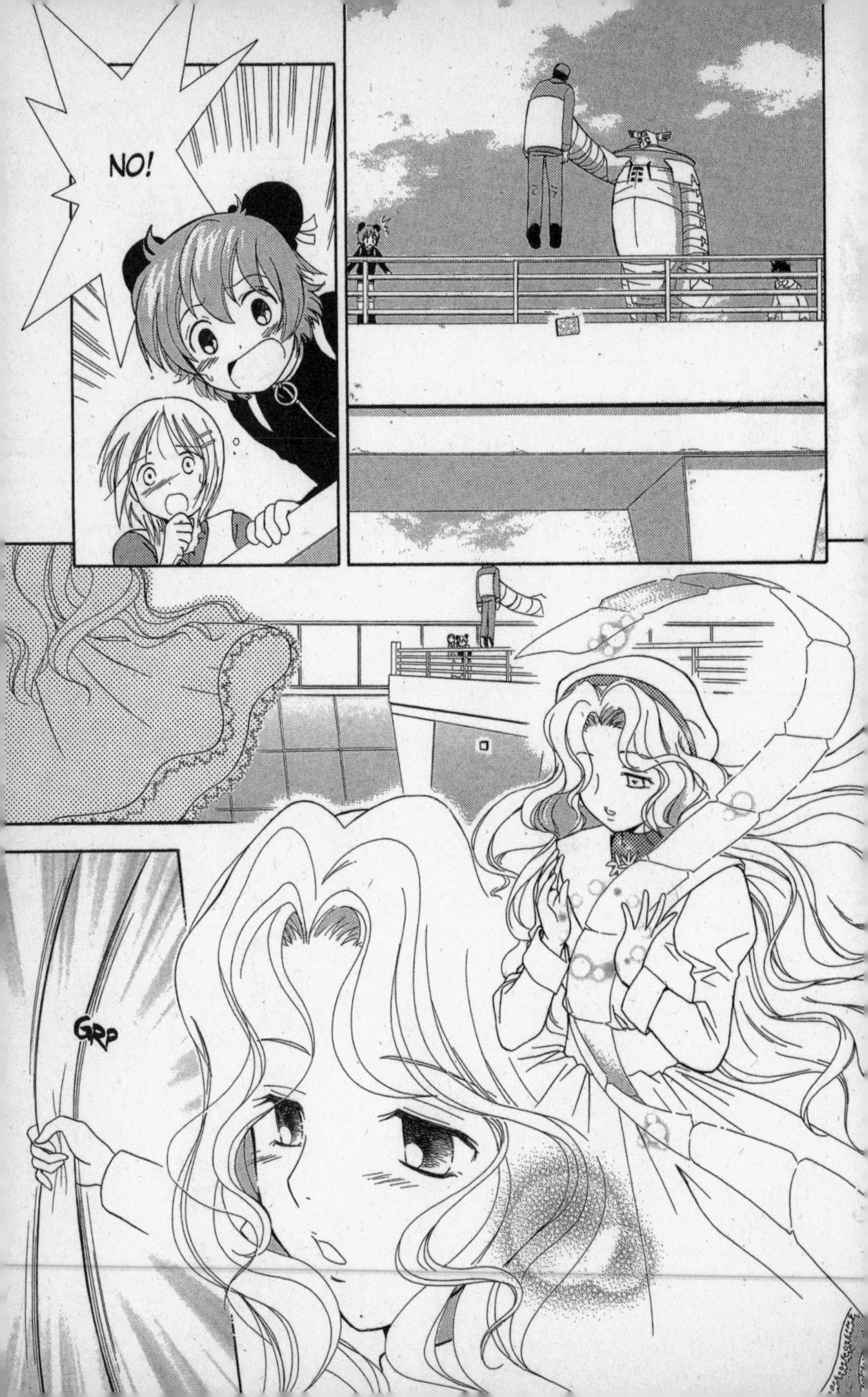
NO!
GRP

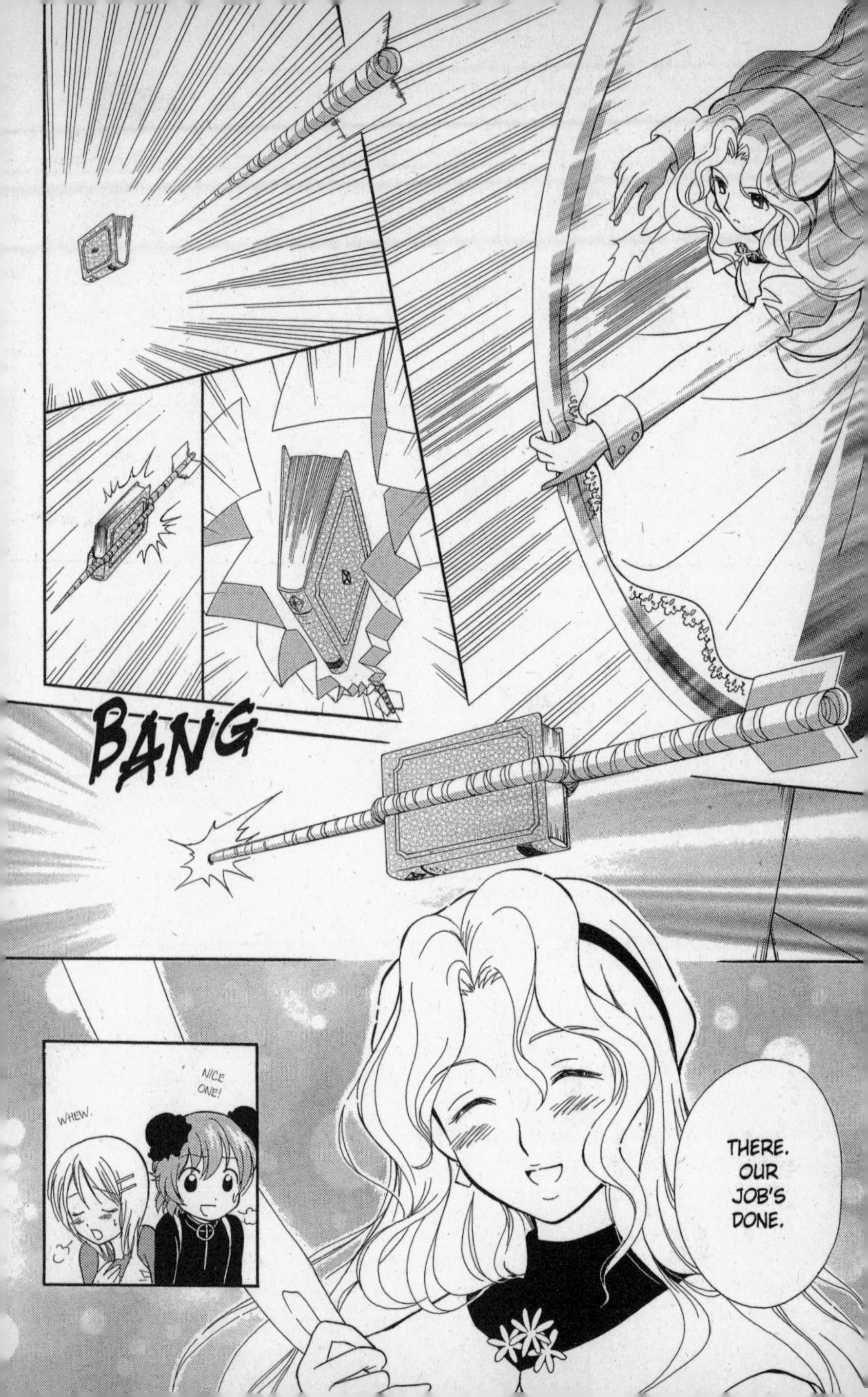
BANG
THERE. OUR JOB'S DONE.
NICE ONE!
WHEW.

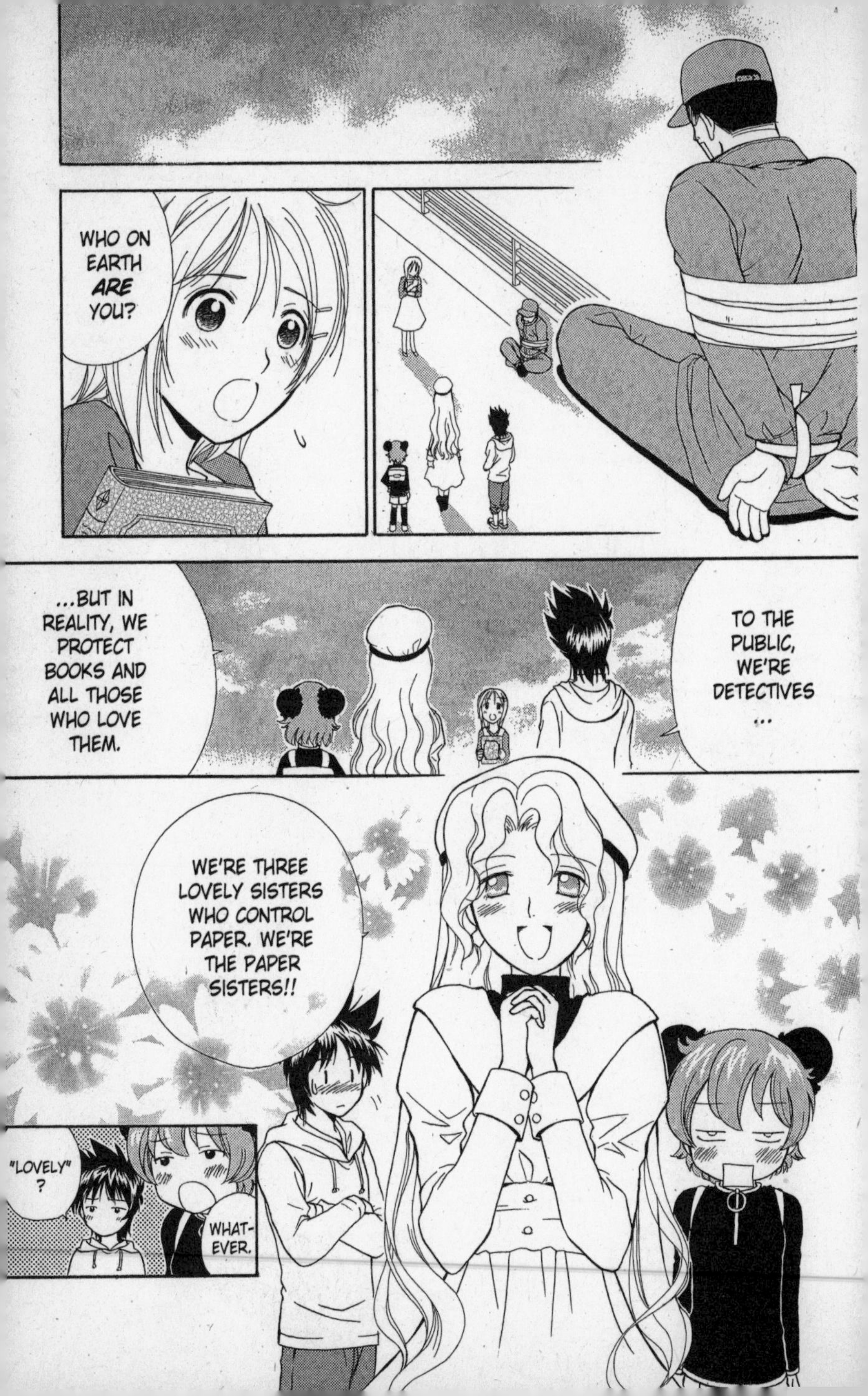
WHO ON EARTH ARE YOU?
TO THE PUBLIC, WE'RE DETECTIVES...
...BUT IN REALITY, WE PROTECT BOOKS AND ALL THOSE WHO LOVE THEM.
WE'RE THREE LOVELY SISTERS WHO CONTROL PAPER. WE'RE THE PAPER SISTERS!!
"LOVELY"?
WHAT-EVER.

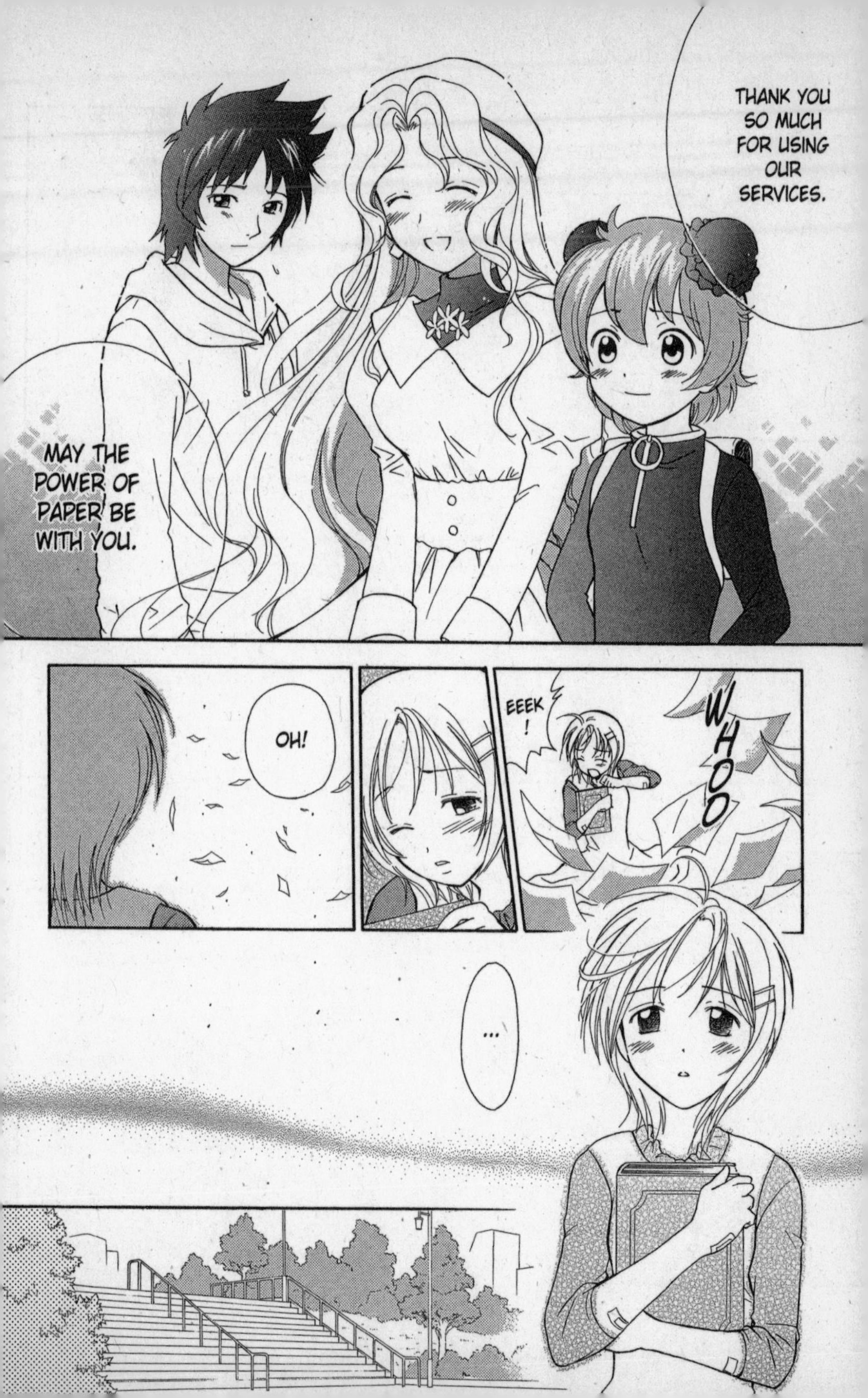
THANK YOU SO MUCH FOR USING OUR SERVICES.
MAY THE POWER OF PAPER BE WITH YOU.
WHOOO
EEEK!
OH!
...

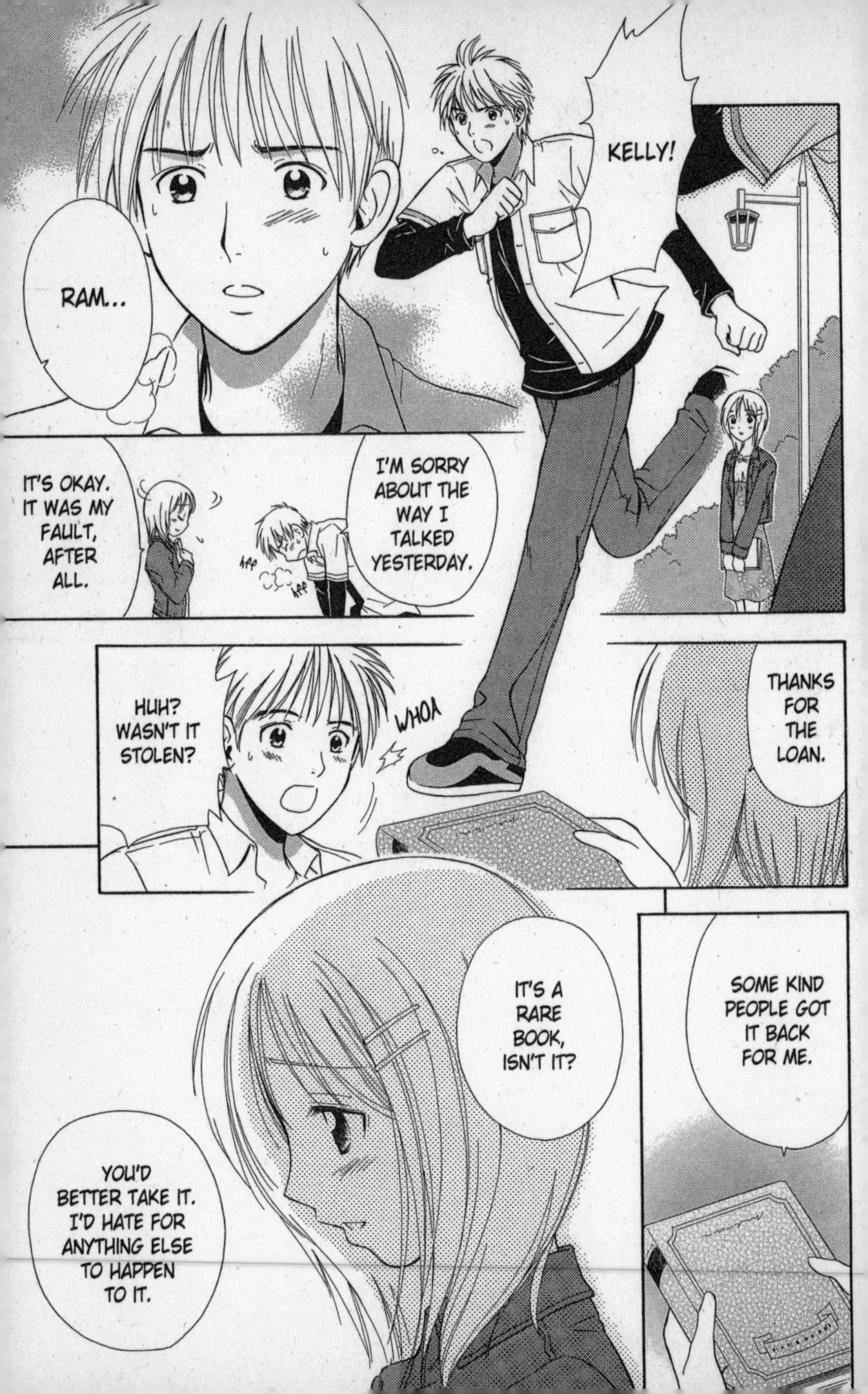
KELLY!
RAM...
I'M SORRY ABOUT THE WAY I TALKED YESTERDAY.
HFF
HFF
IT'S OKAY. IT WAS MY FAULT, AFTER ALL.
THANKS FOR THE LOAN.
WHOA
HUH? WASN'T IT STOLEN?
SOME KIND PEOPLE GOT IT BACK FOR ME.
IT'S A RARE BOOK, ISN'T IT?
YOU'D BETTER TAKE IT. I'D HATE FOR ANYTHING ELSE TO HAPPEN TO IT.

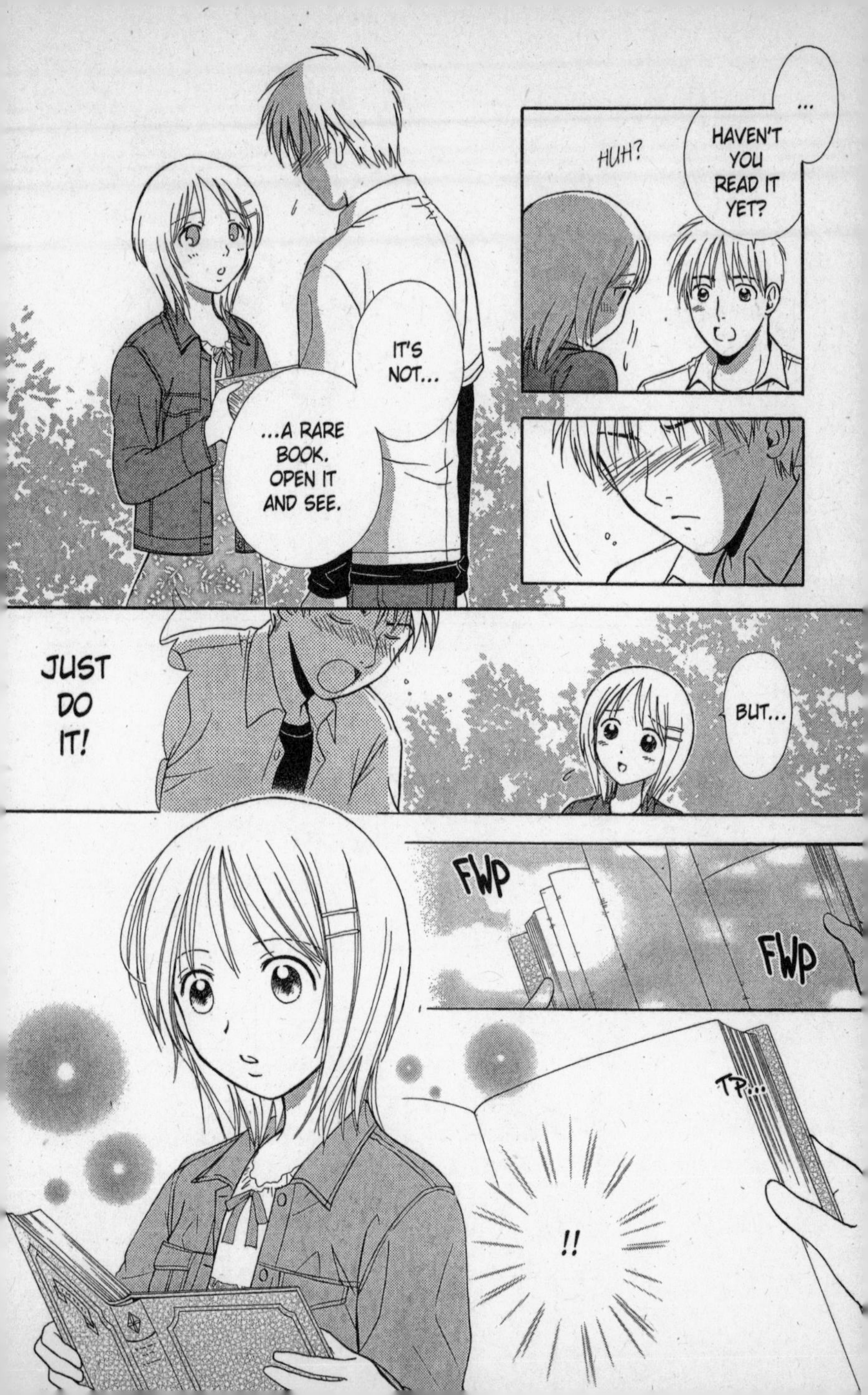
... HAVEN'T YOU READ IT YET?
HUH?
IT'S NOT...
...A RARE BOOK. OPEN IT AND SEE.
BUT...
JUST DO IT!
FWP
FWP
TP...
!!

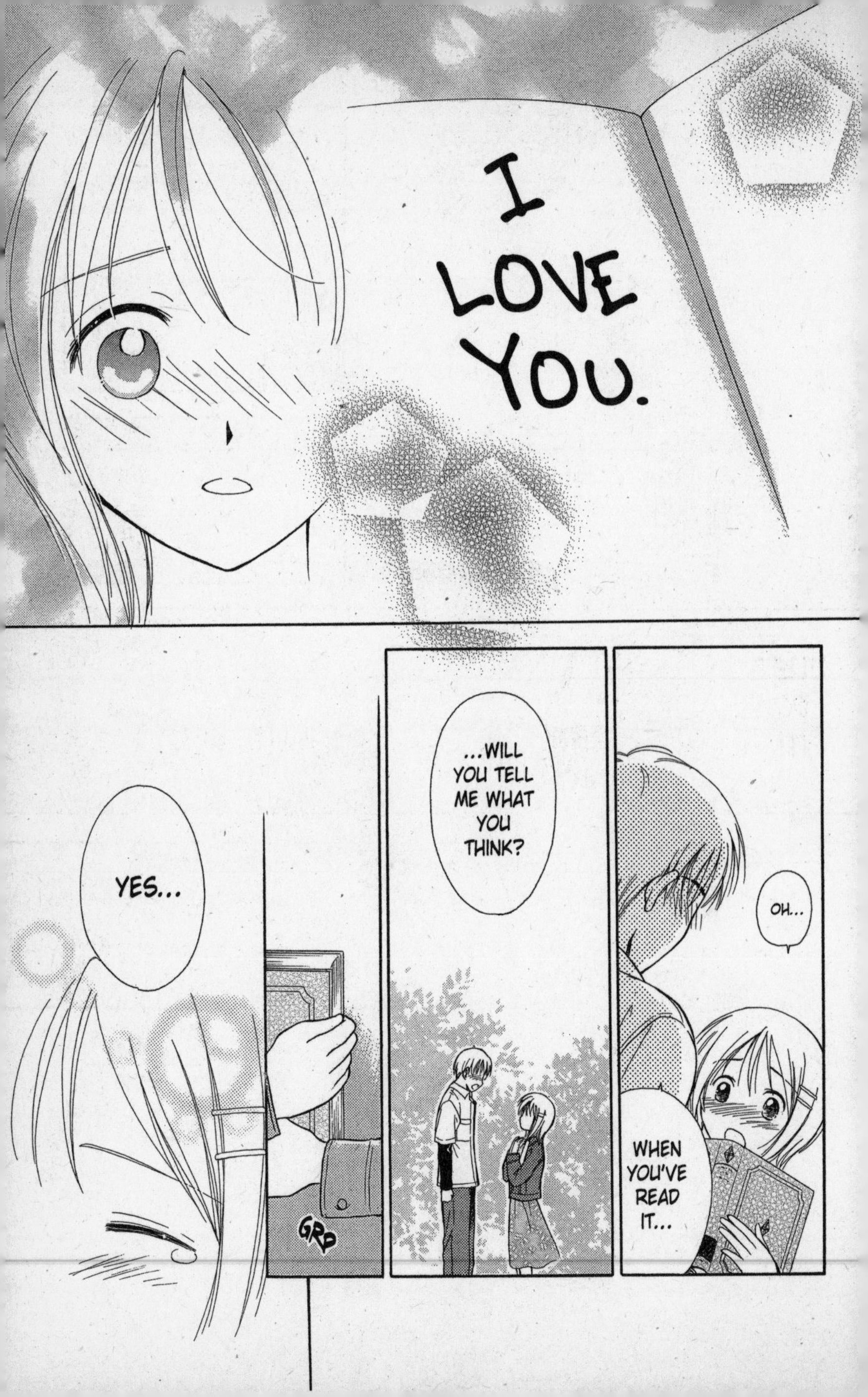
I LOVE YOU.
OH...
WHEN YOU'VE READ IT...
...WILL YOU TELL ME WHAT YOU THINK?
YES...
GRP

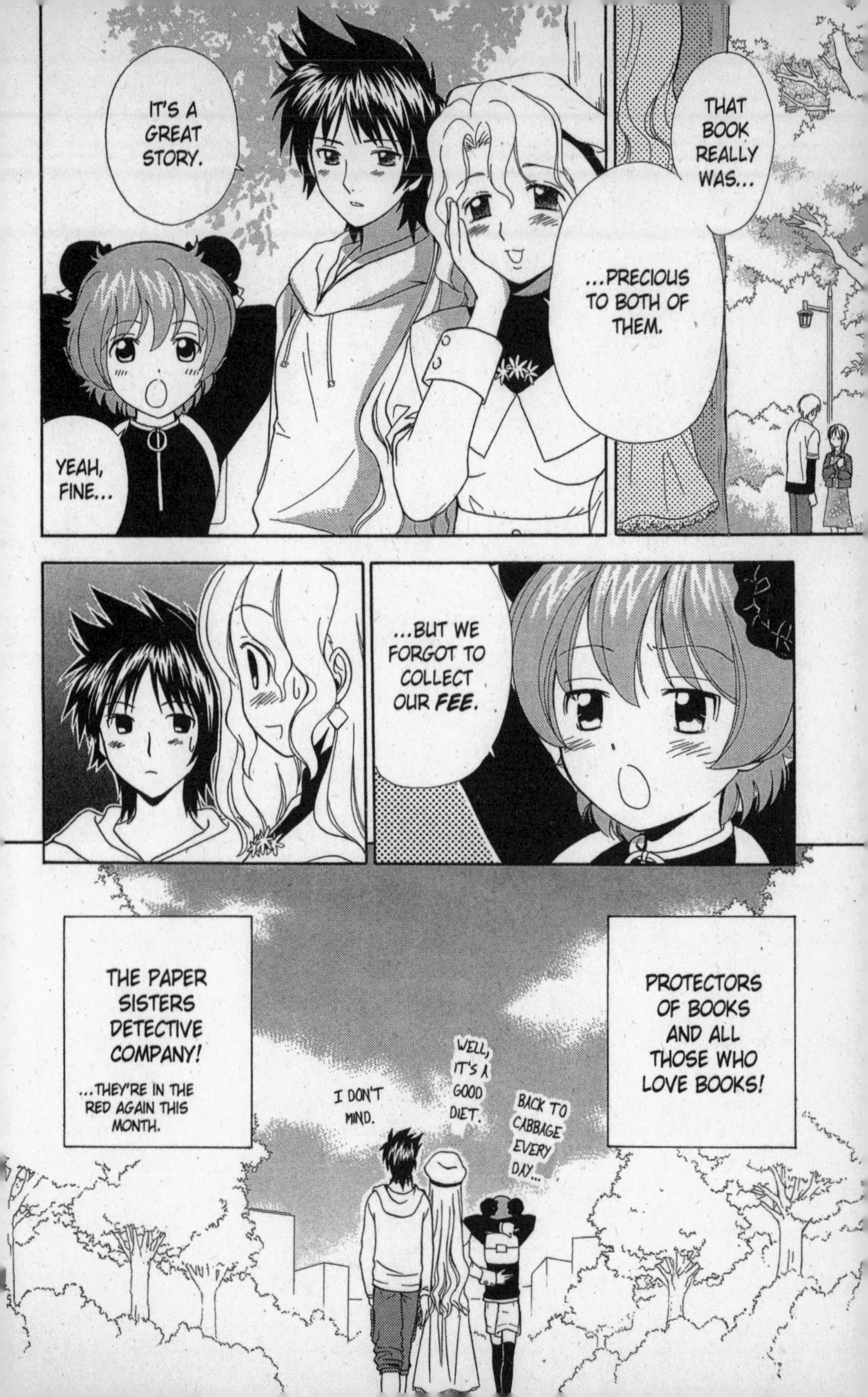

THAT BOOK REALLY WAS...
...PRECIOUS TO BOTH OF THEM.
IT'S A GREAT STORY.
YEAH, FINE...
...BUT WE FORGOT TO COLLECT OUR FEE.
PROTECTORS OF BOOKS AND ALL THOSE WHO LOVE BOOKS!
BACK TO CABBAGE EVERY DAY...
WELL, IT'S A GOOD DIET.
I DON'T MIND.
THE PAPER SISTERS DETECTIVE COMPANY!
...THEY'RE IN THE RED AGAIN THIS MONTH.

CHAPTER 2

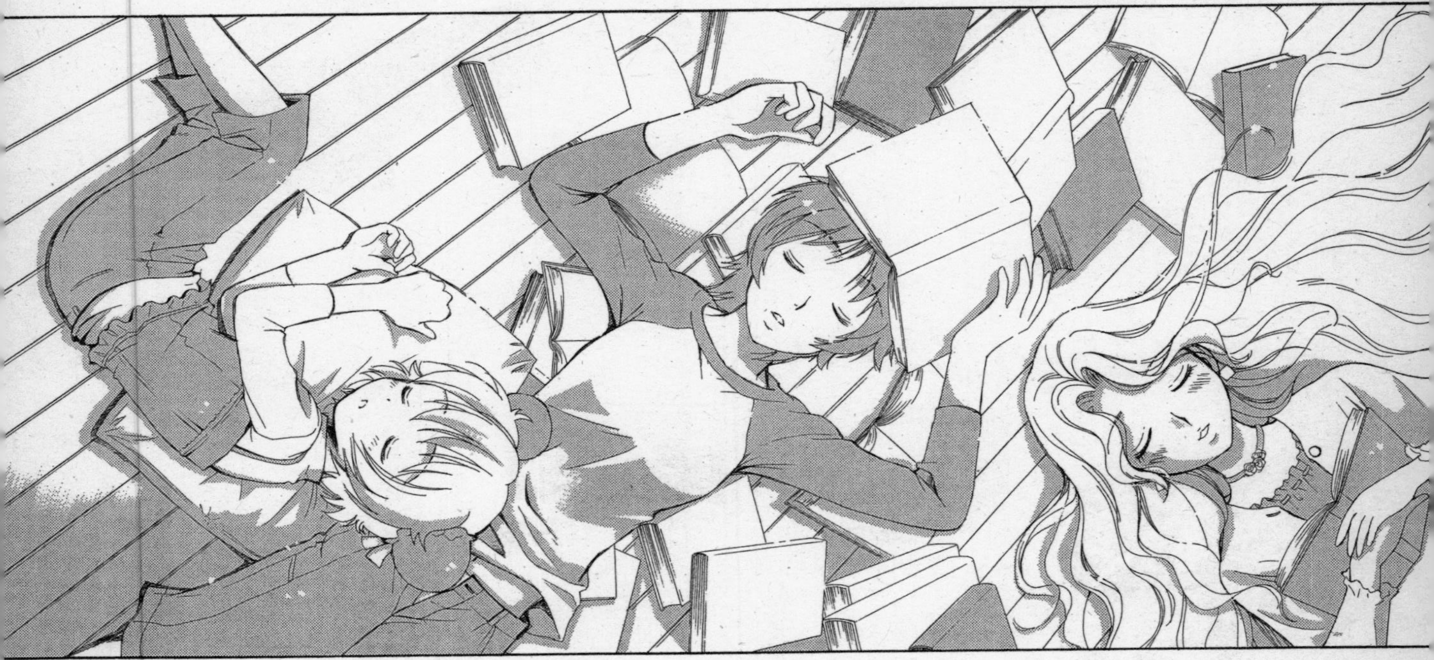

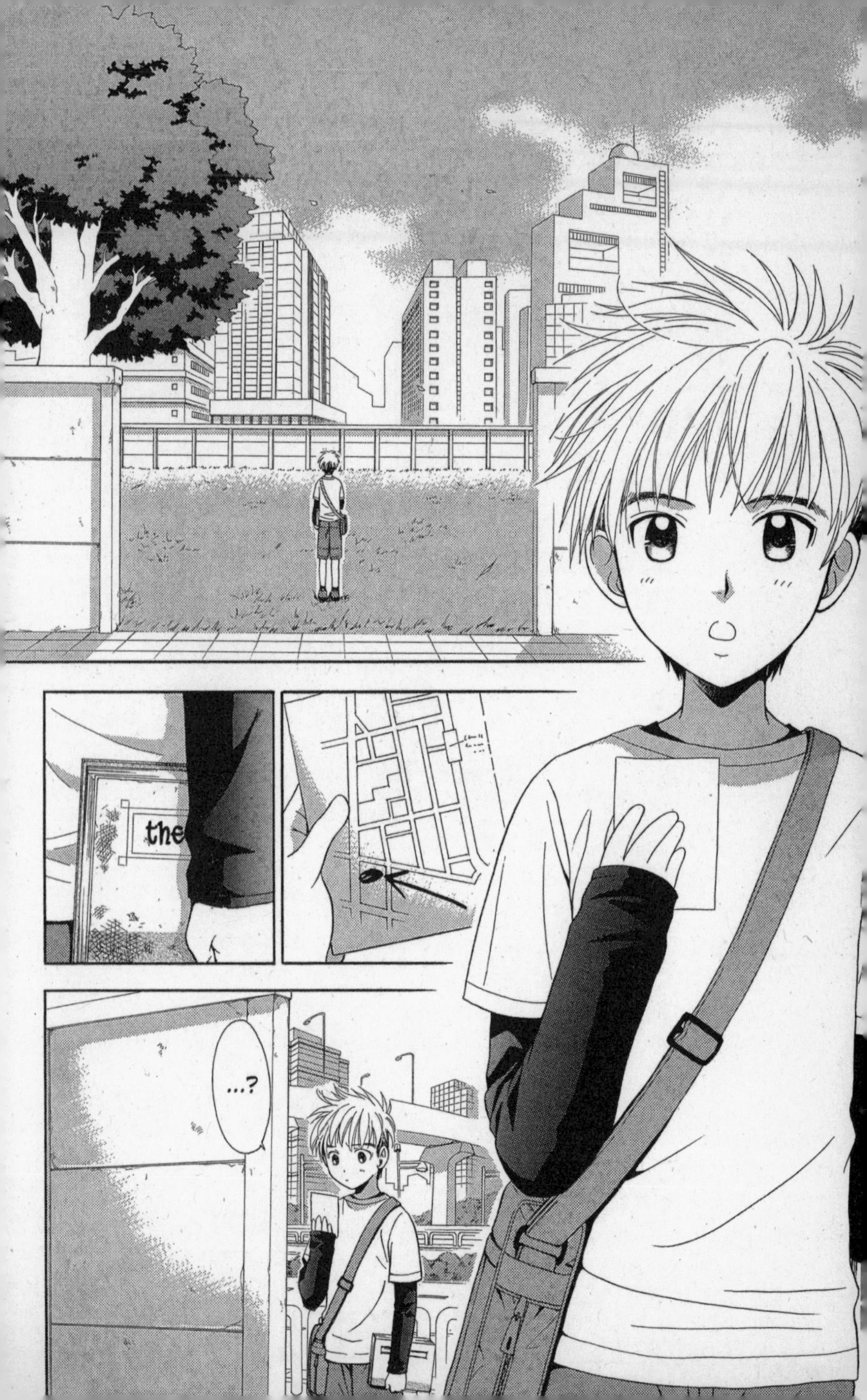
the
...?

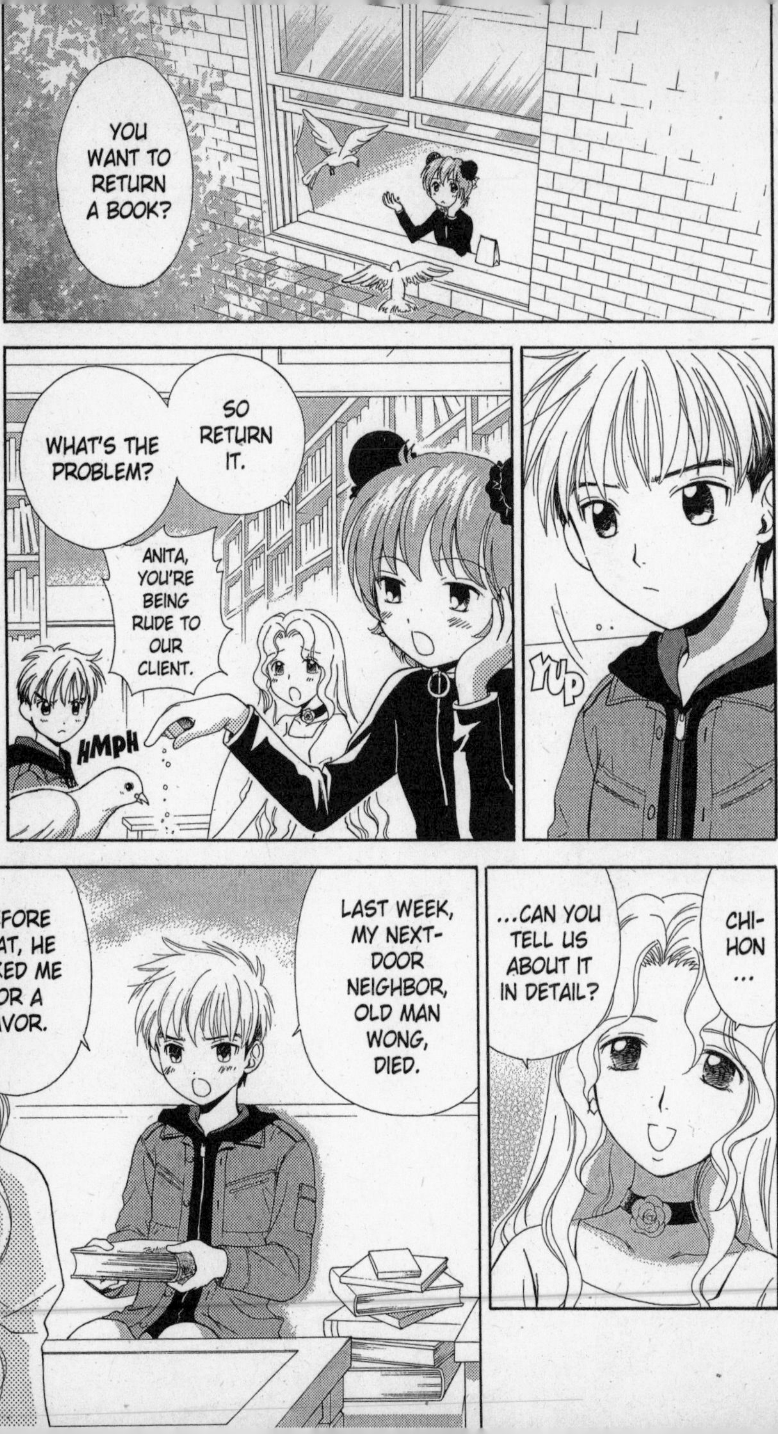
YOU WANT TO RETURN A BOOK?
YUP
SO RETURN IT.
WHAT'S THE PROBLEM?
ANITA, YOU'RE BEING RUDE TO OUR CLIENT.
HMPH
CHI-HON ...
...CAN YOU TELL US ABOUT IT IN DETAIL?
LAST WEEK, MY NEXT-DOOR NEIGHBOR, OLD MAN WONG, DIED.
BEFORE THAT, HE ASKED ME FOR A FAVOR.

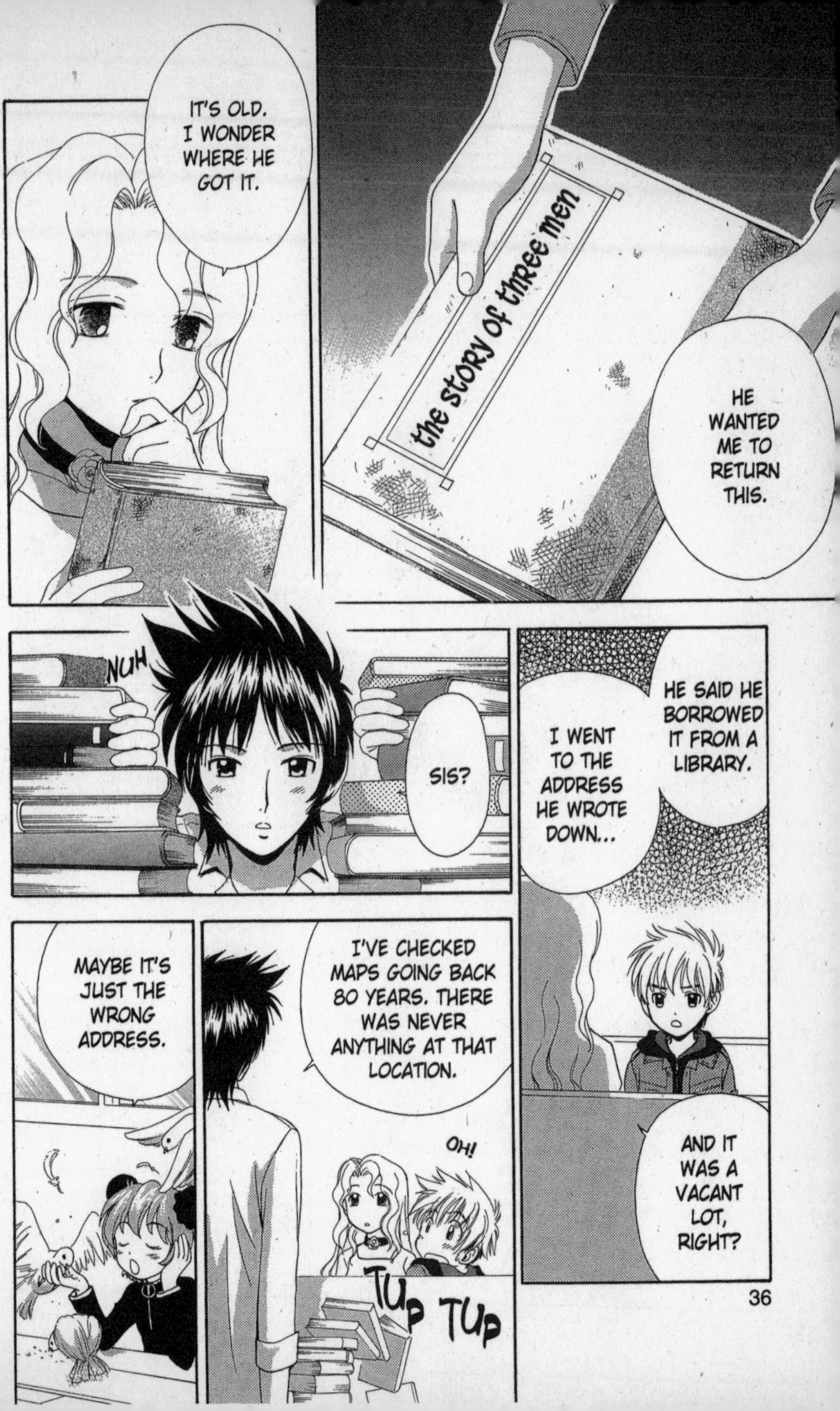

the story of three men
HE WANTED ME TO RETURN THIS.
IT'S OLD. I WONDER WHERE HE GOT IT.
HE SAID HE BORROWED IT FROM A LIBRARY.
I WENT TO THE ADDRESS HE WROTE DOWN...
AND IT WAS A VACANT LOT, RIGHT?
NUH
SIS?
I'VE CHECKED MAPS GOING BACK 80 YEARS. THERE WAS NEVER ANYTHING AT THAT LOCATION.
OH!
TUP TUP
MAYBE IT'S JUST THE WRONG ADDRESS.

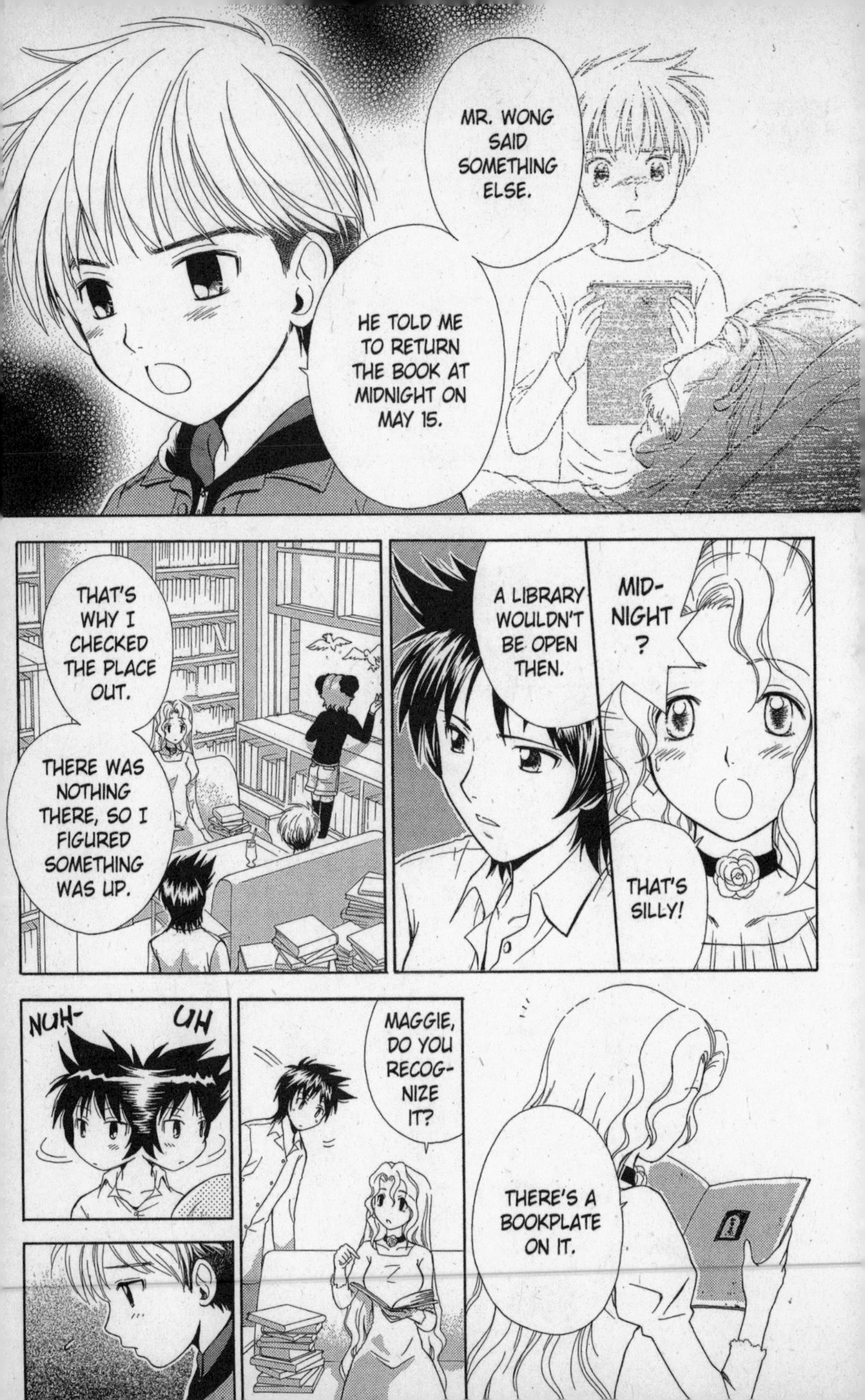
MR. WONG SAID SOMETHING ELSE.
HE TOLD ME TO RETURN THE BOOK AT MIDNIGHT ON MAY 15.
MID-NIGHT?
A LIBRARY WOULDN'T BE OPEN THEN.
THAT'S SILLY!
THAT'S WHY I CHECKED THE PLACE OUT.
THERE WAS NOTHING THERE, SO I FIGURED SOMETHING WAS UP.
THERE'S A BOOKPLATE ON IT.
MAGGIE, DO YOU RECOGNIZE IT?
NUH-UH

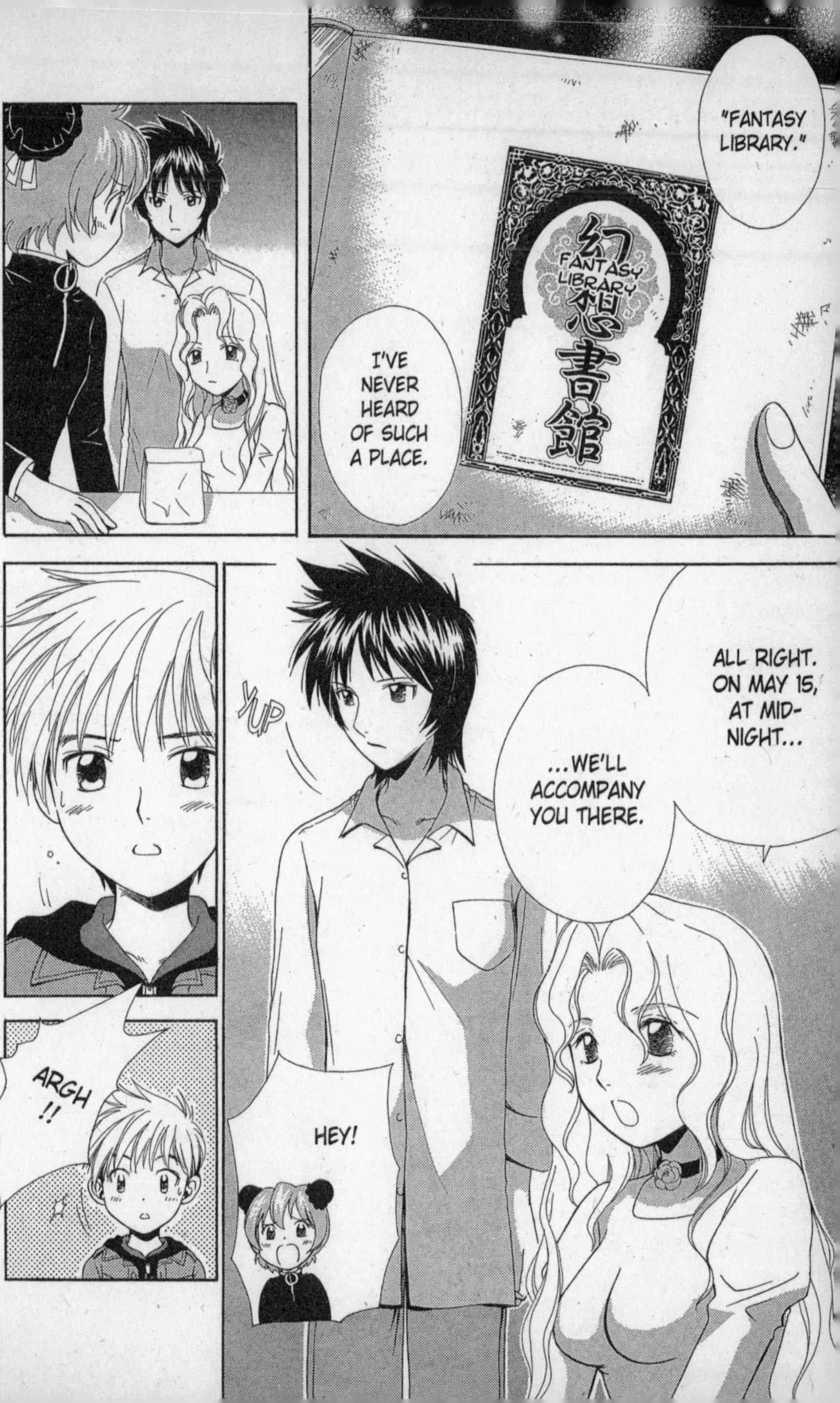
"FANTASY LIBRARY."
幻想書館
FANTASY LIBRARY
I'VE NEVER HEARD OF SUCH A PLACE.
ALL RIGHT. ON MAY 15, AT MID-NIGHT...
...WE'LL ACCOMPANY YOU THERE.
YUP
HEY!
ARGH !!

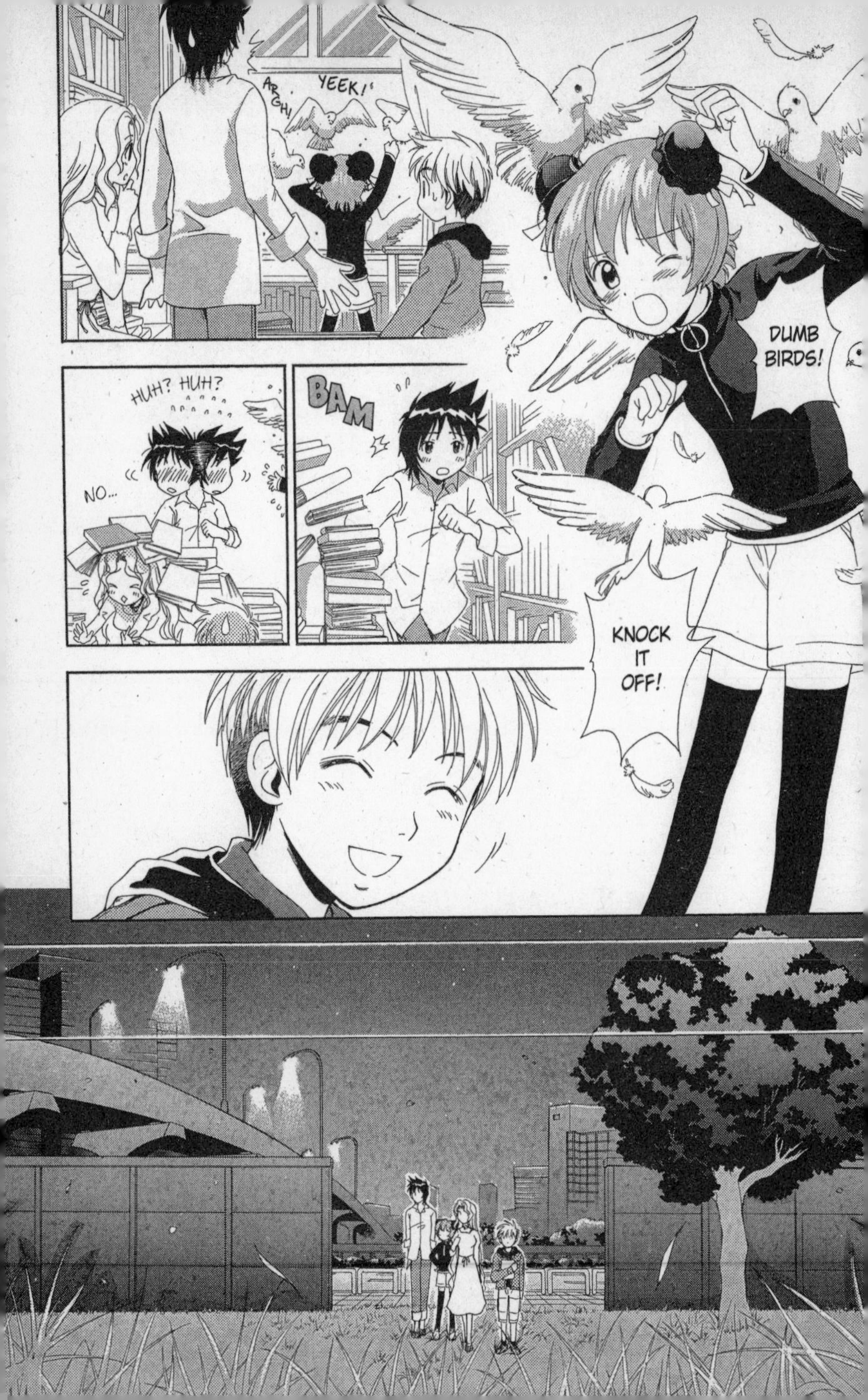
DUMB BIRDS!
KNOCK IT OFF!
YEEK!
ARGH!
BAM
HUH? HUH?
NO...

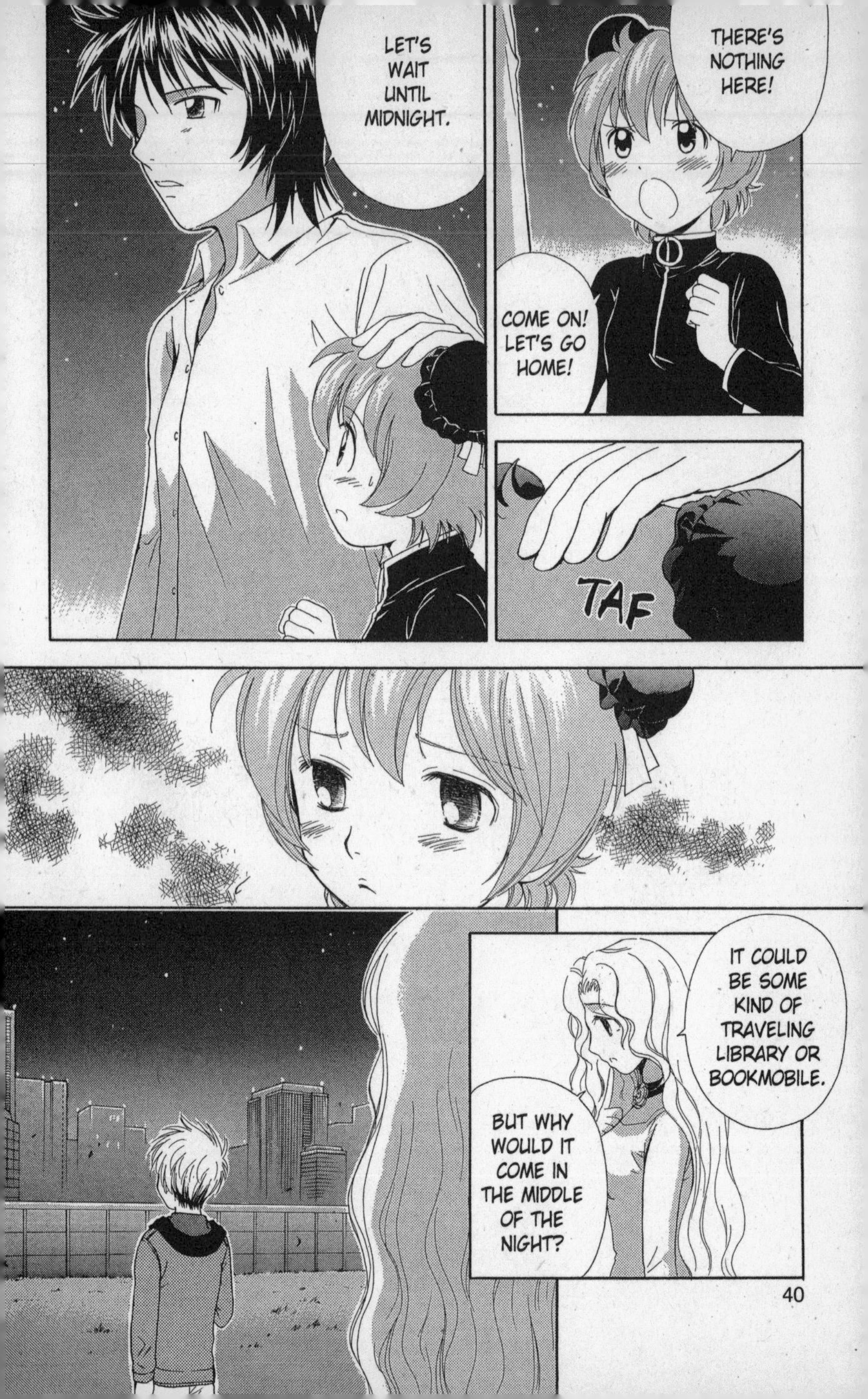
THERE'S NOTHING HERE!
COME ON! LET'S GO HOME!
TAF
LET'S WAIT UNTIL MIDNIGHT.
IT COULD BE SOME KIND OF TRAVELING LIBRARY OR BOOKMOBILE.
BUT WHY WOULD IT COME IN THE MIDDLE OF THE NIGHT?

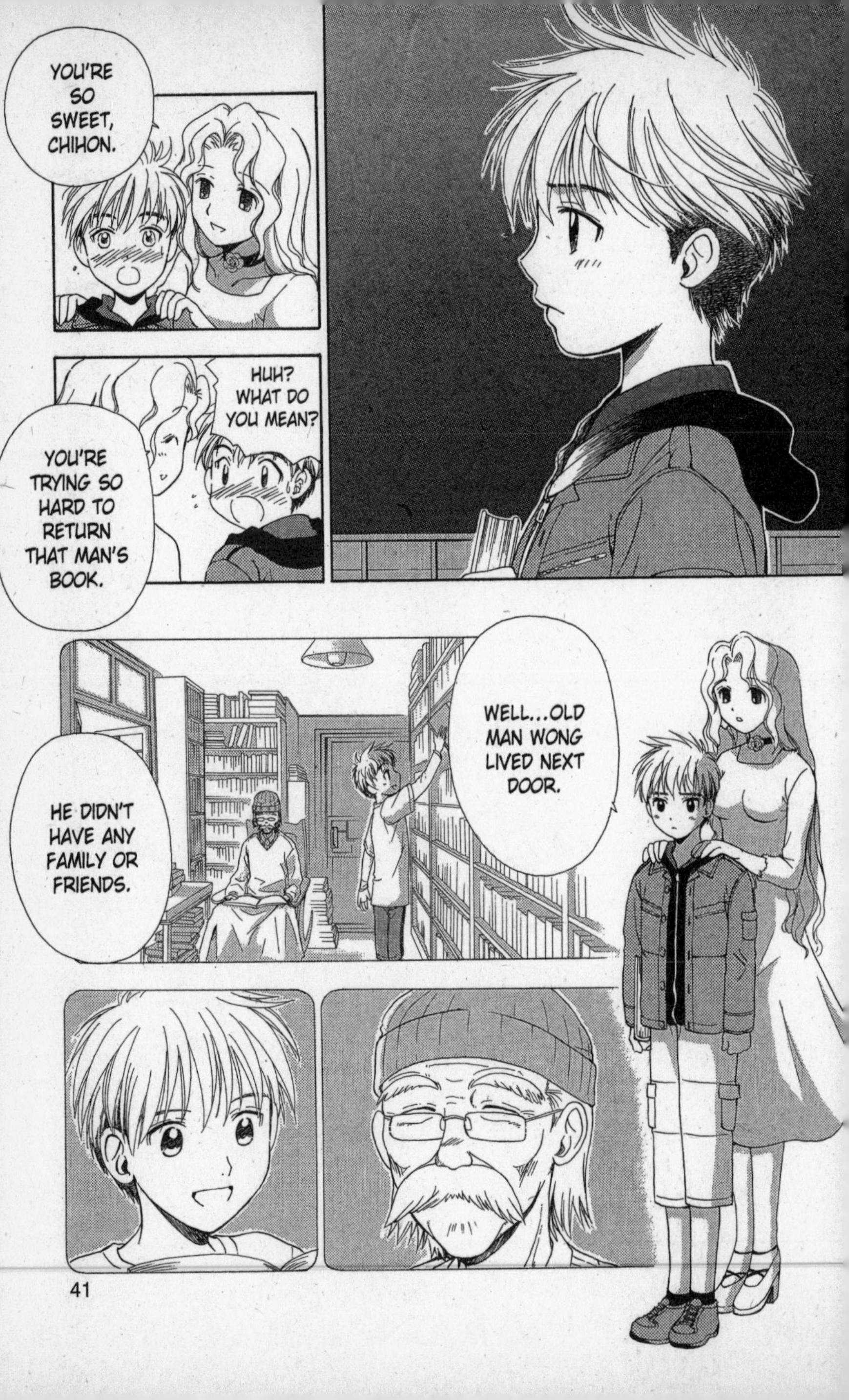
YOU'RE SO SWEET, CHIHON.
HUH? WHAT DO YOU MEAN?
YOU'RE TRYING SO HARD TO RETURN THAT MAN'S BOOK.
WELL...OLD MAN WONG LIVED NEXT DOOR.
HE DIDN'T HAVE ANY FAMILY OR FRIENDS.

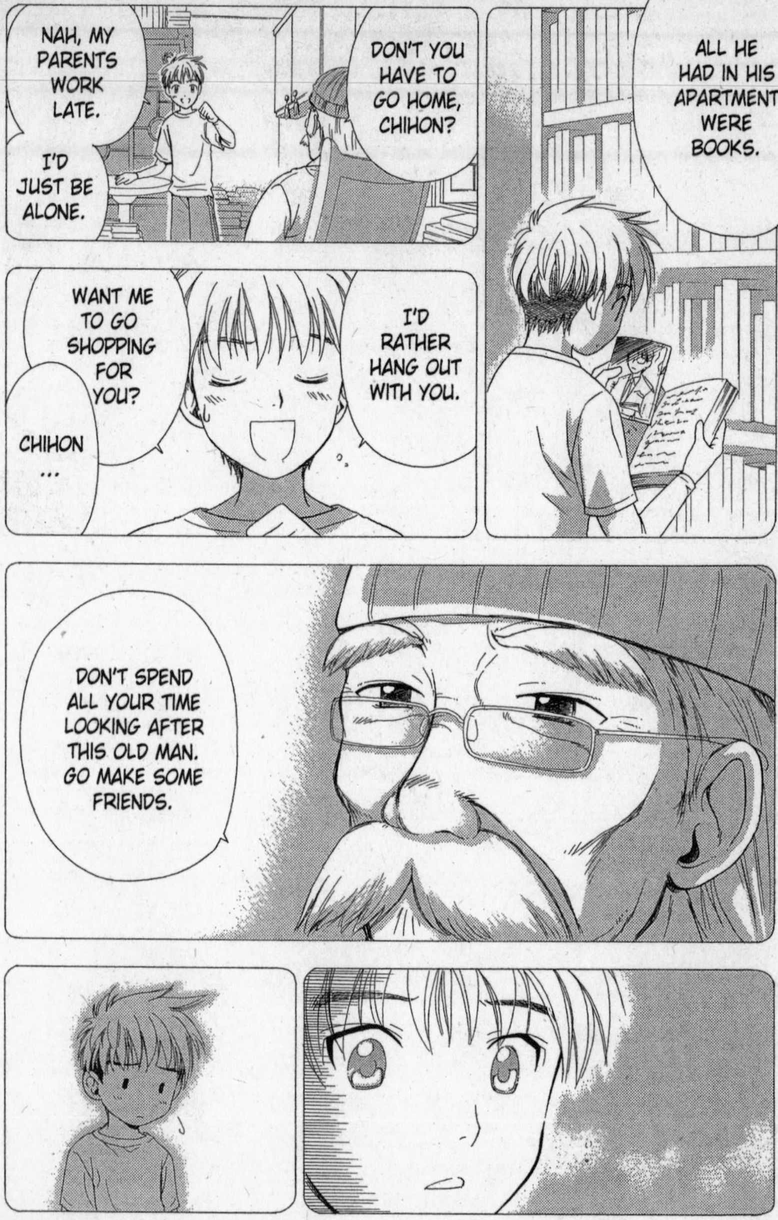
ALL HE HAD IN HIS APARTMENT WERE BOOKS.
DON'T YOU HAVE TO GO HOME, CHIHON?
NAH, MY PARENTS WORK LATE.
I'D JUST BE ALONE.
I'D RATHER HANG OUT WITH YOU.
WANT ME TO GO SHOPPING FOR YOU?
CHIHON ...
DON'T SPEND ALL YOUR TIME LOOKING AFTER THIS OLD MAN. GO MAKE SOME FRIENDS.

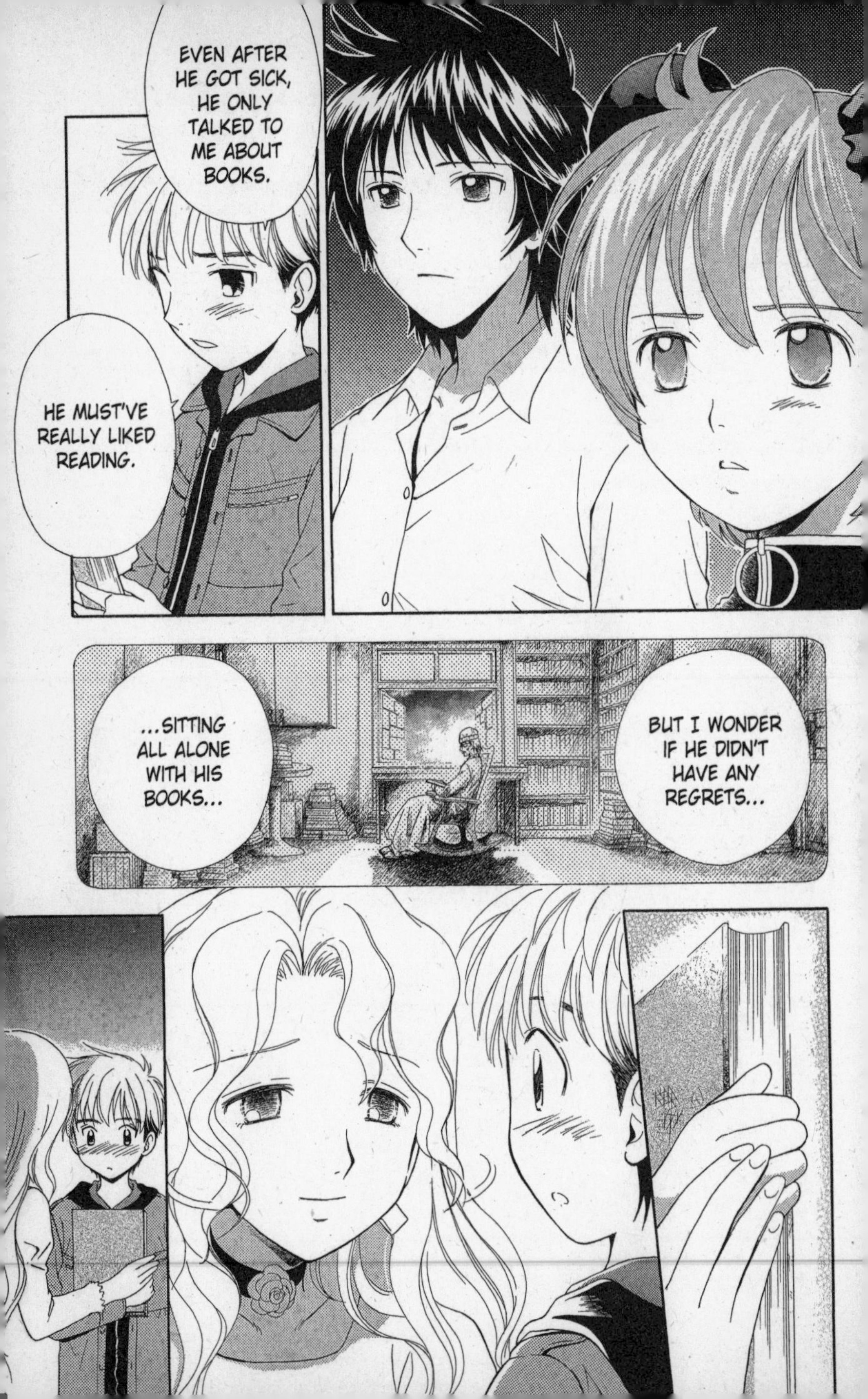
EVEN AFTER HE GOT SICK, HE ONLY TALKED TO ME ABOUT BOOKS.
HE MUST'VE REALLY LIKED READING.
BUT I WONDER IF HE DIDN'T HAVE ANY REGRETS...
...SITTING ALL ALONE WITH HIS BOOKS...

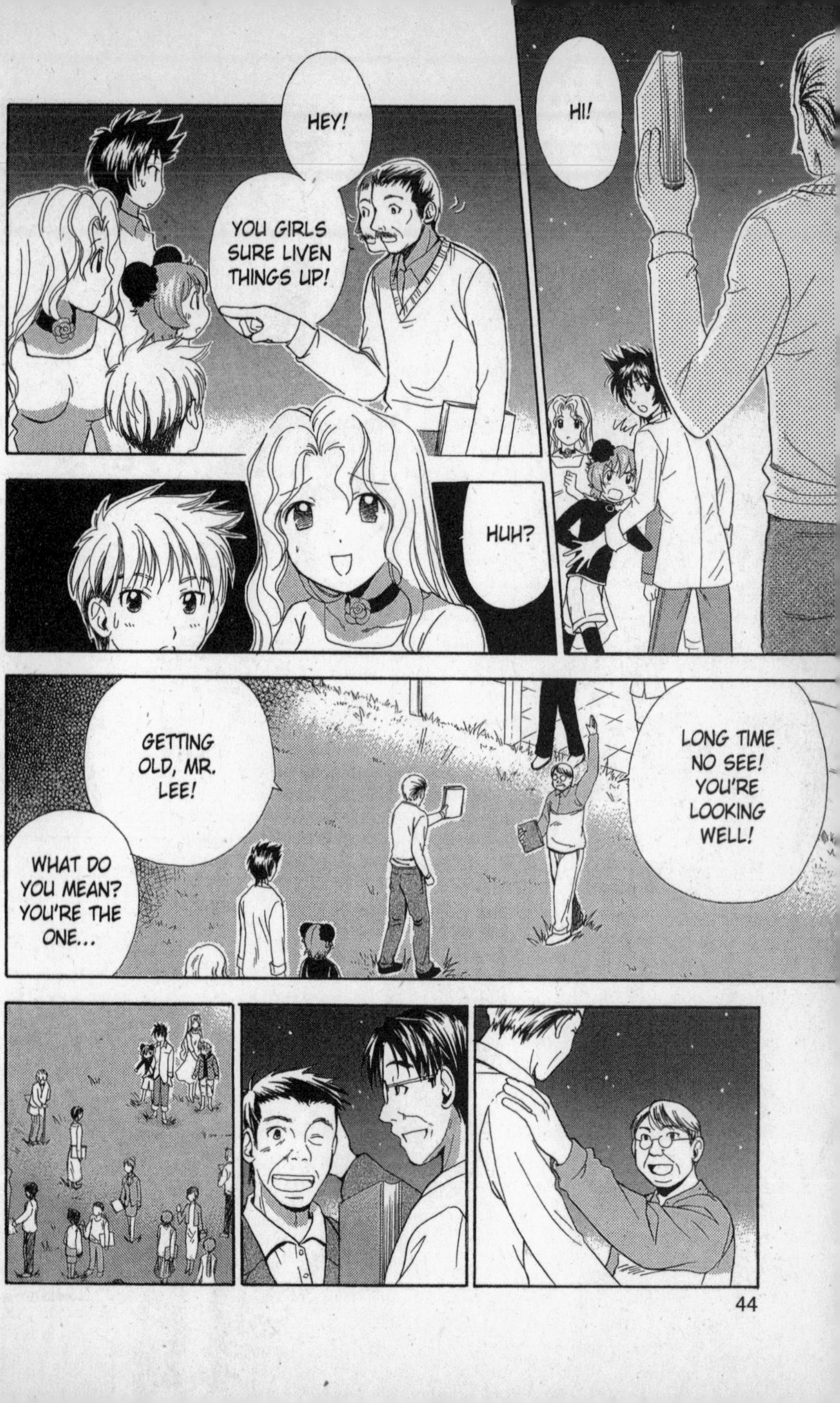
HI!
HEY!
YOU GIRLS SURE LIVEN THINGS UP!
HUH?
LONG TIME NO SEE! YOU'RE LOOKING WELL!
GETTING OLD, MR. LEE!
WHAT DO YOU MEAN? YOU'RE THE ONE...

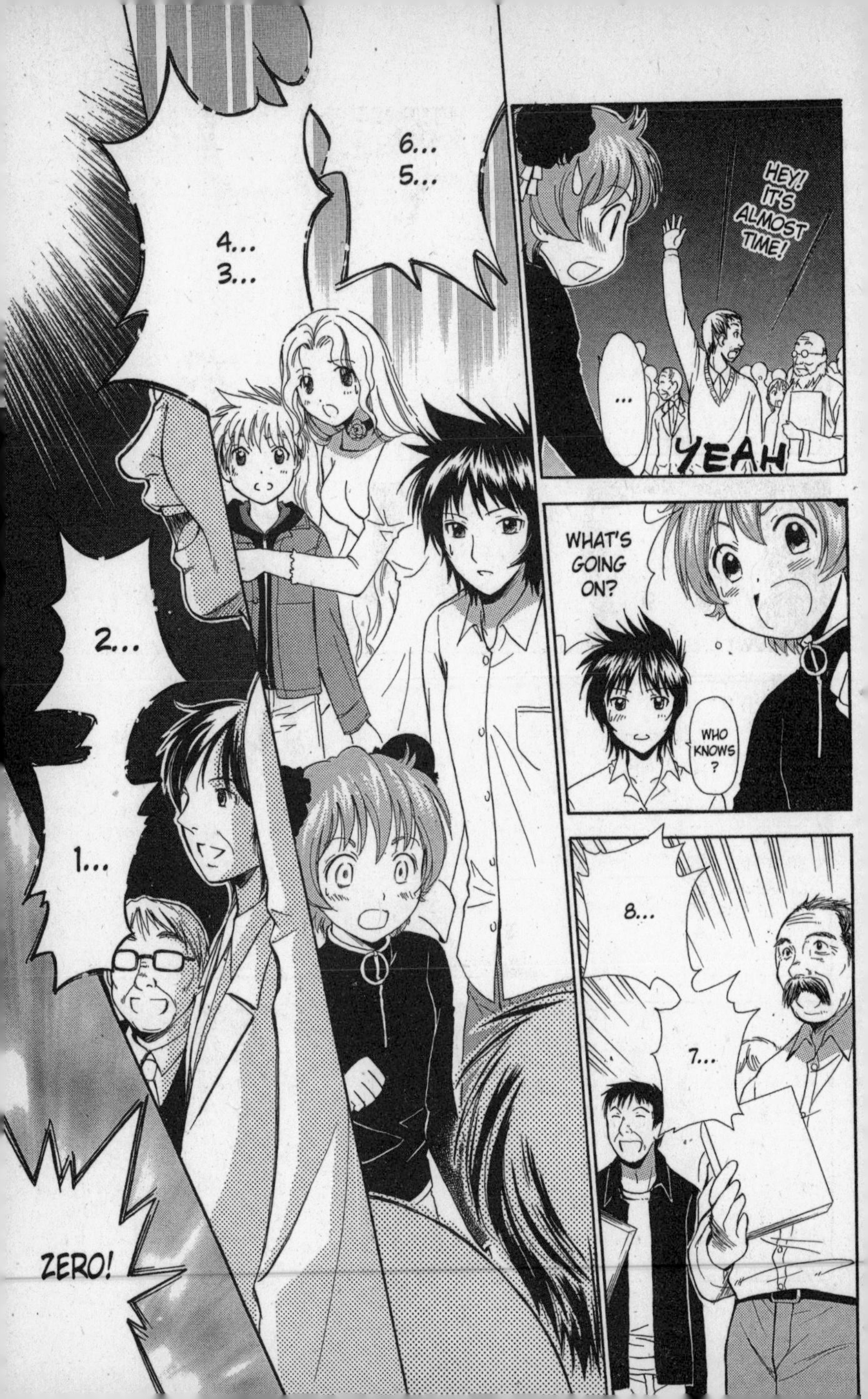
HEY! IT'S ALMOST TIME!
...
YEAH
WHAT'S GOING ON?
WHO KNOWS?
8...
7...
6...
5...
4...
3...
2...
1...
ZERO!

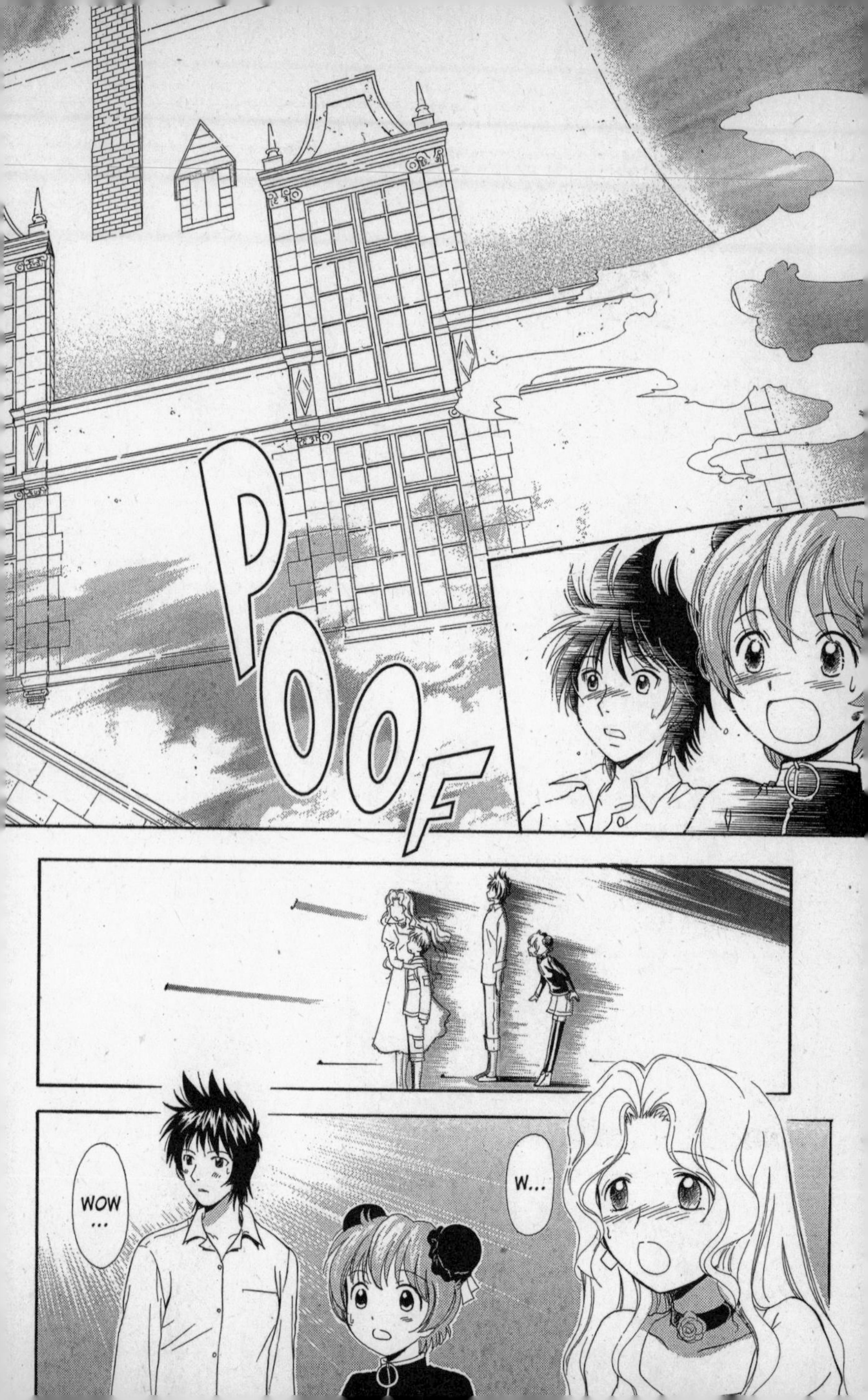
POOOF
W...
WOW ...

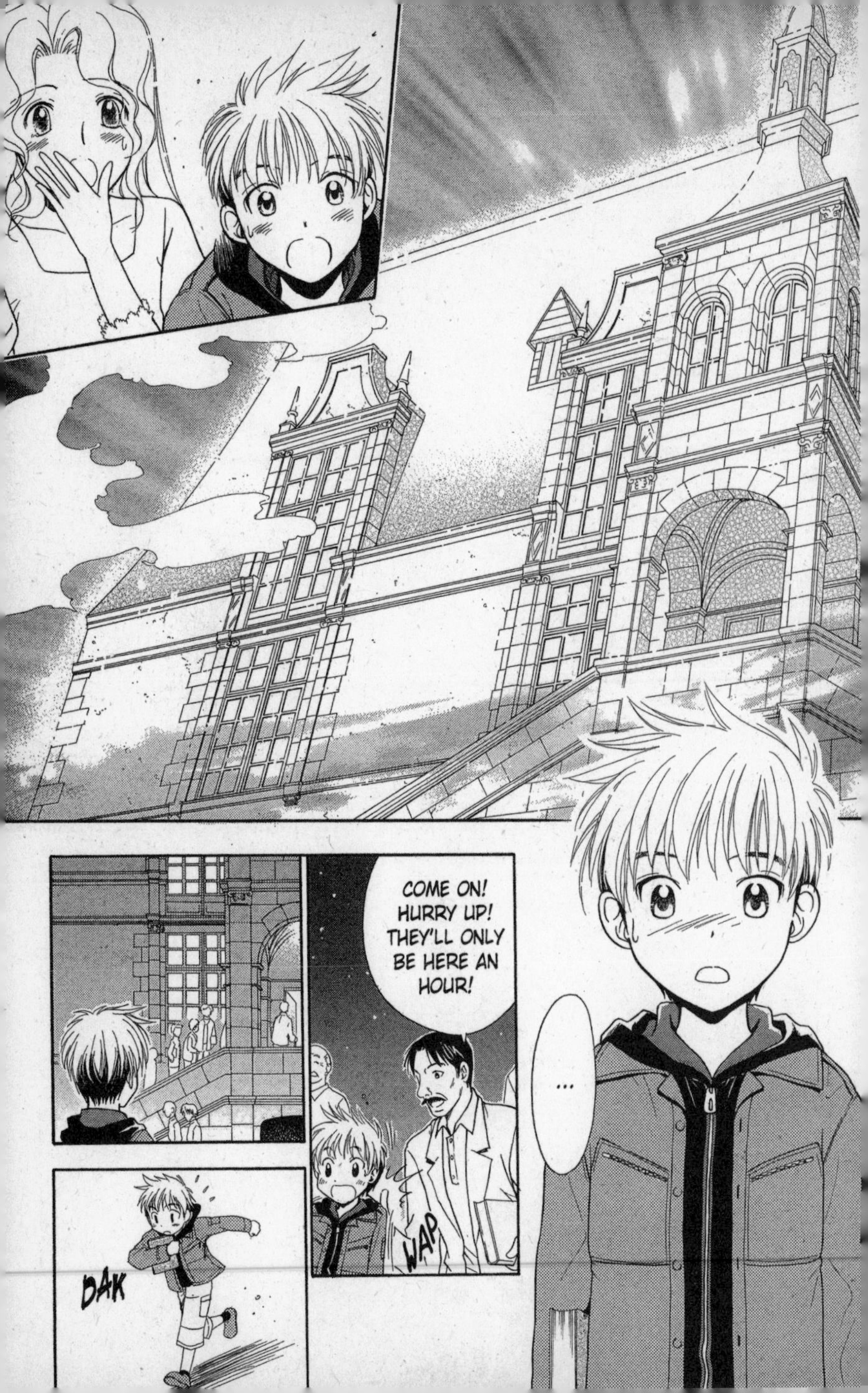
...
COME ON! HURRY UP! THEY'LL ONLY BE HERE AN HOUR!
WAP
DAK

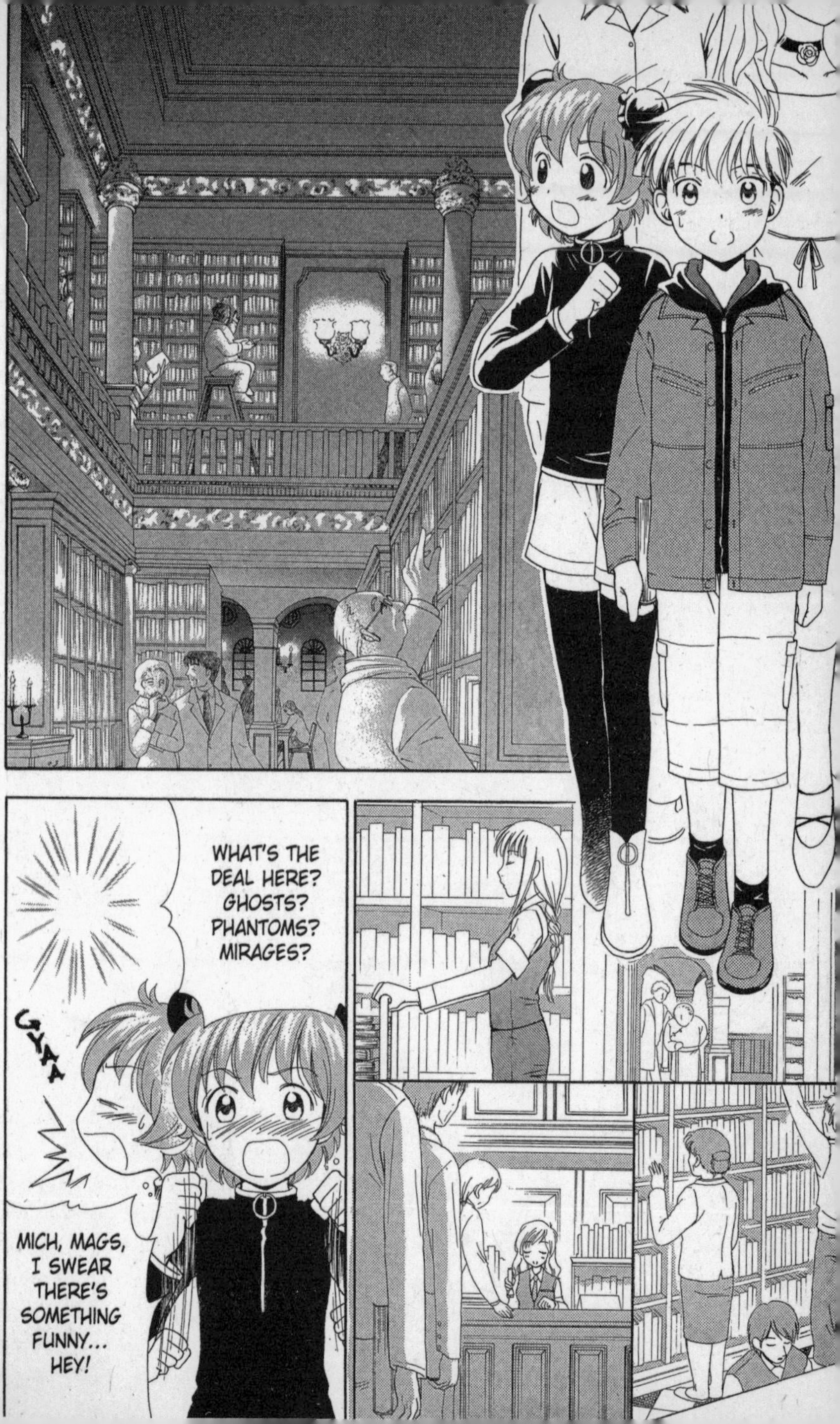
WHAT'S THE DEAL HERE? GHOSTS? PHANTOMS? MIRAGES?
GYAA
MICH, MAGS, I SWEAR THERE'S SOMETHING FUNNY... HEY!

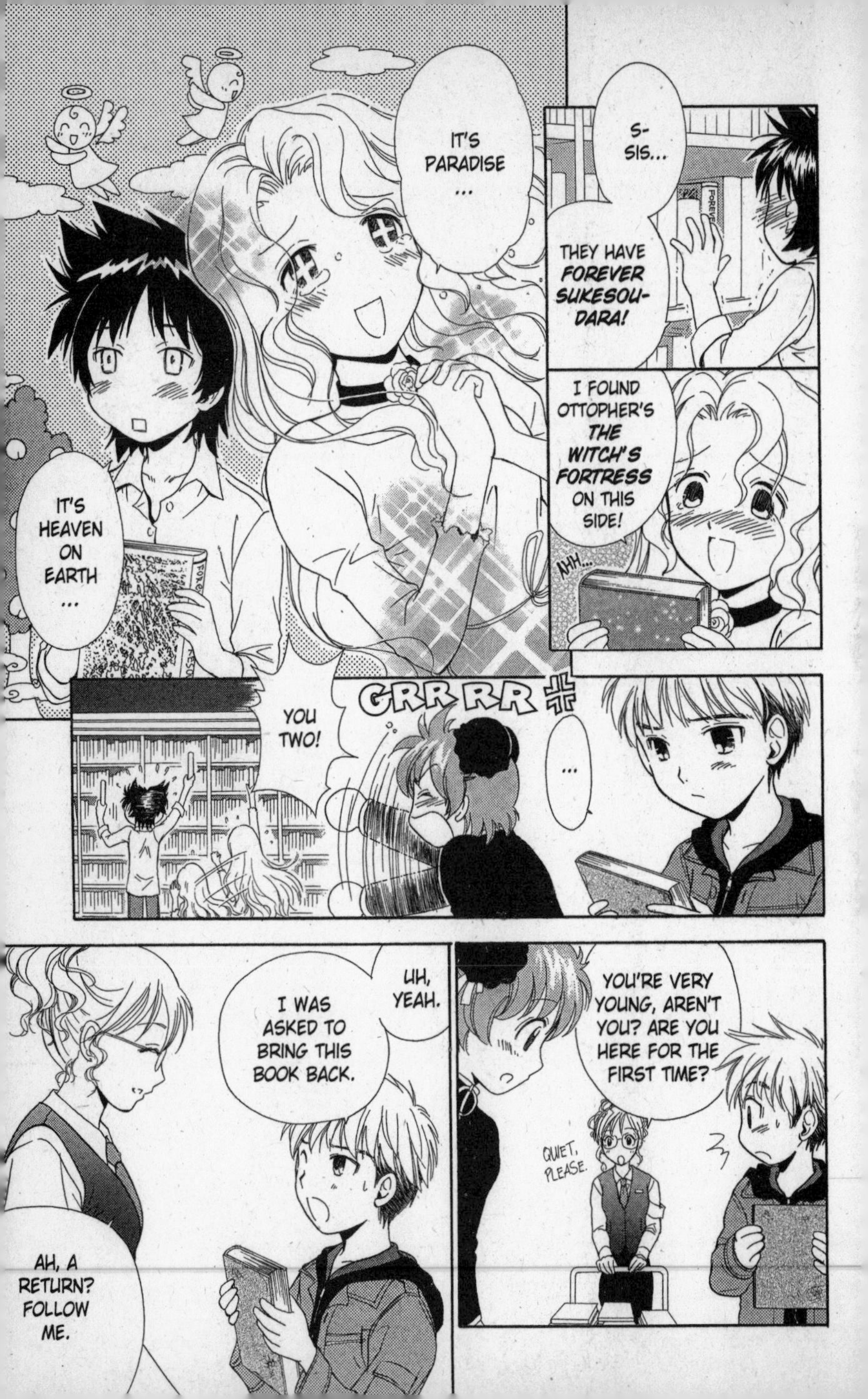
S-SIS...
THEY HAVE FOREVER SUKESOUDARA!
I FOUND OTTOPHER'S THE WITCH'S FORTRESS ON THIS SIDE!
AHH...
IT'S PARADISE...
IT'S HEAVEN ON EARTH...
GRRRRR
...
YOU TWO!
YOU'RE VERY YOUNG, AREN'T YOU? ARE YOU HERE FOR THE FIRST TIME?
QUIET, PLEASE.
UH, YEAH.
I WAS ASKED TO BRING THIS BOOK BACK.
AH, A RETURN? FOLLOW ME.

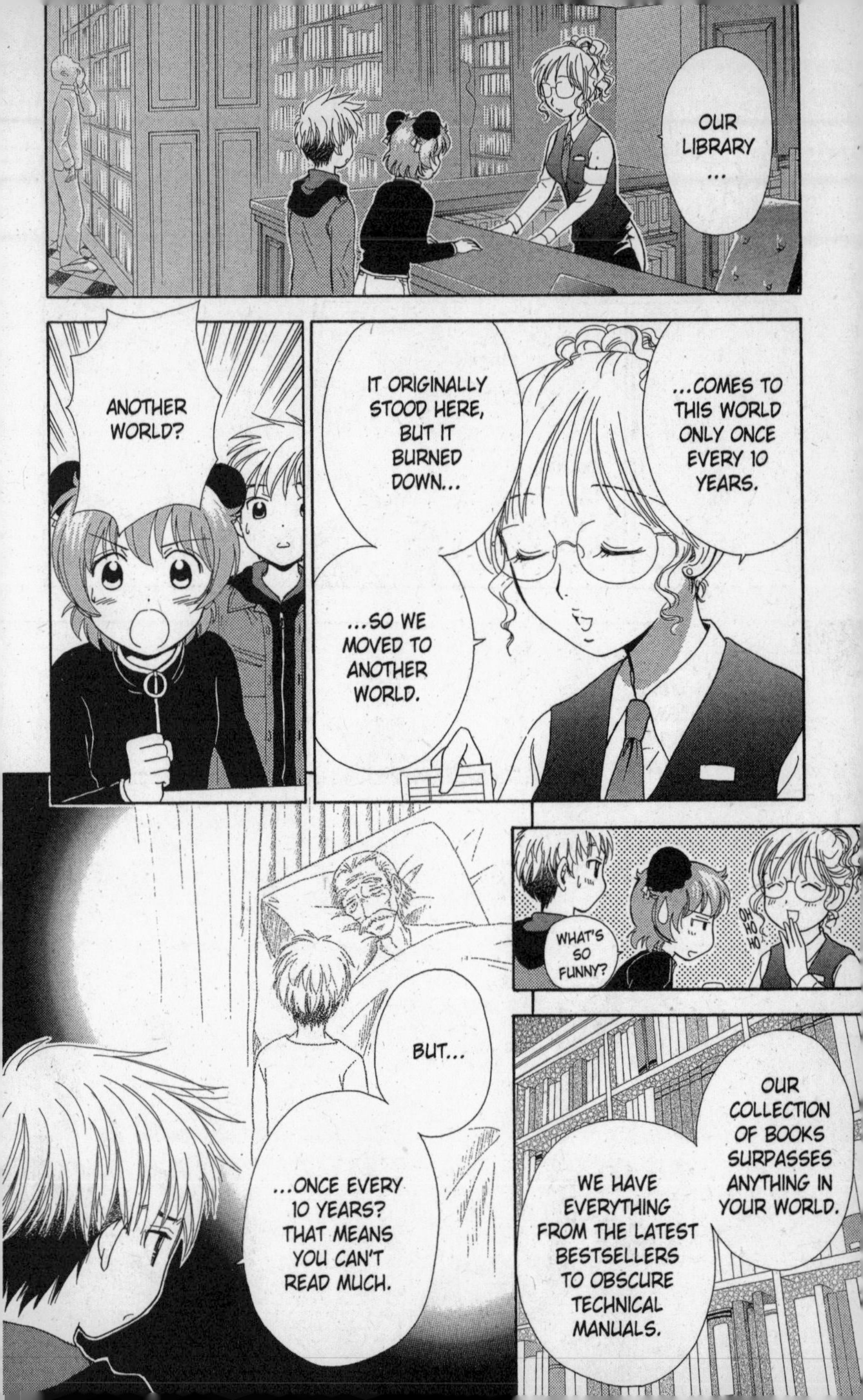
OUR LIBRARY ...
...COMES TO THIS WORLD ONLY ONCE EVERY 10 YEARS.
IT ORIGINALLY STOOD HERE, BUT IT BURNED DOWN...
...SO WE MOVED TO ANOTHER WORLD.
ANOTHER WORLD?
OH HO HO
WHAT'S SO FUNNY?
OUR COLLECTION OF BOOKS SURPASSES ANYTHING IN YOUR WORLD.
WE HAVE EVERYTHING FROM THE LATEST BESTSELLERS TO OBSCURE TECHNICAL MANUALS.
BUT...
...ONCE EVERY 10 YEARS? THAT MEANS YOU CAN'T READ MUCH.

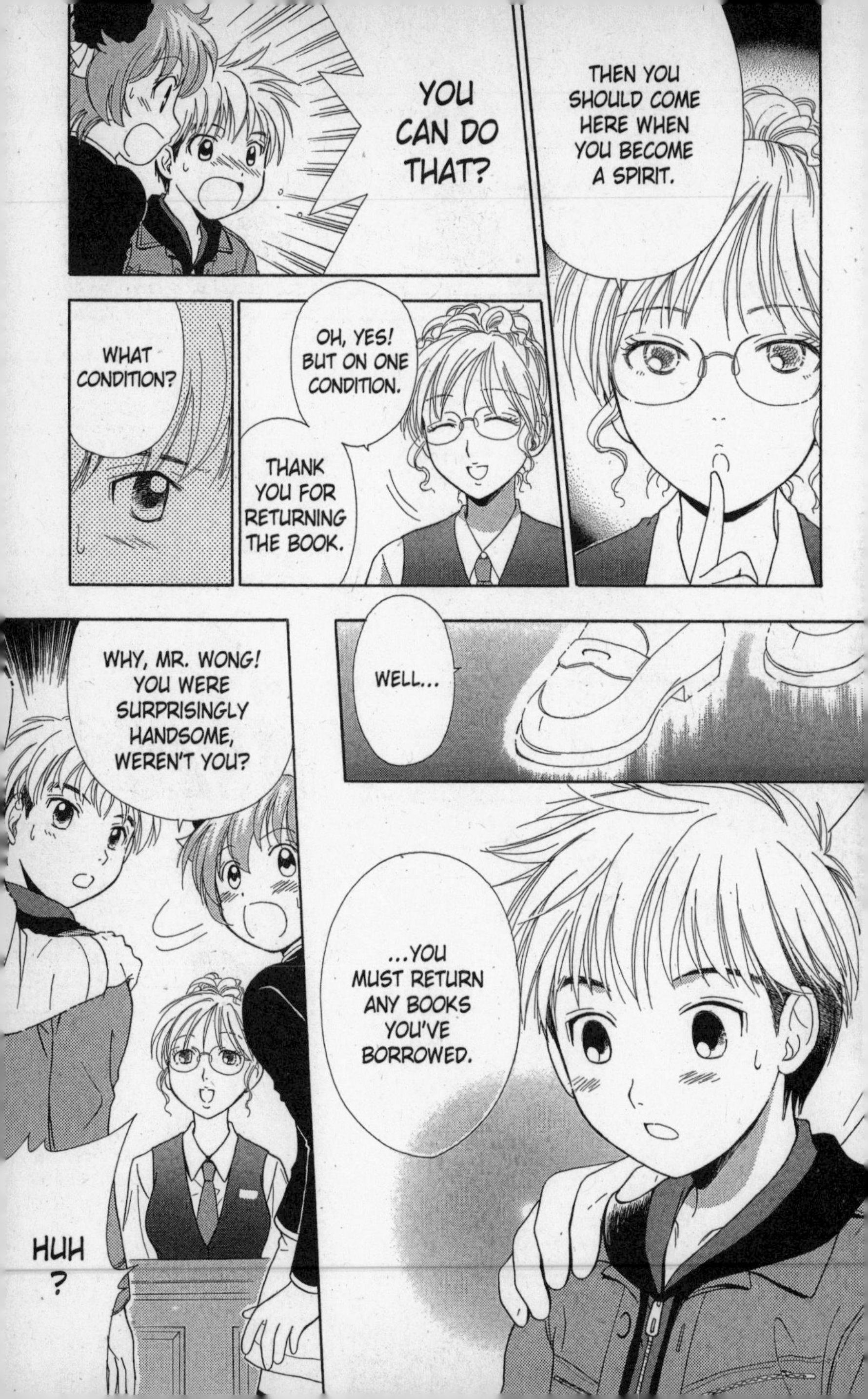
THEN YOU SHOULD COME HERE WHEN YOU BECOME A SPIRIT.
YOU CAN DO THAT?
OH, YES! BUT ON ONE CONDITION.
THANK YOU FOR RETURNING THE BOOK.
WHAT CONDITION?
WELL...
...YOU MUST RETURN ANY BOOKS YOU'VE BORROWED.
WHY, MR. WONG! YOU WERE SURPRISINGLY HANDSOME, WEREN'T YOU?
HUH ?

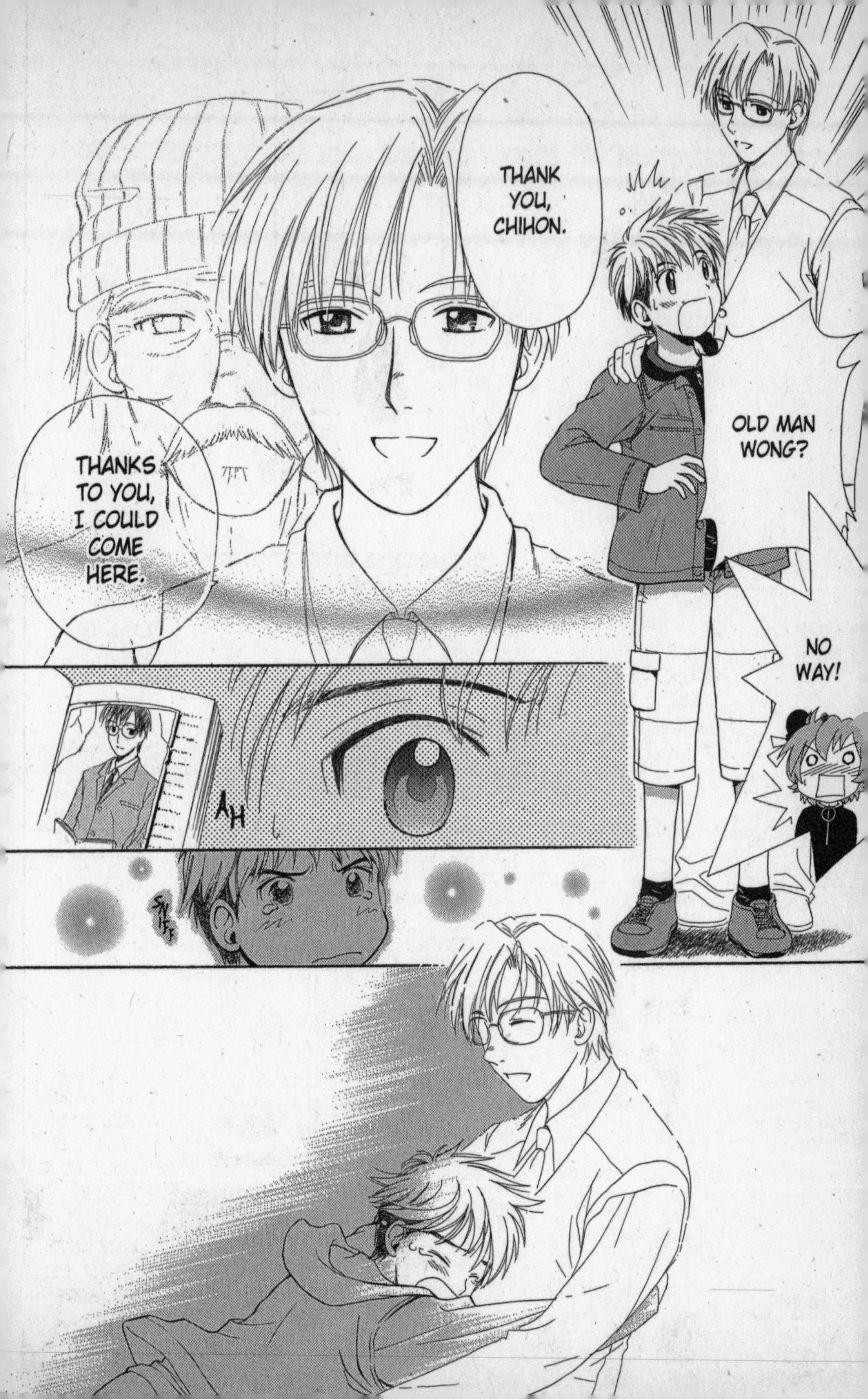
OLD MAN WONG?
NO WAY!
THANK YOU, CHIHON.
THANKS TO YOU, I COULD COME HERE.
AH
SNIFF

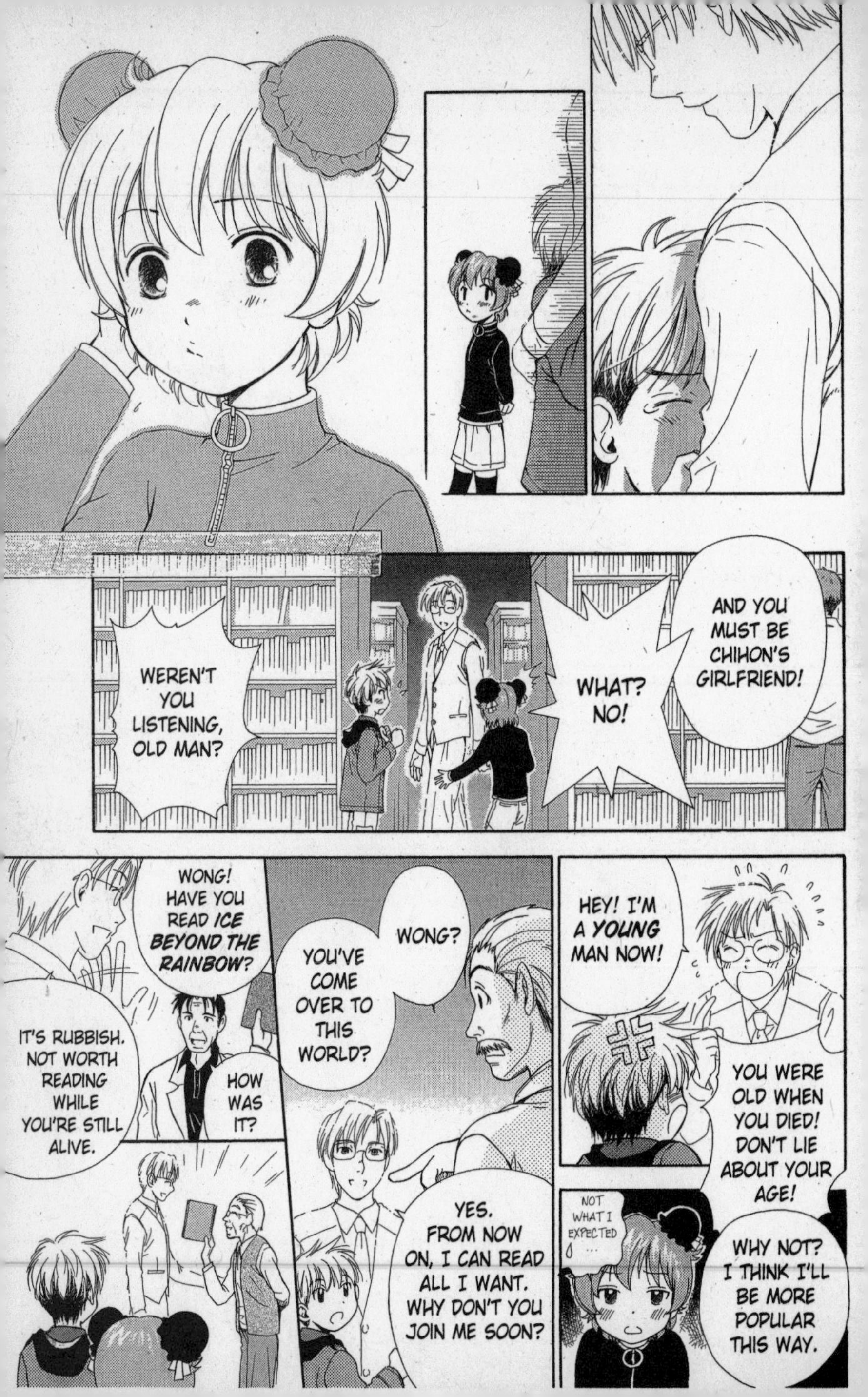
AND YOU MUST BE CHIHON'S GIRLFRIEND!
WHAT? NO!
WEREN'T YOU LISTENING, OLD MAN?
HEY! I'M A *YOUNG* MAN NOW!
YOU WERE OLD WHEN YOU DIED! DON'T LIE ABOUT YOUR AGE!
WHY NOT? I THINK I'LL BE MORE POPULAR THIS WAY.
NOT WHAT I EXPECTED ...
WONG?
YOU'VE COME OVER TO THIS WORLD?
YES. FROM NOW ON, I CAN READ ALL I WANT. WHY DON'T YOU JOIN ME SOON?
WONG! HAVE YOU READ *ICE BEYOND THE RAINBOW*?
HOW WAS IT?
IT'S RUBBISH. NOT WORTH READING WHILE YOU'RE STILL ALIVE.

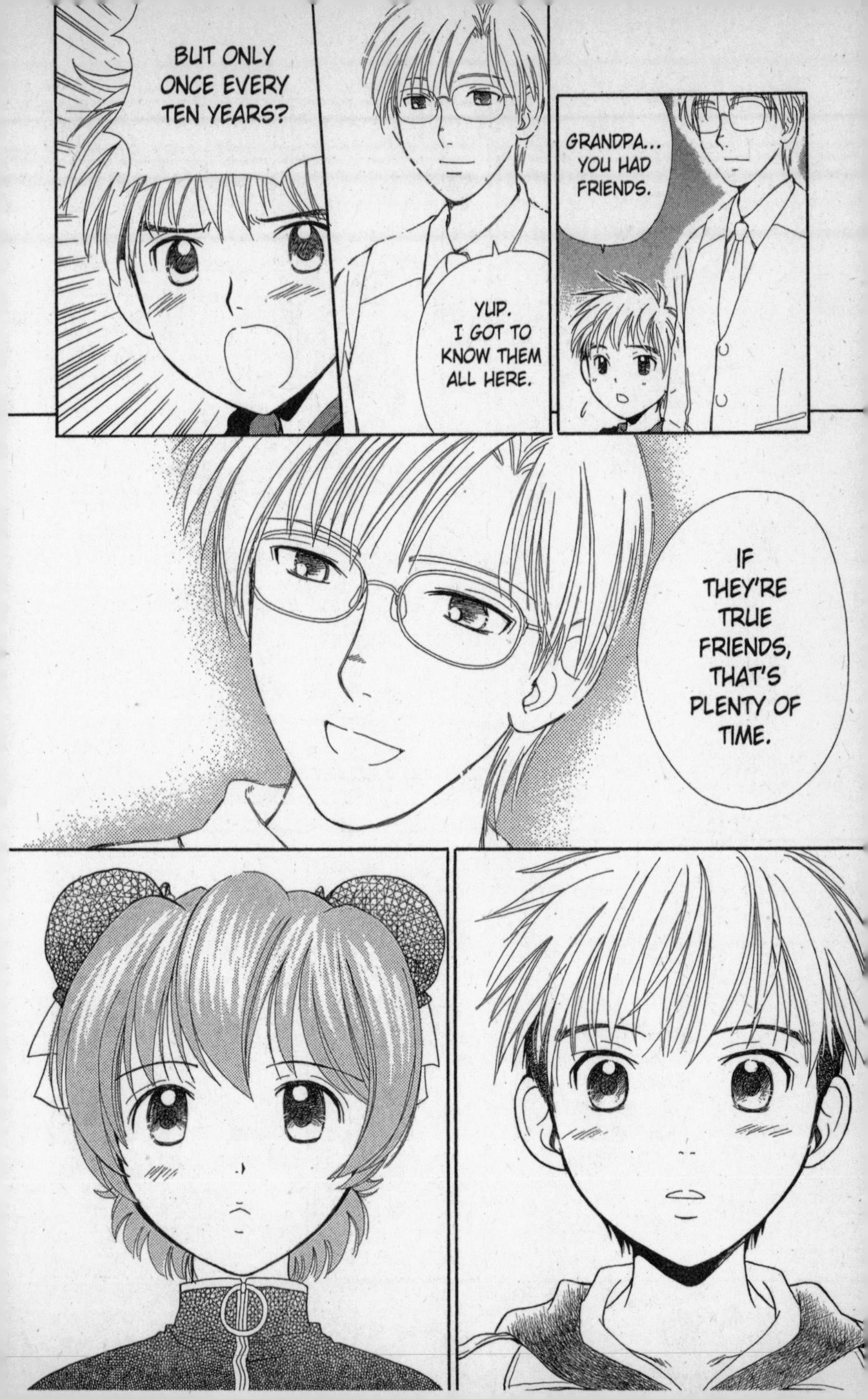
GRANDPA... YOU HAD FRIENDS.
BUT ONLY ONCE EVERY TEN YEARS?
YUP. I GOT TO KNOW THEM ALL HERE.
IF THEY'RE TRUE FRIENDS, THAT'S PLENTY OF TIME.

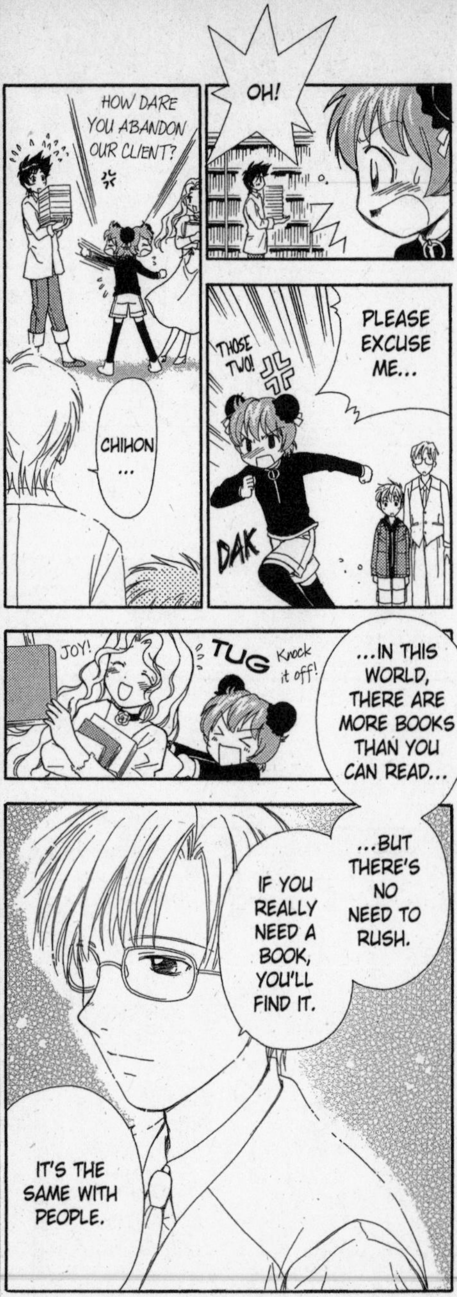
OH!
PLEASE EXCUSE ME...
THOSE TWO!
DAK
HOW DARE YOU ABANDON OUR CLIENT?
CHIHON...
...IN THIS WORLD, THERE ARE MORE BOOKS THAN YOU CAN READ...
Knock it off!
TUG
JOY!
...BUT THERE'S NO NEED TO RUSH.
IF YOU REALLY NEED A BOOK, YOU'LL FIND IT.
IT'S THE SAME WITH PEOPLE.

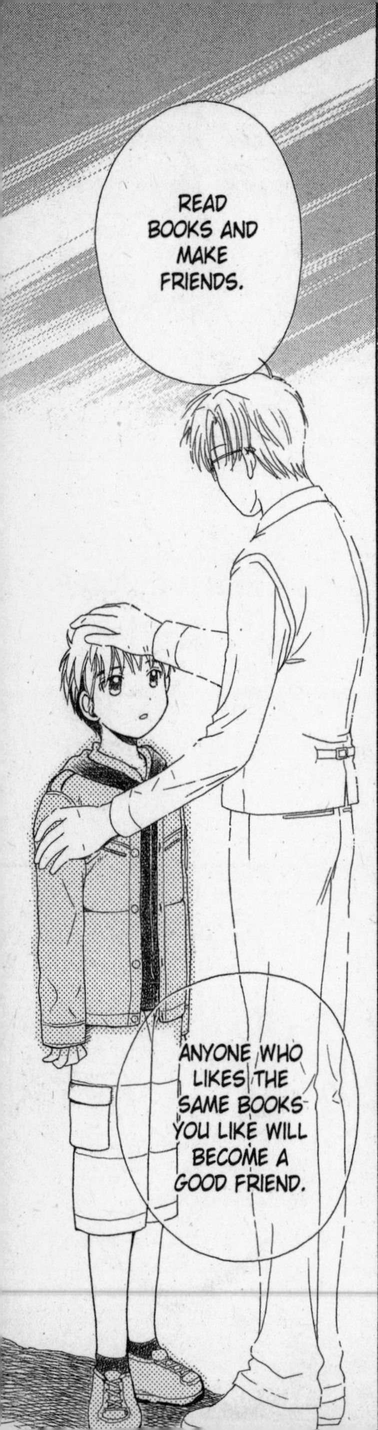
READ BOOKS AND MAKE FRIENDS.
ANYONE WHO LIKES THE SAME BOOKS YOU LIKE WILL BECOME A GOOD FRIEND.

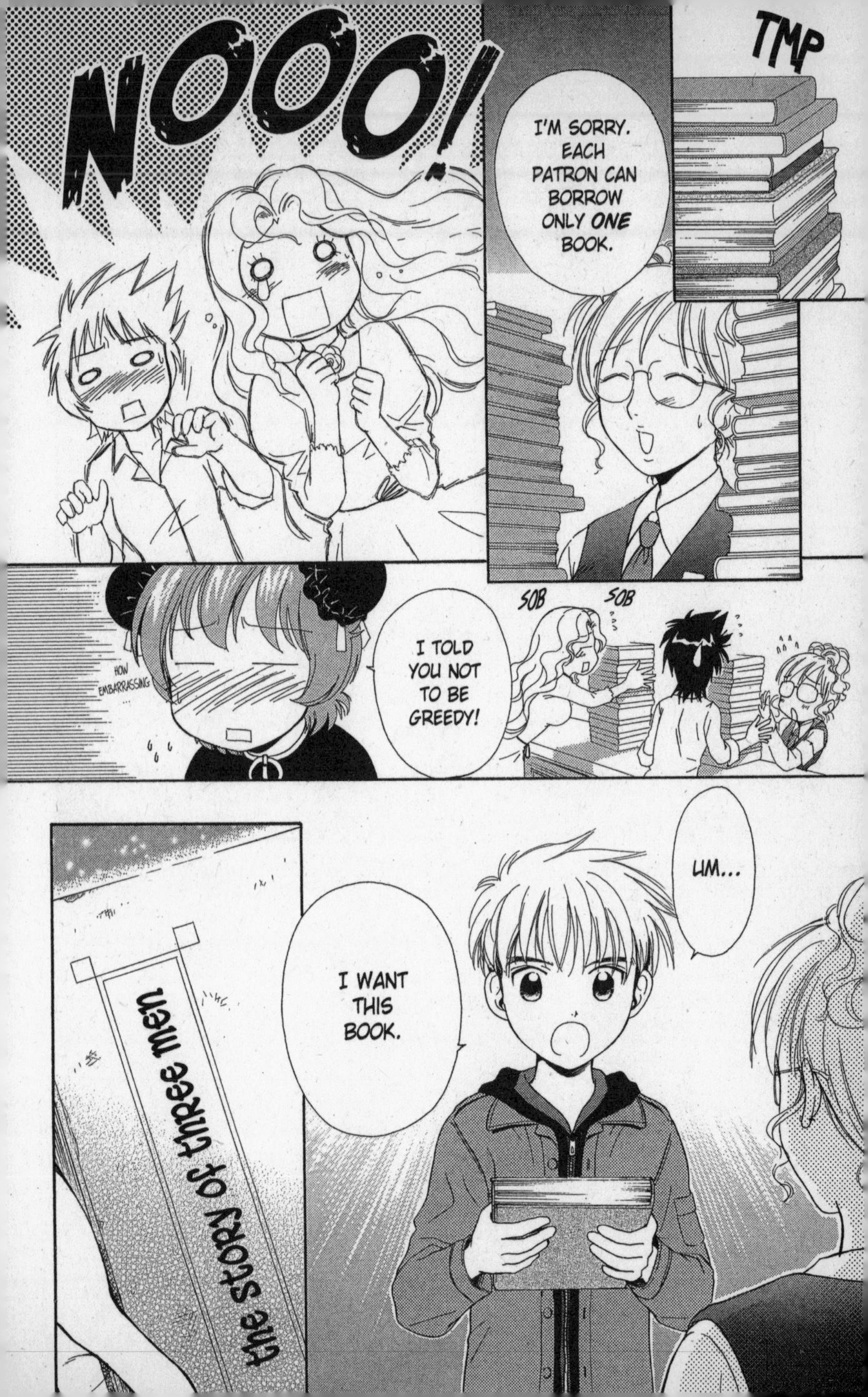
TMP
I'M SORRY. EACH PATRON CAN BORROW ONLY **ONE** BOOK.
NOOO!
SOB SOB
I TOLD YOU NOT TO BE GREEDY!
HOW EMBARRASSING...
UM...
I WANT THIS BOOK.
the story of three men

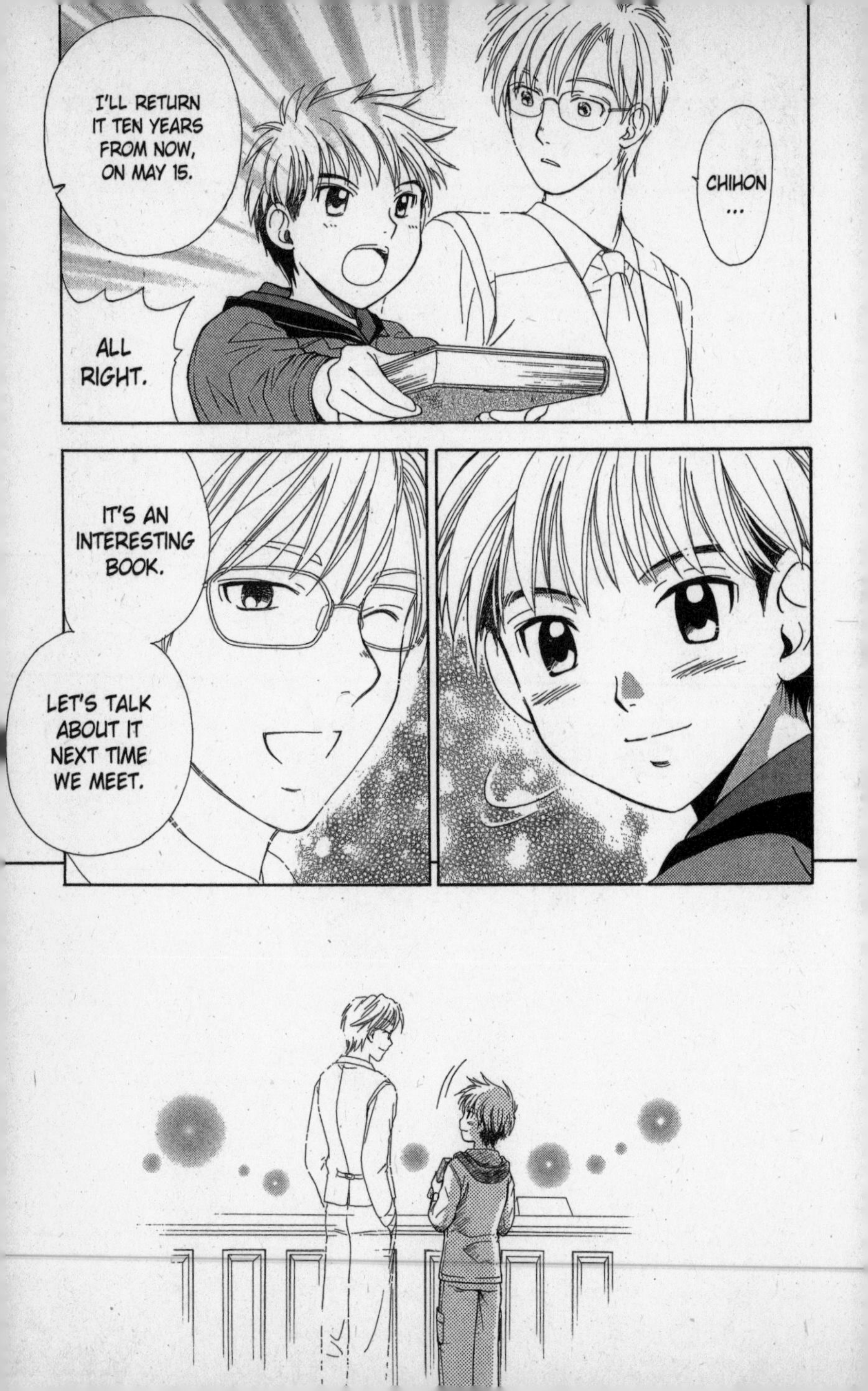
CHIHON ...
I'LL RETURN IT TEN YEARS FROM NOW, ON MAY 15.
ALL RIGHT.
IT'S AN INTERESTING BOOK.
LET'S TALK ABOUT IT NEXT TIME WE MEET.

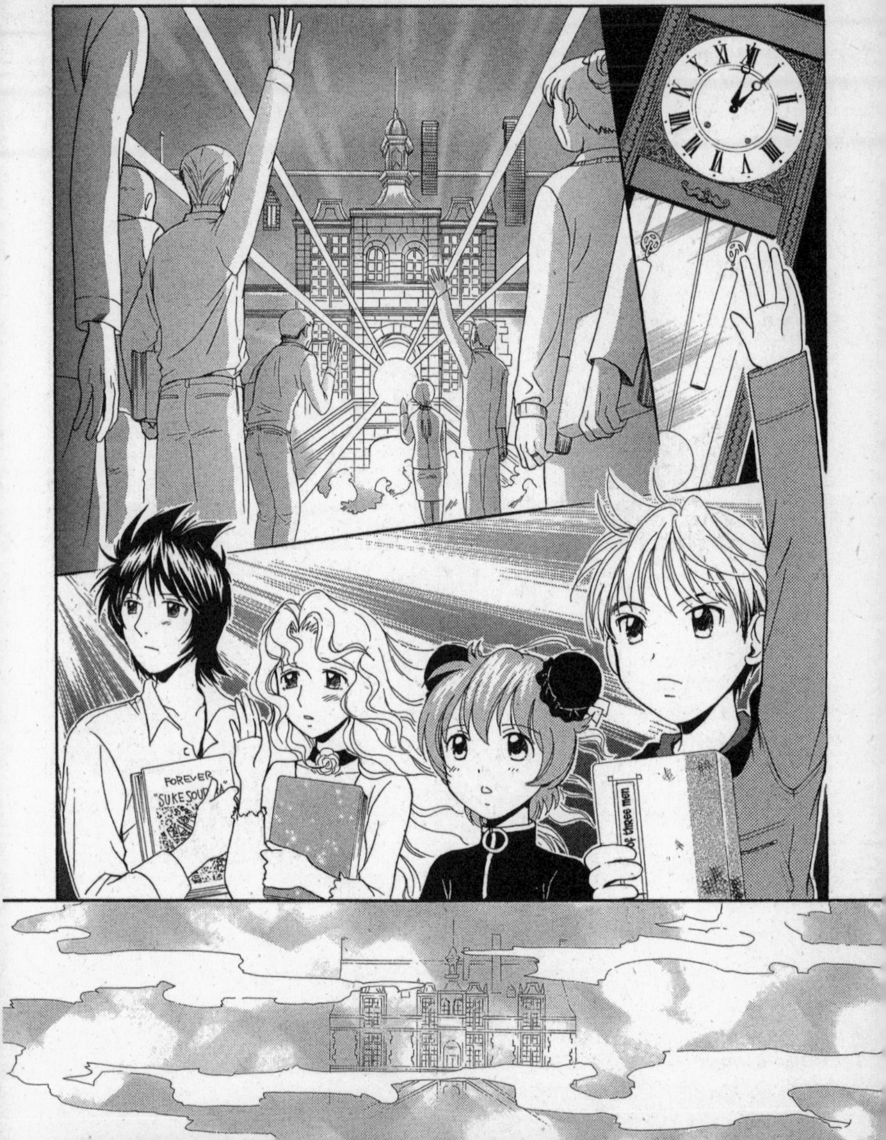
of three men
FOREVER

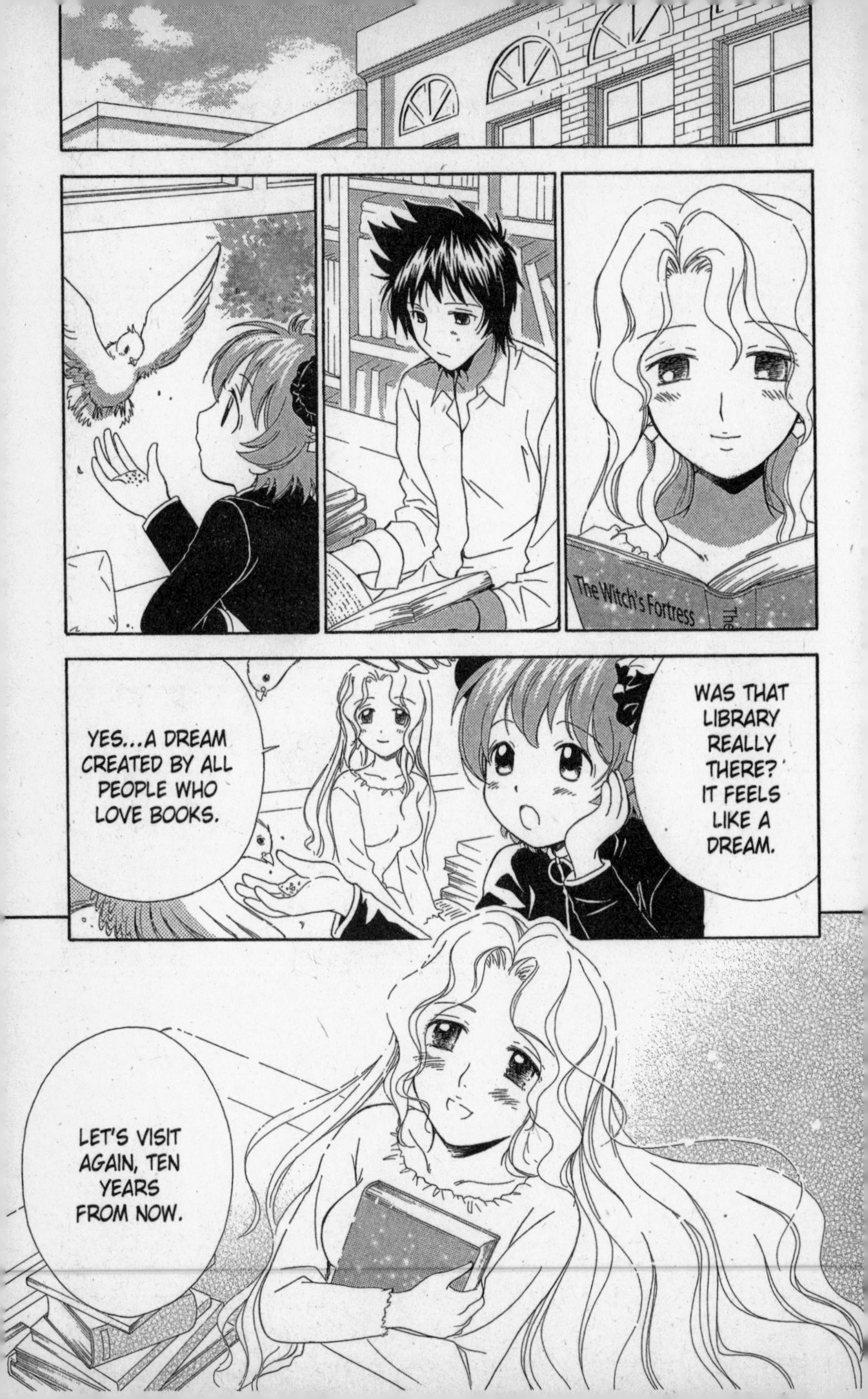
The Witch's Fortress
WAS THAT LIBRARY REALLY THERE? IT FEELS LIKE A DREAM.
YES...A DREAM CREATED BY ALL PEOPLE WHO LOVE BOOKS.
LET'S VISIT AGAIN, TEN YEARS FROM NOW.

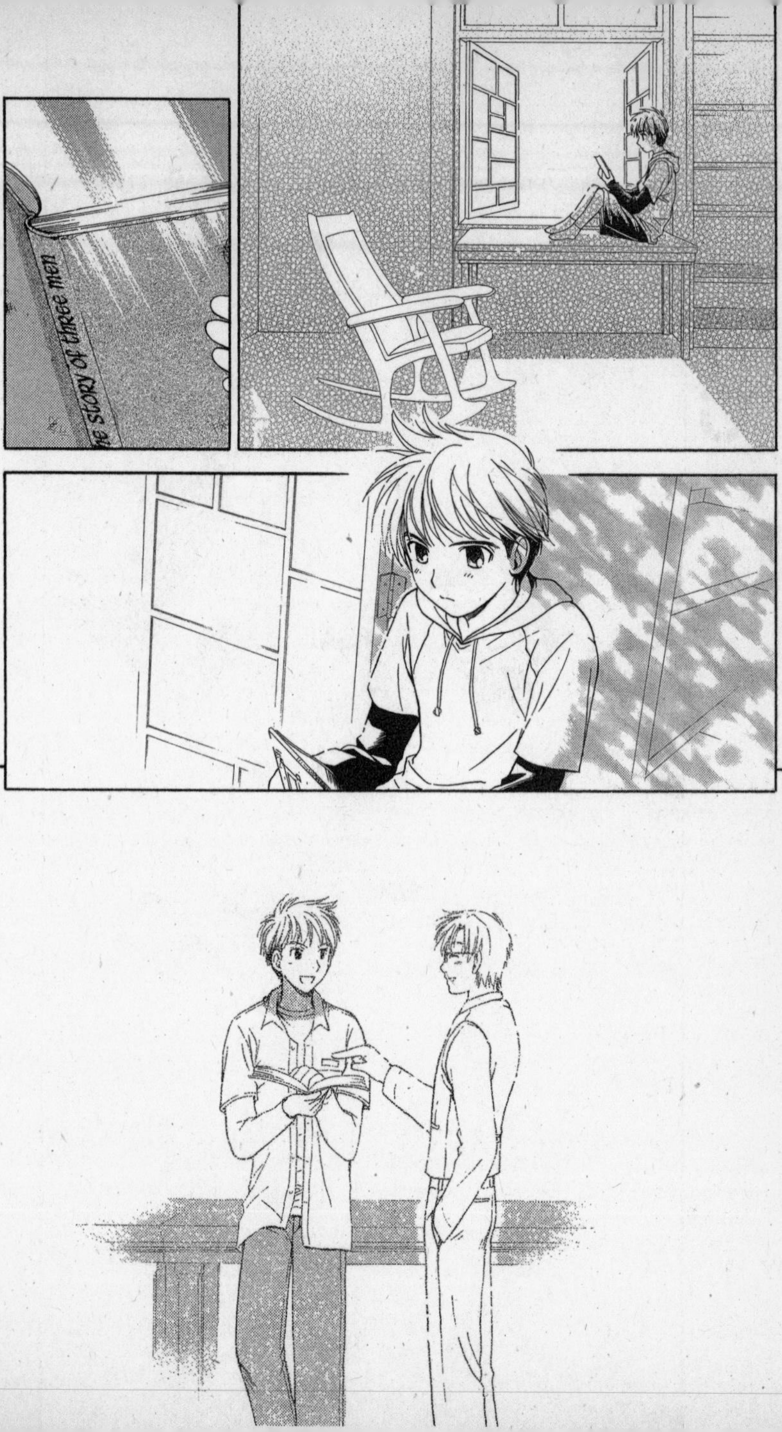
he story of three men

CHAPTER 3

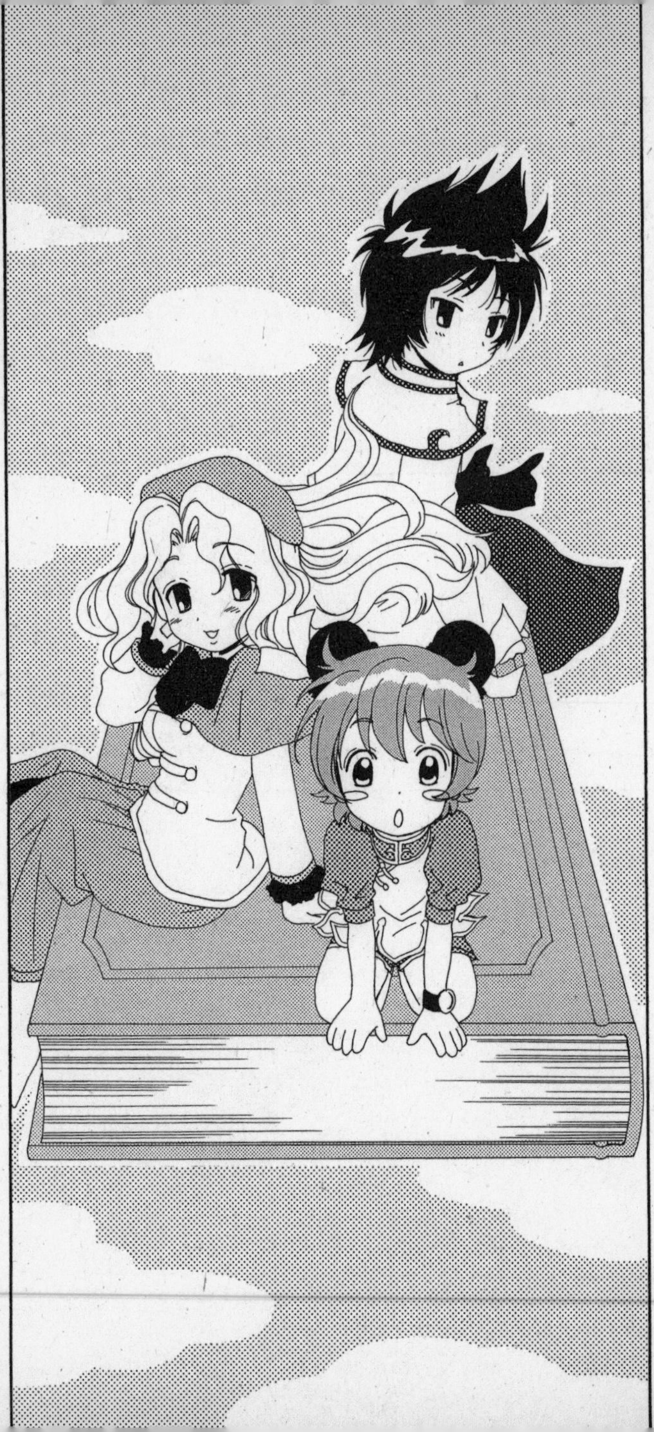

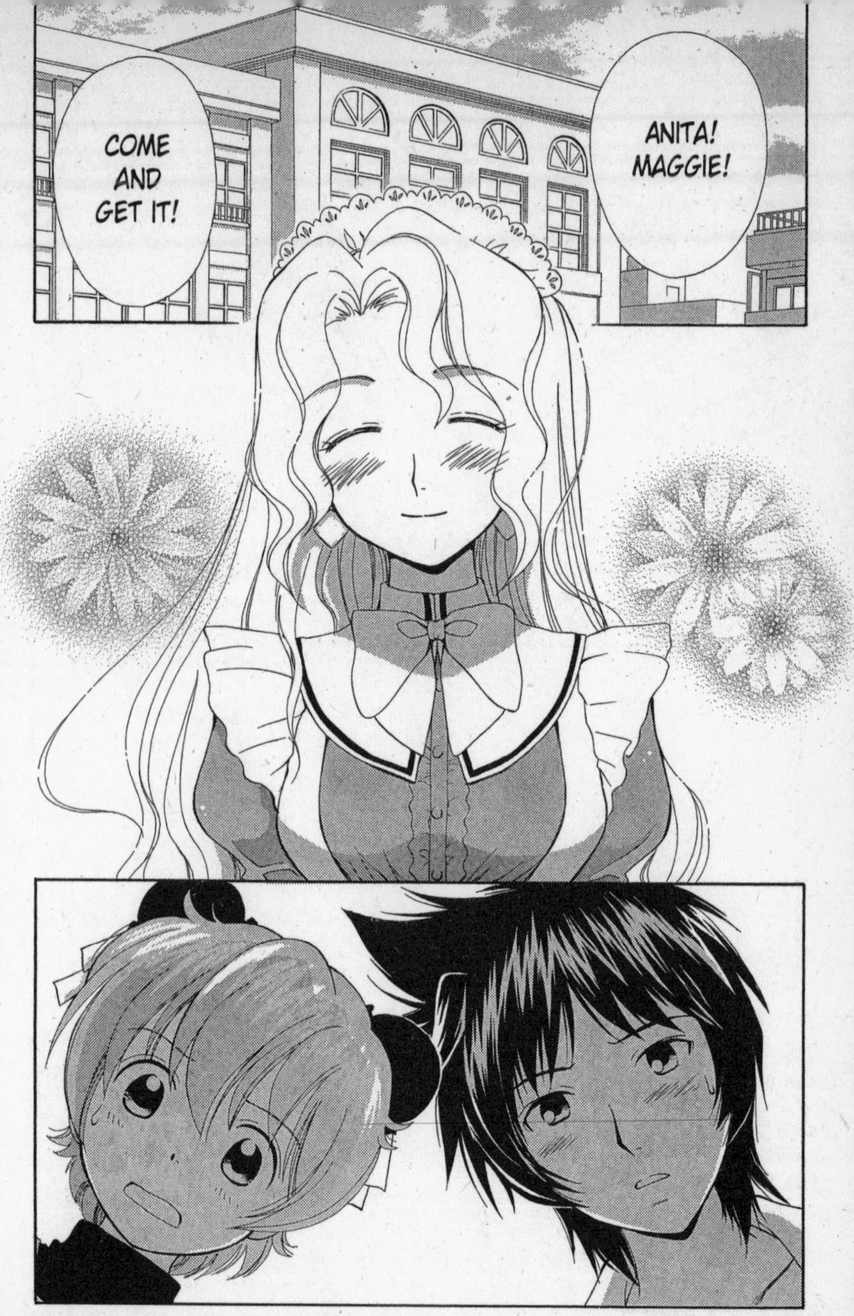
ANITA! MAGGIE!
COME AND GET IT!

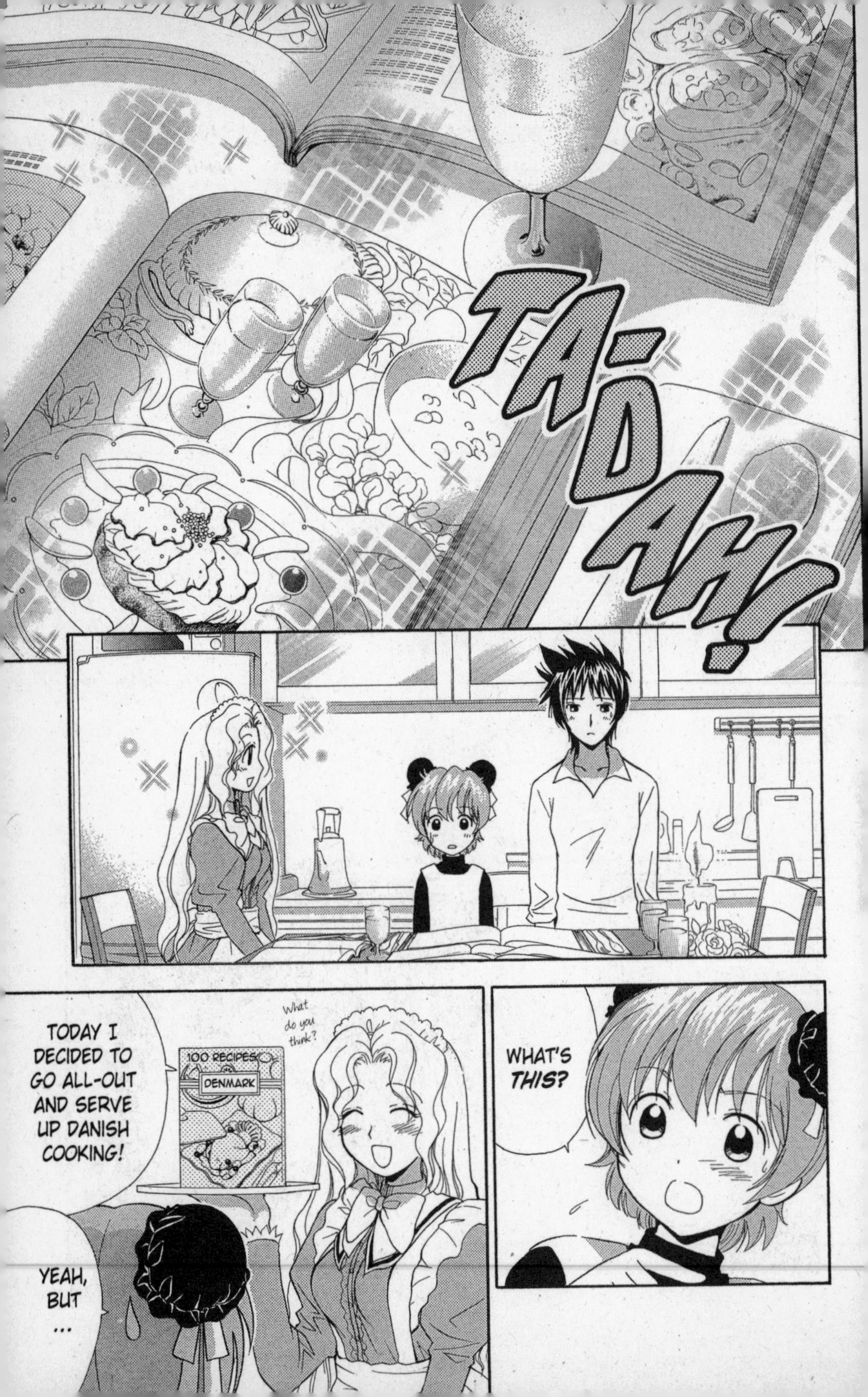
TA-DAH!
WHAT'S THIS?
What do you think?
100 RECIPES
DENMARK
TODAY I DECIDED TO GO ALL-OUT AND SERVE UP DANISH COOKING!
YEAH, BUT ...

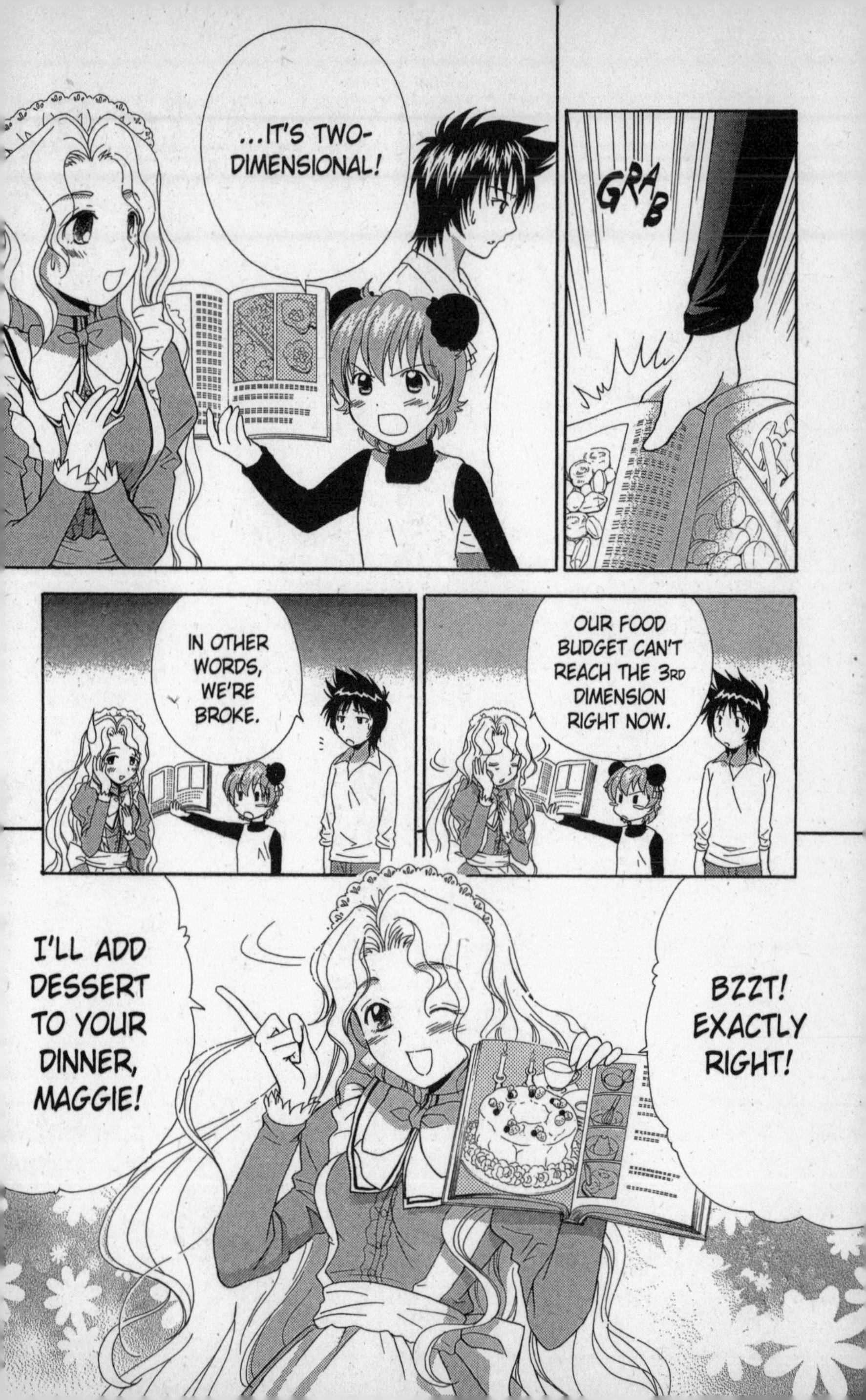
GRAB
...IT'S TWO-DIMENSIONAL!
OUR FOOD BUDGET CAN'T REACH THE 3RD DIMENSION RIGHT NOW.
IN OTHER WORDS, WE'RE BROKE.
BZZT! EXACTLY RIGHT!
I'LL ADD DESSERT TO YOUR DINNER, MAGGIE!

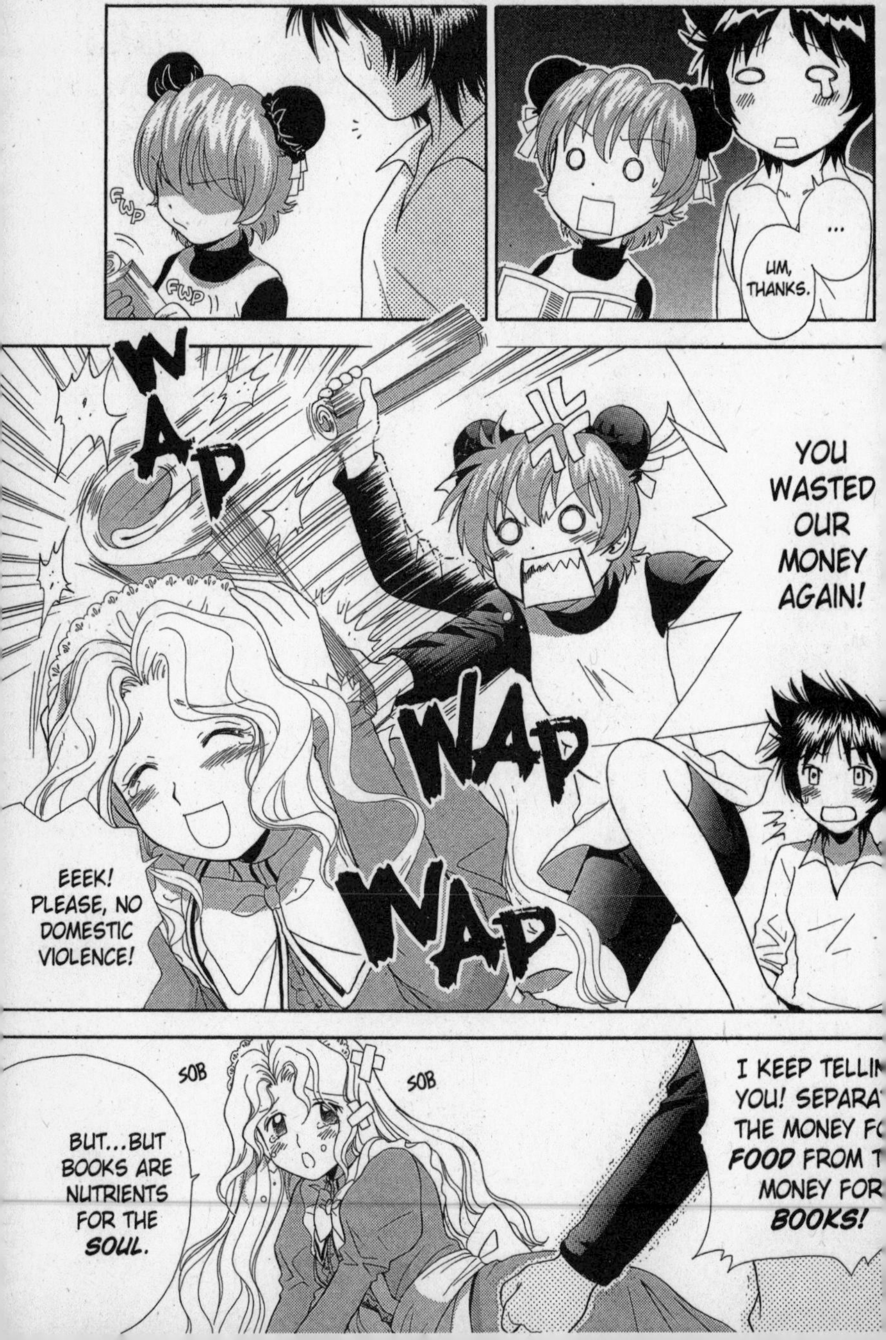
...
UM, THANKS.
FWP
FWP
YOU WASTED OUR MONEY AGAIN!
WAP
WAP
WAP
EEEK! PLEASE, NO DOMESTIC VIOLENCE!
I KEEP TELLI YOU! SEPARA THE MONEY FO FOOD FROM T MONEY FOR BOOKS!
SOB
SOB
BUT...BUT BOOKS ARE NUTRIENTS FOR THE SOUL.

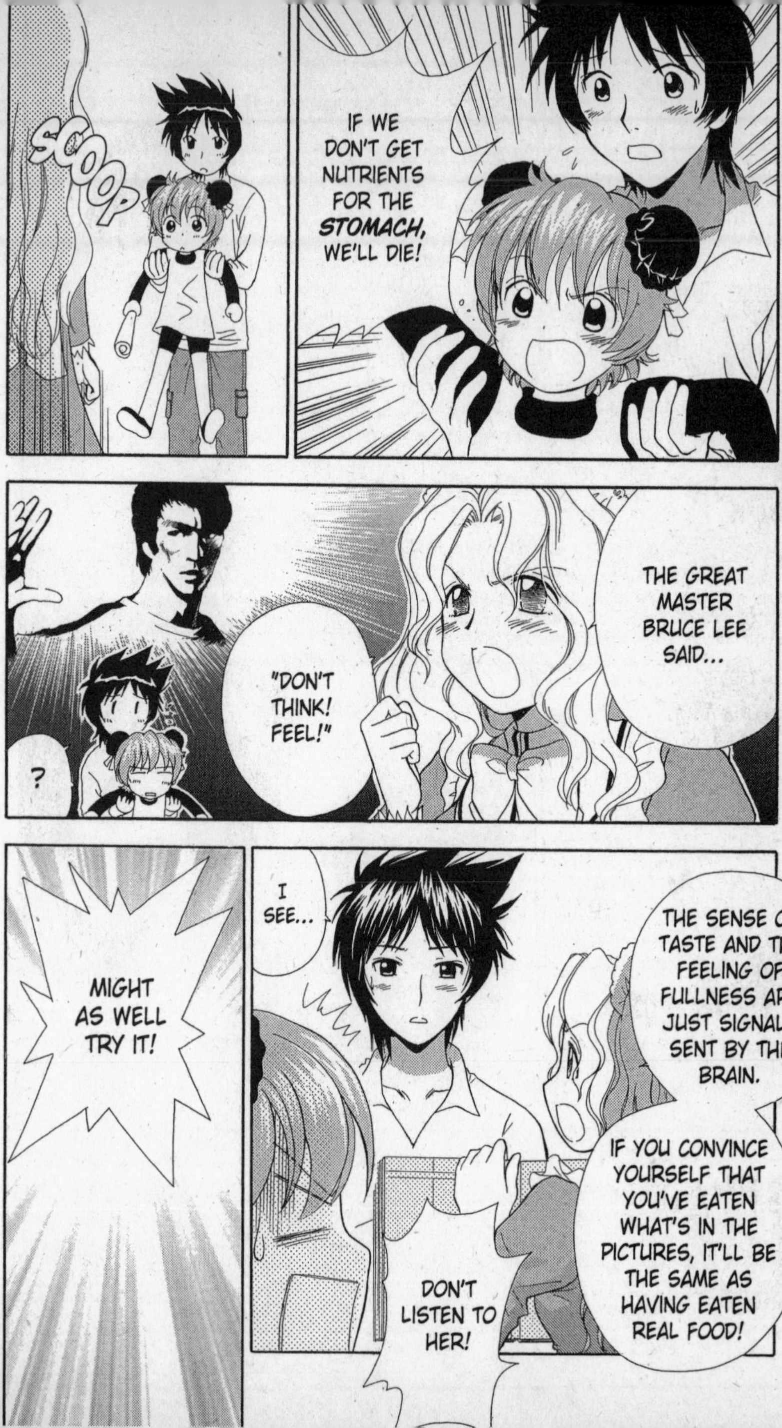
IF WE DON'T GET NUTRIENTS FOR THE *STOMACH*, WE'LL DIE!
SCOOP
THE GREAT MASTER BRUCE LEE SAID...
"DON'T THINK! FEEL!"
?
THE SENSE OF TASTE AND THE FEELING OF FULLNESS ARE JUST SIGNALS SENT BY THE BRAIN.
I SEE...
IF YOU CONVINCE YOURSELF THAT YOU'VE EATEN WHAT'S IN THE PICTURES, IT'LL BE THE SAME AS HAVING EATEN REAL FOOD!
DON'T LISTEN TO HER!
MIGHT AS WELL TRY IT!

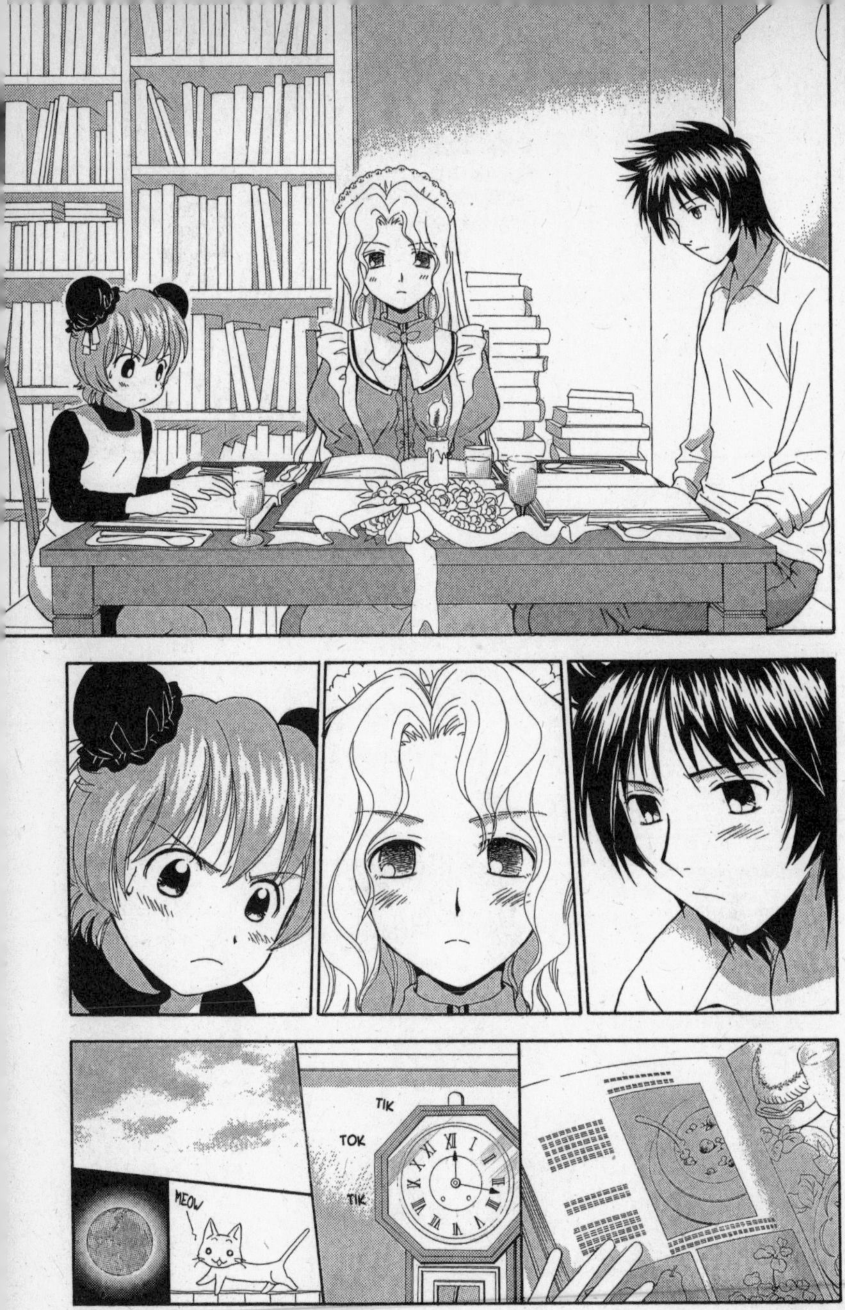
TIK
TOK
TIK
MEOW

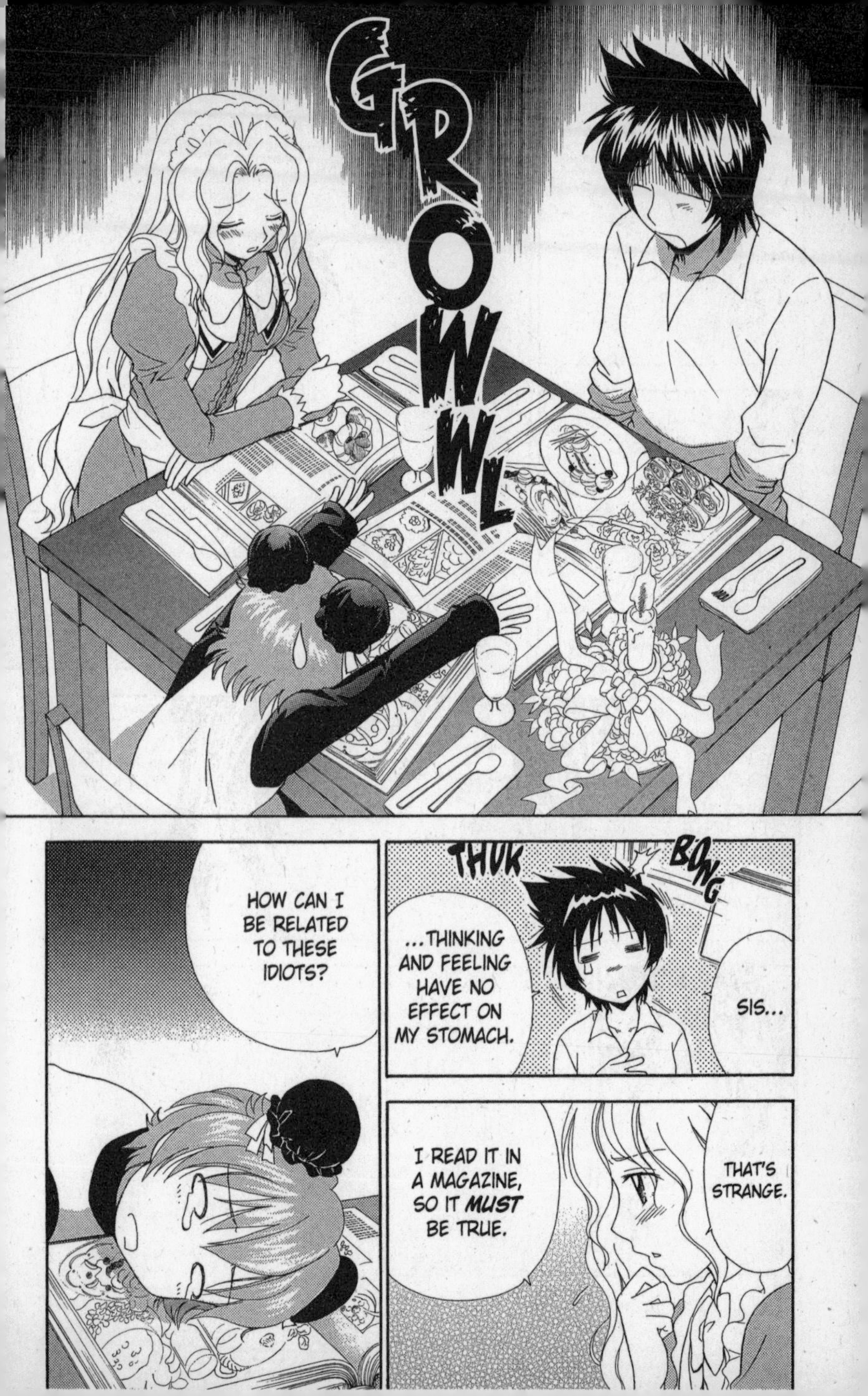
GROWL
BONG
SIS...
THUK
...THINKING AND FEELING HAVE NO EFFECT ON MY STOMACH.
THAT'S STRANGE.
I READ IT IN A MAGAZINE, SO IT *MUST* BE TRUE.
HOW CAN I BE RELATED TO THESE IDIOTS?

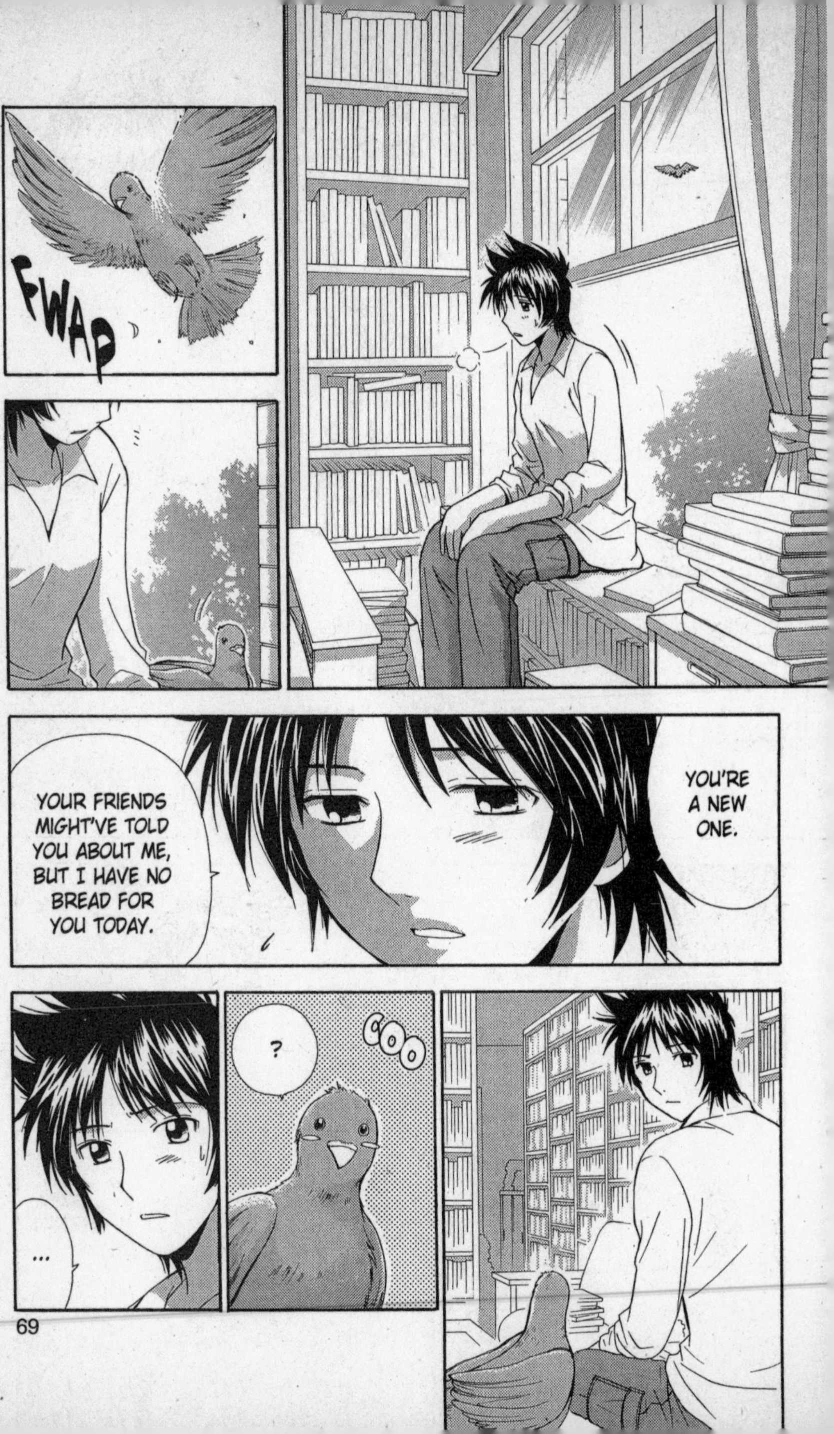
FWAP
YOU'RE A NEW ONE.
YOUR FRIENDS MIGHT'VE TOLD YOU ABOUT ME, BUT I HAVE NO BREAD FOR YOU TODAY.
?
COO
...

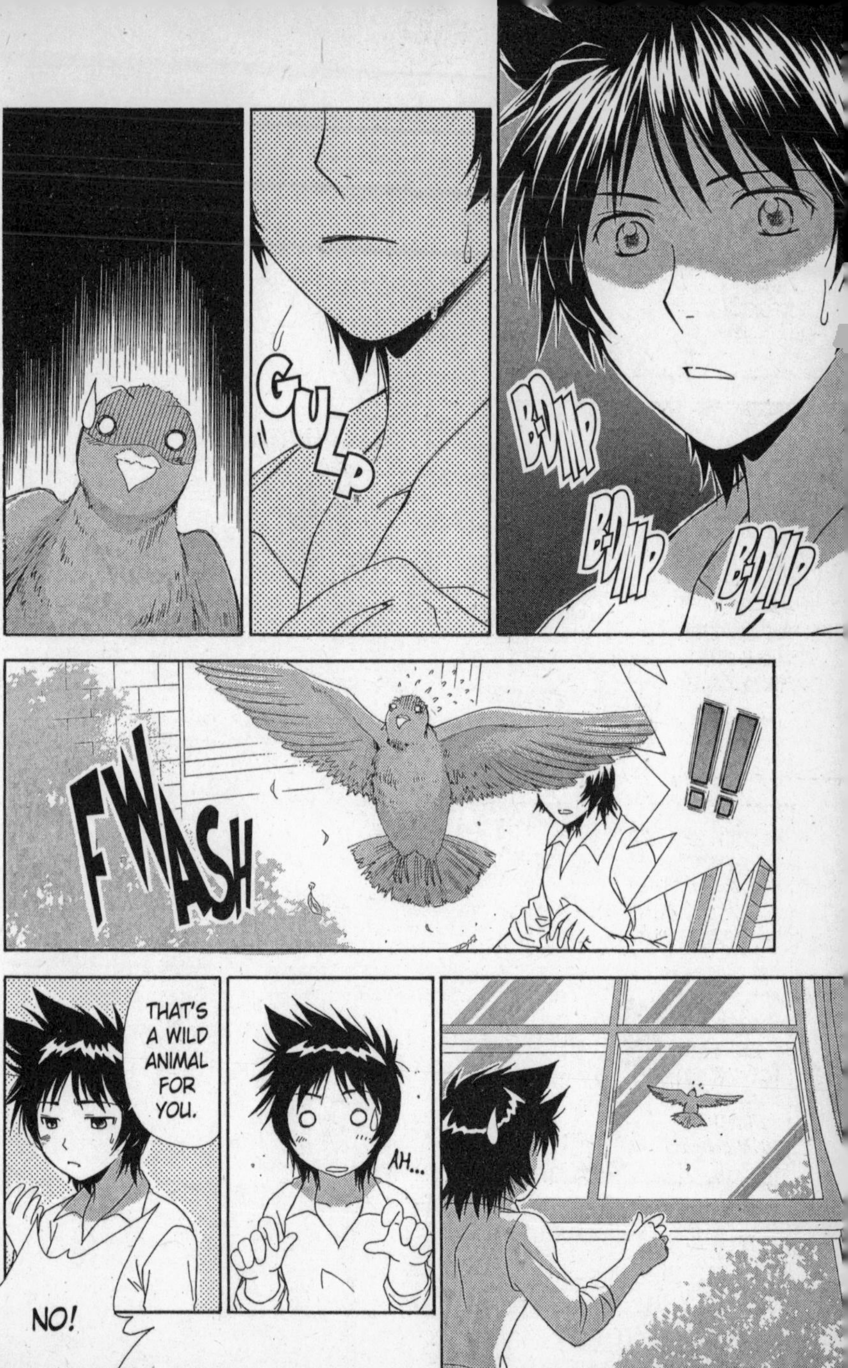
B-DMP
B-DMP
B-DMP
GULP
!!
FWASH
AH...
THAT'S A WILD ANIMAL FOR YOU.
NO!

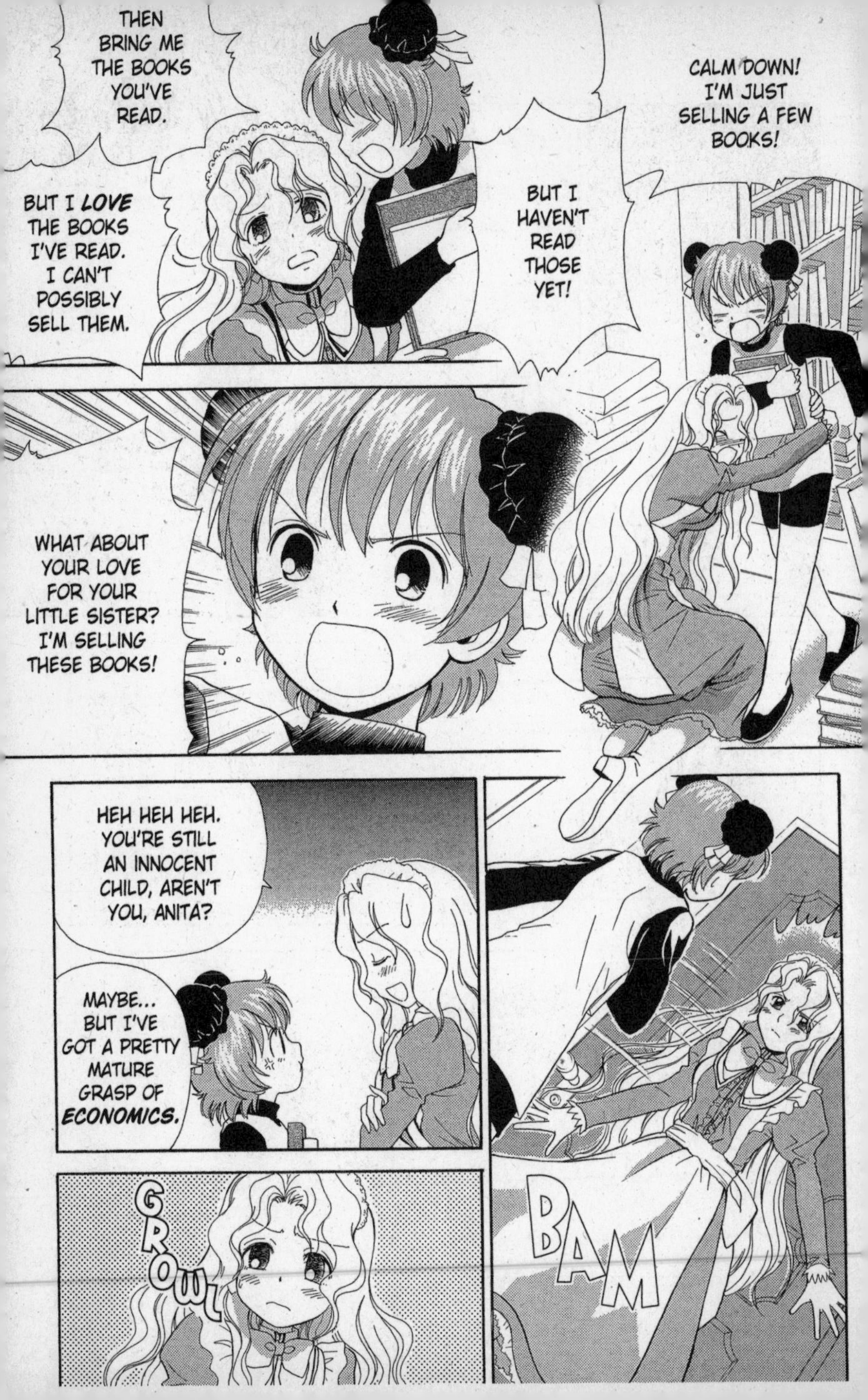
CALM DOWN! I'M JUST SELLING A FEW BOOKS!
BUT I HAVEN'T READ THOSE YET!
THEN BRING ME THE BOOKS YOU'VE READ.
BUT I LOVE THE BOOKS I'VE READ. I CAN'T POSSIBLY SELL THEM.
WHAT ABOUT YOUR LOVE FOR YOUR LITTLE SISTER? I'M SELLING THESE BOOKS!
BAM
HEH HEH HEH. YOU'RE STILL AN INNOCENT CHILD, AREN'T YOU, ANITA?
MAYBE... BUT I'VE GOT A PRETTY MATURE GRASP OF ECONOMICS.
GROWL

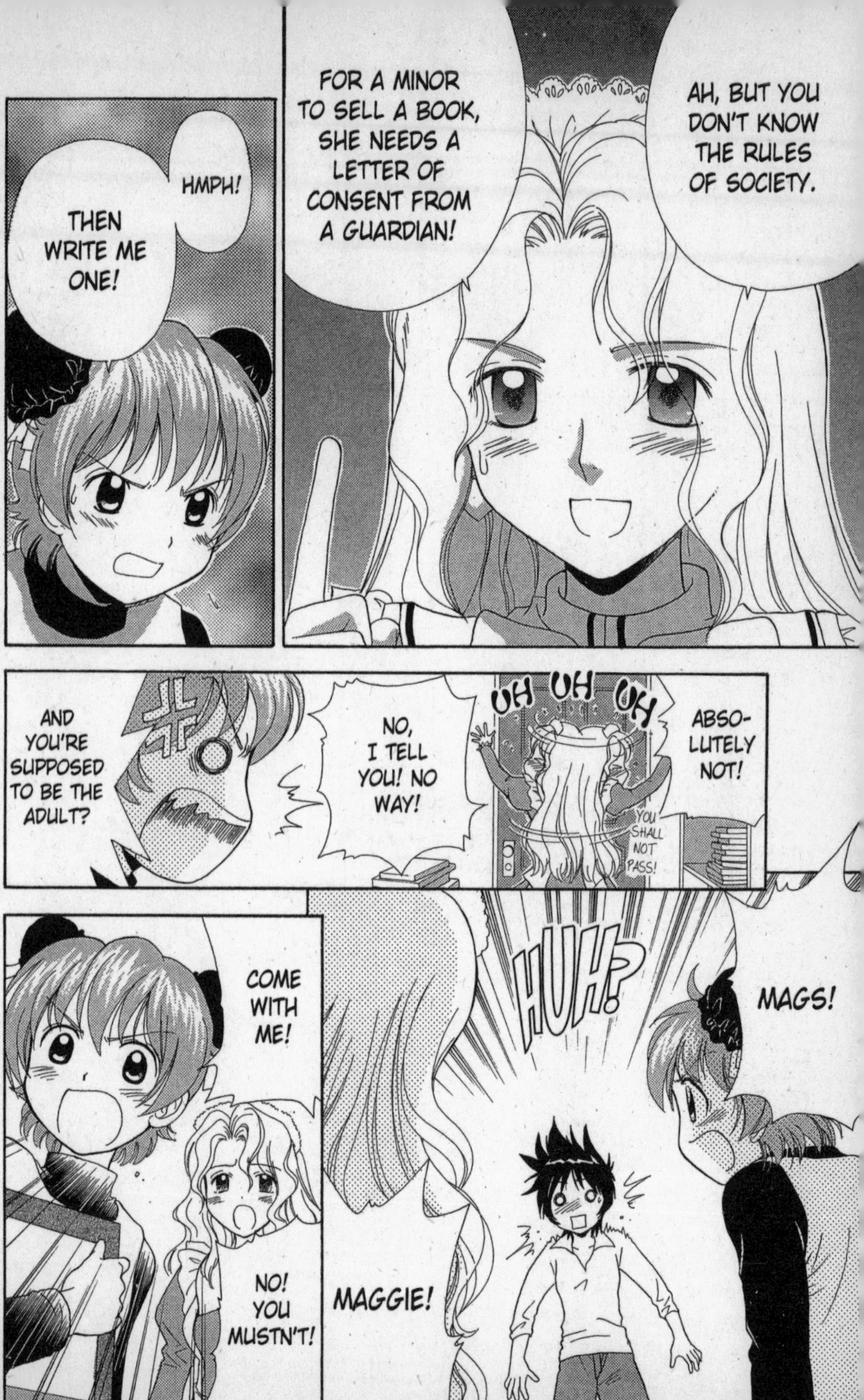
AH, BUT YOU DON'T KNOW THE RULES OF SOCIETY.
FOR A MINOR TO SELL A BOOK, SHE NEEDS A LETTER OF CONSENT FROM A GUARDIAN!
HMPH!
THEN WRITE ME ONE!
ABSO-LUTELY NOT!
UH UH UH
YOU SHALL NOT PASS!
NO, I TELL YOU! NO WAY!
AND YOU'RE SUPPOSED TO BE THE ADULT?
MAGS!
HUH!?
MAGGIE!
COME WITH ME!
NO! YOU MUSTN'T!

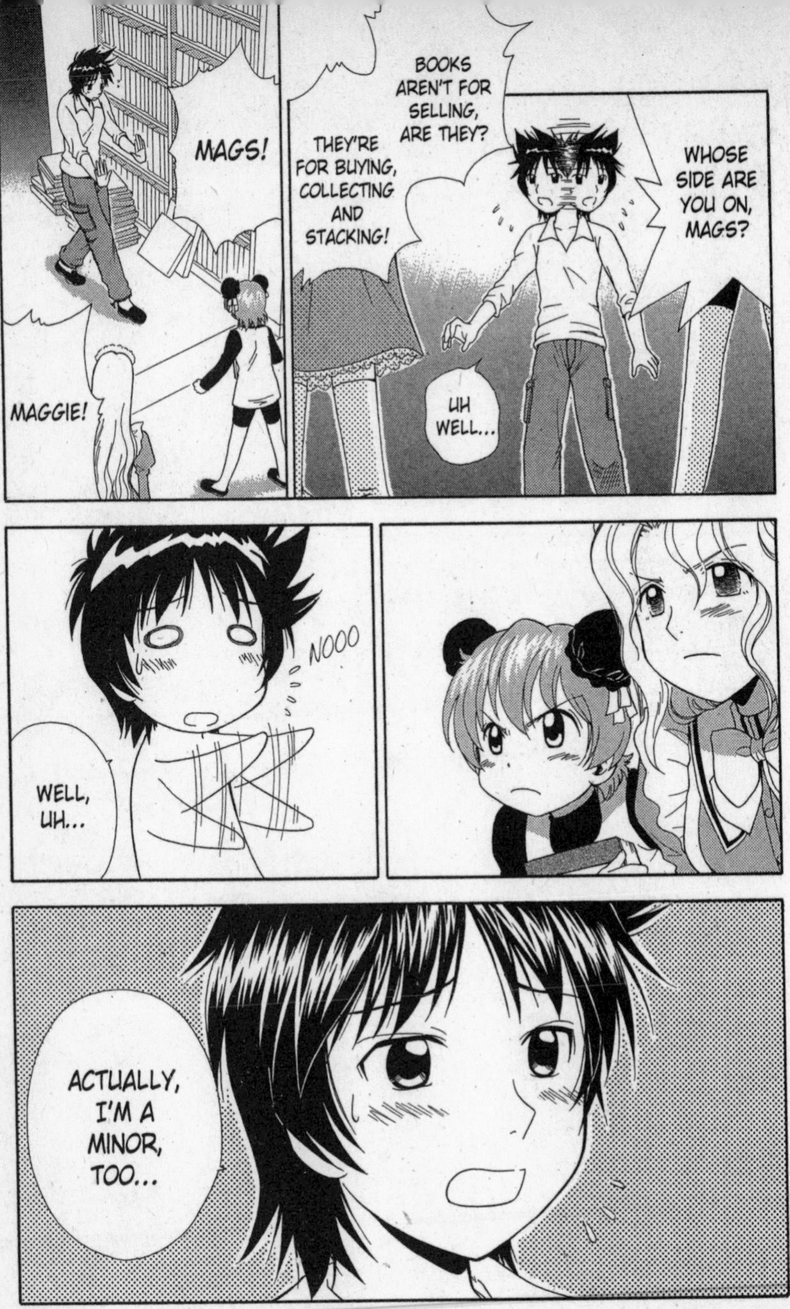
BOOKS AREN'T FOR SELLING, ARE THEY?
THEY'RE FOR BUYING, COLLECTING AND STACKING!
WHOSE SIDE ARE YOU ON, MAGS?
UH WELL...
MAGS!
MAGGIE!
NOOO
WELL, UH...
ACTUALLY, I'M A MINOR, TOO...

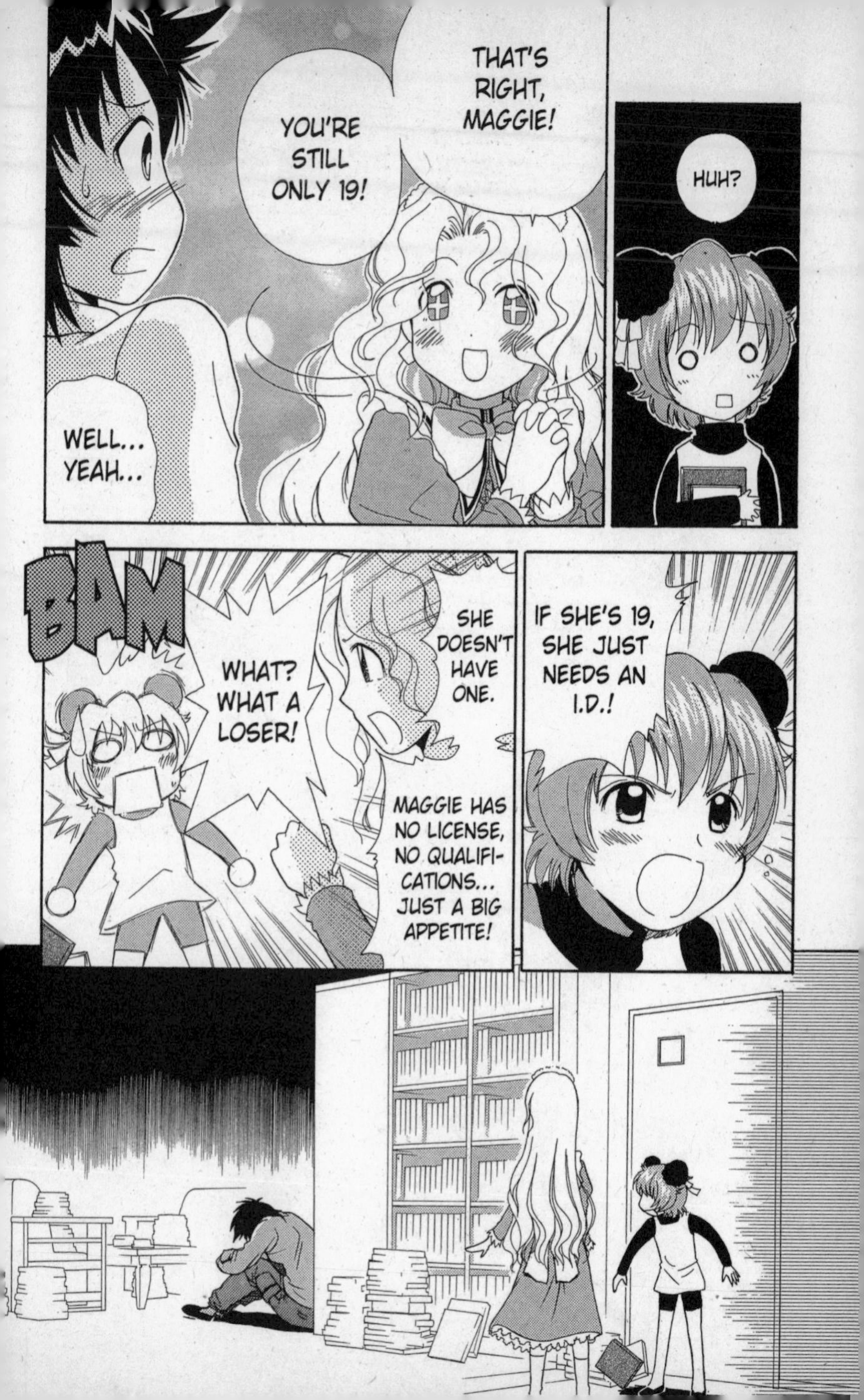
HUH?
THAT'S RIGHT, MAGGIE!
YOU'RE STILL ONLY 19!
WELL... YEAH...
IF SHE'S 19, SHE JUST NEEDS AN I.D.!
SHE DOESN'T HAVE ONE.
BAM
WHAT? WHAT A LOSER!
MAGGIE HAS NO LICENSE, NO QUALIFI- CATIONS... JUST A BIG APPETITE!

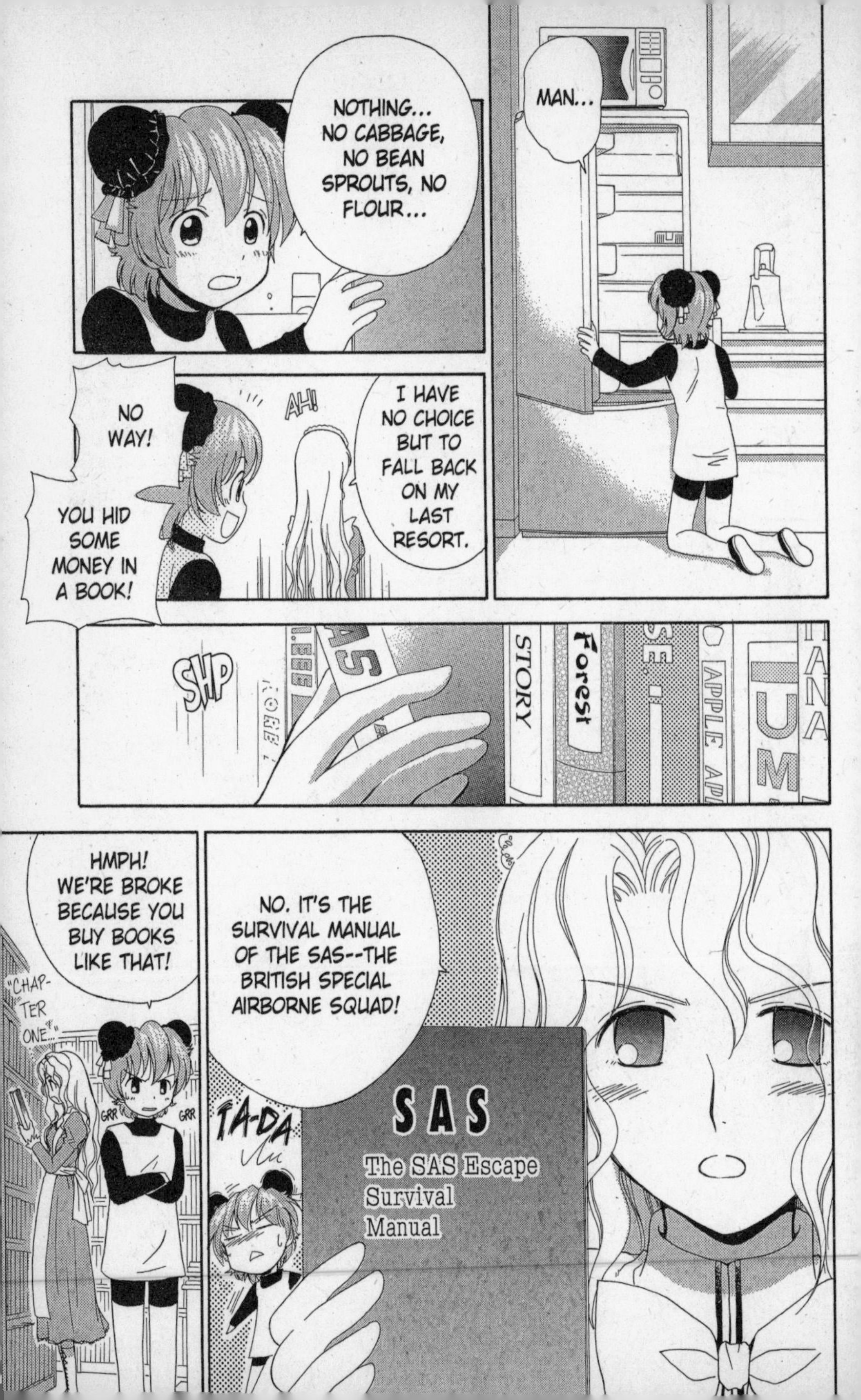
MAN...
NOTHING... NO CABBAGE, NO BEAN SPROUTS, NO FLOUR...
I HAVE NO CHOICE BUT TO FALL BACK ON MY LAST RESORT.
AH!
NO WAY!
YOU HID SOME MONEY IN A BOOK!
STORY
Forest
APPLE
SHP
NO. IT'S THE SURVIVAL MANUAL OF THE SAS--THE BRITISH SPECIAL AIRBORNE SQUAD!
SAS
The SAS Escape Survival Manual
TA-DA
HMPH! WE'RE BROKE BECAUSE YOU BUY BOOKS LIKE THAT!
"CHAPTER ONE..."
GRR
GRR

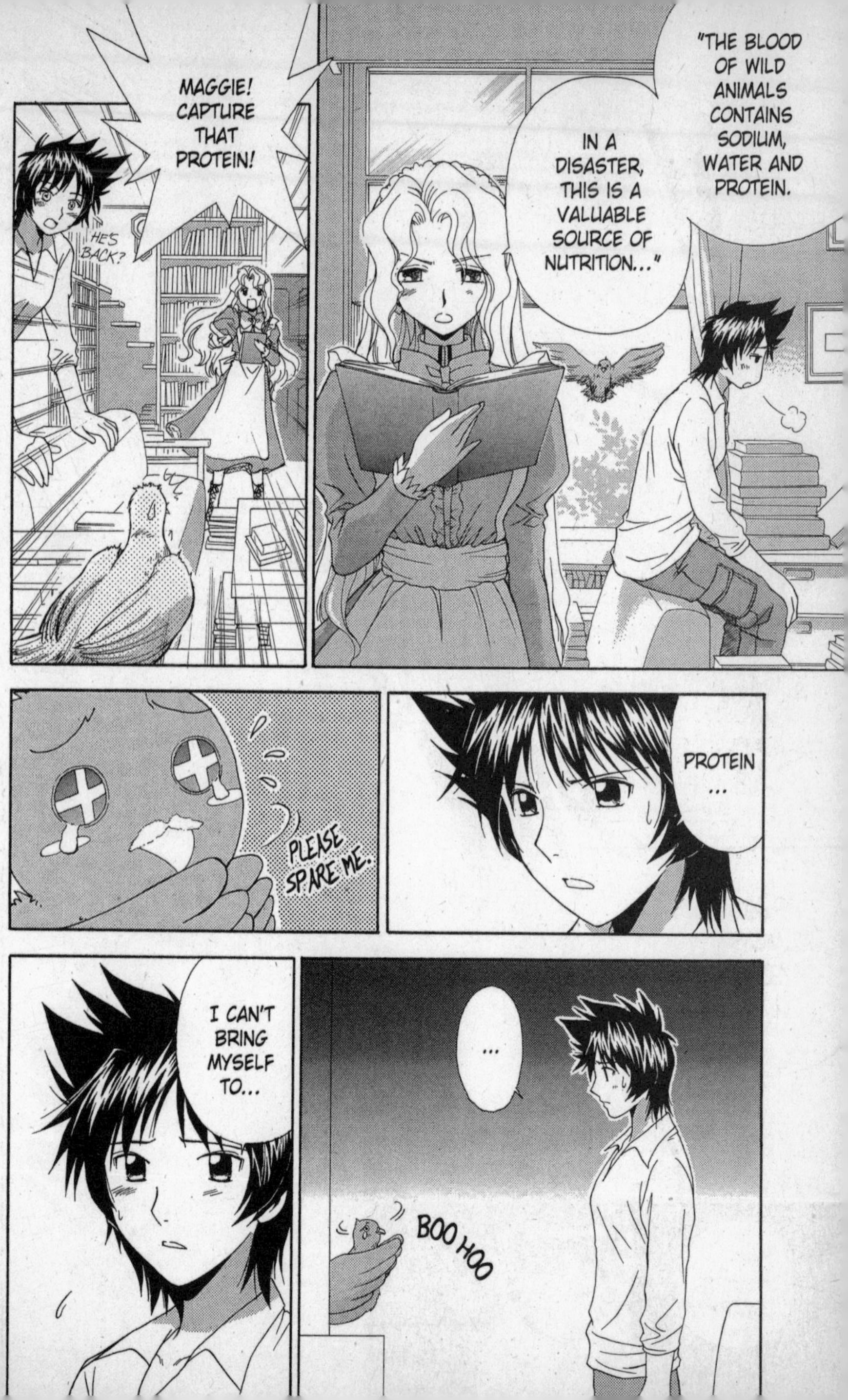
"THE BLOOD OF WILD ANIMALS CONTAINS SODIUM, WATER AND PROTEIN.
IN A DISASTER, THIS IS A VALUABLE SOURCE OF NUTRITION..."
MAGGIE! CAPTURE THAT PROTEIN!
HE'S BACK?
PROTEIN ...
PLEASE SPARE ME.
...
BOO HOO
I CAN'T BRING MYSELF TO...

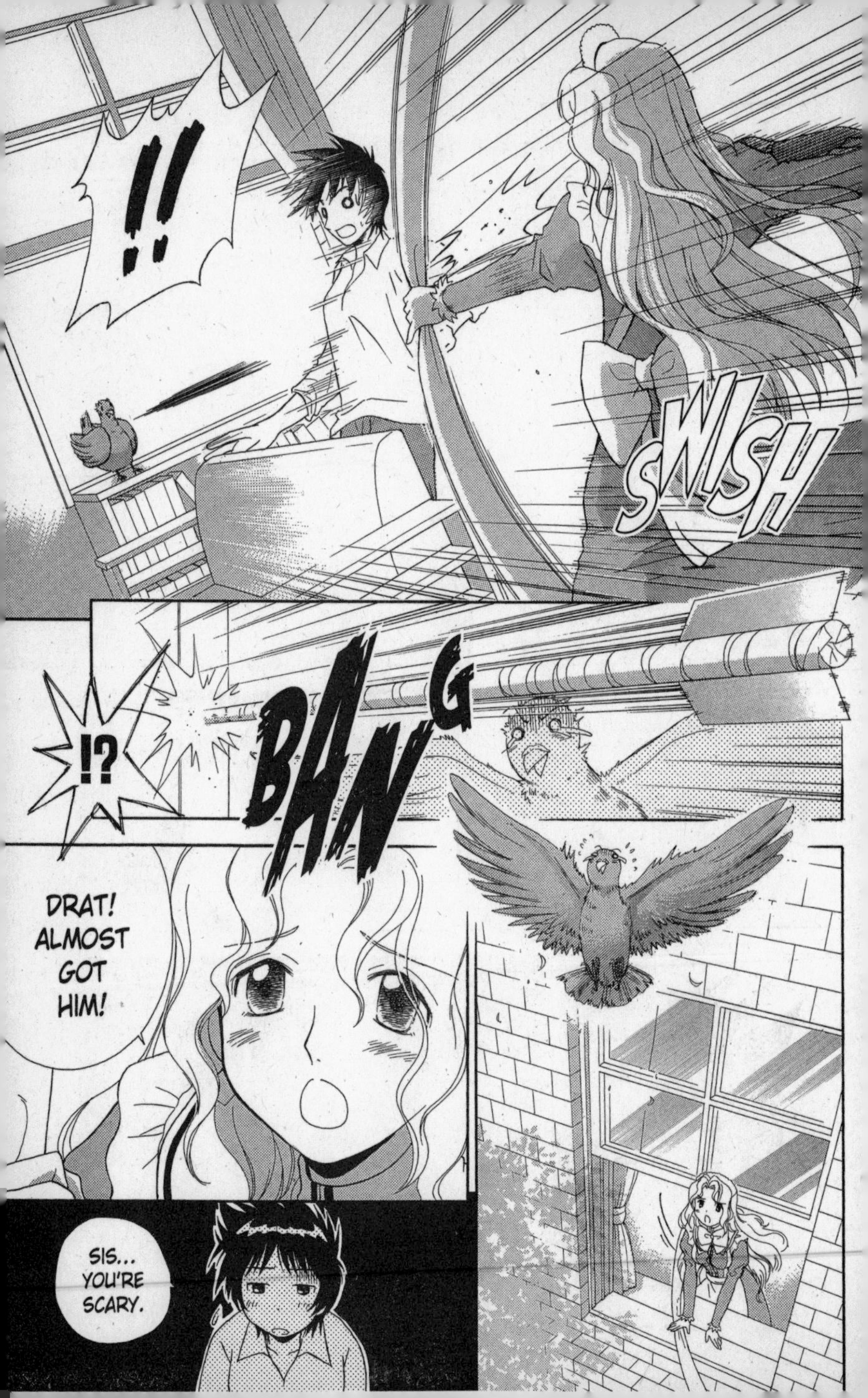
SWISH
!!
BANG
!?
DRAT! ALMOST GOT HIM!
SIS... YOU'RE SCARY.

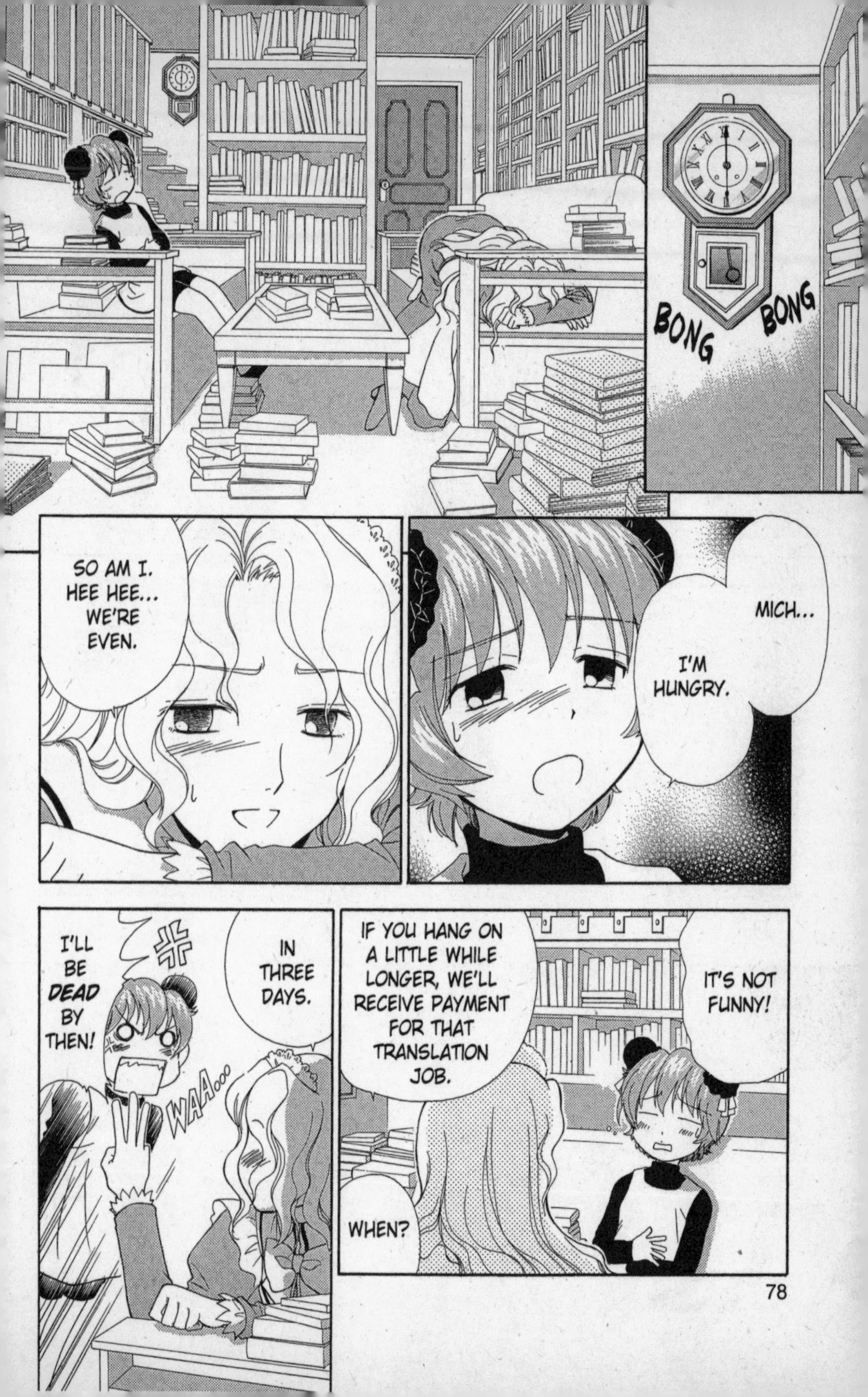
BONG
BONG
MICH...
I'M HUNGRY.
SO AM I. HEE HEE... WE'RE EVEN.
IT'S NOT FUNNY!
IF YOU HANG ON A LITTLE WHILE LONGER, WE'LL RECEIVE PAYMENT FOR THAT TRANSLATION JOB.
WHEN?
IN THREE DAYS.
I'LL BE ***DEAD*** BY THEN!
WAAooo

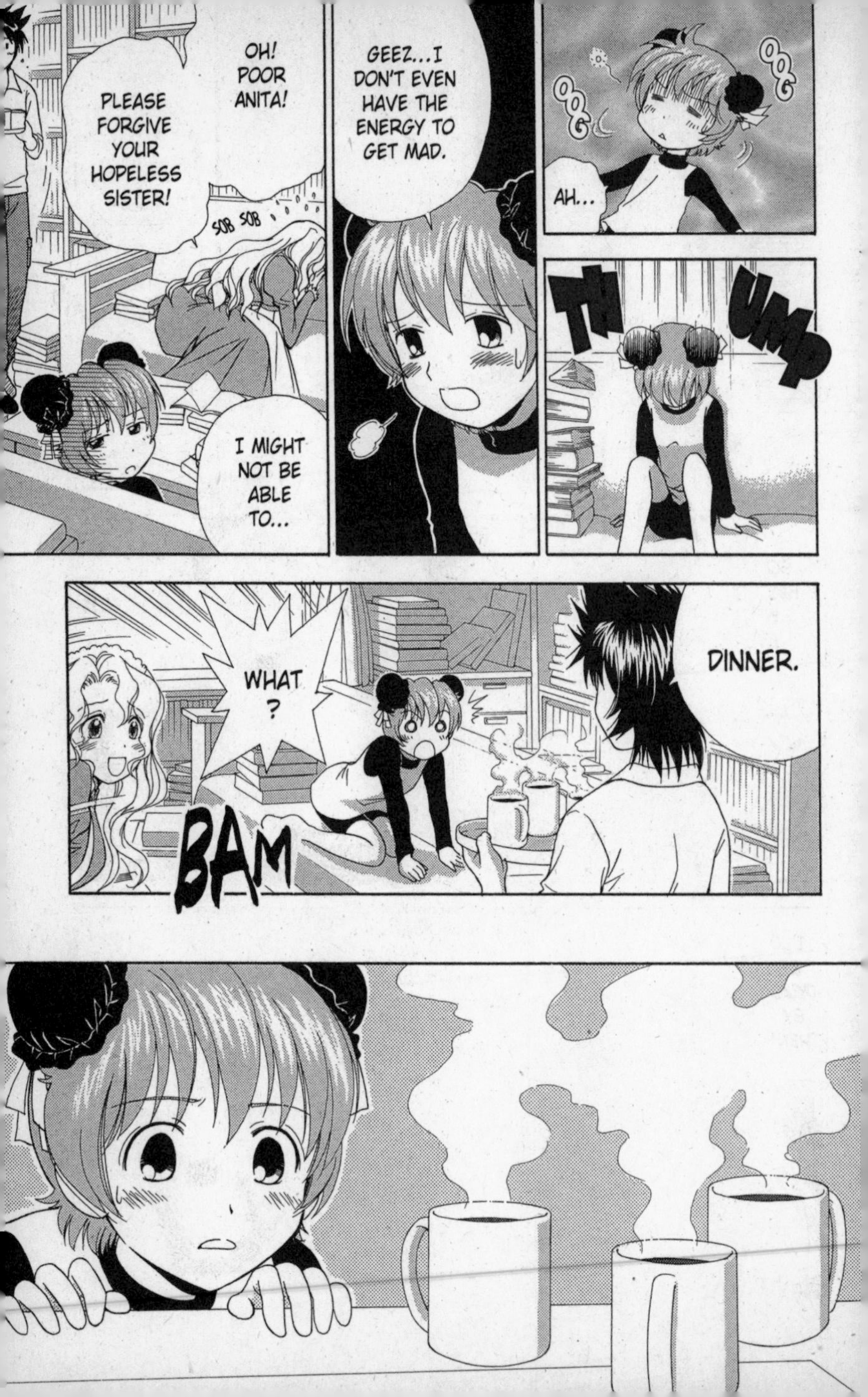
OOG
OOG
AH...
TH UMP
GEEZ...I DON'T EVEN HAVE THE ENERGY TO GET MAD.
OH! POOR ANITA!
PLEASE FORGIVE YOUR HOPELESS SISTER!
SOB SOB
I MIGHT NOT BE ABLE TO...
DINNER.
WHAT?
BAM

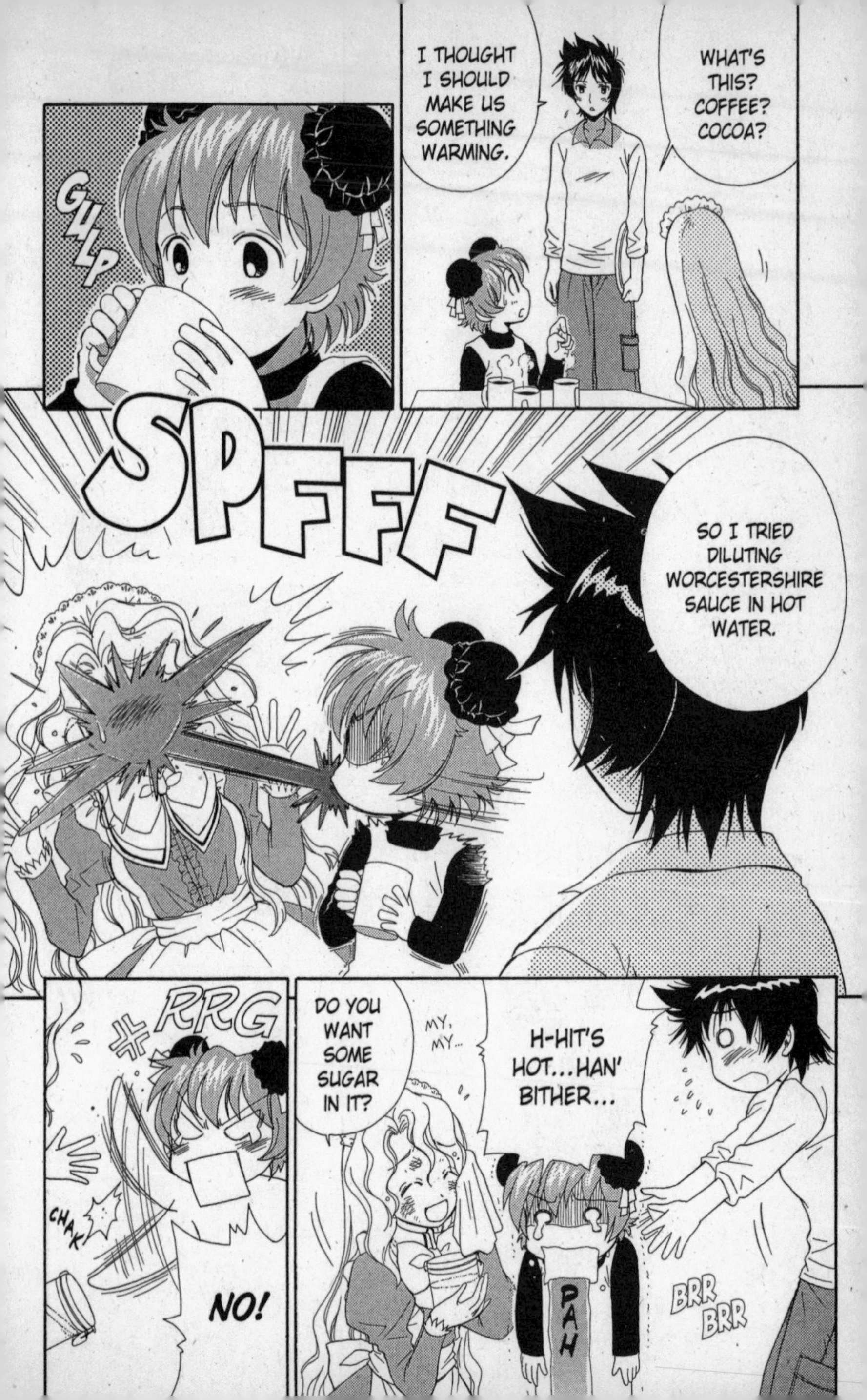
WHAT'S THIS? COFFEE? COCOA?
I THOUGHT I SHOULD MAKE US SOMETHING WARMING.
GULP
SO I TRIED DILUTING WORCESTERSHIRE SAUCE IN HOT WATER.
SPFFF
H-HIT'S HOT...HAN' BITHER...
BRR BRR
PAH
MY, MY...
DO YOU WANT SOME SUGAR IN IT?
RRG
CHAK
NO!

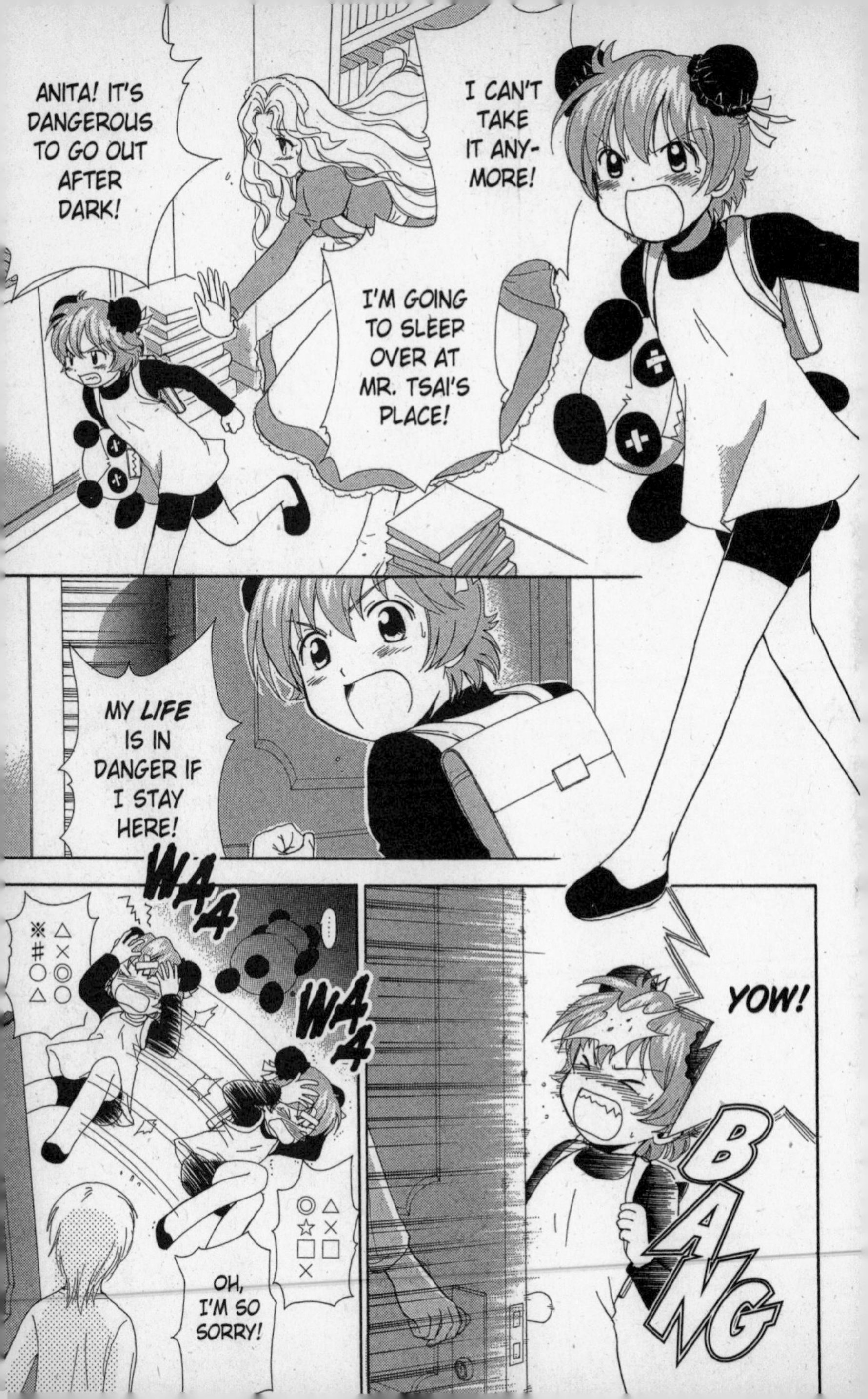
I CAN'T TAKE IT ANY-MORE!
ANITA! IT'S DANGEROUS TO GO OUT AFTER DARK!
I'M GOING TO SLEEP OVER AT MR. TSAI'S PLACE!
MY *LIFE* IS IN DANGER IF I STAY HERE!
YOW!
BANG
WAA
WAA
※△#×○◎△○
...
◎△☆×□□×
OH, I'M SO SORRY!

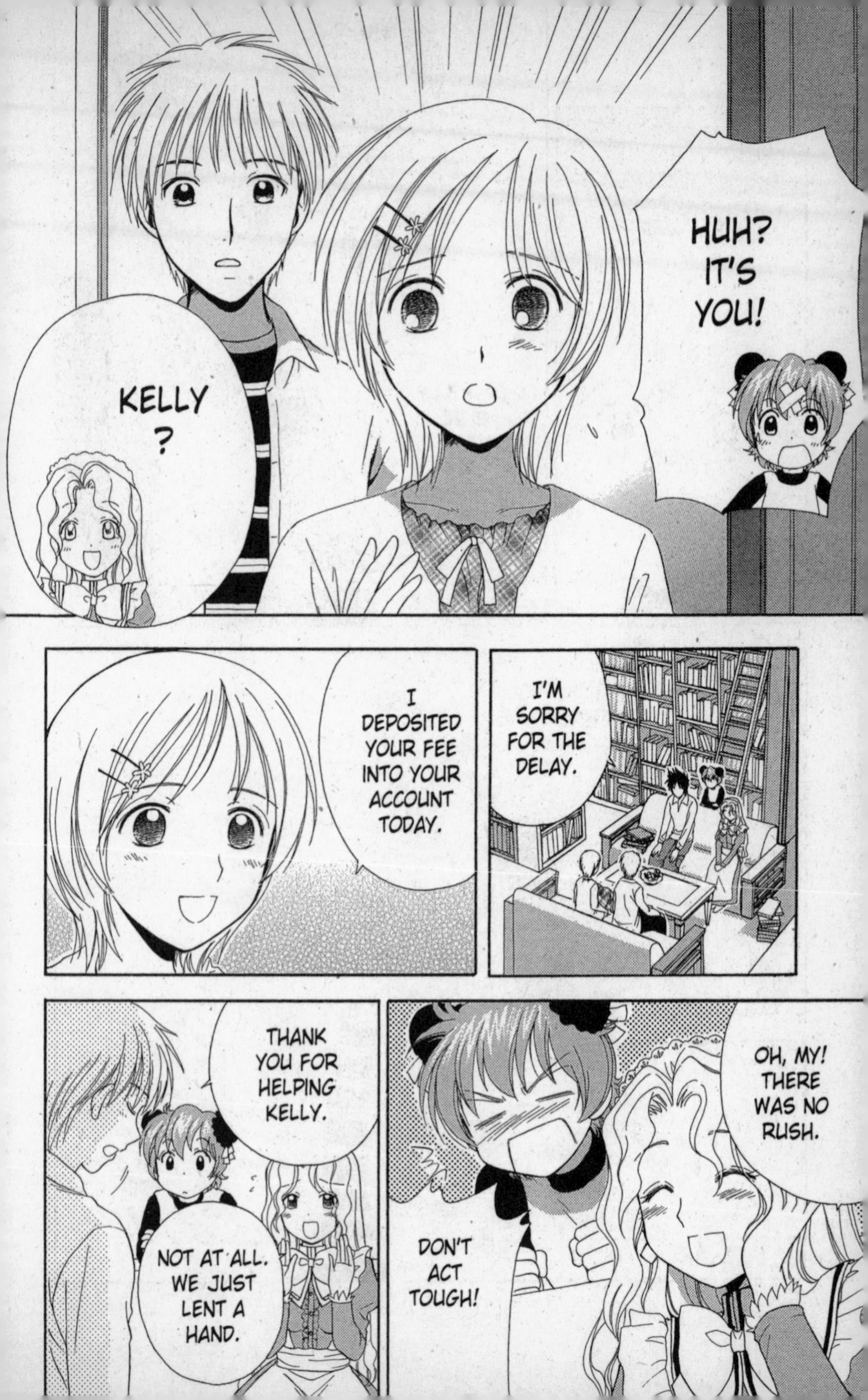
HUH? IT'S YOU!
KELLY?
I'M SORRY FOR THE DELAY.
I DEPOSITED YOUR FEE INTO YOUR ACCOUNT TODAY.
OH, MY! THERE WAS NO RUSH.
DON'T ACT TOUGH!
THANK YOU FOR HELPING KELLY.
NOT AT ALL. WE JUST LENT A HAND.

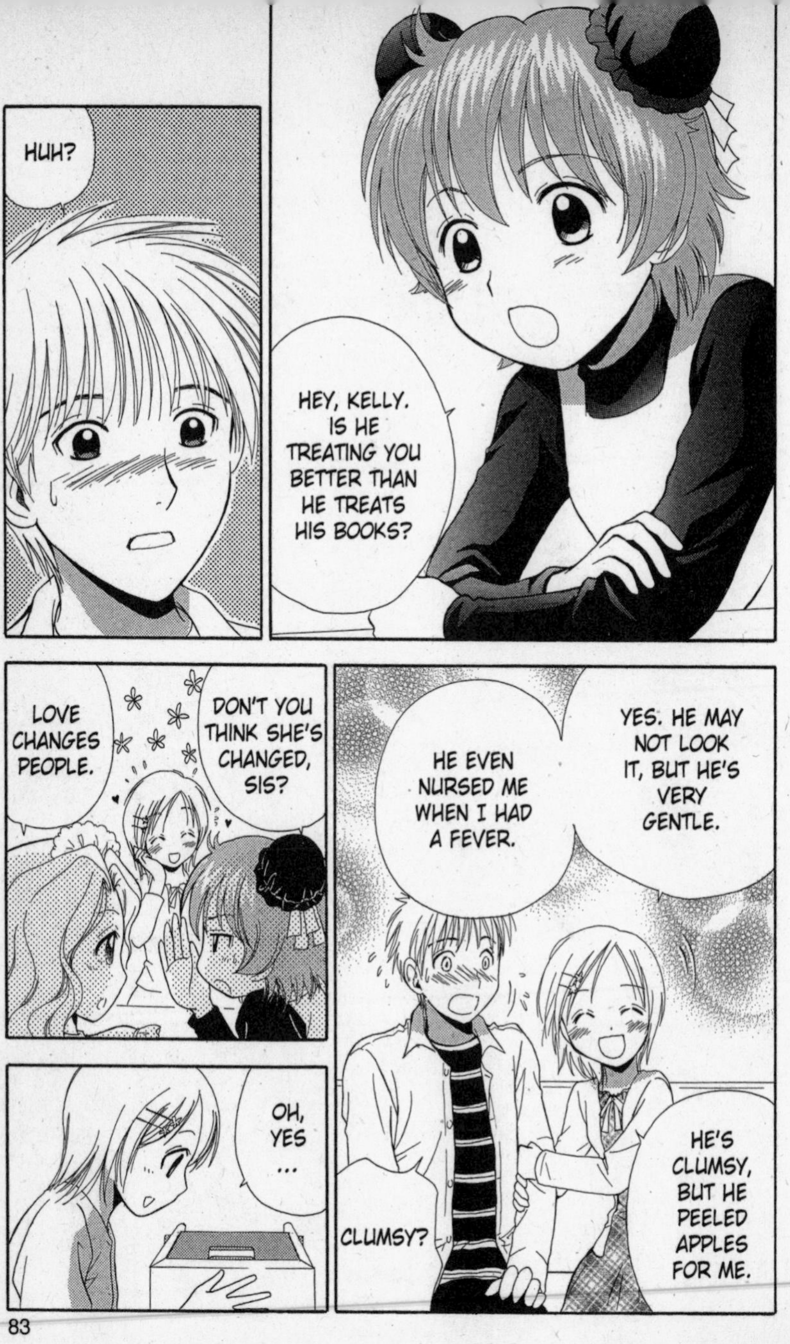
HEY, KELLY. IS HE TREATING YOU BETTER THAN HE TREATS HIS BOOKS?
HUH?
YES. HE MAY NOT LOOK IT, BUT HE'S VERY GENTLE.
HE EVEN NURSED ME WHEN I HAD A FEVER.
HE'S CLUMSY, BUT HE PEELED APPLES FOR ME.
CLUMSY?
DON'T YOU THINK SHE'S CHANGED, SIS?
LOVE CHANGES PEOPLE.
OH, YES ...

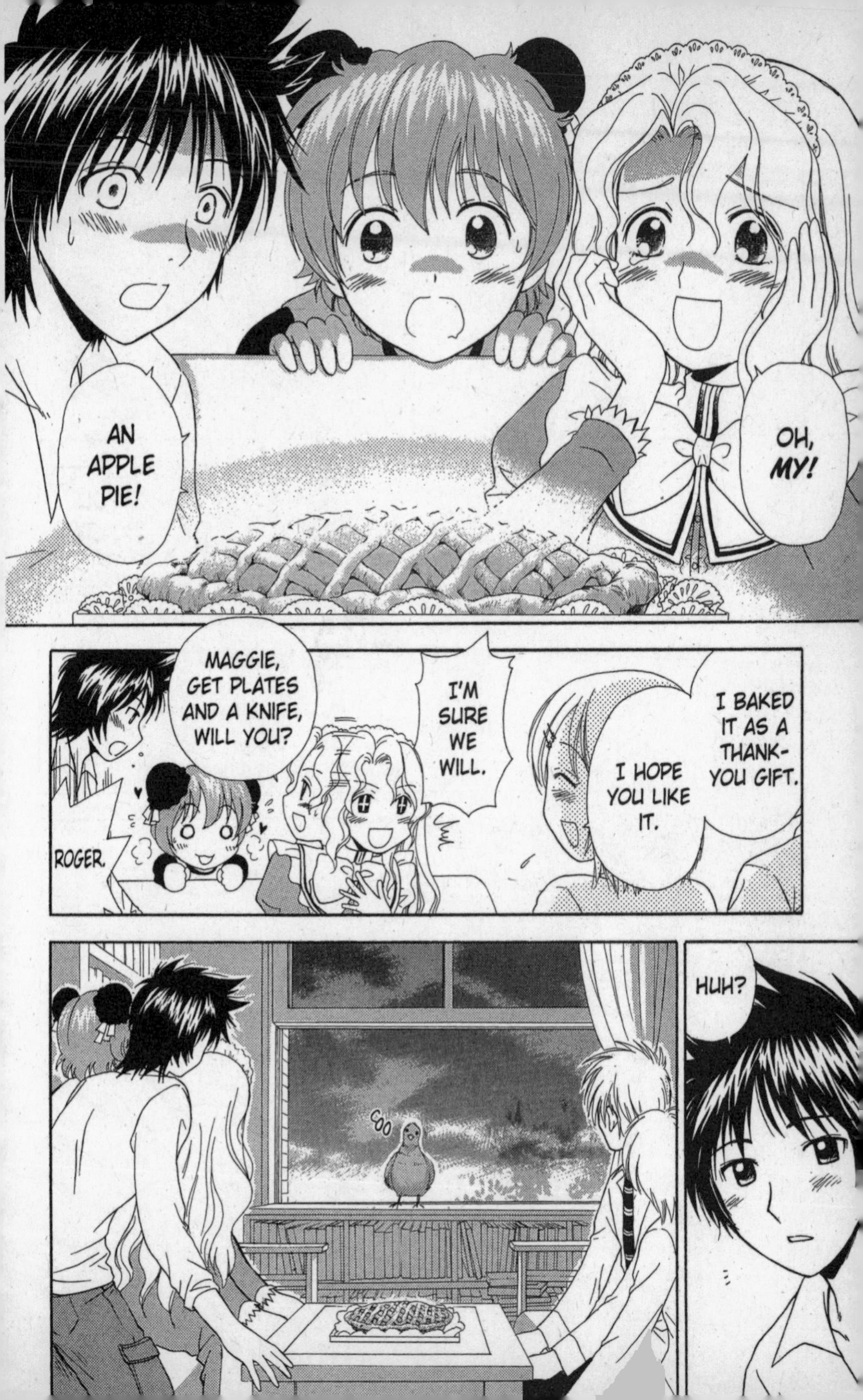
OH, MY!
AN APPLE PIE!
I BAKED IT AS A THANK-YOU GIFT.
I HOPE YOU LIKE IT.
I'M SURE WE WILL.
MAGGIE, GET PLATES AND A KNIFE, WILL YOU?
ROGER.
HUH?
COO

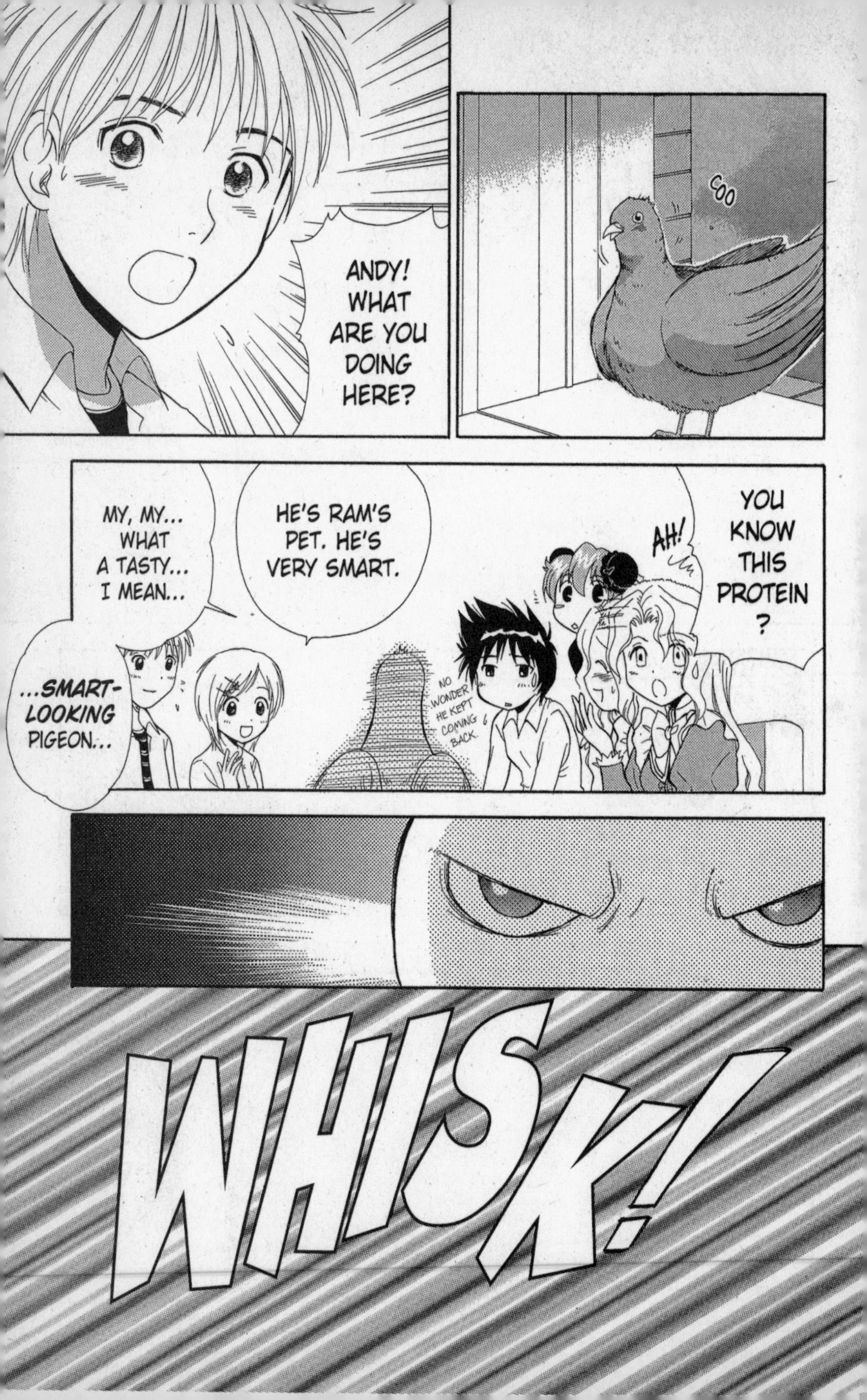
COO
ANDY! WHAT ARE YOU DOING HERE?
YOU KNOW THIS PROTEIN?
AH!
NO WONDER HE KEPT COMING BACK.
HE'S RAM'S PET. HE'S VERY SMART.
MY, MY... WHAT A TASTY... I MEAN...
...SMART-LOOKING PIGEON...
WHISK!

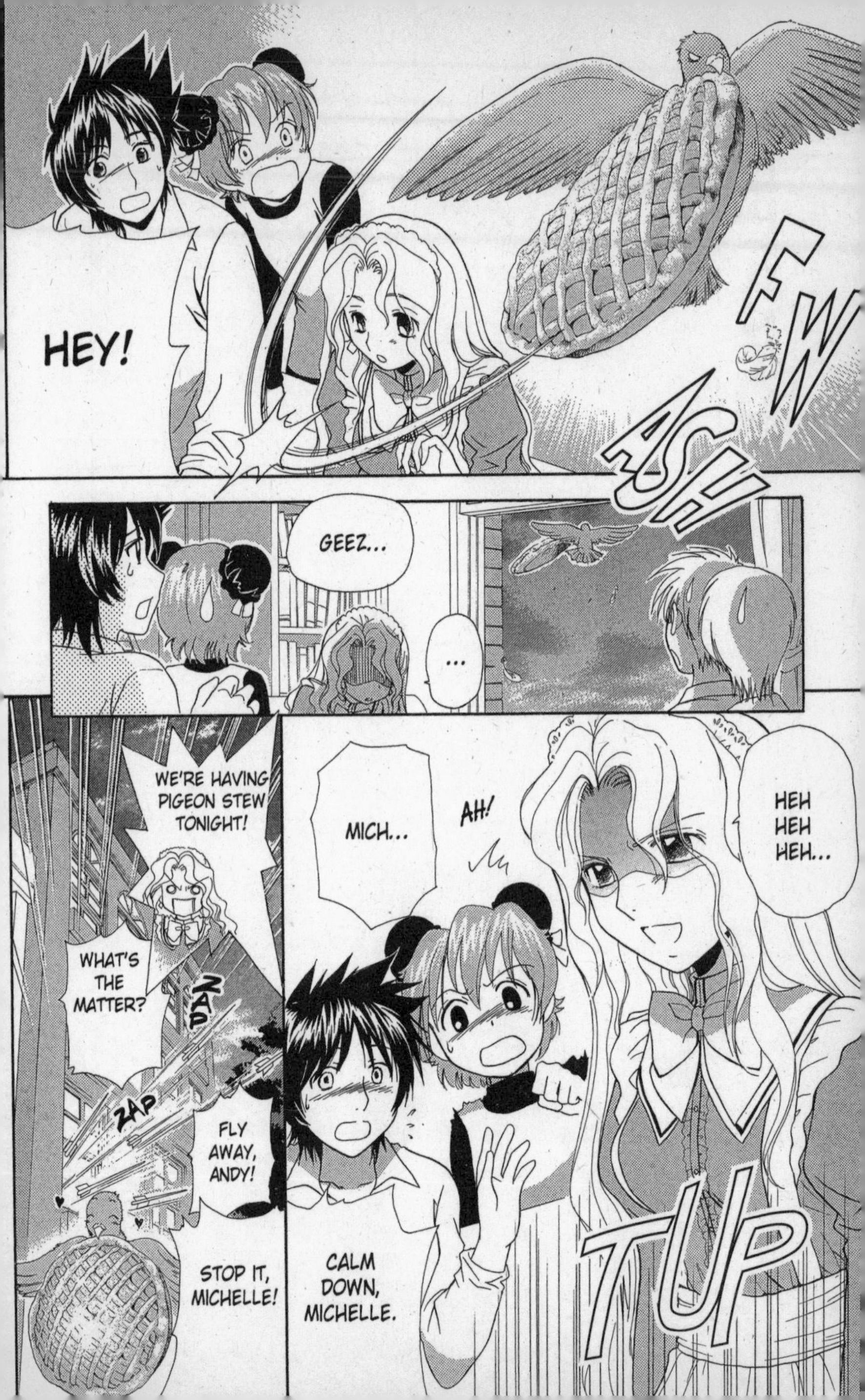
FWASH
HEY!
GEEZ...
...
HEH HEH HEH...
AH!
MICH...
TUP
CALM DOWN, MICHELLE.
WE'RE HAVING PIGEON STEW TONIGHT!
WHAT'S THE MATTER?
ZAP
ZAP
FLY AWAY, ANDY!
STOP IT, MICHELLE!

CHAPTER 4

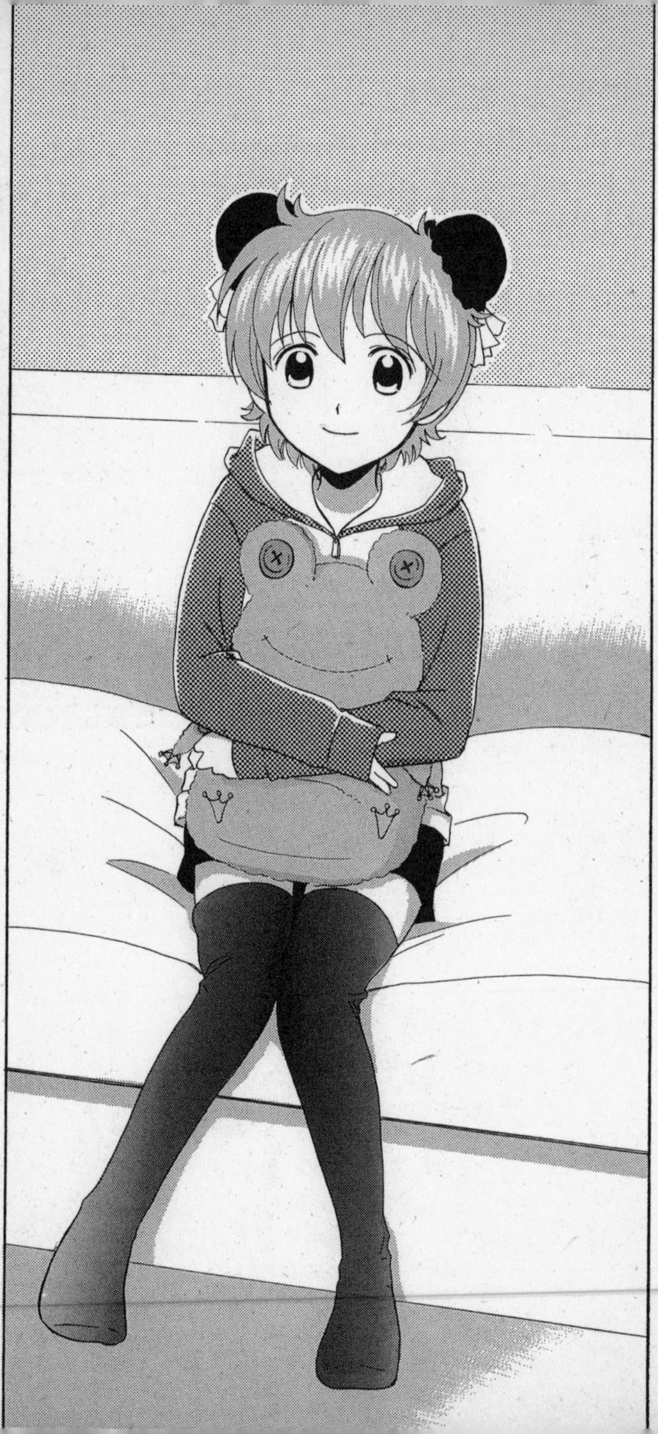

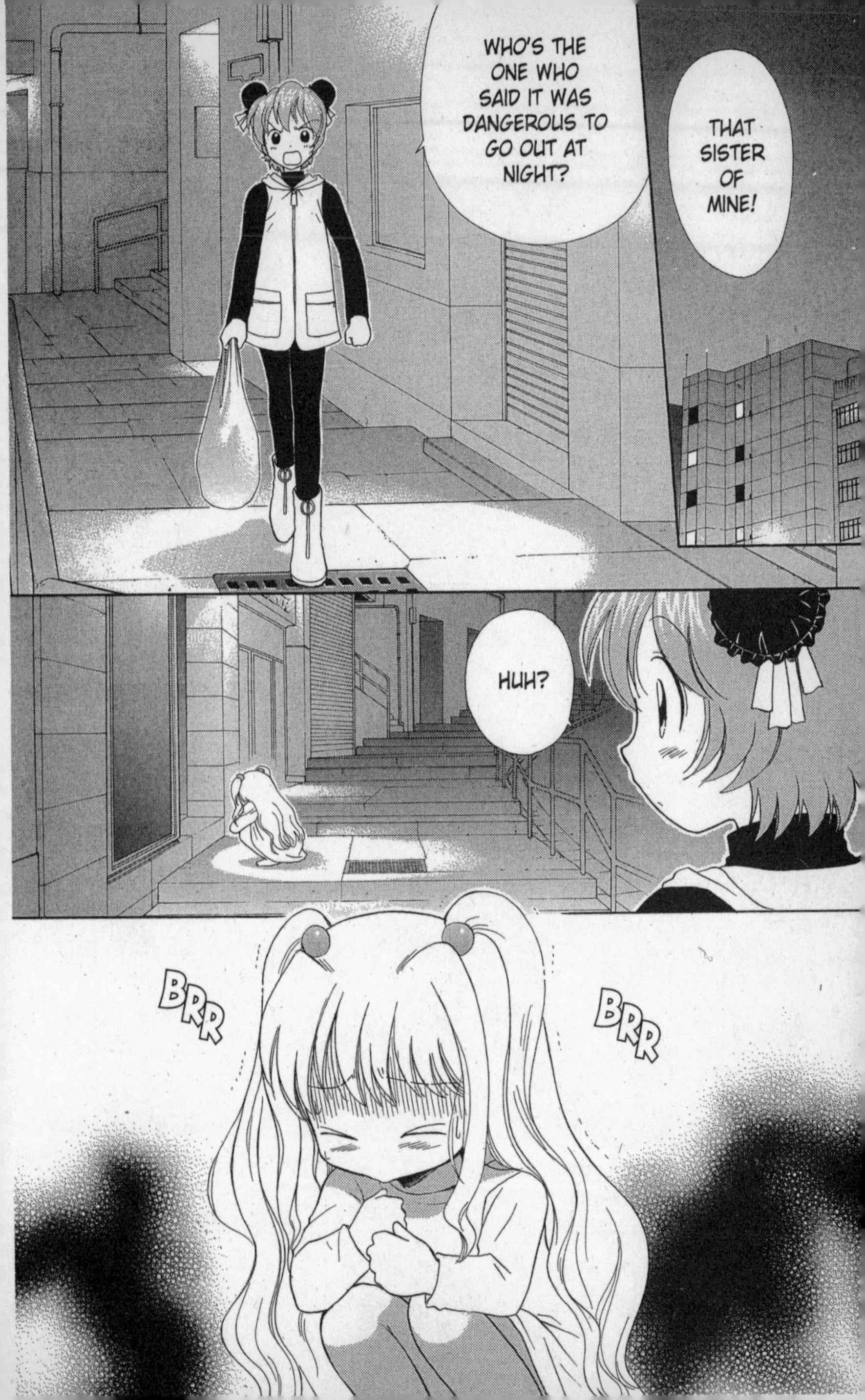
THAT SISTER OF MINE!
WHO'S THE ONE WHO SAID IT WAS DANGEROUS TO GO OUT AT NIGHT?
HUH?
BRR
BRR

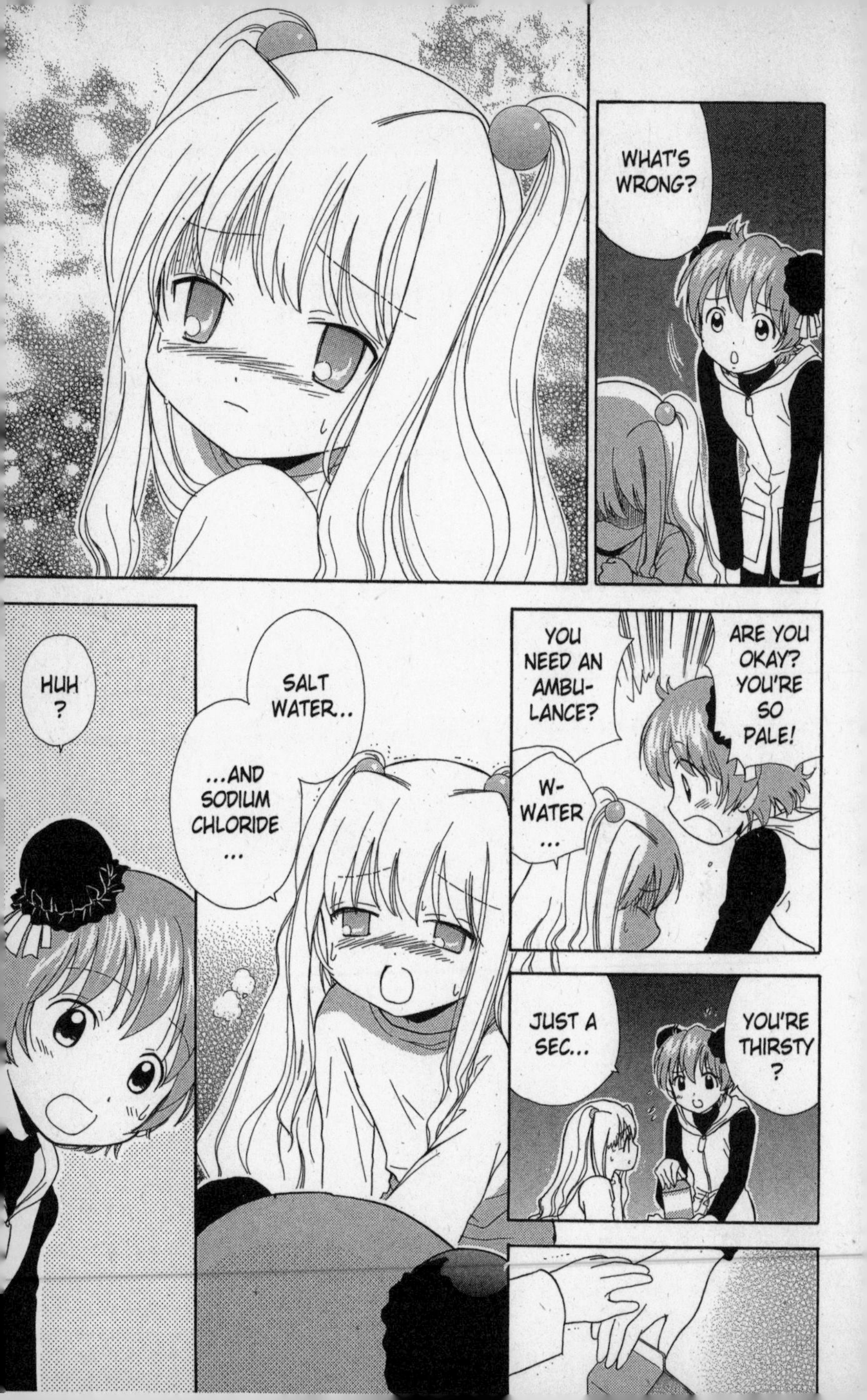
WHAT'S WRONG?
ARE YOU OKAY? YOU'RE SO PALE!
YOU NEED AN AMBU-LANCE?
W-WATER ...
YOU'RE THIRSTY ?
JUST A SEC...
SALT WATER...
...AND SODIUM CHLORIDE ...
HUH ?

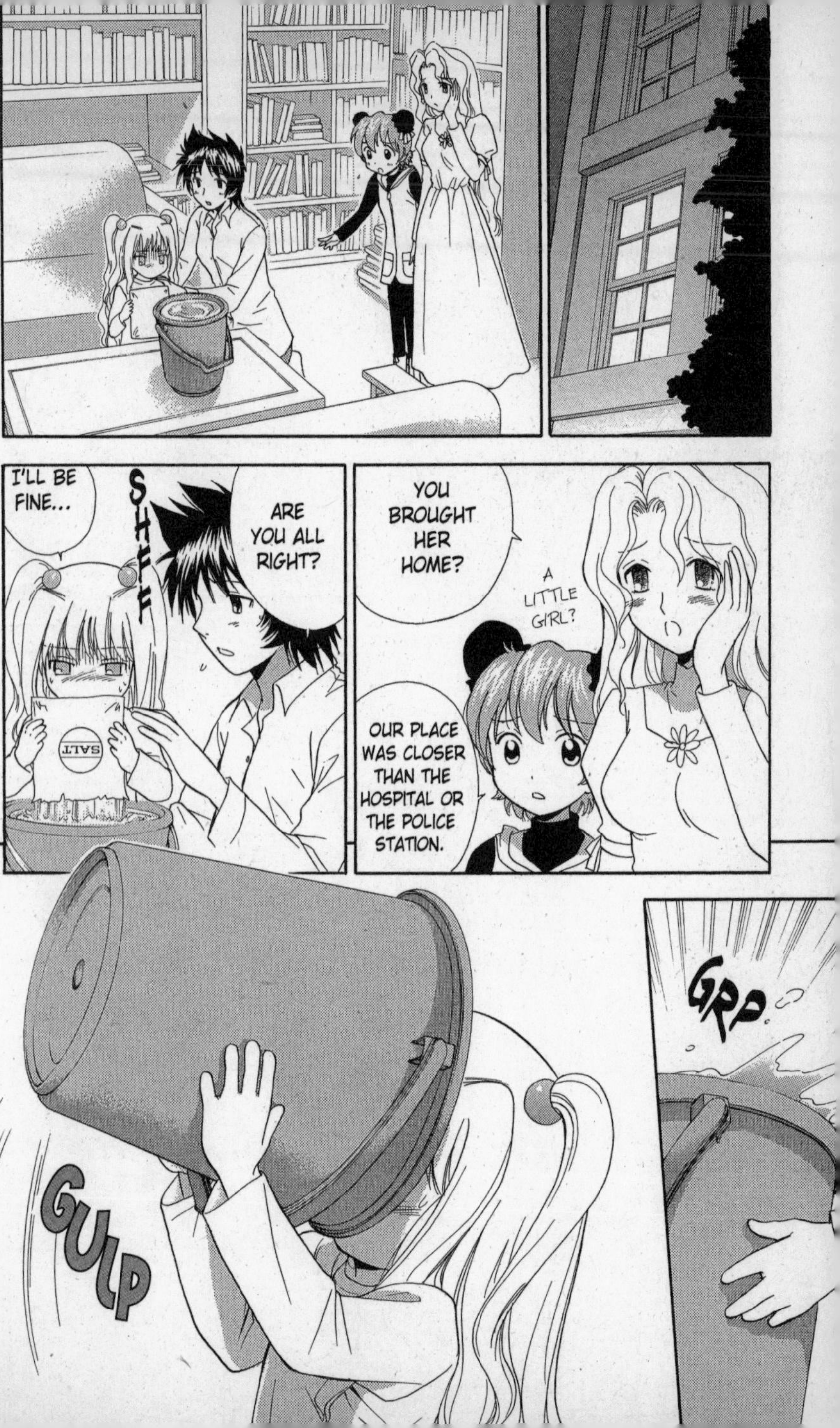
YOU BROUGHT HER HOME?
A LITTLE GIRL?
OUR PLACE WAS CLOSER THAN THE HOSPITAL OR THE POLICE STATION.
ARE YOU ALL RIGHT?
SHFF
I'LL BE FINE...
SALT
GRP
GULP

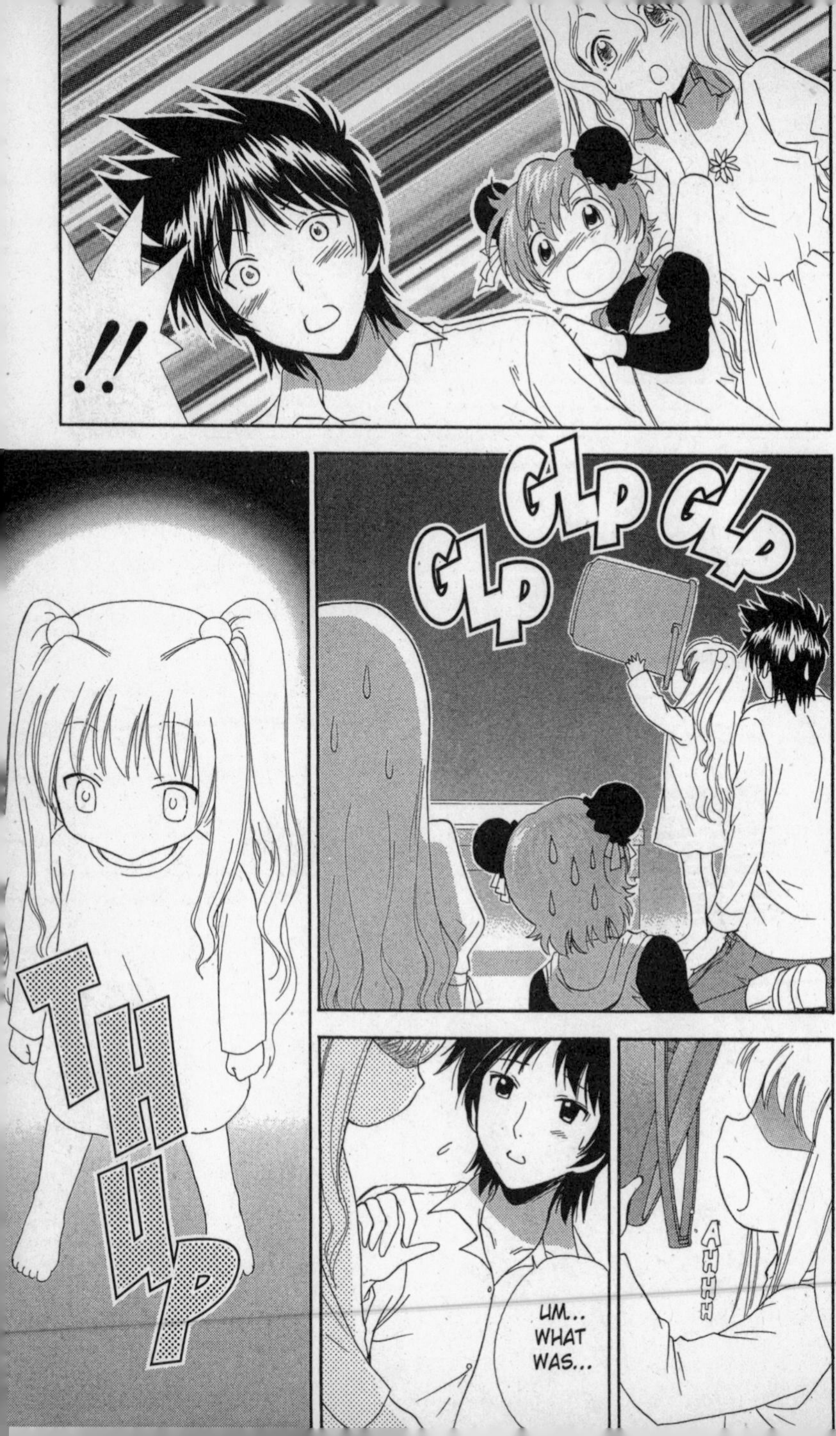
!!
GLP GLP GLP
AHHHH
UM... WHAT WAS...
THUP

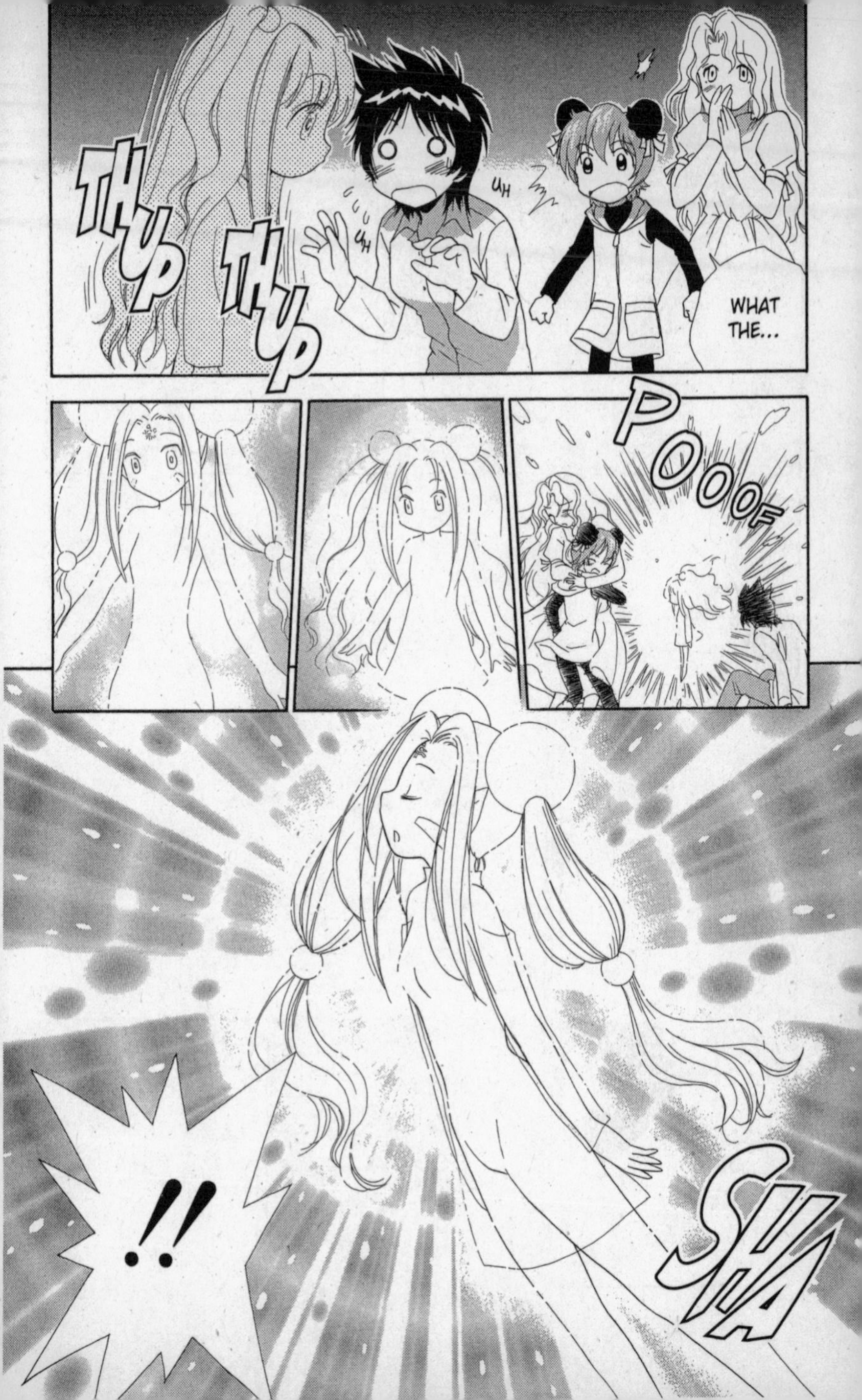
WHAT THE...
UH
UH
THUP
THUP
POOOF
SHA
!!

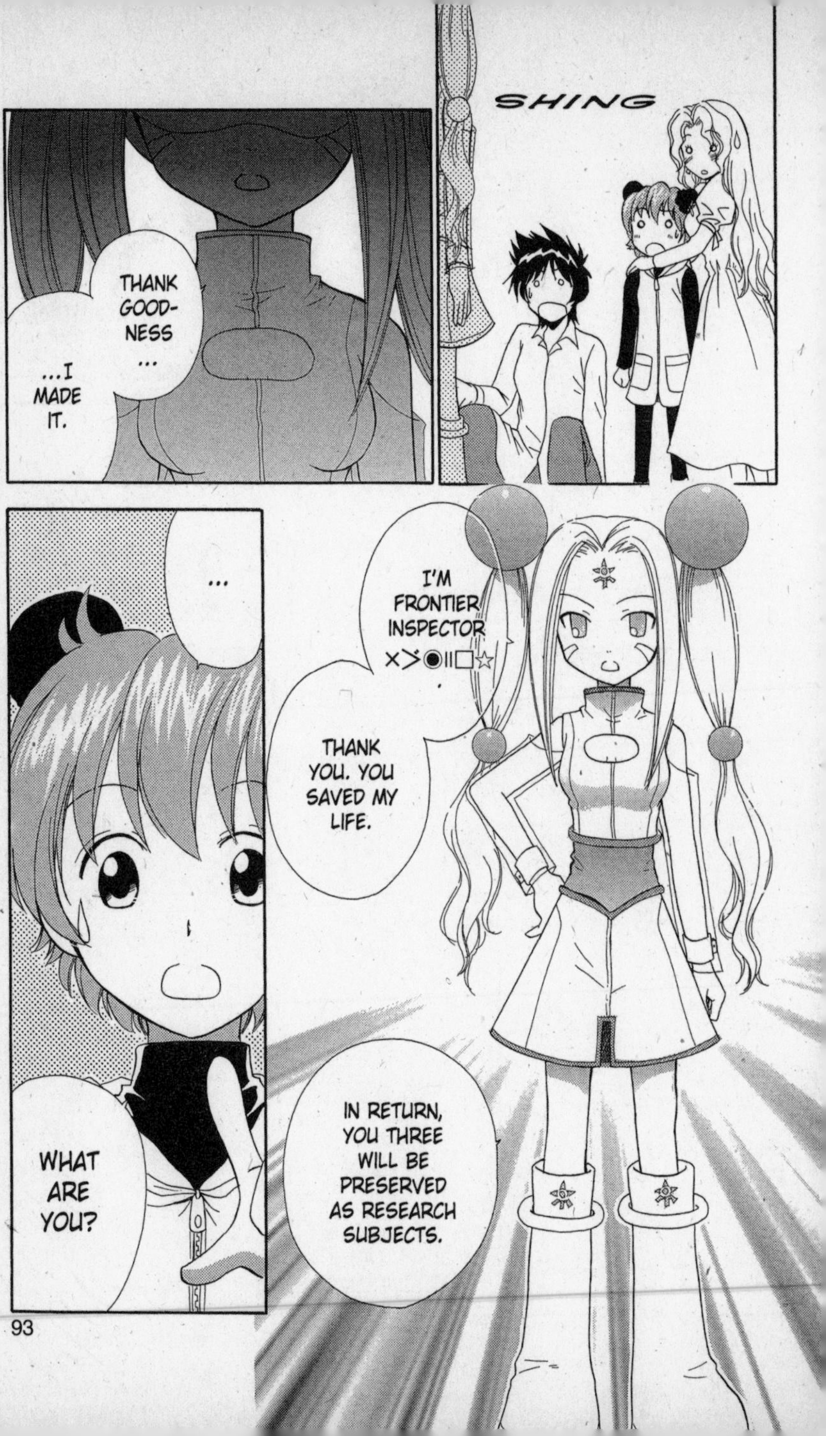

SHING
THANK GOODNESS ...
...I MADE IT.
I'M FRONTIER INSPECTOR ×ゞ◉II□☆.
THANK YOU. YOU SAVED MY LIFE.
IN RETURN, YOU THREE WILL BE PRESERVED AS RESEARCH SUBJECTS.
...
WHAT ARE YOU?

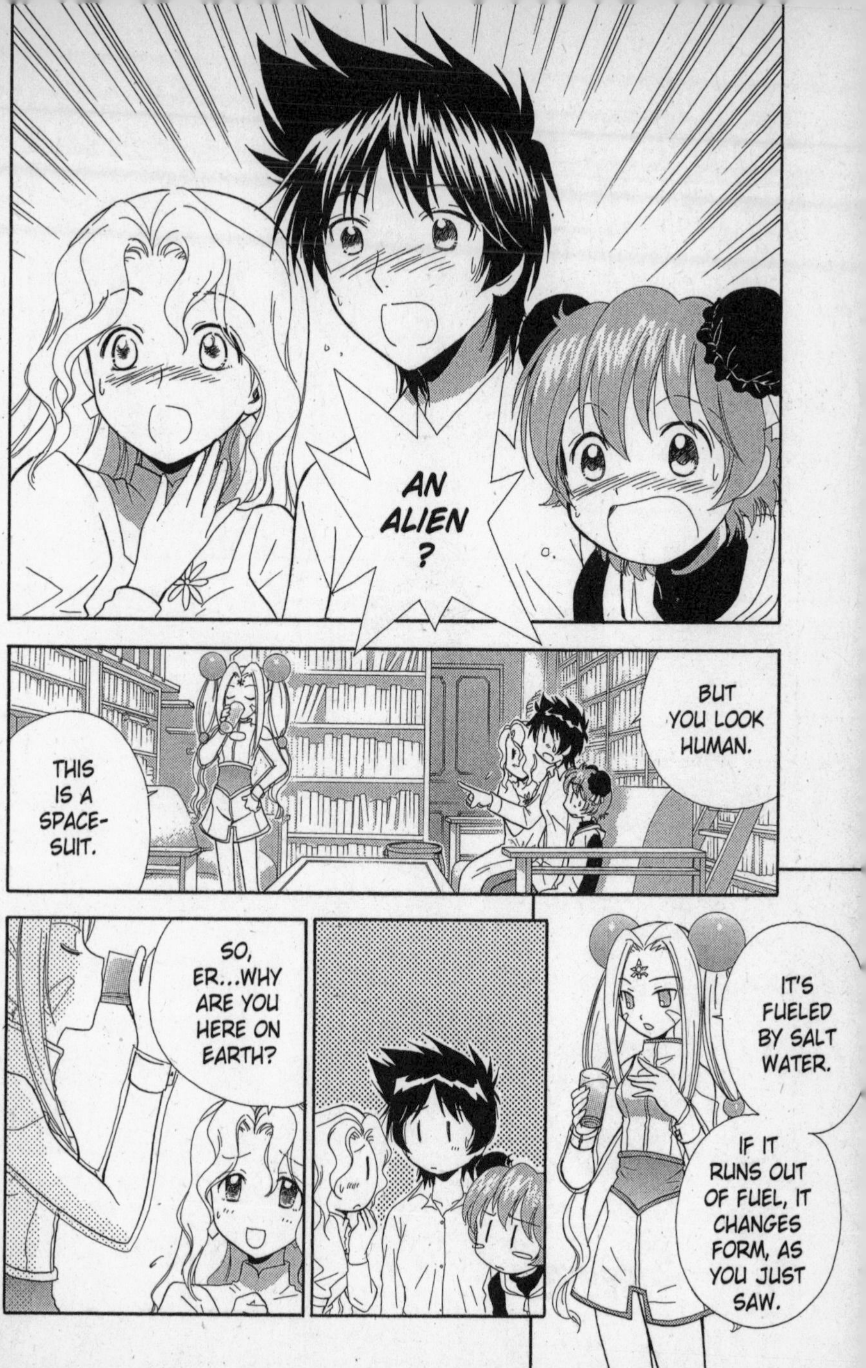
AN ALIEN?
BUT YOU LOOK HUMAN.
THIS IS A SPACE-SUIT.
IT'S FUELED BY SALT WATER.
IF IT RUNS OUT OF FUEL, IT CHANGES FORM, AS YOU JUST SAW.
SO, ER...WHY ARE YOU HERE ON EARTH?

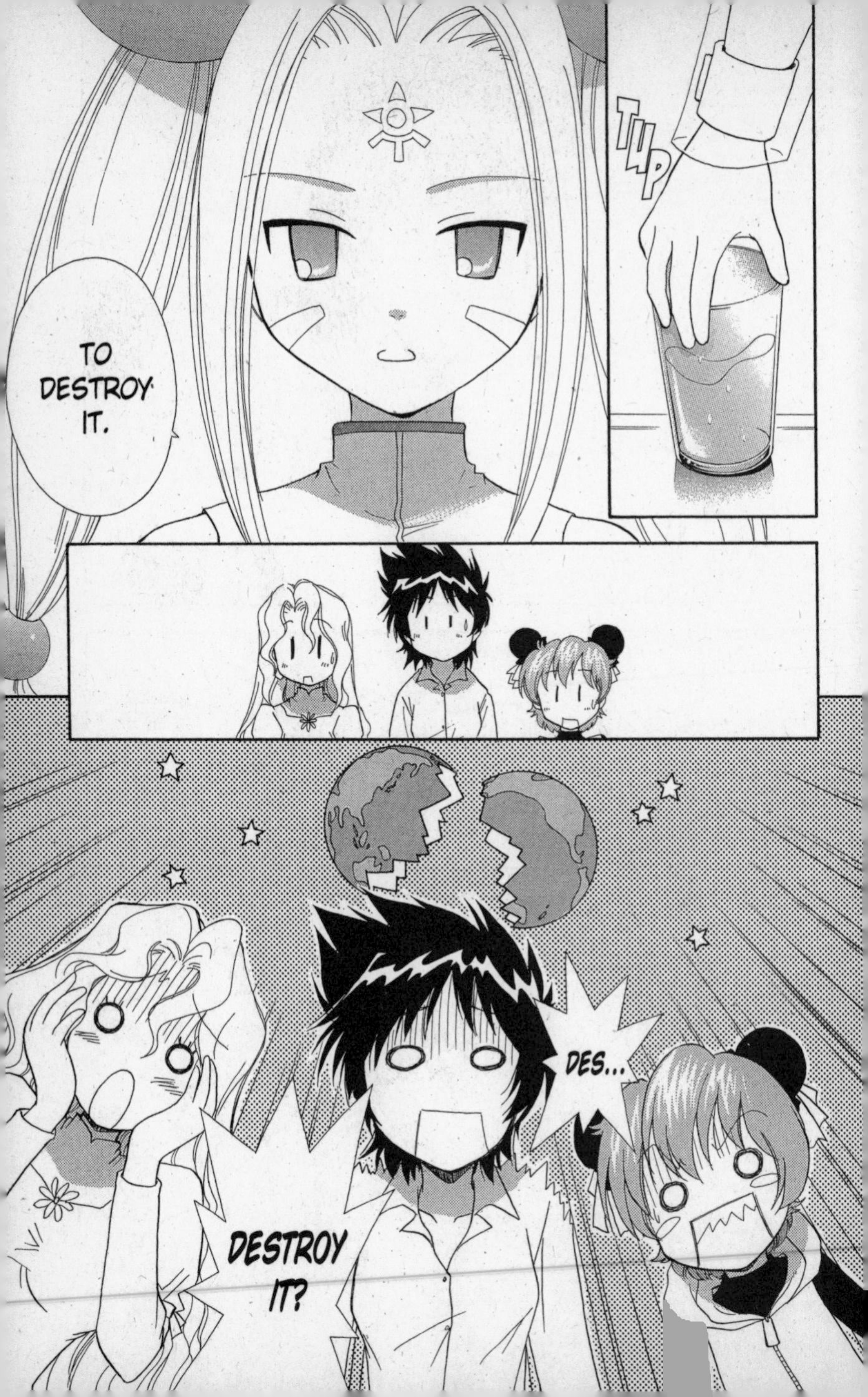
TUP
TO DESTROY IT.
DES...
DESTROY IT?

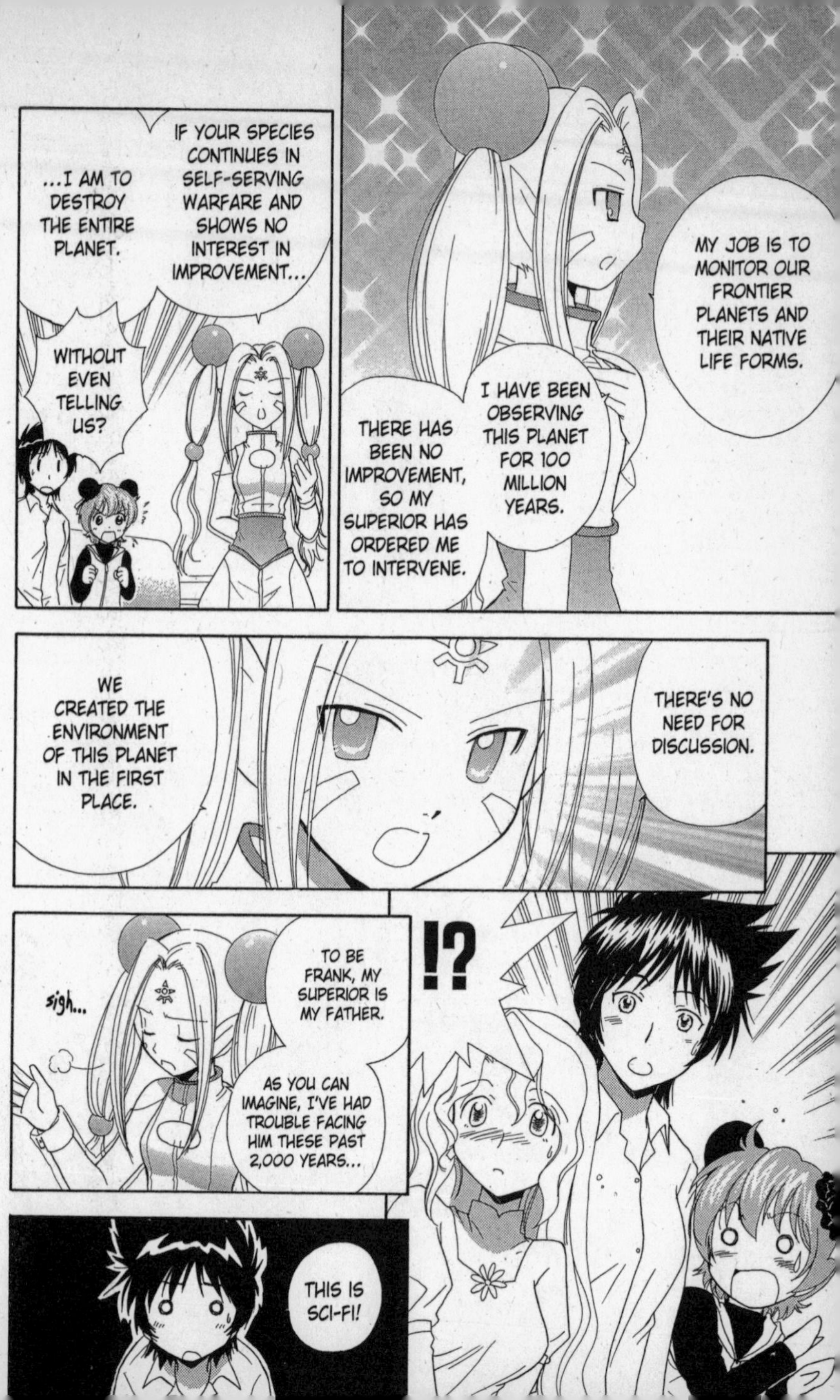
MY JOB IS TO MONITOR OUR FRONTIER PLANETS AND THEIR NATIVE LIFE FORMS.
I HAVE BEEN OBSERVING THIS PLANET FOR 100 MILLION YEARS.
THERE HAS BEEN NO IMPROVEMENT, SO MY SUPERIOR HAS ORDERED ME TO INTERVENE.
IF YOUR SPECIES CONTINUES IN SELF-SERVING WARFARE AND SHOWS NO INTEREST IN IMPROVEMENT...
...I AM TO DESTROY THE ENTIRE PLANET.
WITHOUT EVEN TELLING US?
THERE'S NO NEED FOR DISCUSSION.
WE CREATED THE ENVIRONMENT OF THIS PLANET IN THE FIRST PLACE.
!?
TO BE FRANK, MY SUPERIOR IS MY FATHER.
AS YOU CAN IMAGINE, I'VE HAD TROUBLE FACING HIM THESE PAST 2,000 YEARS...
sigh...
THIS IS SCI-FI!

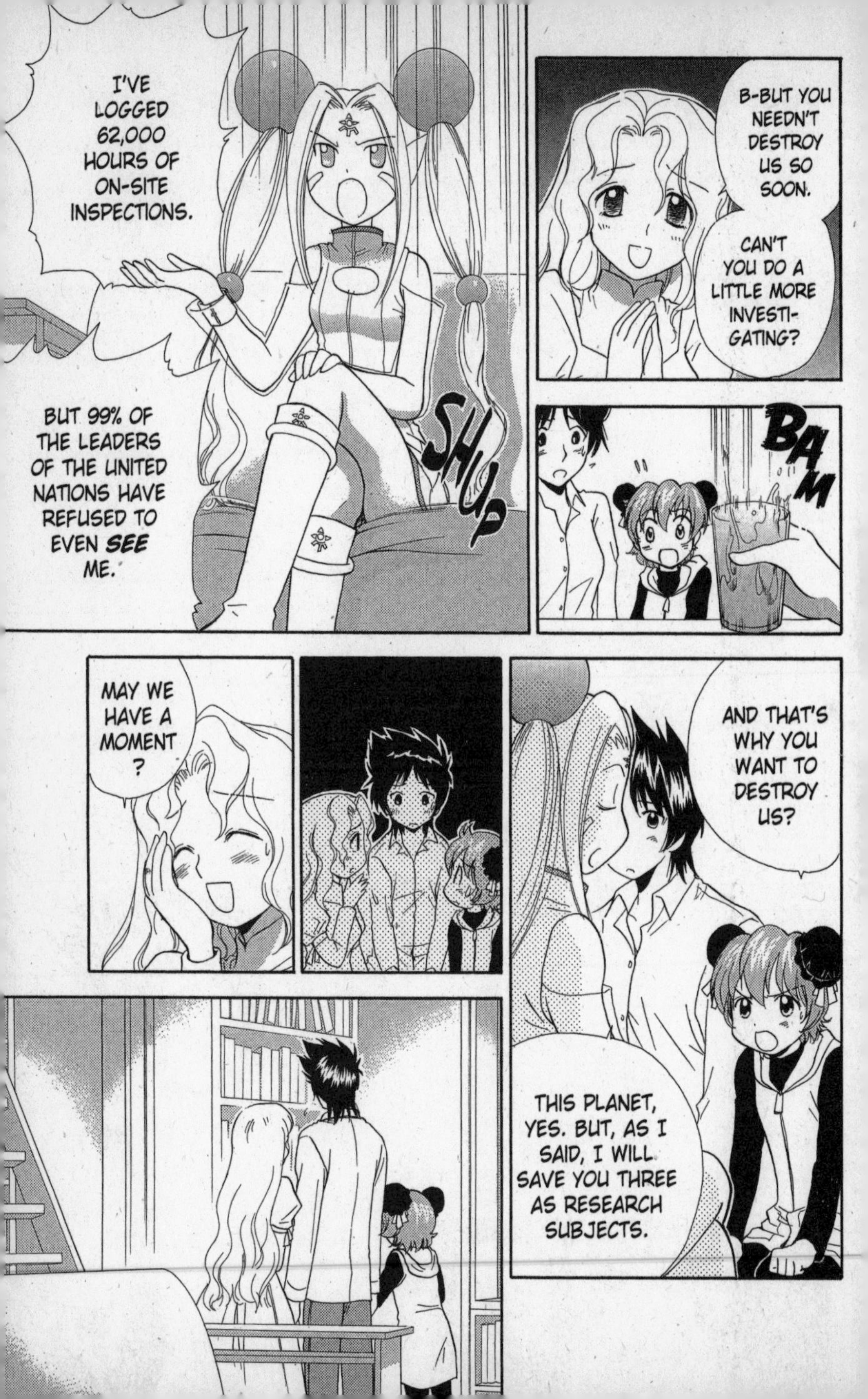
B-BUT YOU NEEDN'T DESTROY US SO SOON.
CAN'T YOU DO A LITTLE MORE INVESTI-GATING?
BAM
I'VE LOGGED 62,000 HOURS OF ON-SITE INSPECTIONS.
SHUP
BUT 99% OF THE LEADERS OF THE UNITED NATIONS HAVE REFUSED TO EVEN SEE ME.
AND THAT'S WHY YOU WANT TO DESTROY US?
THIS PLANET, YES. BUT, AS I SAID, I WILL SAVE YOU THREE AS RESEARCH SUBJECTS.
MAY WE HAVE A MOMENT?

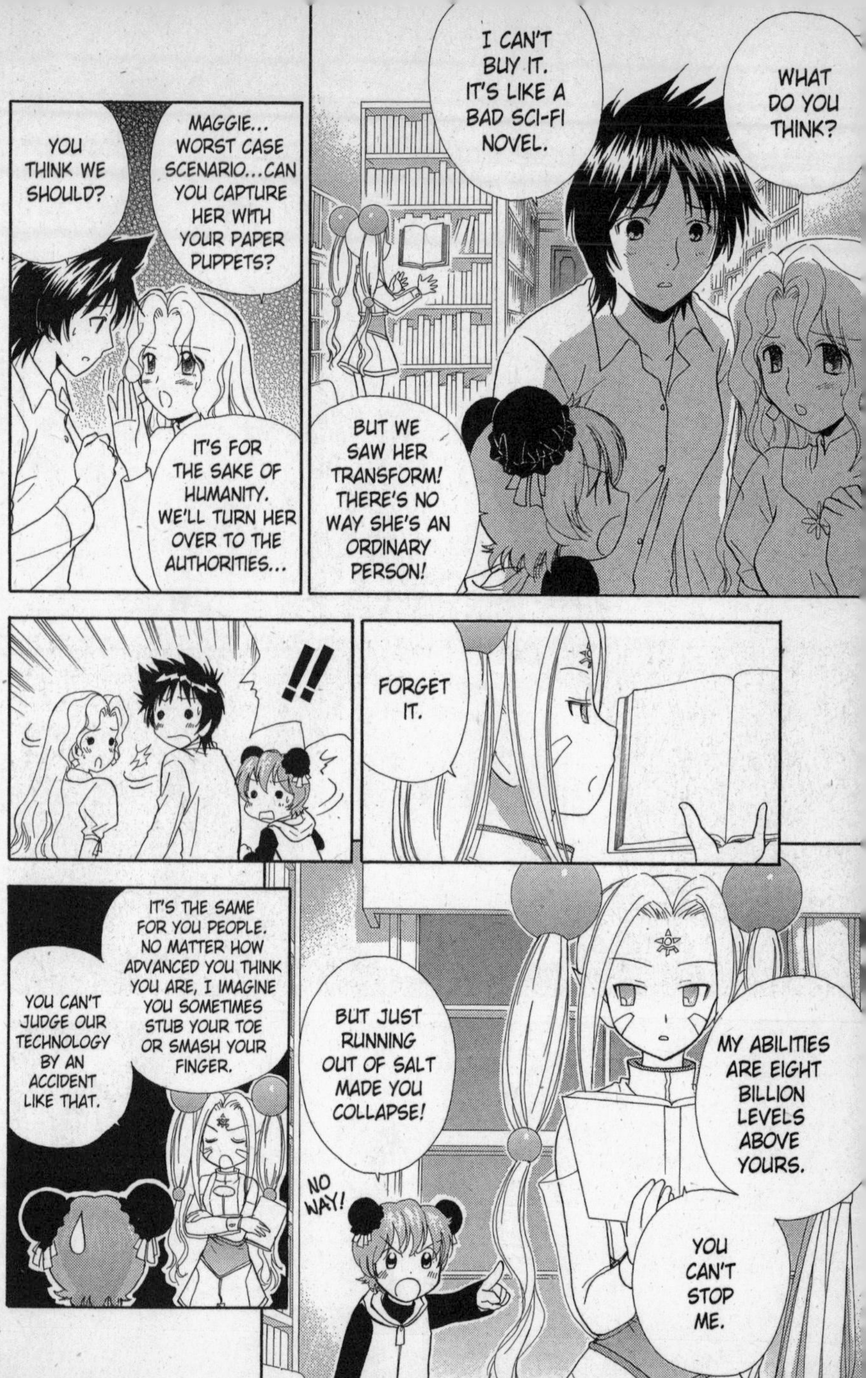
WHAT DO YOU THINK?
I CAN'T BUY IT. IT'S LIKE A BAD SCI-FI NOVEL.
BUT WE SAW HER TRANSFORM! THERE'S NO WAY SHE'S AN ORDINARY PERSON!
MAGGIE... WORST CASE SCENARIO...CAN YOU CAPTURE HER WITH YOUR PAPER PUPPETS?
YOU THINK WE SHOULD?
IT'S FOR THE SAKE OF HUMANITY. WE'LL TURN HER OVER TO THE AUTHORITIES...
FORGET IT.
!!
MY ABILITIES ARE EIGHT BILLION LEVELS ABOVE YOURS.
YOU CAN'T STOP ME.
BUT JUST RUNNING OUT OF SALT MADE YOU COLLAPSE!
NO WAY!
IT'S THE SAME FOR YOU PEOPLE. NO MATTER HOW ADVANCED YOU THINK YOU ARE, I IMAGINE YOU SOMETIMES STUB YOUR TOE OR SMASH YOUR FINGER.
YOU CAN'T JUDGE OUR TECHNOLOGY BY AN ACCIDENT LIKE THAT.

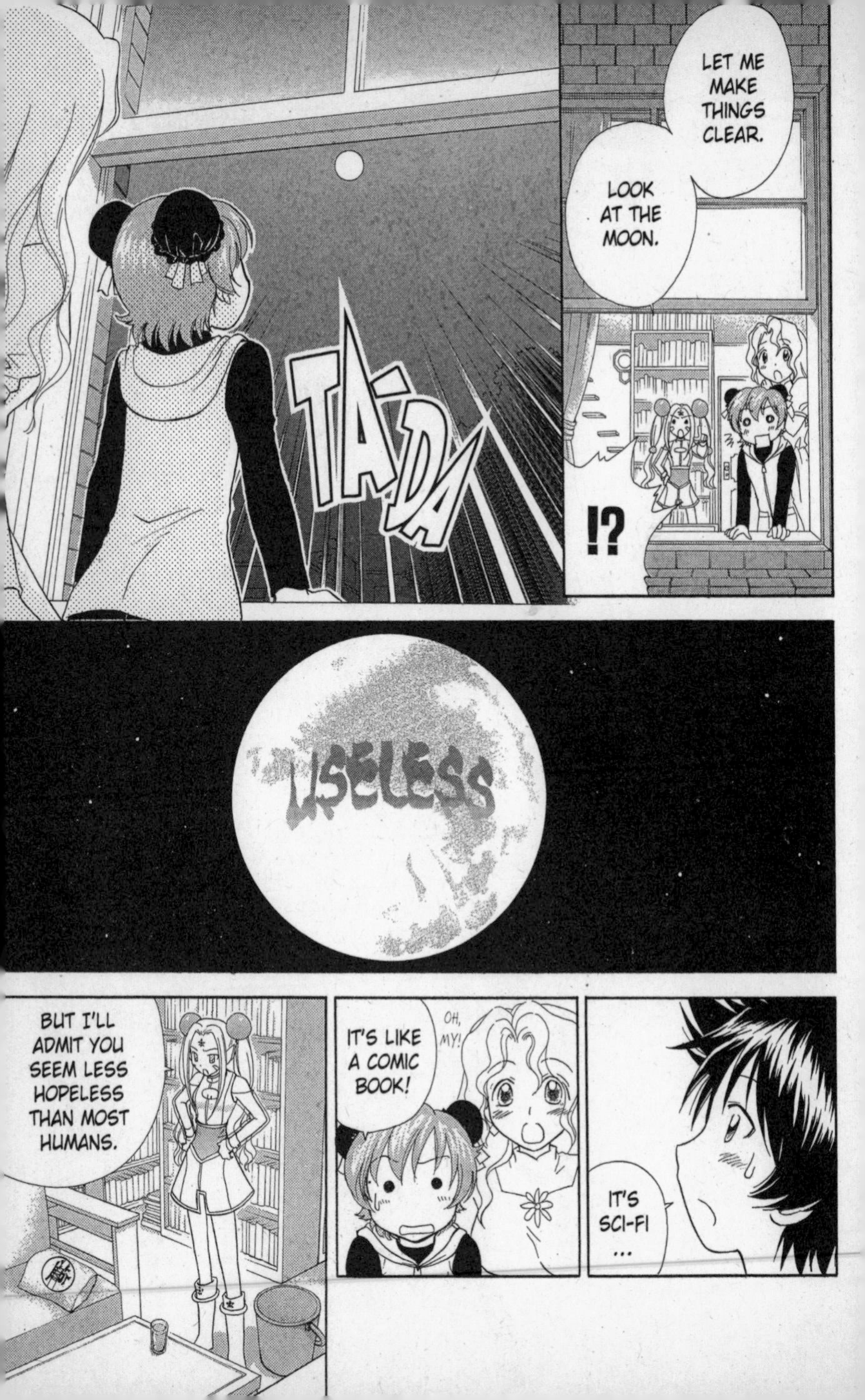
LET ME MAKE THINGS CLEAR.
LOOK AT THE MOON.
!?
TA-DA
USELESS
IT'S SCI-FI ...
OH, MY!
IT'S LIKE A COMIC BOOK!
BUT I'LL ADMIT YOU SEEM LESS HOPELESS THAN MOST HUMANS.

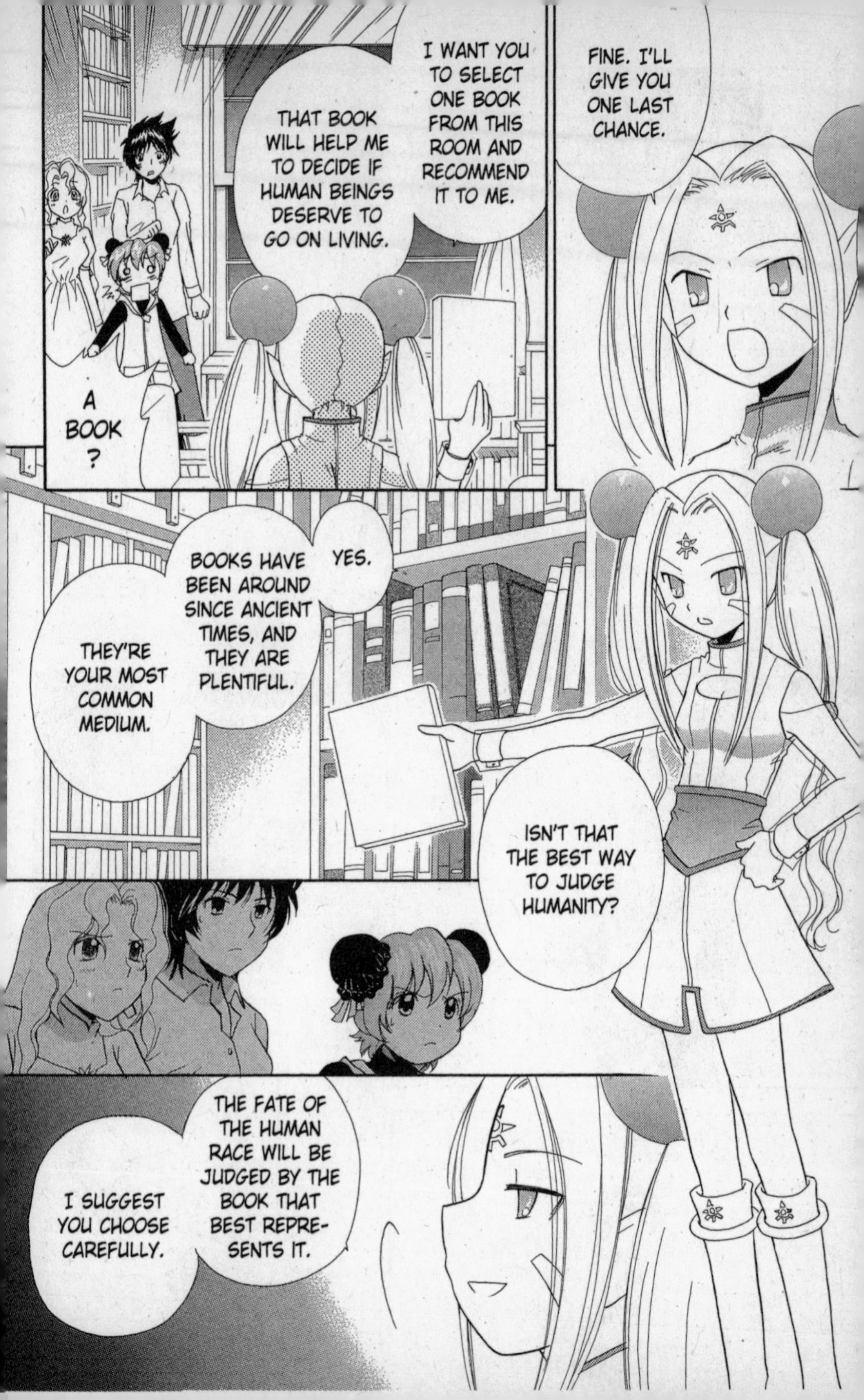
FINE. I'LL GIVE YOU ONE LAST CHANCE.
I WANT YOU TO SELECT ONE BOOK FROM THIS ROOM AND RECOMMEND IT TO ME.
THAT BOOK WILL HELP ME TO DECIDE IF HUMAN BEINGS DESERVE TO GO ON LIVING.
A BOOK?
YES.
BOOKS HAVE BEEN AROUND SINCE ANCIENT TIMES, AND THEY ARE PLENTIFUL.
THEY'RE YOUR MOST COMMON MEDIUM.
ISN'T THAT THE BEST WAY TO JUDGE HUMANITY?
THE FATE OF THE HUMAN RACE WILL BE JUDGED BY THE BOOK THAT BEST REPRESENTS IT.
I SUGGEST YOU CHOOSE CAREFULLY.

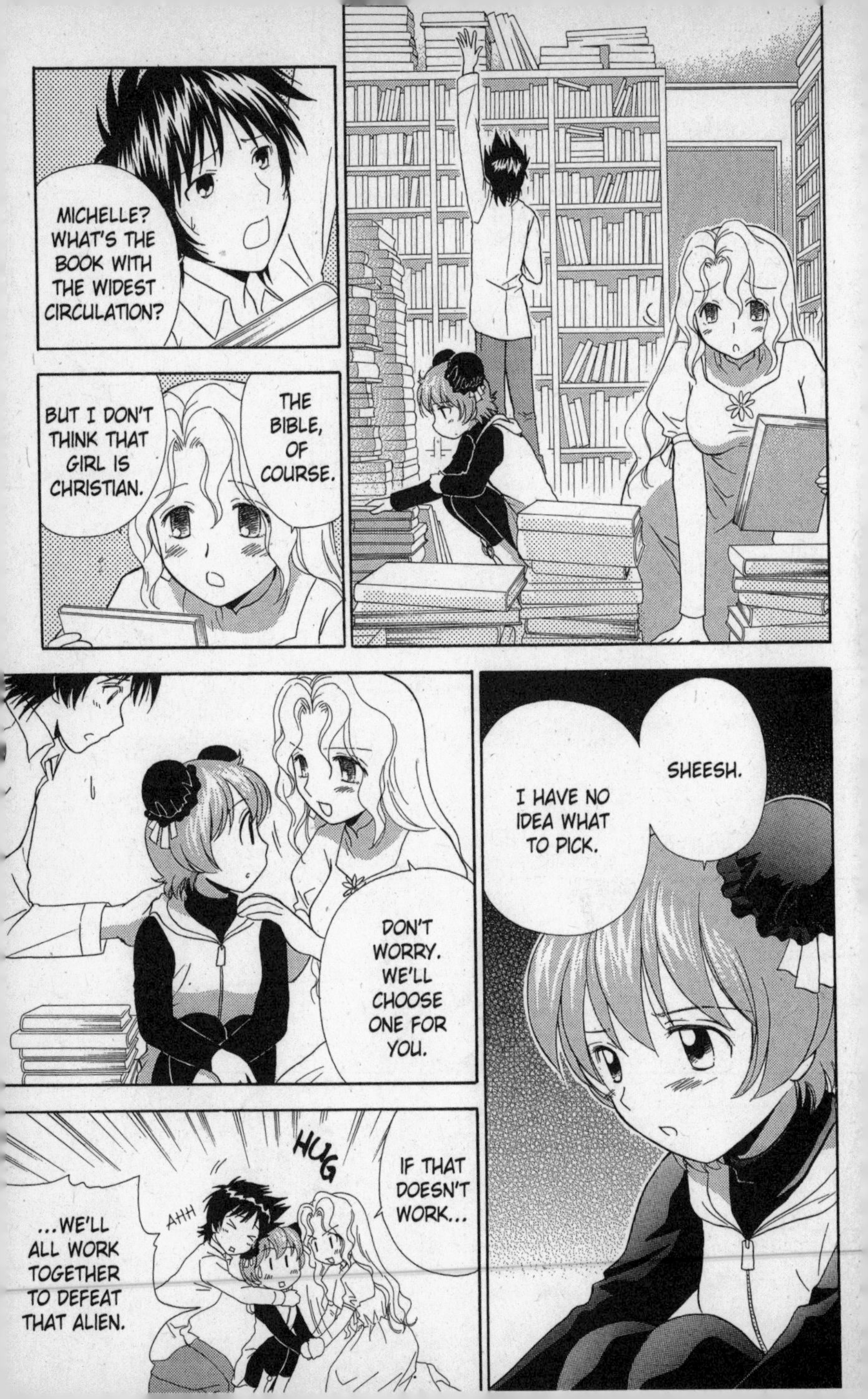
MICHELLE? WHAT'S THE BOOK WITH THE WIDEST CIRCULATION?
THE BIBLE, OF COURSE.
BUT I DON'T THINK THAT GIRL IS CHRISTIAN.
SHEESH.
I HAVE NO IDEA WHAT TO PICK.
DON'T WORRY. WE'LL CHOOSE ONE FOR YOU.
HUG
IF THAT DOESN'T WORK...
AHH
...WE'LL ALL WORK TOGETHER TO DEFEAT THAT ALIEN.

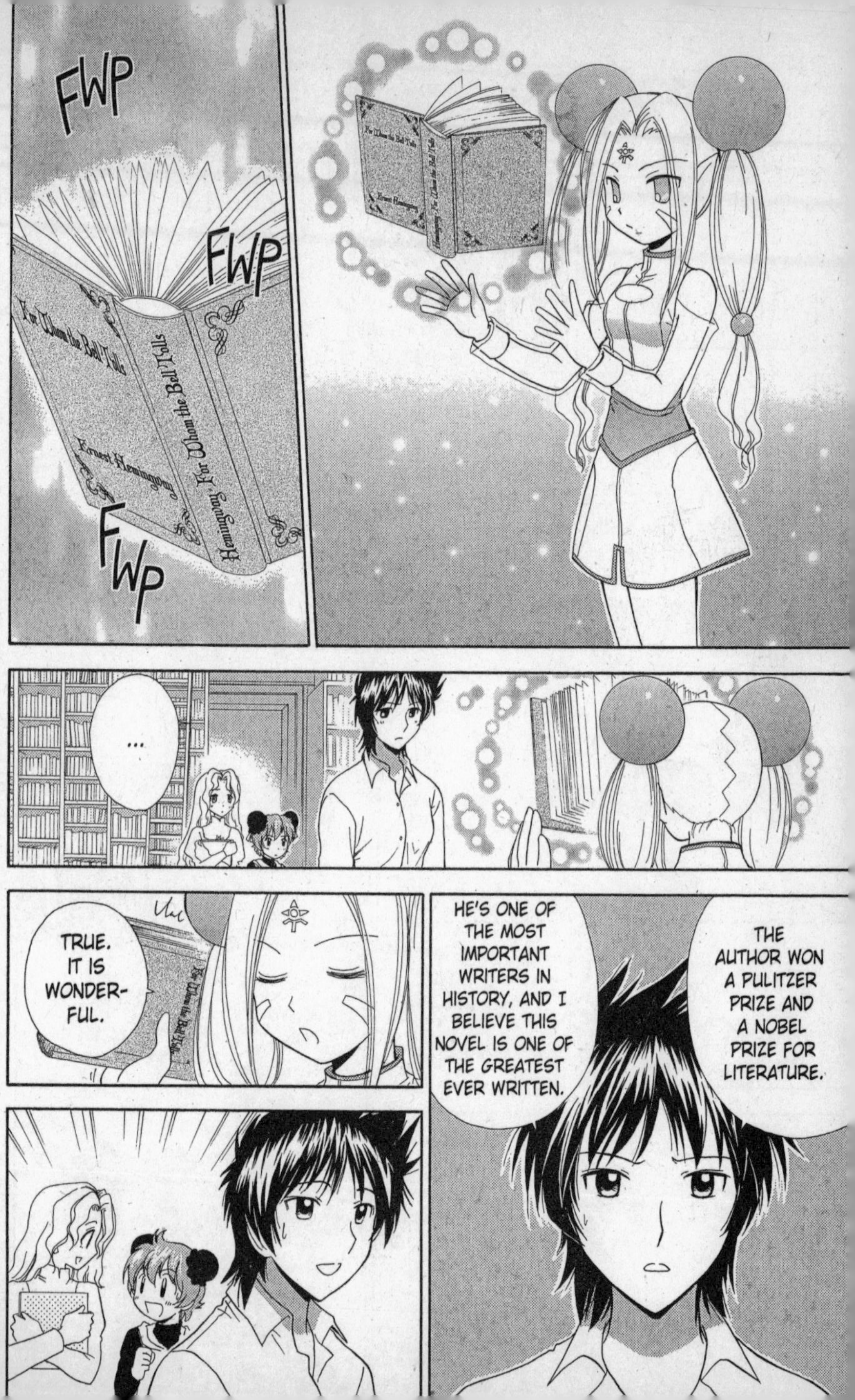
FWP
FWP
FWP
For Whom the Bell Tolls
Ernest Hemingway
Hemingway For Whom the Bell Tolls
...
THE AUTHOR WON A PULITZER PRIZE AND A NOBEL PRIZE FOR LITERATURE.
HE'S ONE OF THE MOST IMPORTANT WRITERS IN HISTORY, AND I BELIEVE THIS NOVEL IS ONE OF THE GREATEST EVER WRITTEN.
TRUE. IT IS WONDERFUL.

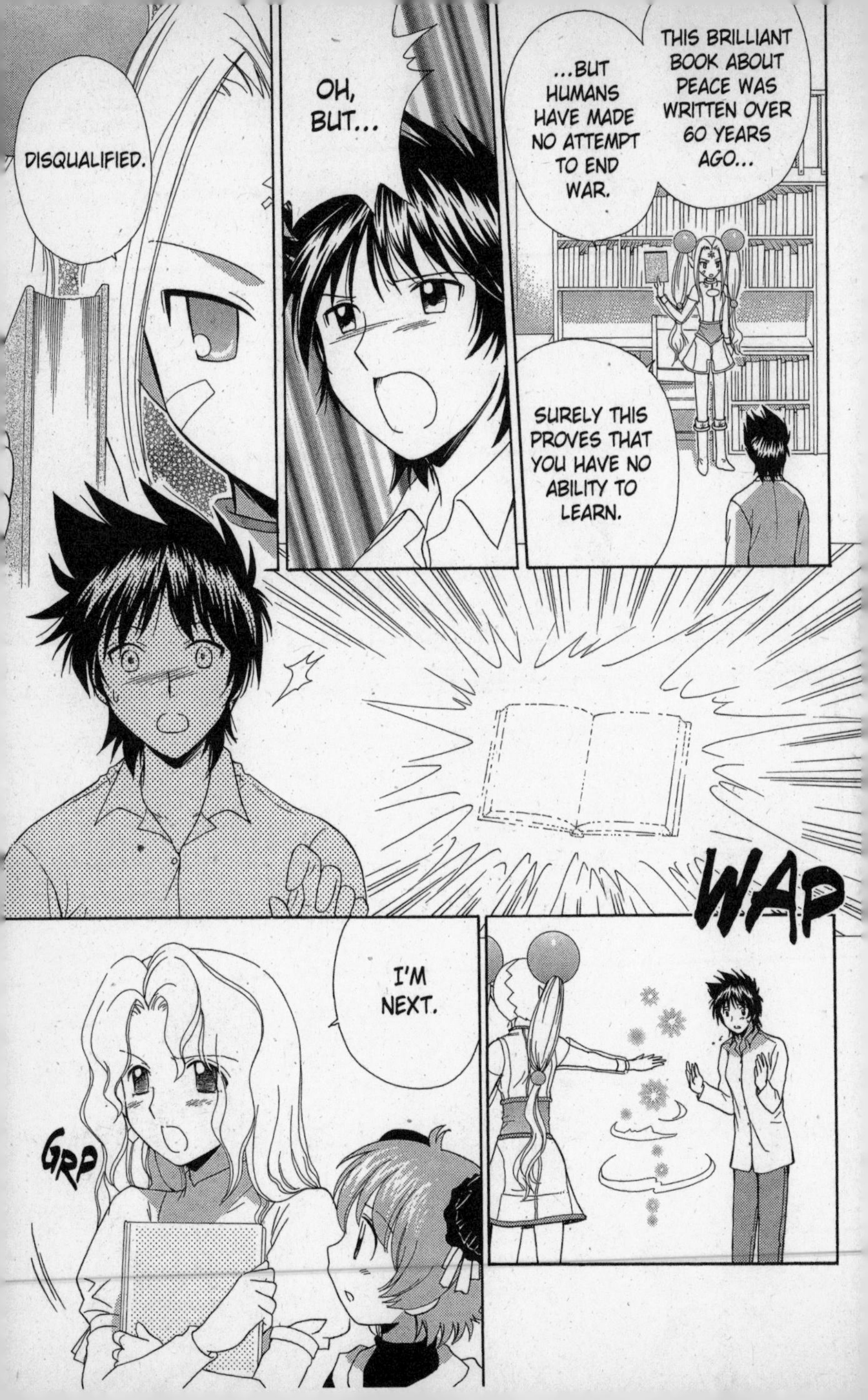
THIS BRILLIANT BOOK ABOUT PEACE WAS WRITTEN OVER 60 YEARS AGO...
...BUT HUMANS HAVE MADE NO ATTEMPT TO END WAR.
SURELY THIS PROVES THAT YOU HAVE NO ABILITY TO LEARN.
OH, BUT...
DISQUALIFIED.
WAP
I'M NEXT.
GRP

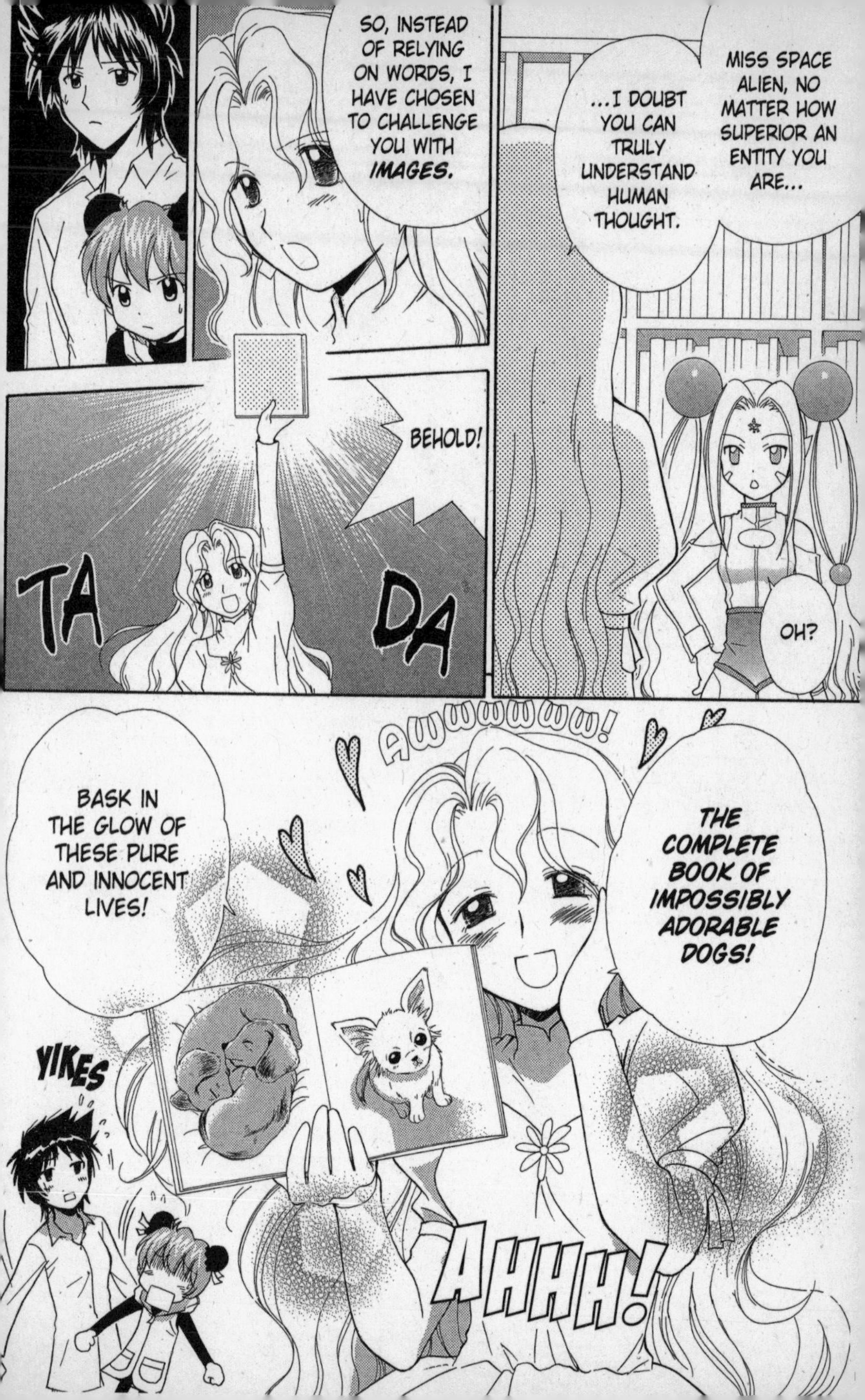
MISS SPACE ALIEN, NO MATTER HOW SUPERIOR AN ENTITY YOU ARE...
...I DOUBT YOU CAN TRULY UNDERSTAND HUMAN THOUGHT.
OH?
SO, INSTEAD OF RELYING ON WORDS, I HAVE CHOSEN TO CHALLENGE YOU WITH *IMAGES.*
BEHOLD!
TA
DA
AWWWWWWW!
THE COMPLETE BOOK OF IMPOSSIBLY ADORABLE DOGS!
BASK IN THE GLOW OF THESE PURE AND INNOCENT LIVES!
YIKES
AHHH!

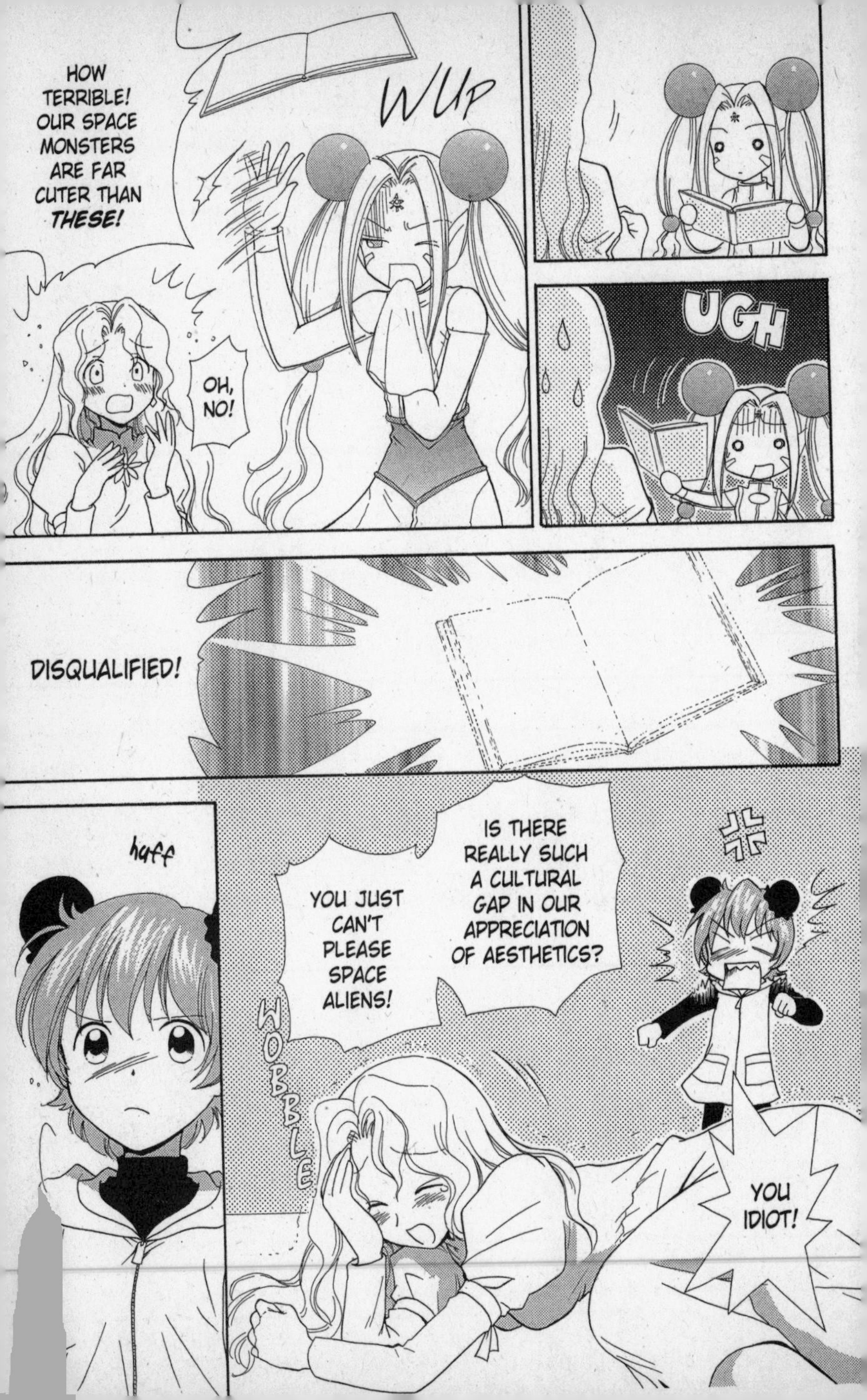
UGH
WUP
HOW TERRIBLE! OUR SPACE MONSTERS ARE FAR CUTER THAN *THESE!*
OH, NO!
DISQUALIFIED!
IS THERE REALLY SUCH A CULTURAL GAP IN OUR APPRECIATION OF AESTHETICS?
YOU JUST CAN'T PLEASE SPACE ALIENS!
WOBBLE
YOU IDIOT!
huff

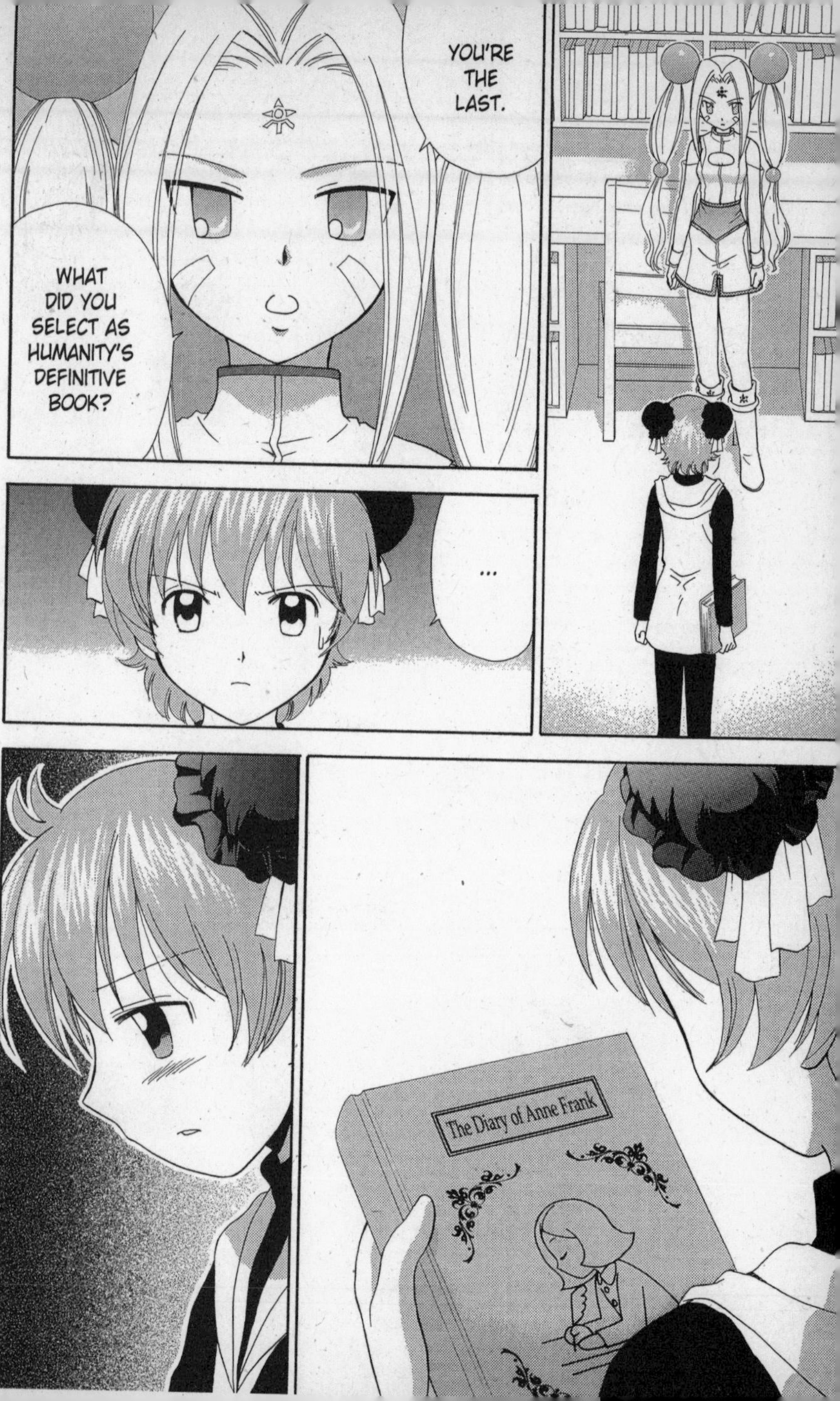
YOU'RE THE LAST.
WHAT DID YOU SELECT AS HUMANITY'S DEFINITIVE BOOK?
...
The Diary of Anne Frank

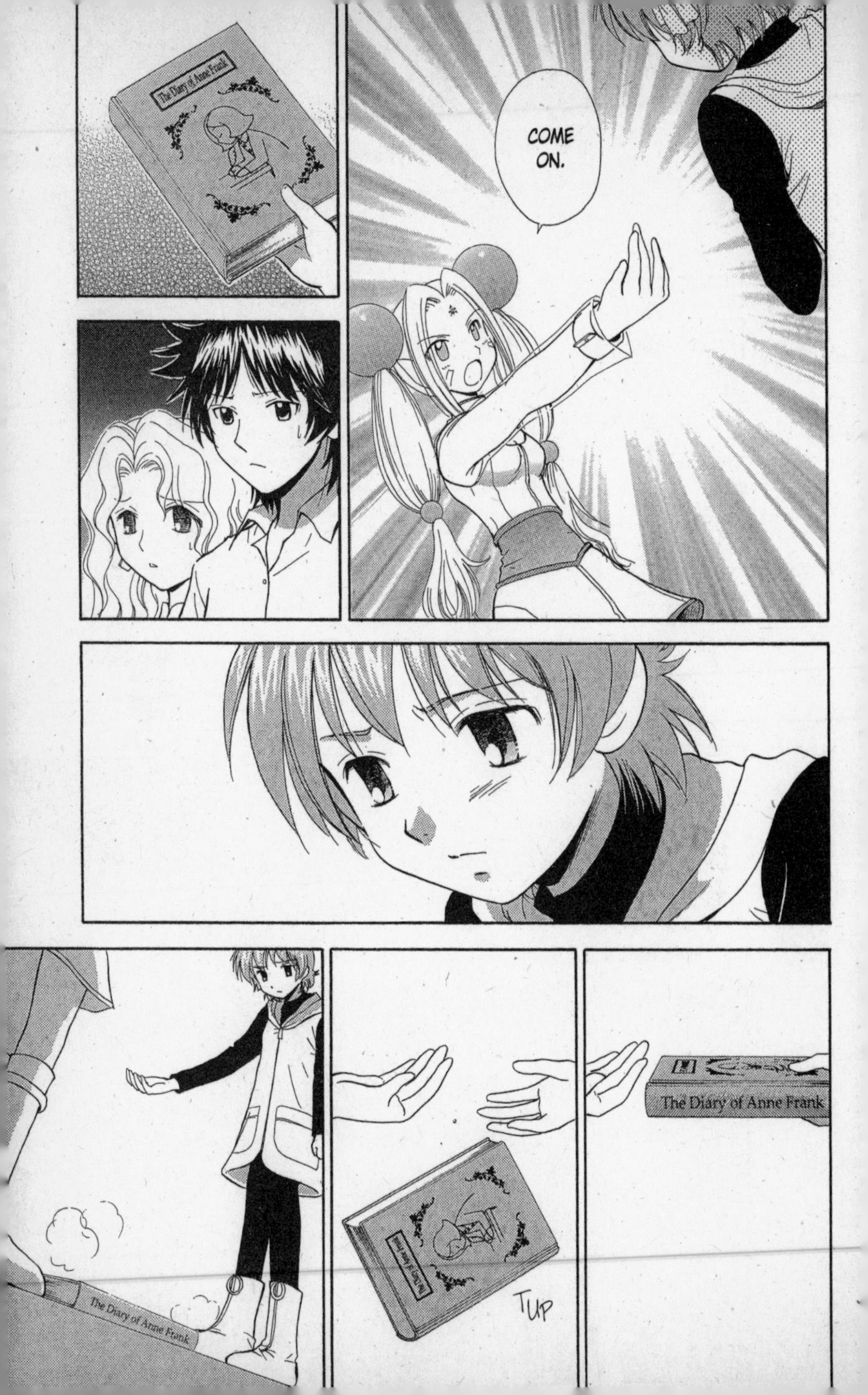
COME ON.
The Diary of Anne Frank
The Diary of Anne Frank
TUP
The Diary of Anne Frank
The Diary of Anne Frank

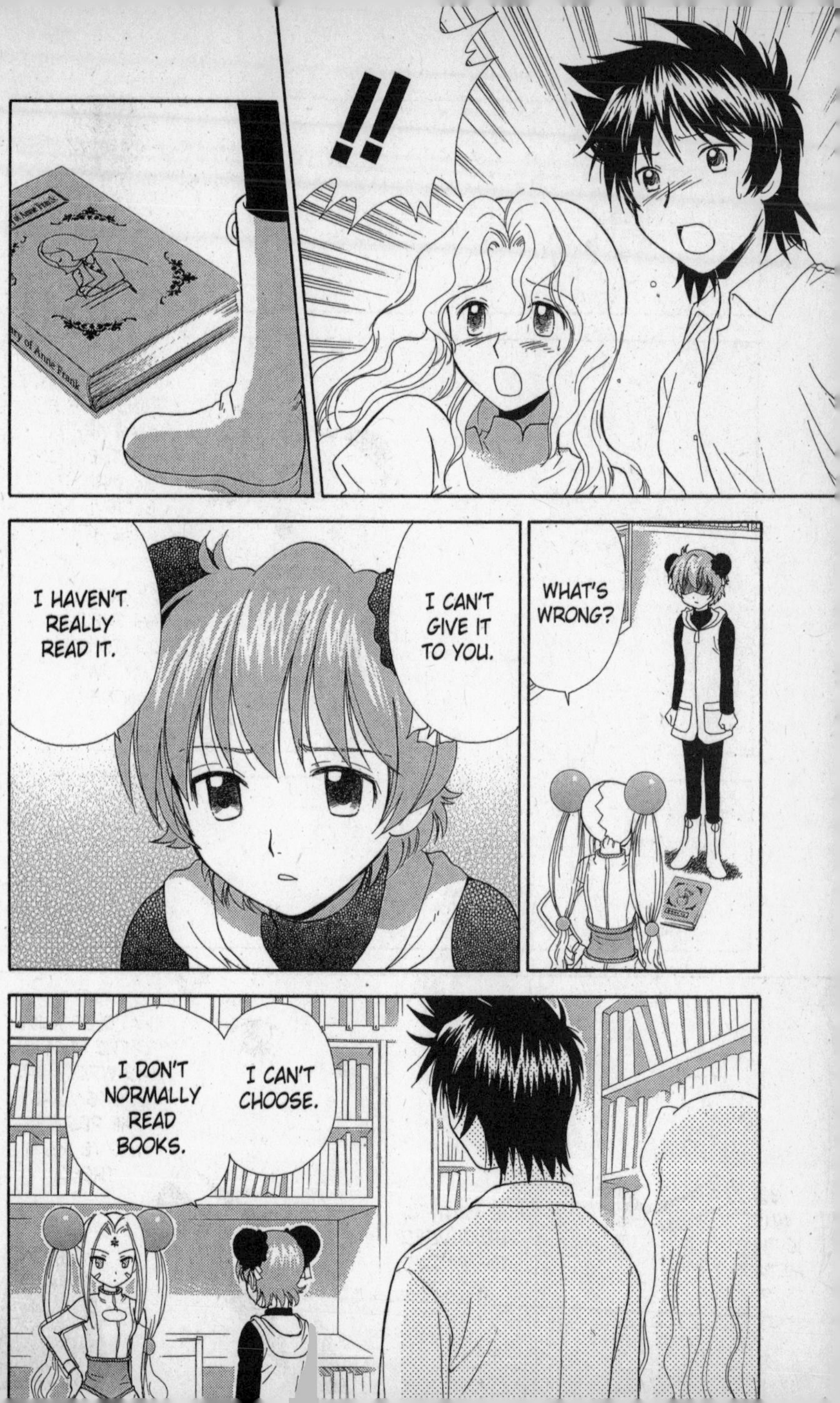
!!
WHAT'S WRONG?
I CAN'T GIVE IT TO YOU.
I HAVEN'T REALLY READ IT.
I CAN'T CHOOSE.
I DON'T NORMALLY READ BOOKS.

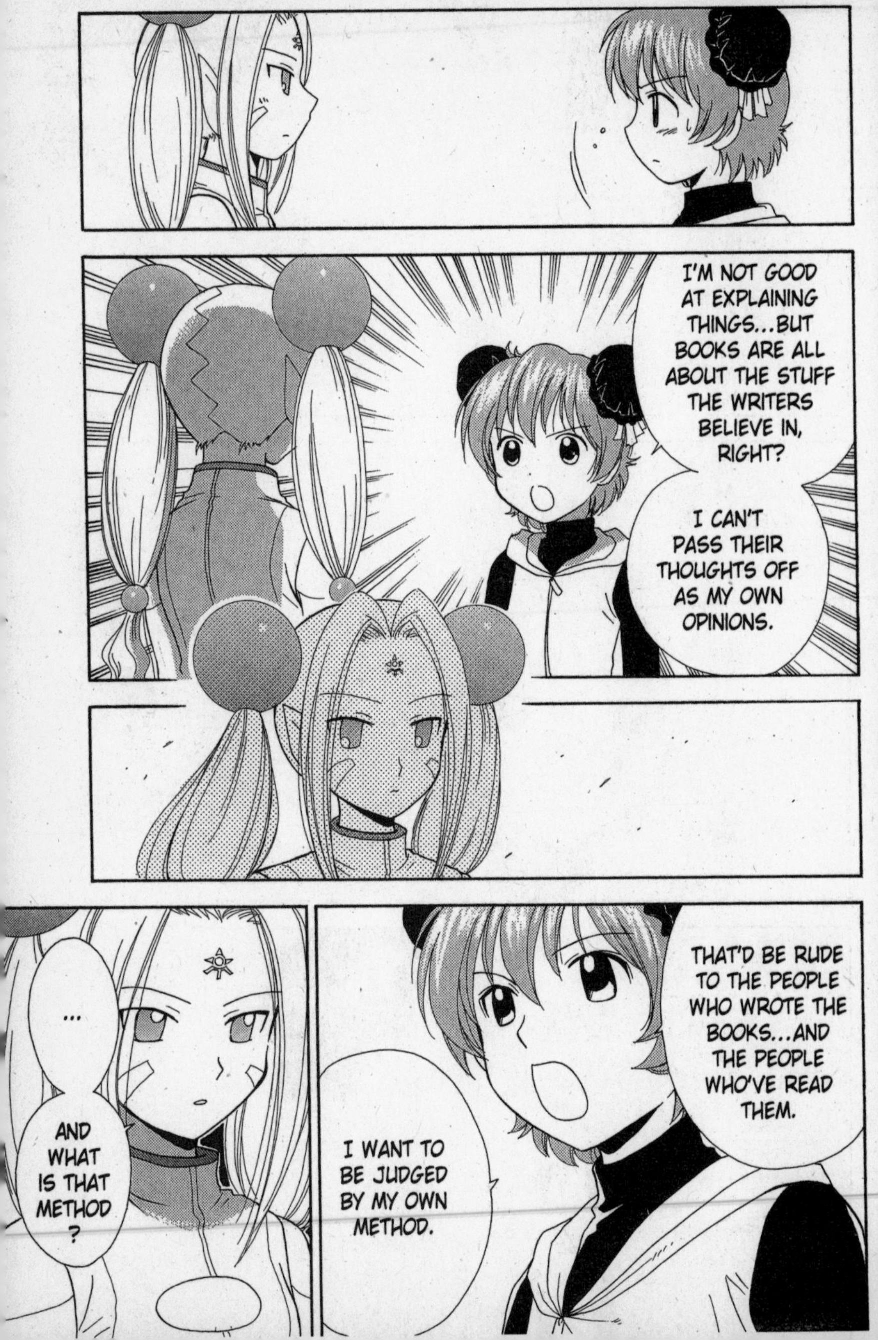
I'M NOT GOOD AT EXPLAINING THINGS...BUT BOOKS ARE ALL ABOUT THE STUFF THE WRITERS BELIEVE IN, RIGHT?
I CAN'T PASS THEIR THOUGHTS OFF AS MY OWN OPINIONS.
THAT'D BE RUDE TO THE PEOPLE WHO WROTE THE BOOKS...AND THE PEOPLE WHO'VE READ THEM.
I WANT TO BE JUDGED BY MY OWN METHOD.
...
AND WHAT IS THAT METHOD ?

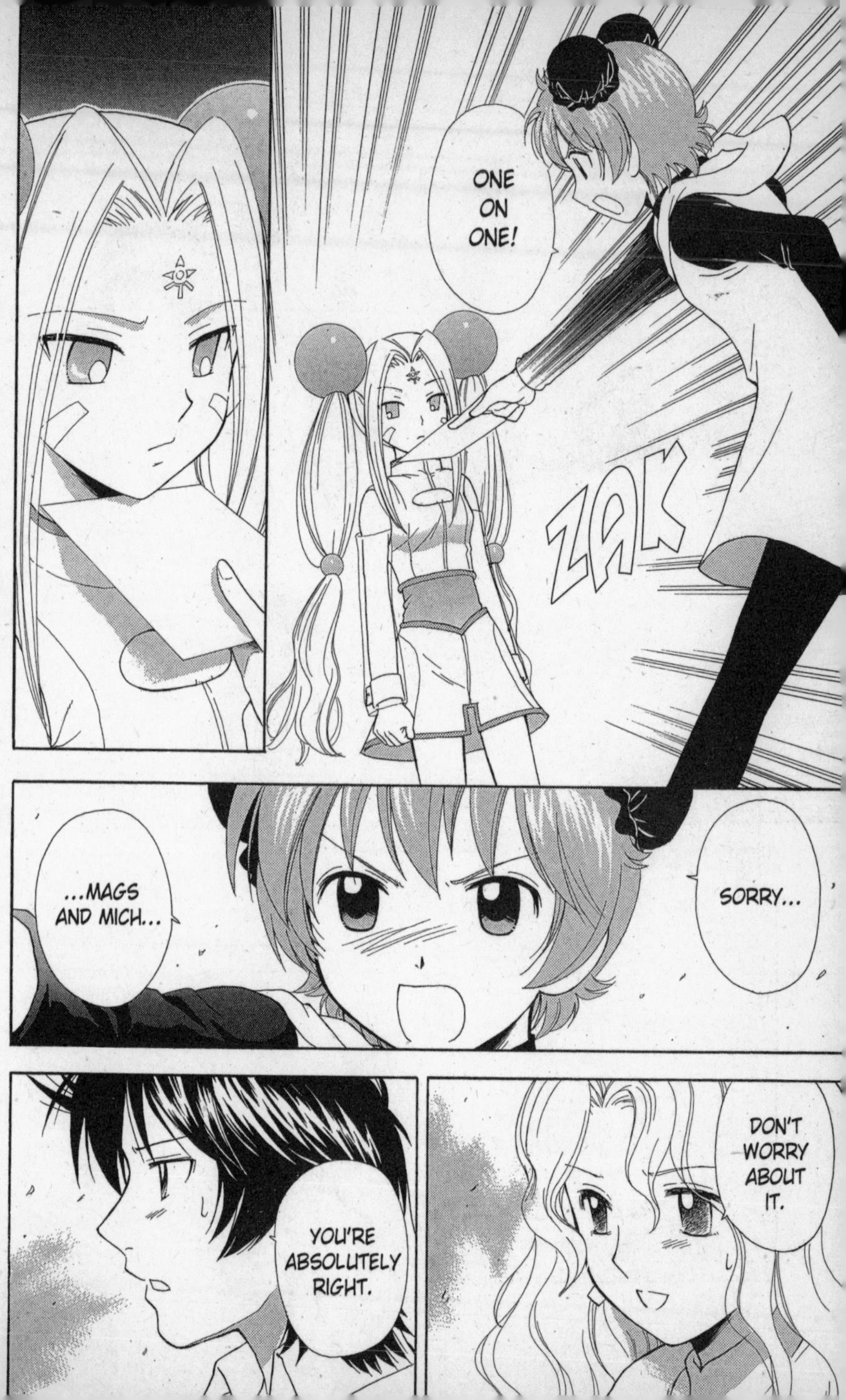
ONE ON ONE!
ZAK
SORRY...
...MAGS AND MICH...
DON'T WORRY ABOUT IT.
YOU'RE ABSOLUTELY RIGHT.

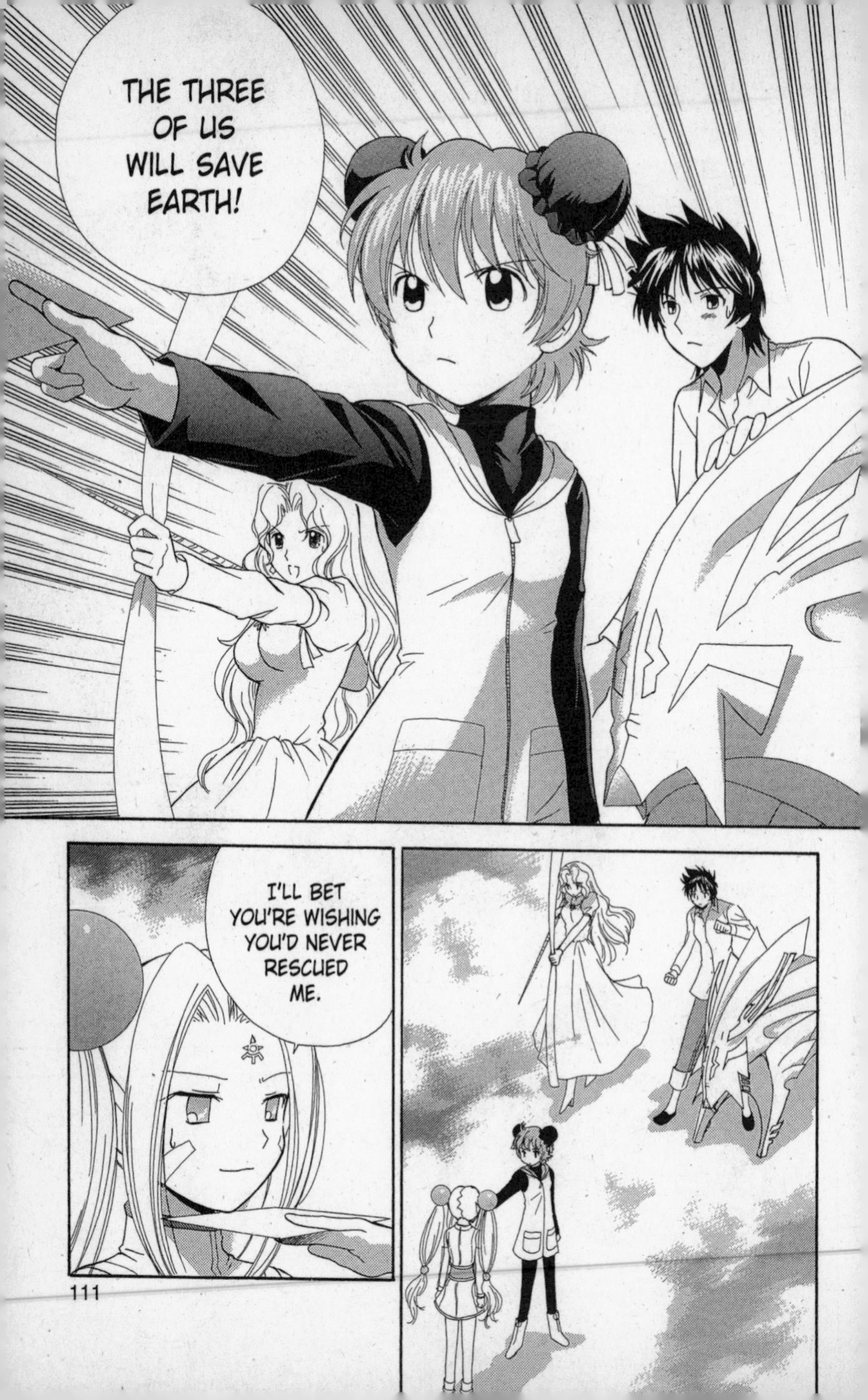
THE THREE OF US WILL SAVE EARTH!
I'LL BET YOU'RE WISHING YOU'D NEVER RESCUED ME.

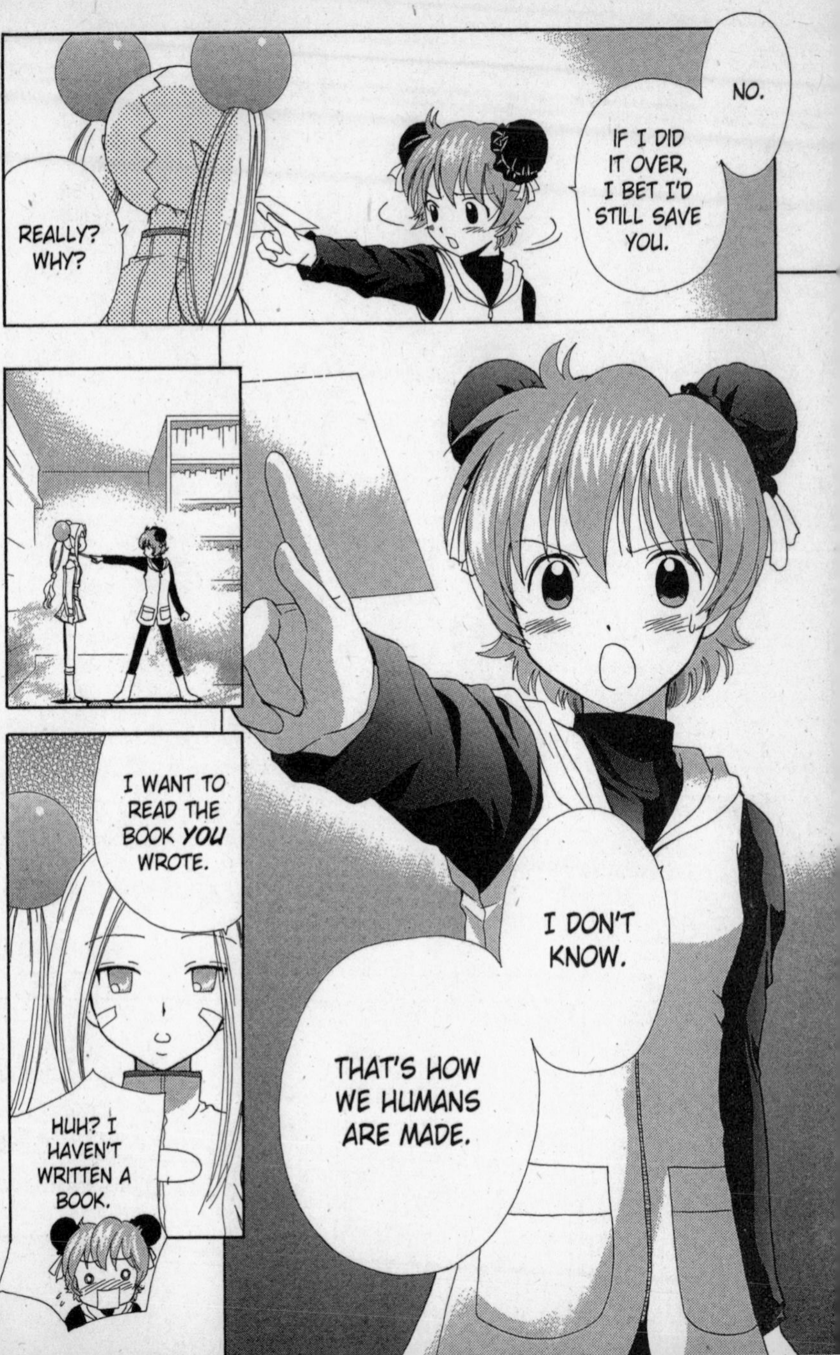
NO.
IF I DID IT OVER, I BET I'D STILL SAVE YOU.
REALLY? WHY?
I DON'T KNOW.
THAT'S HOW WE HUMANS ARE MADE.
I WANT TO READ THE BOOK *YOU* WROTE.
HUH? I HAVEN'T WRITTEN A BOOK.

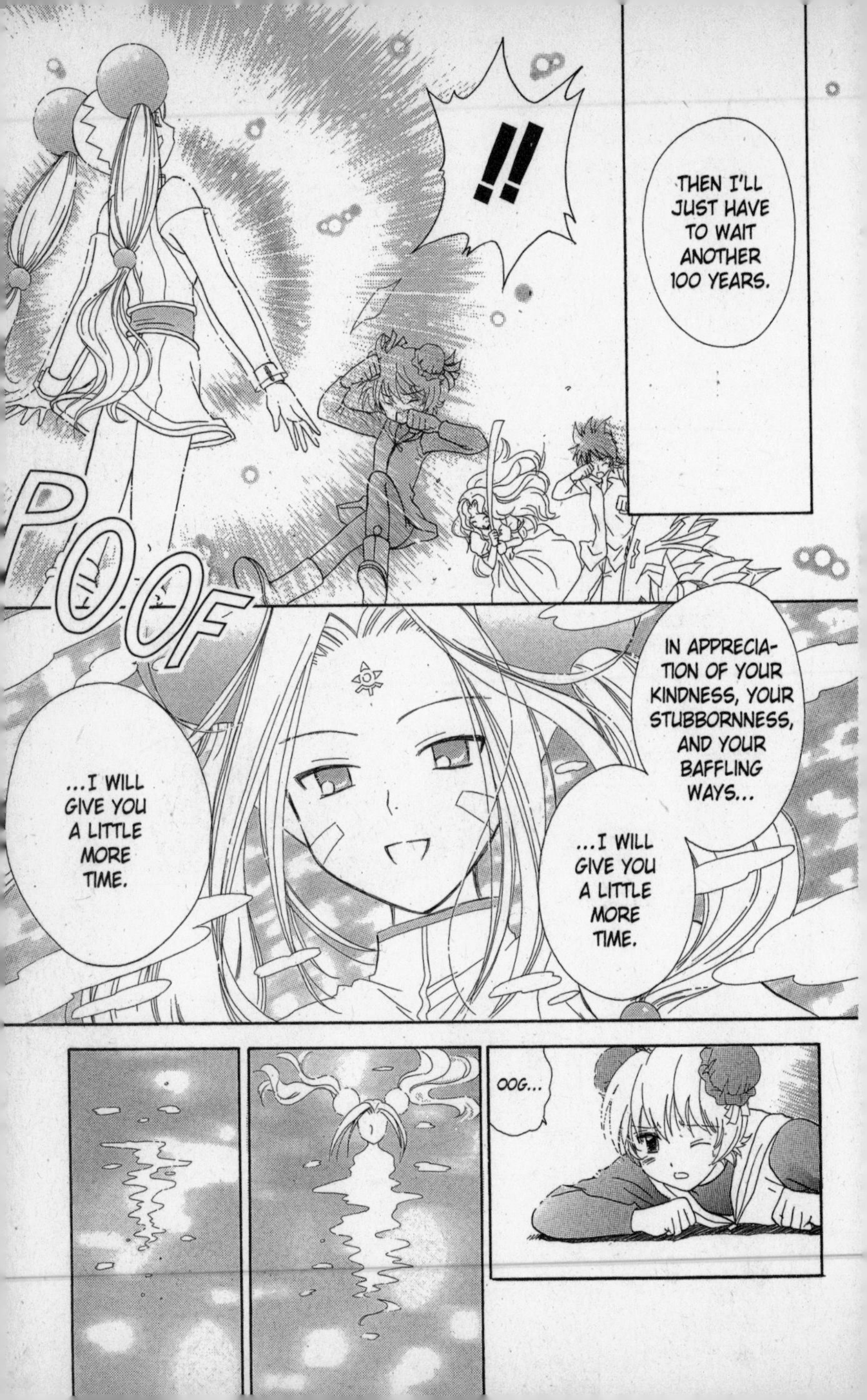
THEN I'LL JUST HAVE TO WAIT ANOTHER 100 YEARS.
!!
POOF
IN APPRECIATION OF YOUR KINDNESS, YOUR STUBBORNNESS, AND YOUR BAFFLING WAYS...
...I WILL GIVE YOU A LITTLE MORE TIME.
...I WILL GIVE YOU A LITTLE MORE TIME.
OOG...

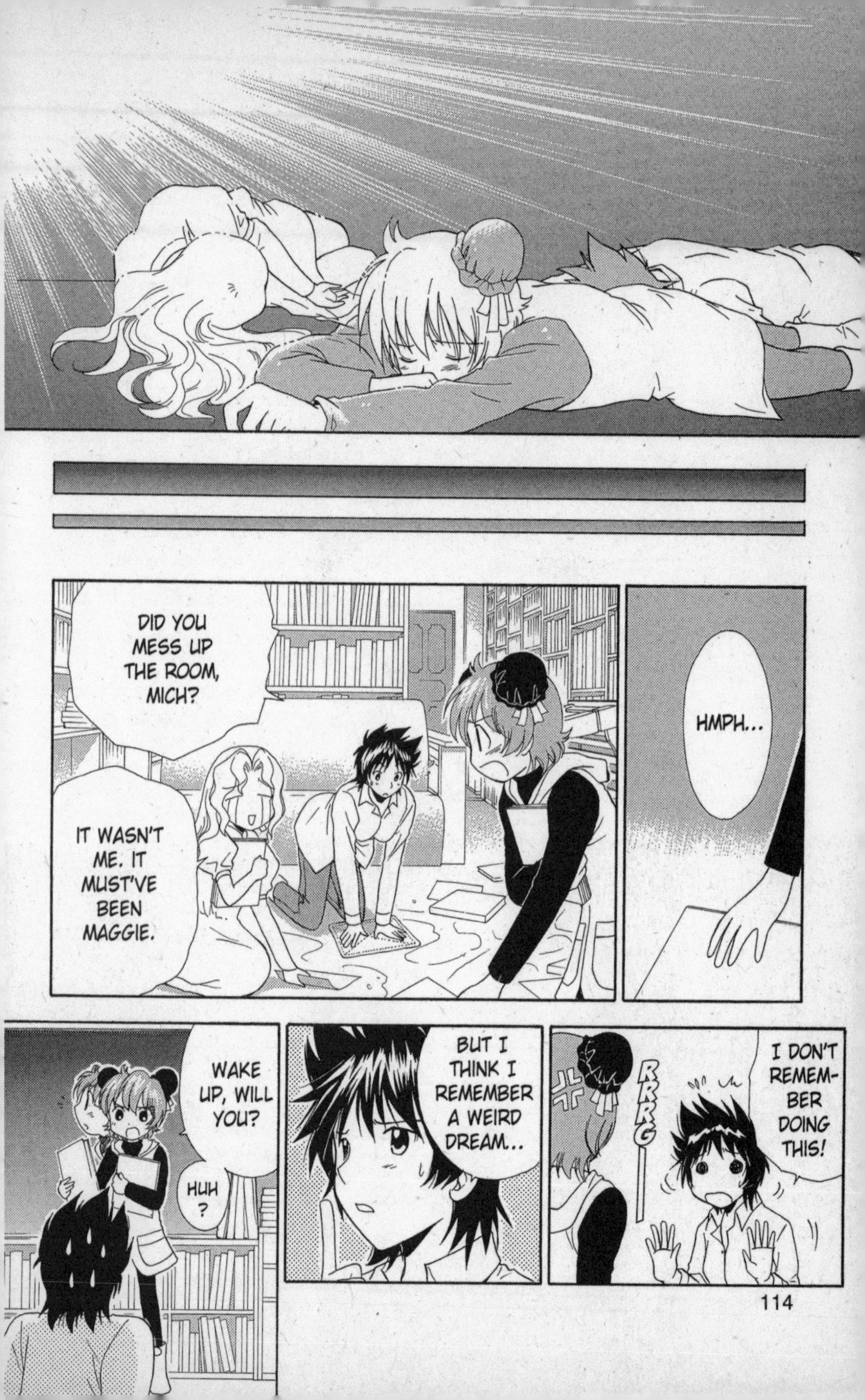
HMPH...
DID YOU MESS UP THE ROOM, MICH?
IT WASN'T ME. IT MUST'VE BEEN MAGGIE.
I DON'T REMEM-BER DOING THIS!
RRRG
BUT I THINK I REMEMBER A WEIRD DREAM...
WAKE UP, WILL YOU?
HUH ?

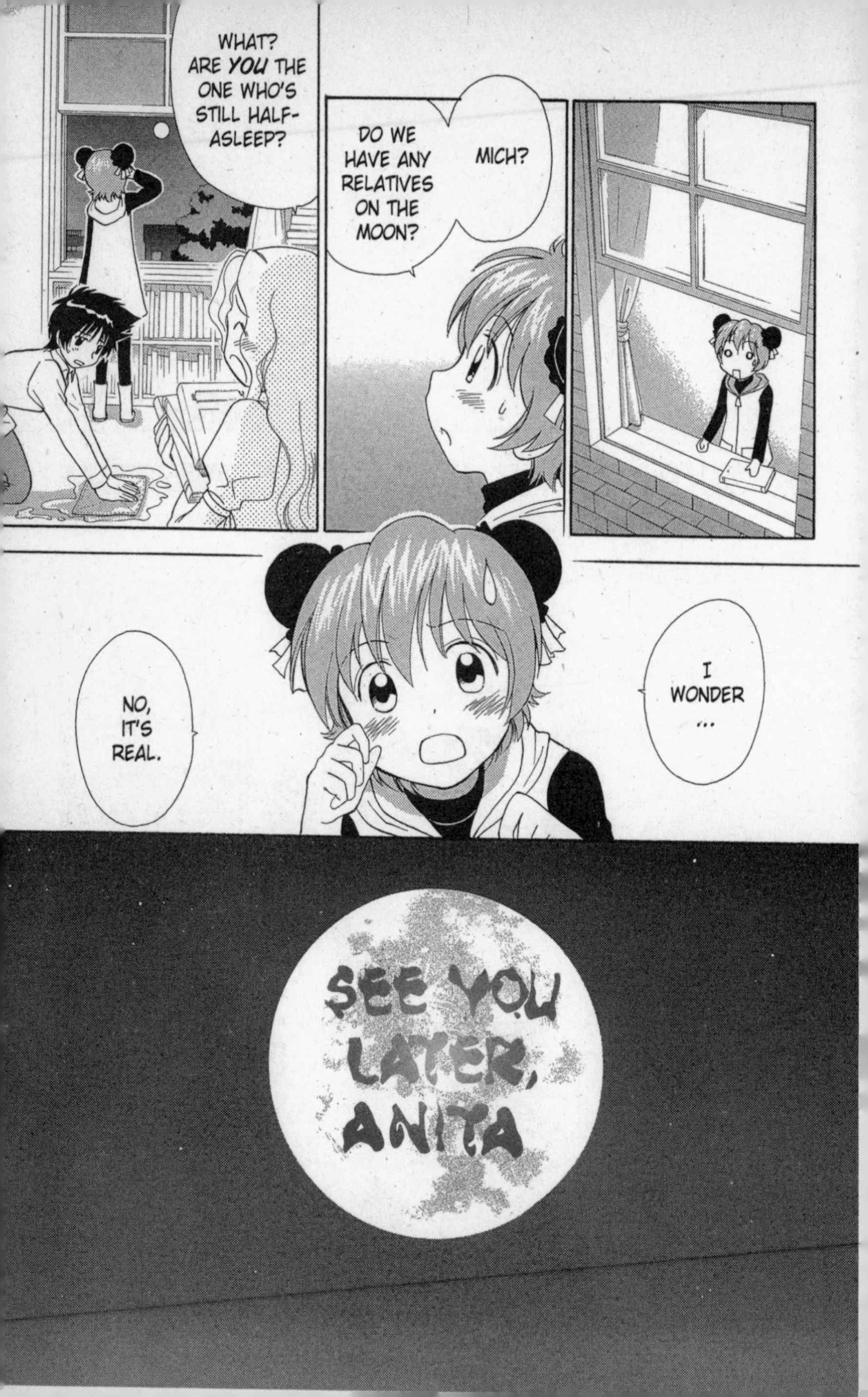
MICH?
DO WE HAVE ANY RELATIVES ON THE MOON?
WHAT? ARE *YOU* THE ONE WHO'S STILL HALF-ASLEEP?
I WONDER ...
NO, IT'S REAL.
SEE YOU LATER, ANITA

THE PAPER SISTERS

R.O.D

•READ OR DREAM•

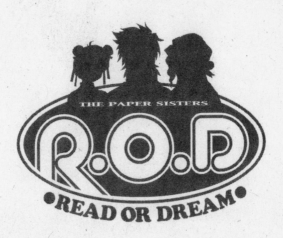

CHAPTER 5

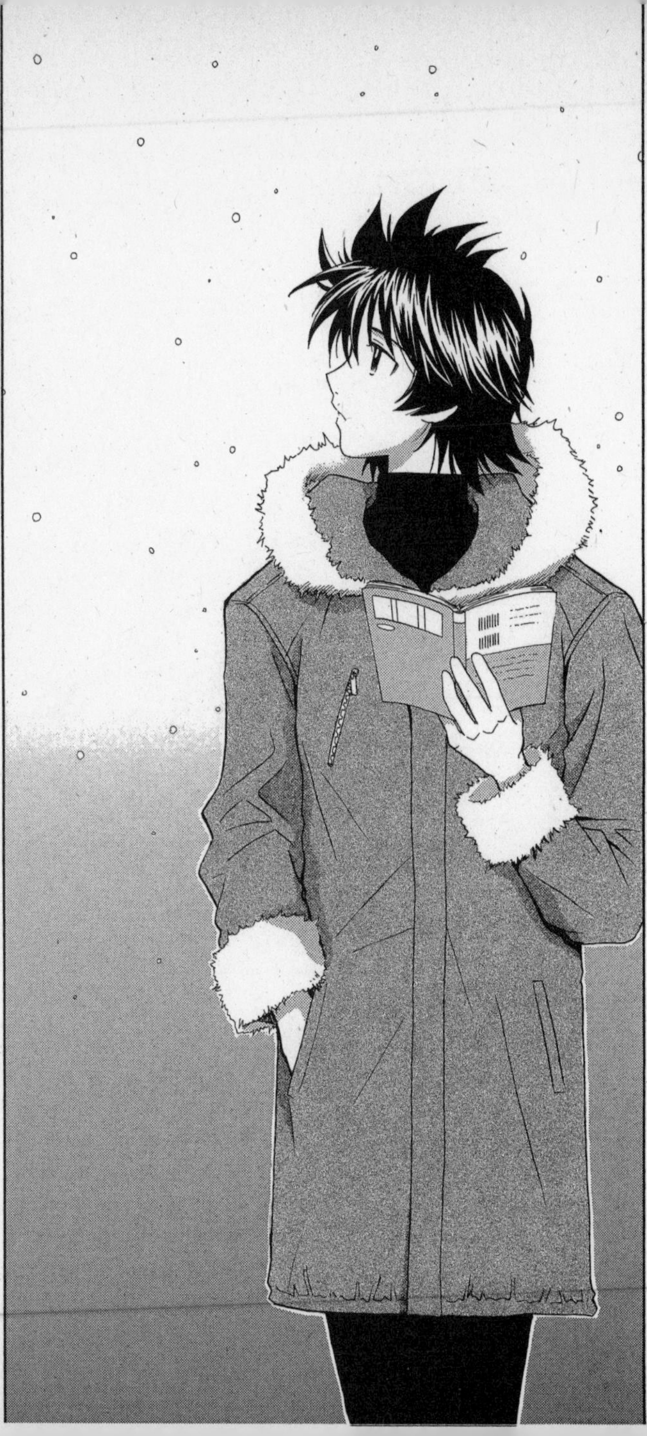

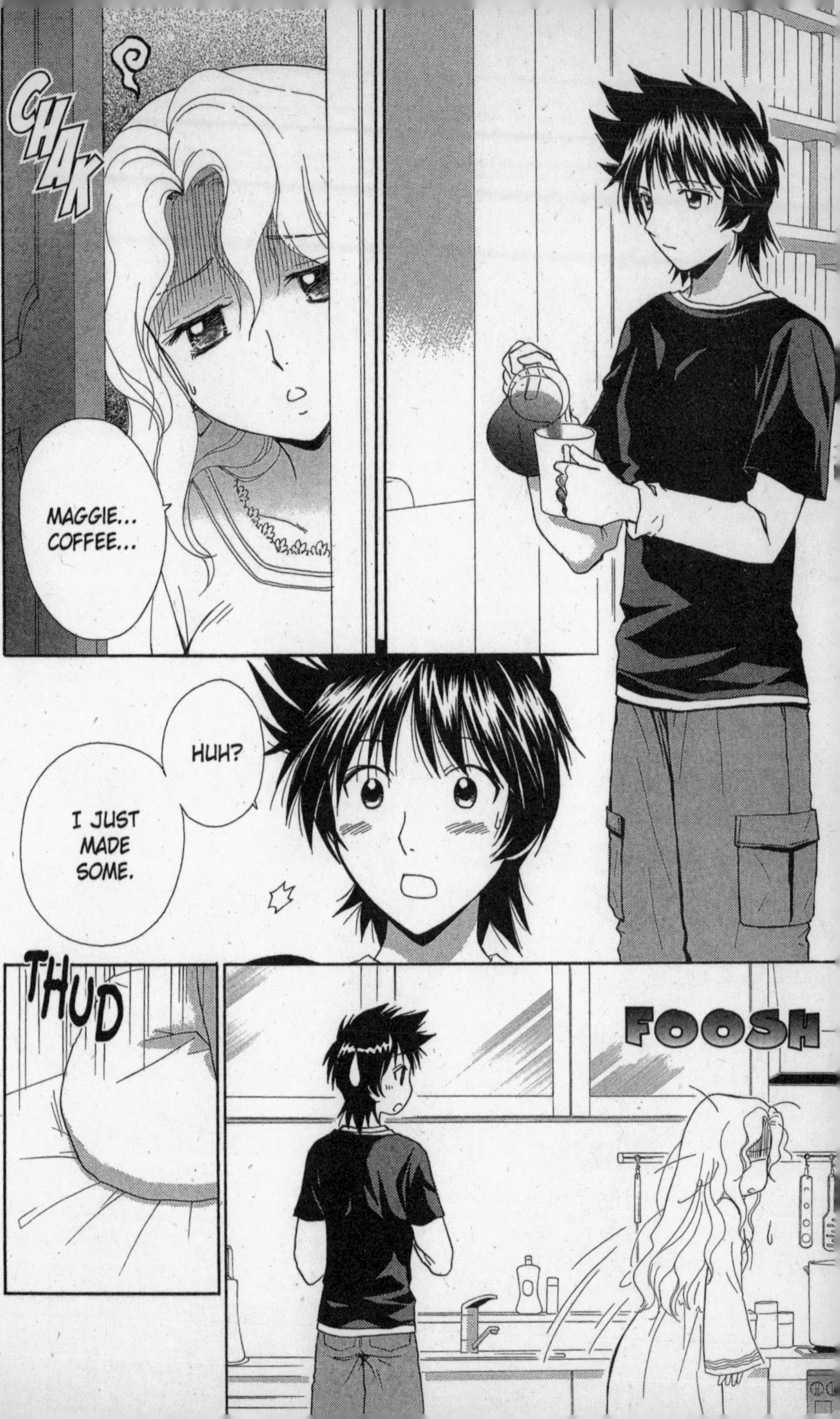
CHAK
MAGGIE... COFFEE...
HUH?
I JUST MADE SOME.
FOOSH
THUD

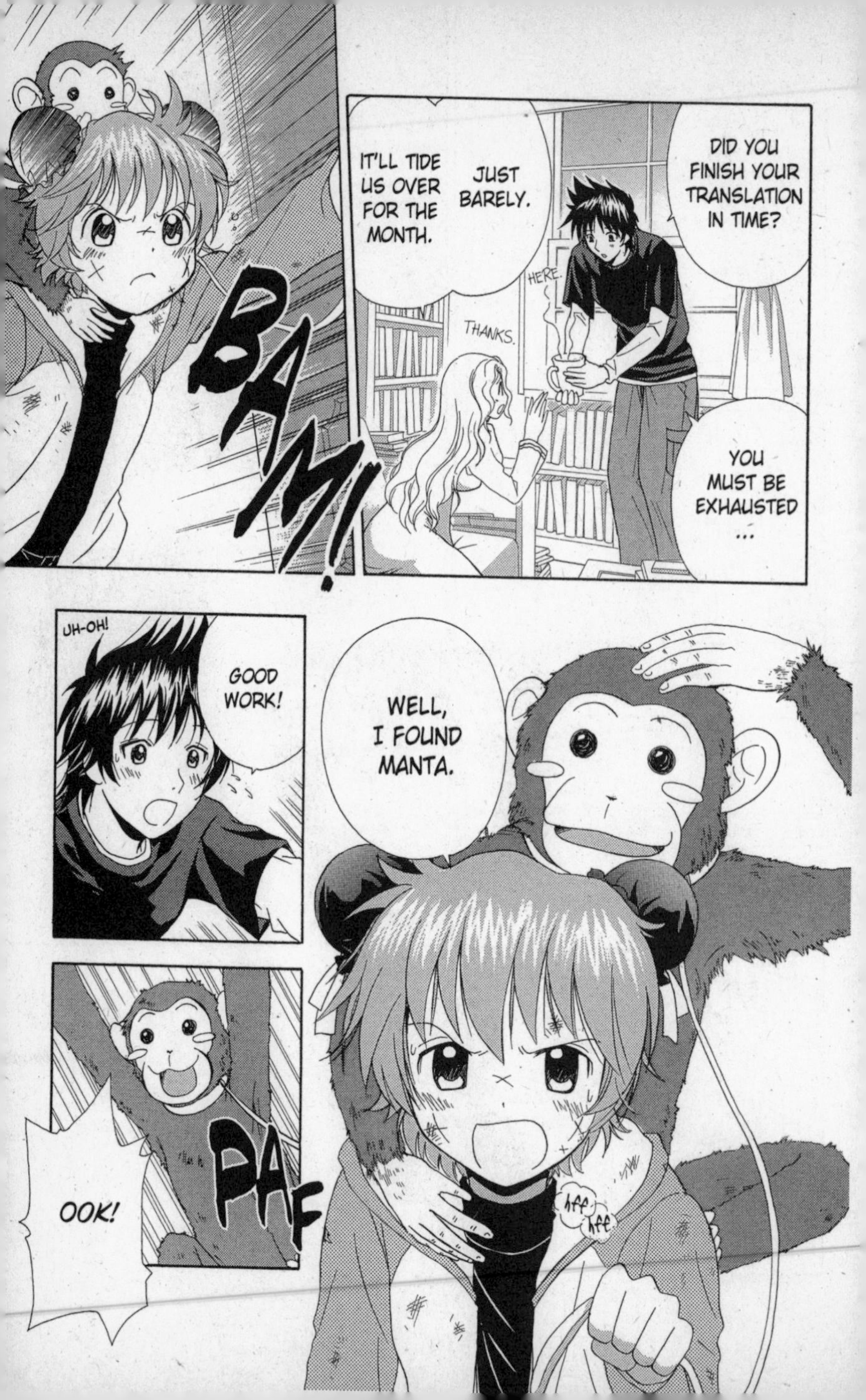
DID YOU FINISH YOUR TRANSLATION IN TIME?
JUST BARELY.
IT'LL TIDE US OVER FOR THE MONTH.
HERE.
THANKS.
YOU MUST BE EXHAUSTED ...
BAM!
WELL, I FOUND MANTA.
hff hff
UH-OH!
GOOD WORK!
PAF
OOK!

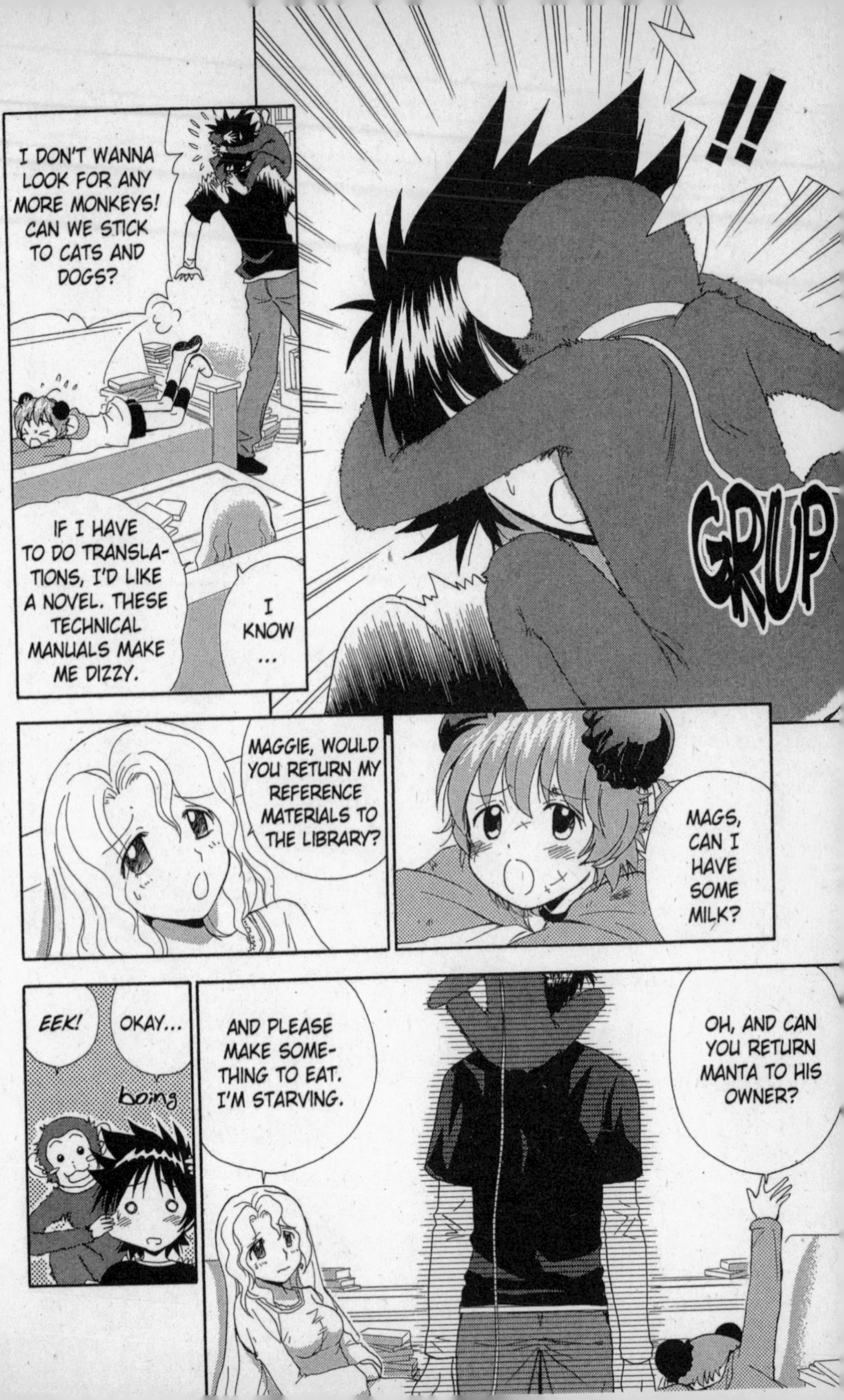
!!
GRUP
I DON'T WANNA LOOK FOR ANY MORE MONKEYS! CAN WE STICK TO CATS AND DOGS?
IF I HAVE TO DO TRANSLA-TIONS, I'D LIKE A NOVEL. THESE TECHNICAL MANUALS MAKE ME DIZZY.
I KNOW ...
MAGS, CAN I HAVE SOME MILK?
MAGGIE, WOULD YOU RETURN MY REFERENCE MATERIALS TO THE LIBRARY?
OH, AND CAN YOU RETURN MANTA TO HIS OWNER?
AND PLEASE MAKE SOME-THING TO EAT. I'M STARVING.
OKAY...
EEK!
boing

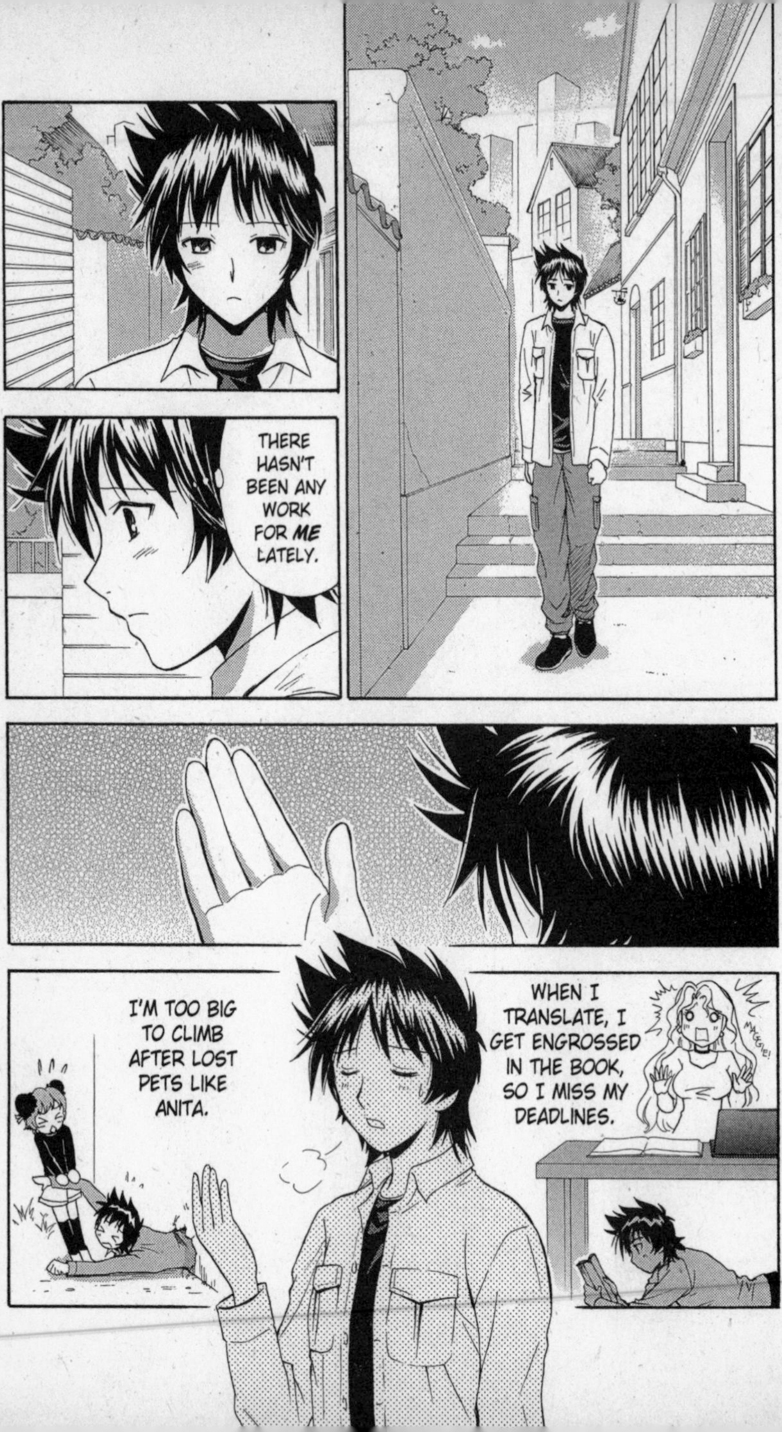
THERE HASN'T BEEN ANY WORK FOR *ME* LATELY.
WHEN I TRANSLATE, I GET ENGROSSED IN THE BOOK, SO I MISS MY DEADLINES.
MAGGIE!
I'M TOO BIG TO CLIMB AFTER LOST PETS LIKE ANITA.

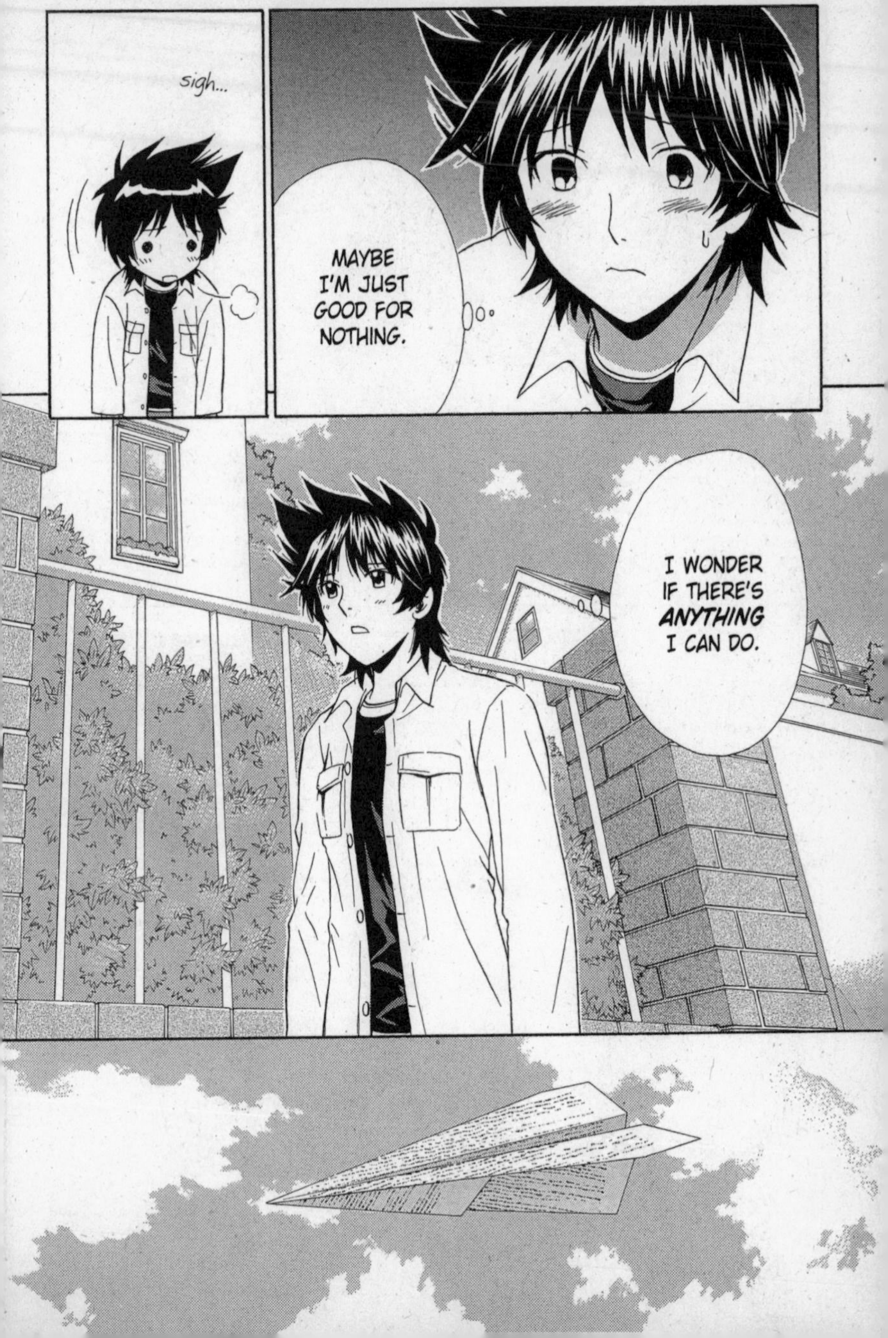
MAYBE I'M JUST GOOD FOR NOTHING.
sigh...
I WONDER IF THERE'S ANYTHING I CAN DO.

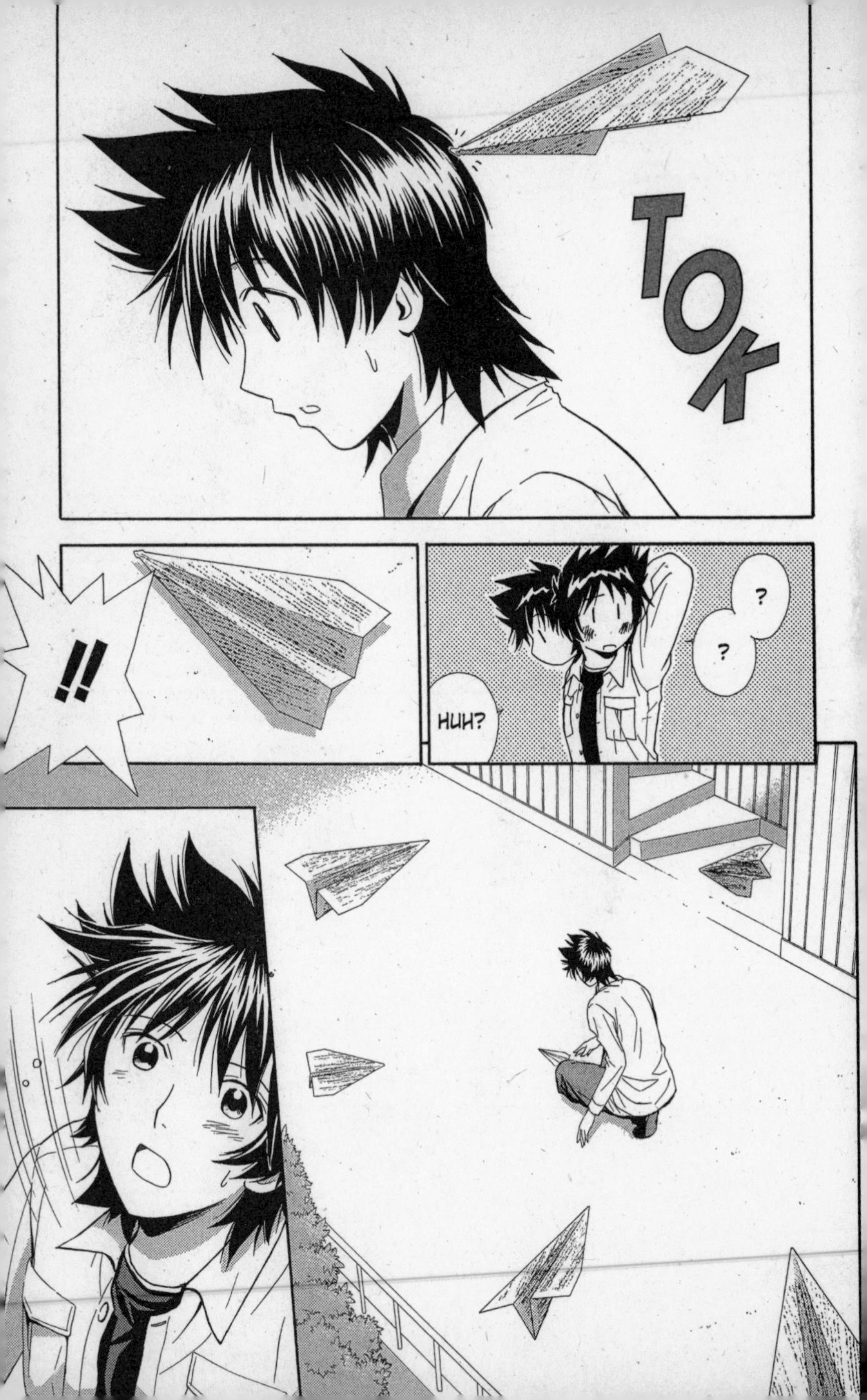
TOK
?
?
HUH?
!!

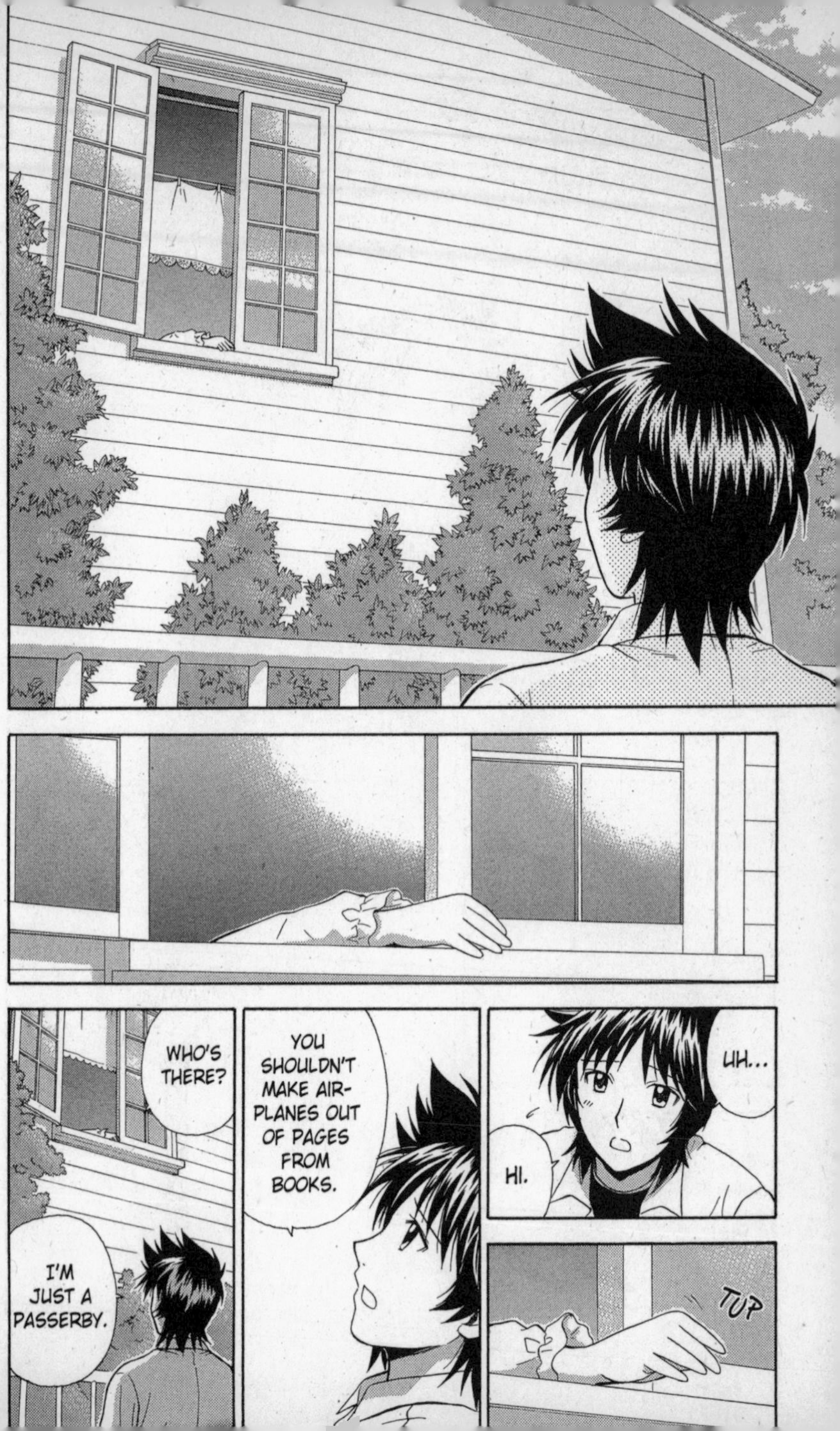
UH...
HI.
TUP
YOU SHOULDN'T MAKE AIR-PLANES OUT OF PAGES FROM BOOKS.
WHO'S THERE?
I'M JUST A PASSERBY.

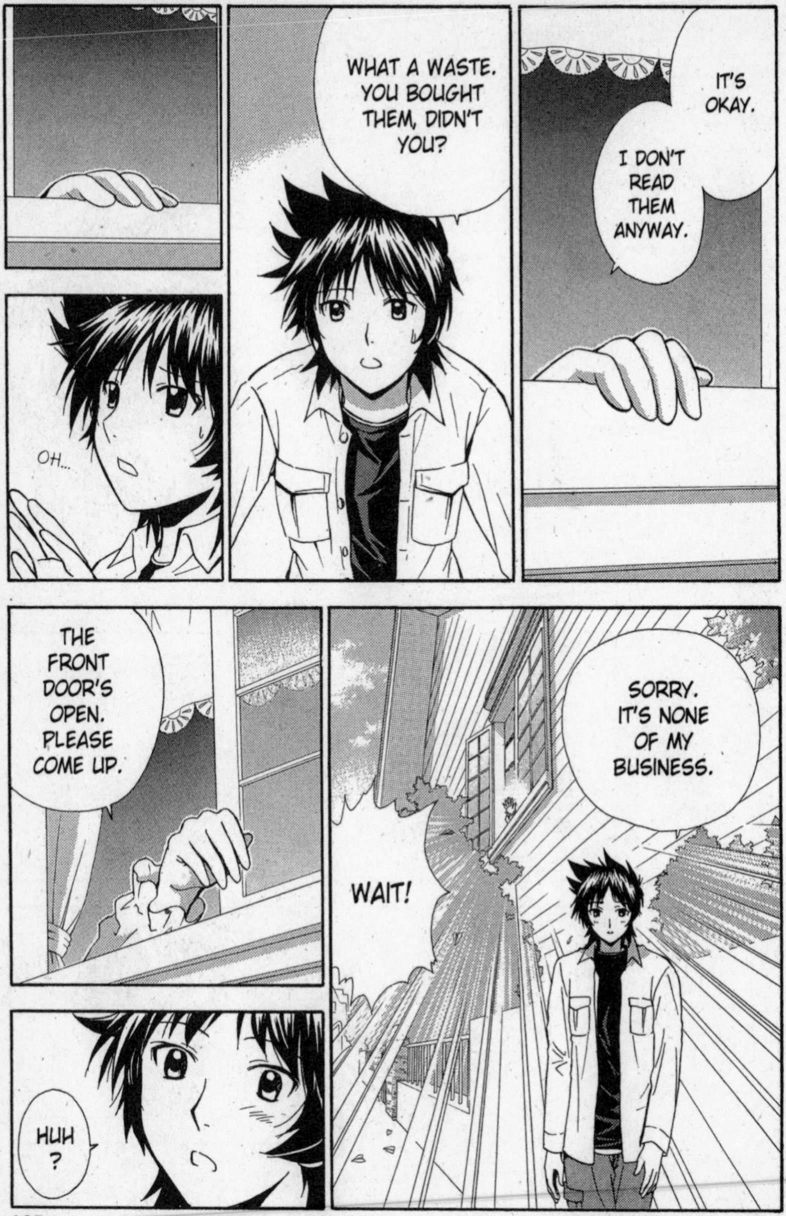
IT'S OKAY.
I DON'T READ THEM ANYWAY.
WHAT A WASTE. YOU BOUGHT THEM, DIDN'T YOU?
OH...
SORRY. IT'S NONE OF MY BUSINESS.
WAIT!
THE FRONT DOOR'S OPEN. PLEASE COME UP.
HUH?

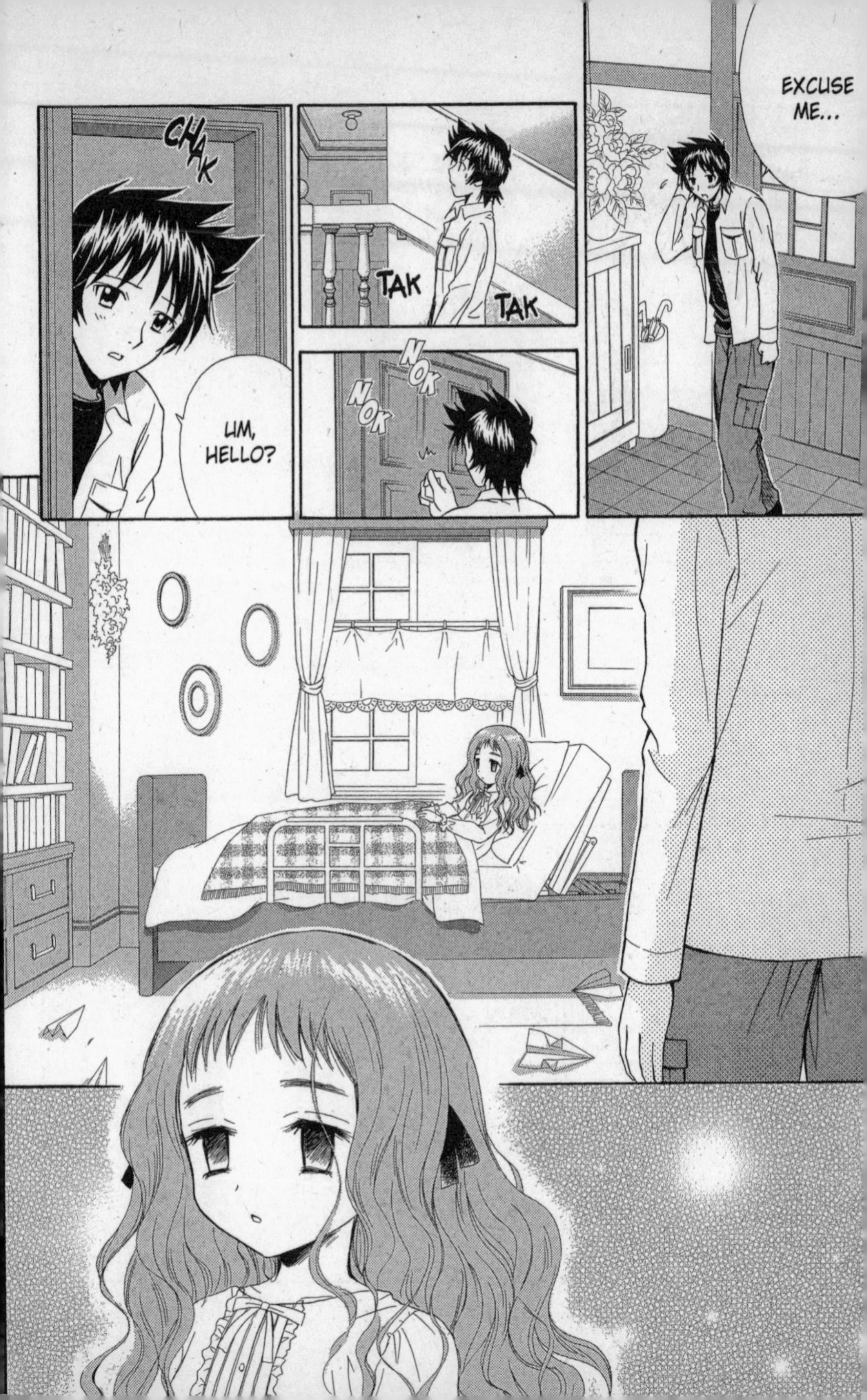
EXCUSE ME...
TAK
TAK
NOK
NOK
CHAK
UM, HELLO?

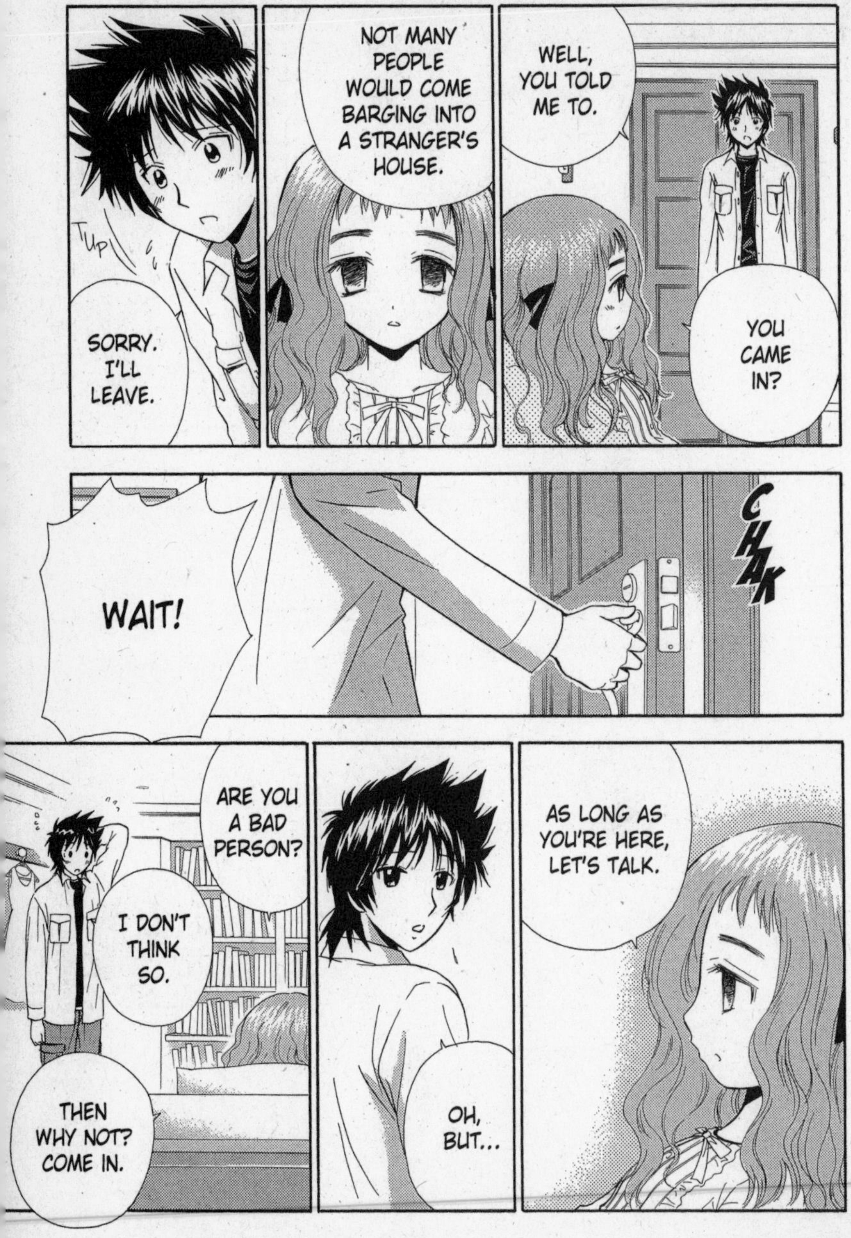
YOU CAME IN?
WELL, YOU TOLD ME TO.
NOT MANY PEOPLE WOULD COME BARGING INTO A STRANGER'S HOUSE.
TUP
SORRY. I'LL LEAVE.
CHAK
WAIT!
AS LONG AS YOU'RE HERE, LET'S TALK.
OH, BUT...
ARE YOU A BAD PERSON?
I DON'T THINK SO.
THEN WHY NOT? COME IN.

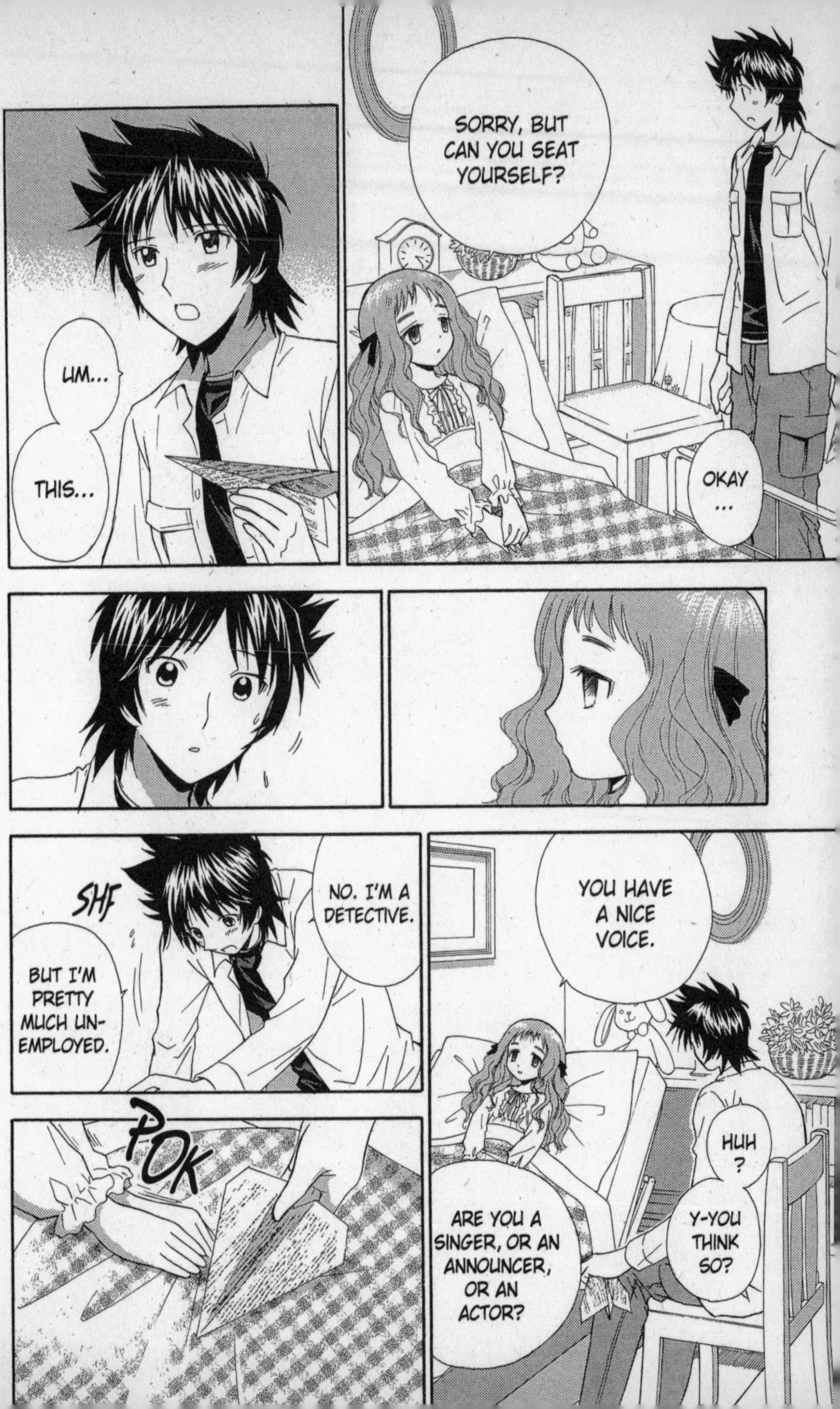
SORRY, BUT CAN YOU SEAT YOURSELF?
OKAY ...
UM...
THIS...
YOU HAVE A NICE VOICE.
HUH?
Y-YOU THINK SO?
ARE YOU A SINGER, OR AN ANNOUNCER, OR AN ACTOR?
SHF
NO. I'M A DETECTIVE.
BUT I'M PRETTY MUCH UN-EMPLOYED.
POK

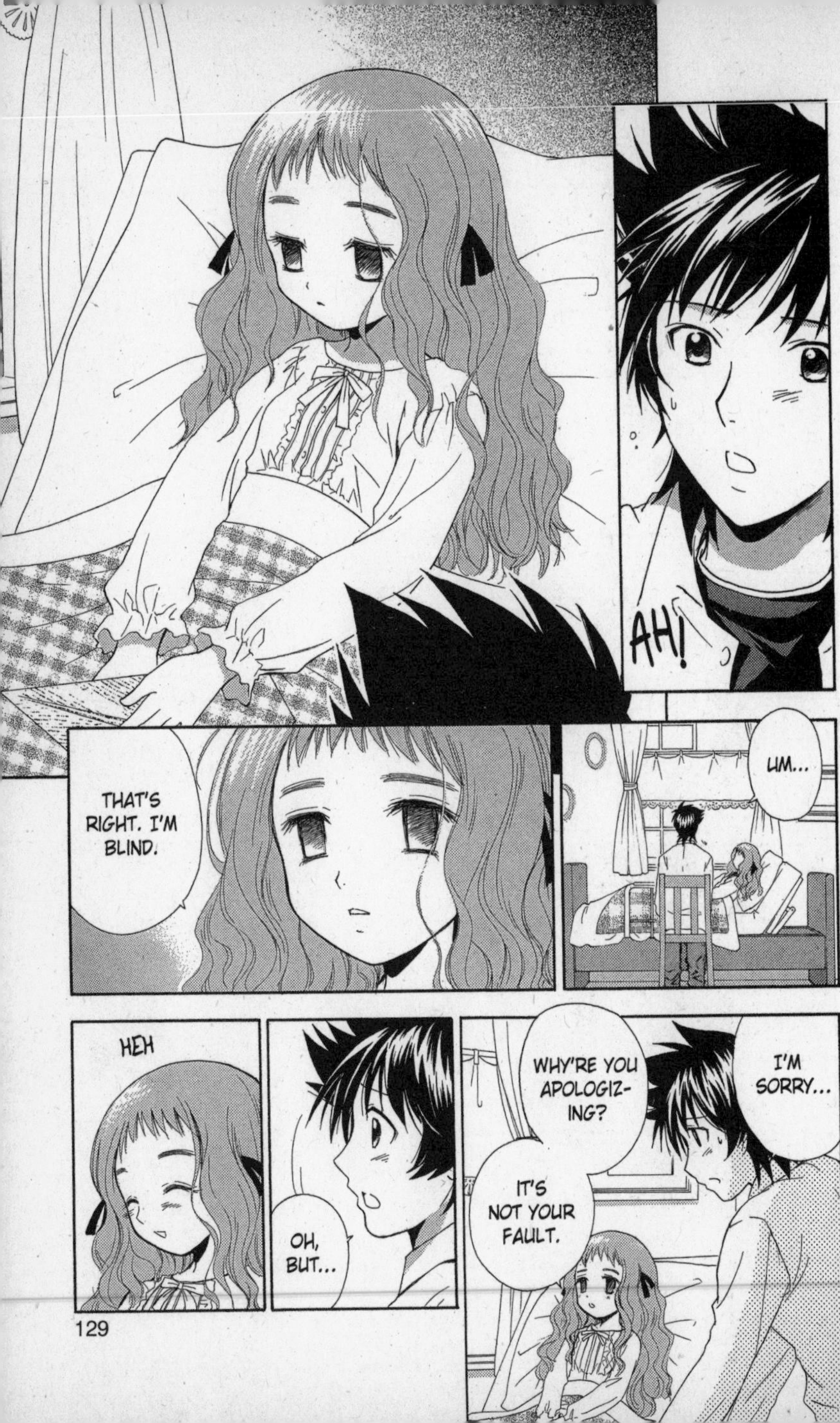
AH!
UM...
THAT'S RIGHT. I'M BLIND.
I'M SORRY...
WHY'RE YOU APOLOGIZING?
IT'S NOT YOUR FAULT.
OH, BUT...
HEH

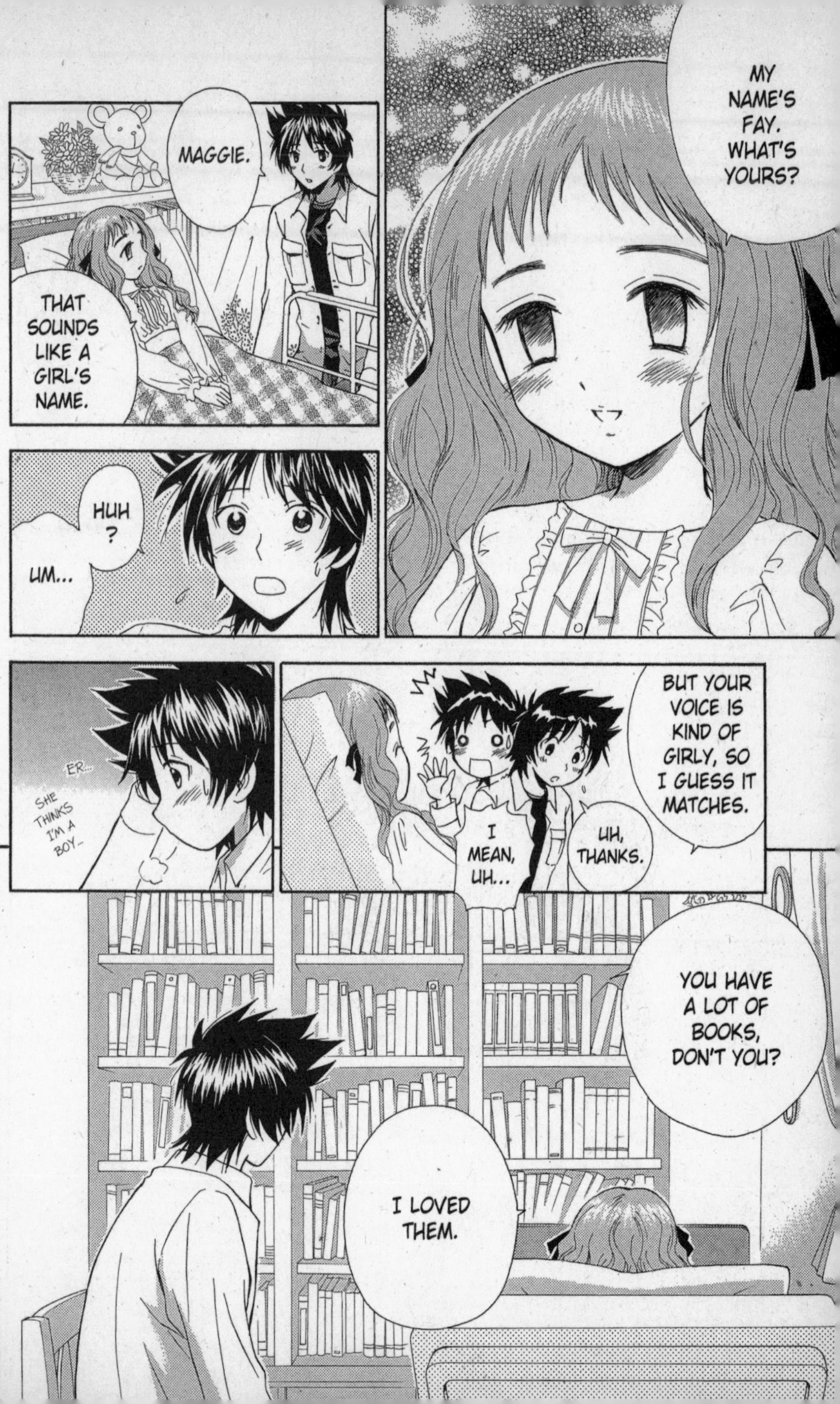

MY NAME'S FAY. WHAT'S YOURS?
MAGGIE.
THAT SOUNDS LIKE A GIRL'S NAME.
HUH?
UM...
BUT YOUR VOICE IS KIND OF GIRLY, SO I GUESS IT MATCHES.
UH, THANKS.
I MEAN, UH...
ER...
SHE THINKS I'M A BOY...
YOU HAVE A LOT OF BOOKS, DON'T YOU?
I LOVED THEM.

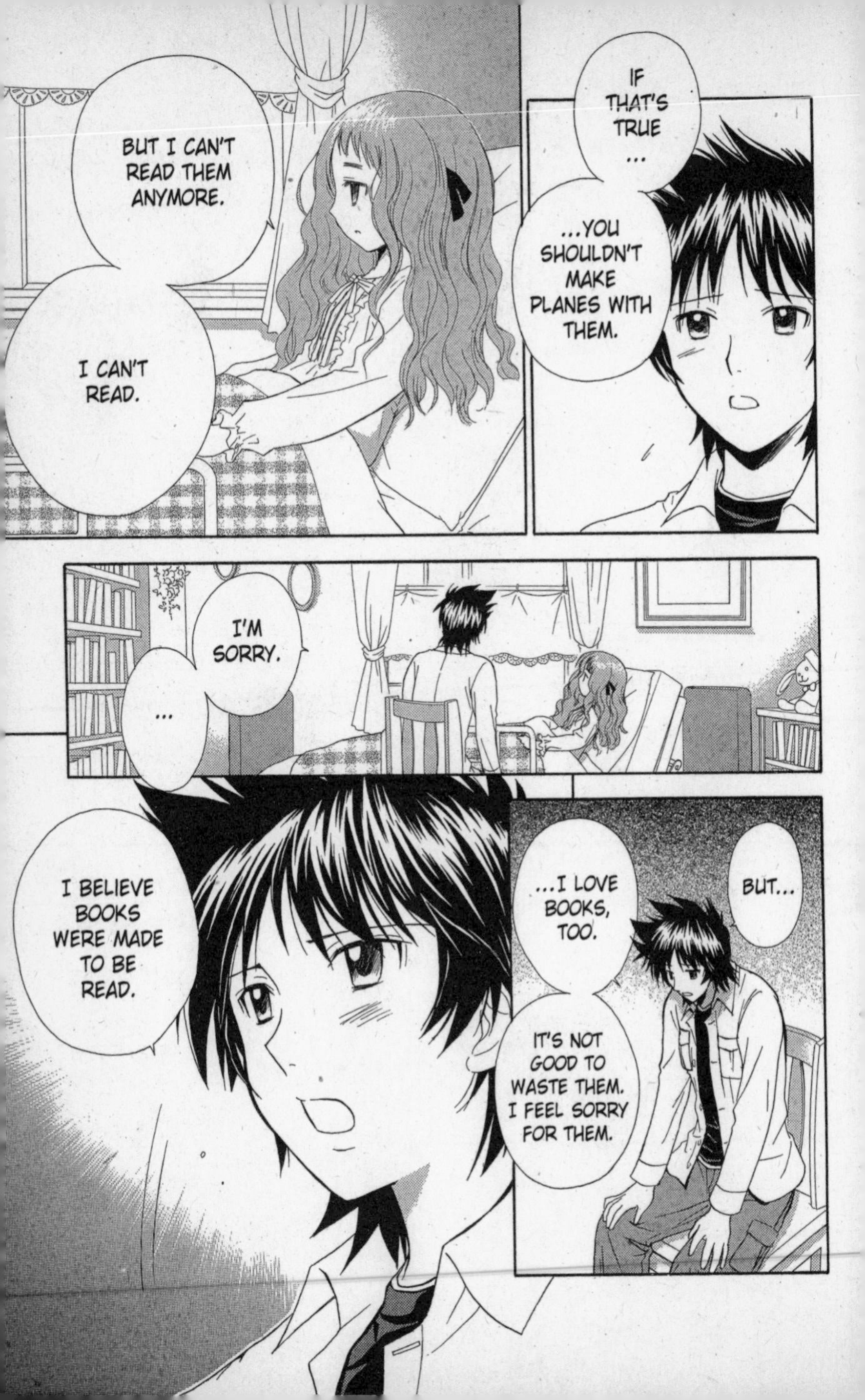
IF THAT'S TRUE ...
...YOU SHOULDN'T MAKE PLANES WITH THEM.
BUT I CAN'T READ THEM ANYMORE.
I CAN'T READ.
I'M SORRY.
...
BUT...
...I LOVE BOOKS, TOO.
IT'S NOT GOOD TO WASTE THEM. I FEEL SORRY FOR THEM.
I BELIEVE BOOKS WERE MADE TO BE READ.

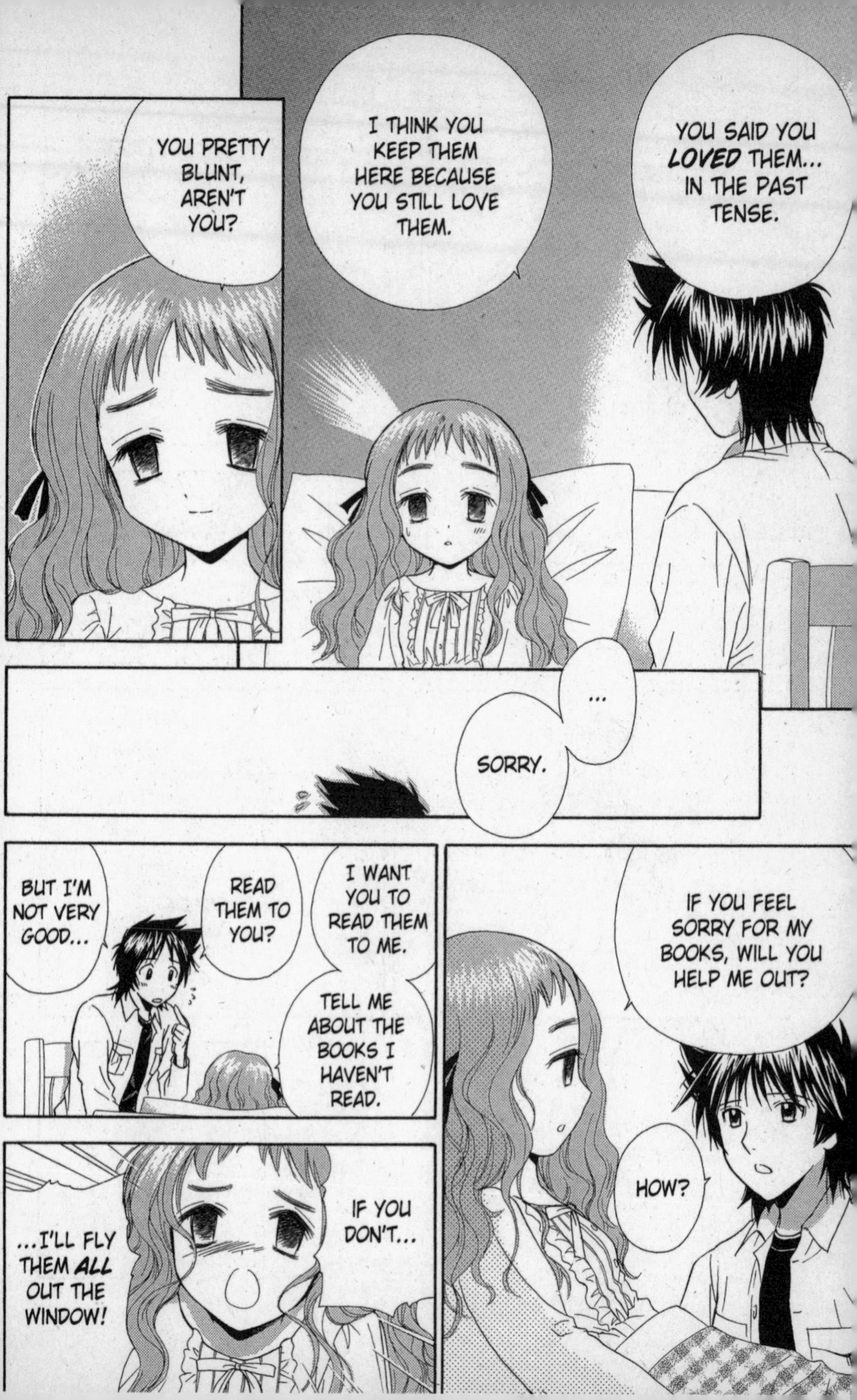
YOU SAID YOU LOVED THEM... IN THE PAST TENSE.
I THINK YOU KEEP THEM HERE BECAUSE YOU STILL LOVE THEM.
YOU PRETTY BLUNT, AREN'T YOU?
...
SORRY.
IF YOU FEEL SORRY FOR MY BOOKS, WILL YOU HELP ME OUT?
HOW?
I WANT YOU TO READ THEM TO ME.
TELL ME ABOUT THE BOOKS I HAVEN'T READ.
READ THEM TO YOU?
BUT I'M NOT VERY GOOD...
IF YOU DON'T...
...I'LL FLY THEM ALL OUT THE WINDOW!

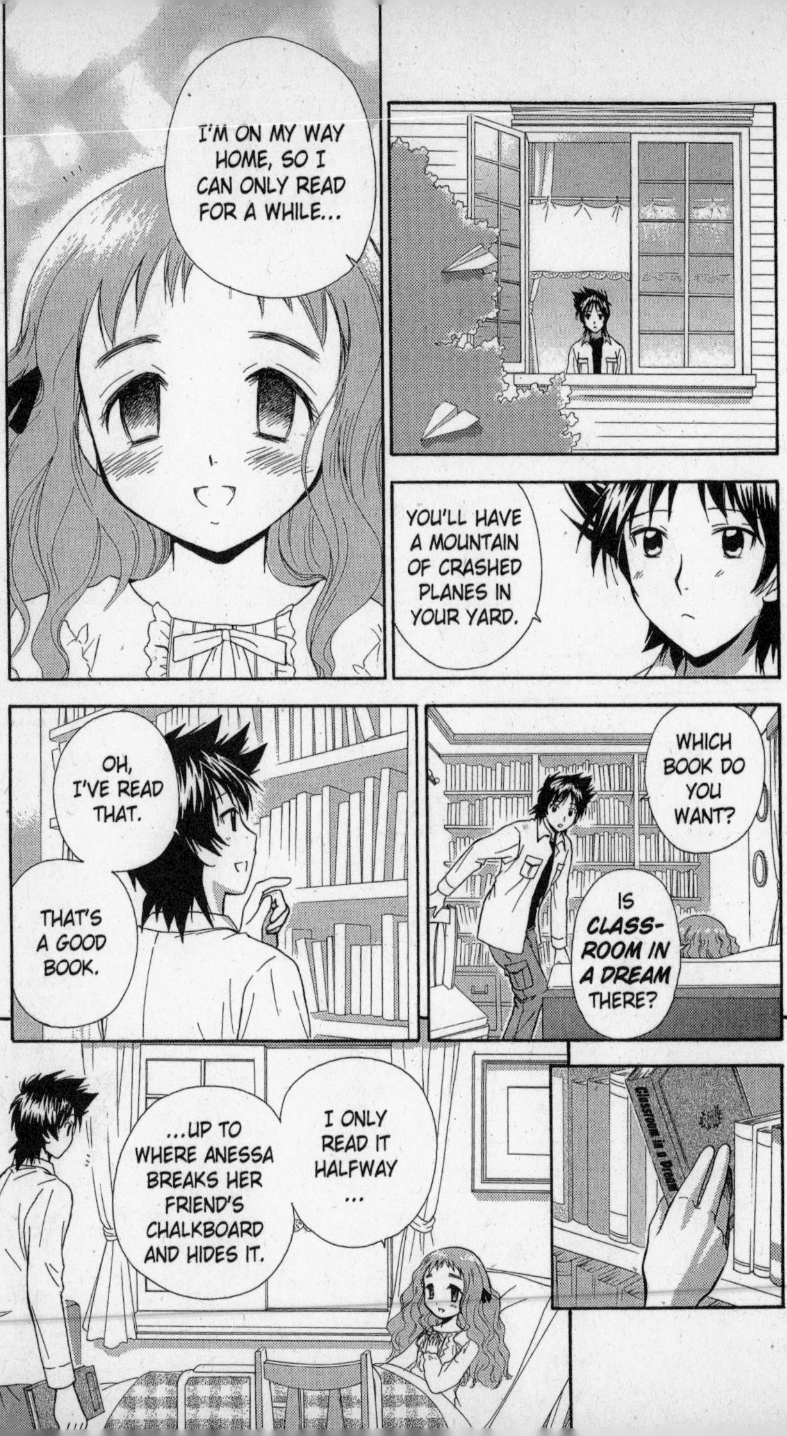
YOU'LL HAVE A MOUNTAIN OF CRASHED PLANES IN YOUR YARD.
I'M ON MY WAY HOME, SO I CAN ONLY READ FOR A WHILE...
WHICH BOOK DO YOU WANT?
IS CLASSROOM IN A DREAM THERE?
OH, I'VE READ THAT.
THAT'S A GOOD BOOK.
Classroom in a Dream
I ONLY READ IT HALFWAY...
...UP TO WHERE ANESSA BREAKS HER FRIEND'S CHALKBOARD AND HIDES IT.

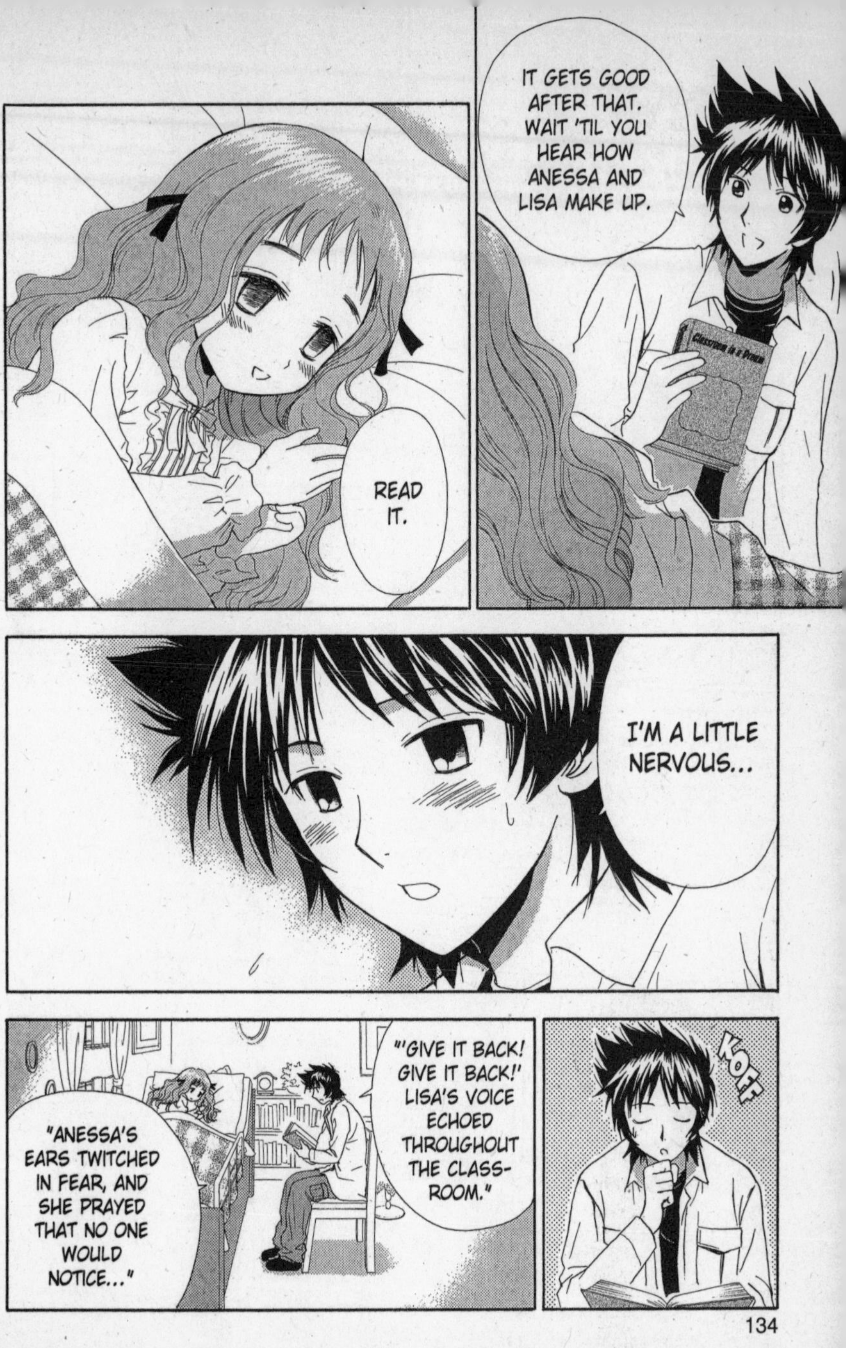
IT GETS GOOD AFTER THAT. WAIT 'TIL YOU HEAR HOW ANESSA AND LISA MAKE UP.
READ IT.
I'M A LITTLE NERVOUS...
KOFF
"'GIVE IT BACK! GIVE IT BACK!' LISA'S VOICE ECHOED THROUGHOUT THE CLASS-ROOM."
"ANESSA'S EARS TWITCHED IN FEAR, AND SHE PRAYED THAT NO ONE WOULD NOTICE..."

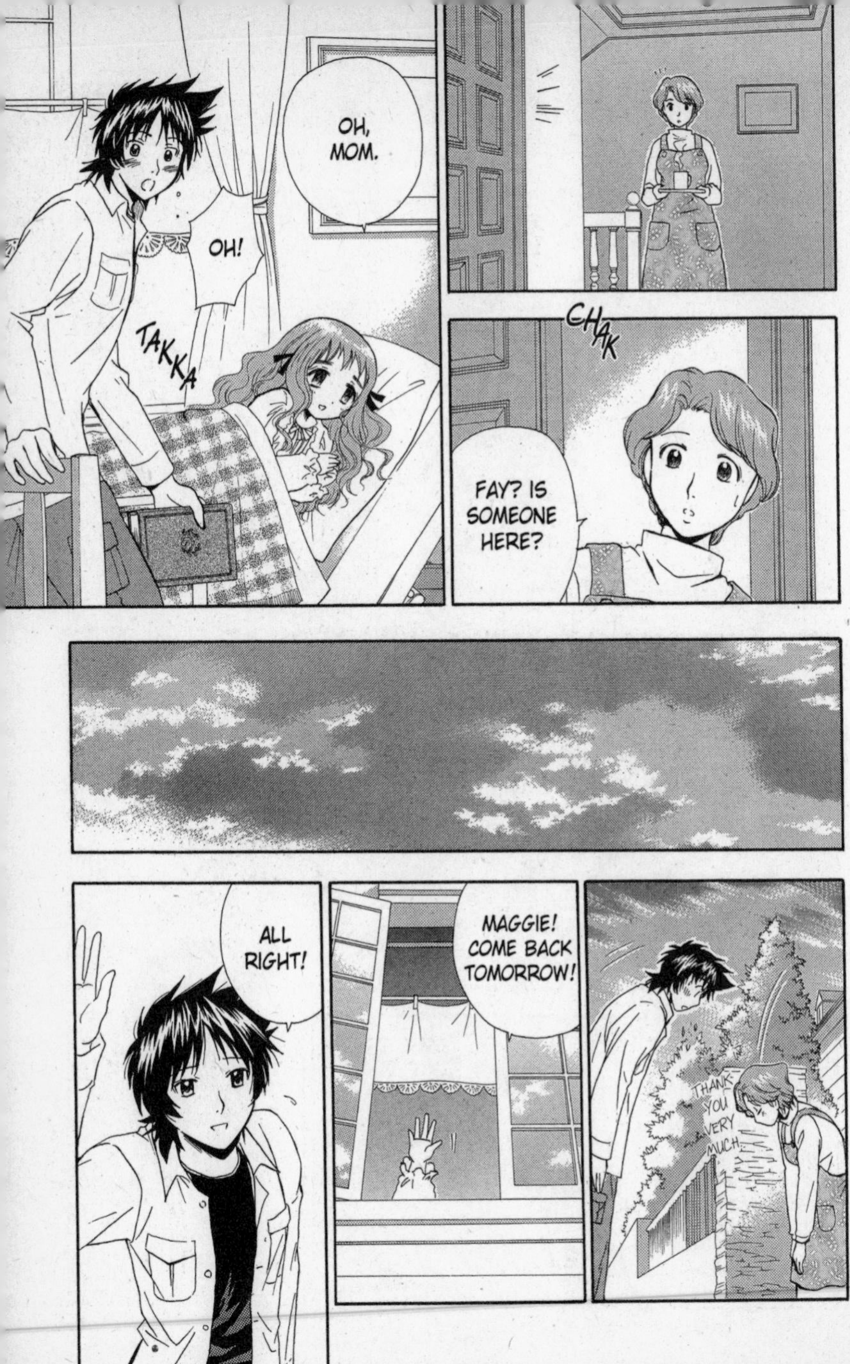
CHAK
FAY? IS SOMEONE HERE?
OH, MOM.
OH!
TAKKA
THANK YOU VERY MUCH.
MAGGIE! COME BACK TOMORROW!
ALL RIGHT!

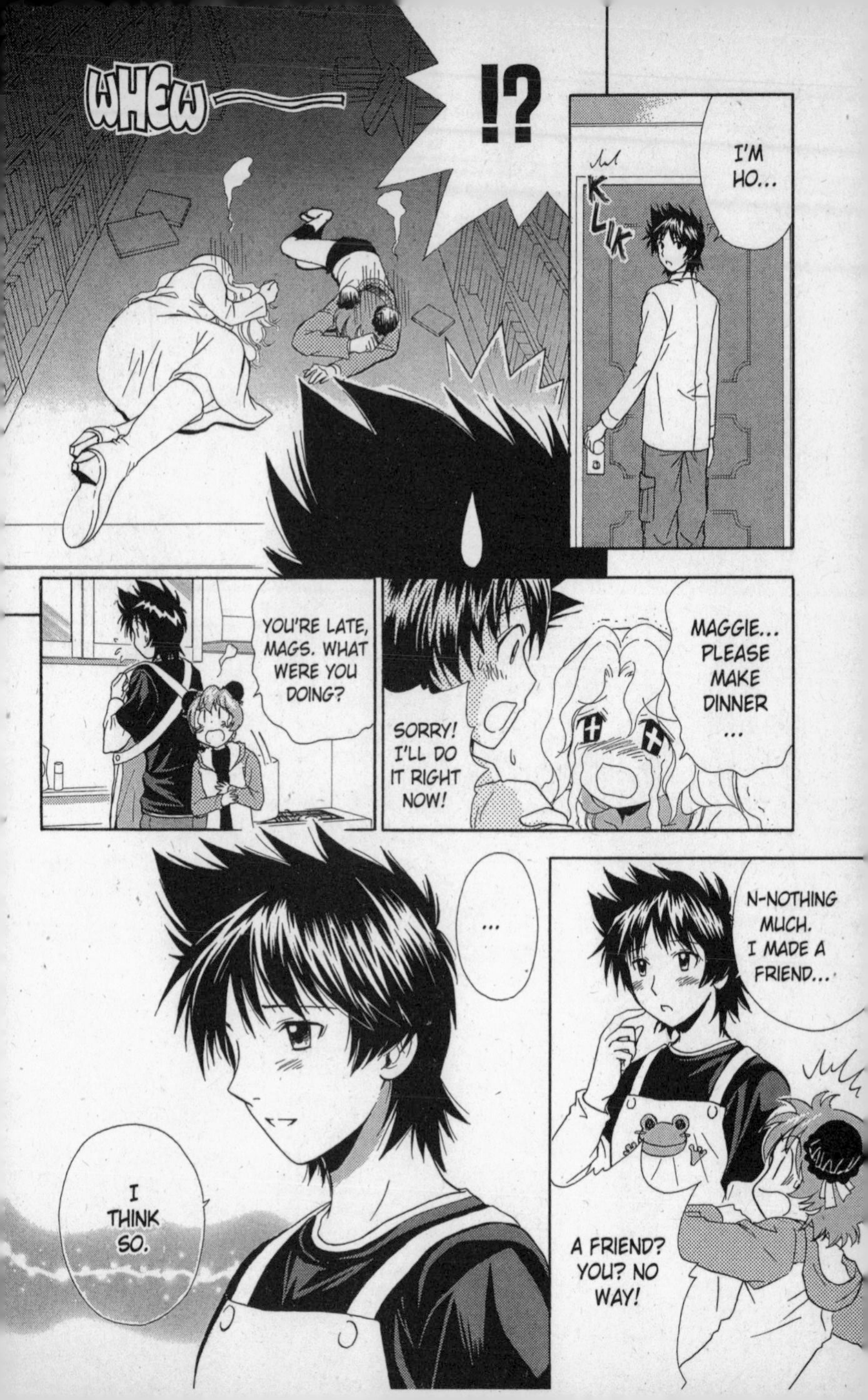
KLIK
I'M HO...
!?
WHEW—
MAGGIE... PLEASE MAKE DINNER ...
SORRY! I'LL DO IT RIGHT NOW!
YOU'RE LATE, MAGS. WHAT WERE YOU DOING?
N-NOTHING MUCH. I MADE A FRIEND...
A FRIEND? YOU? NO WAY!
...
I THINK SO.

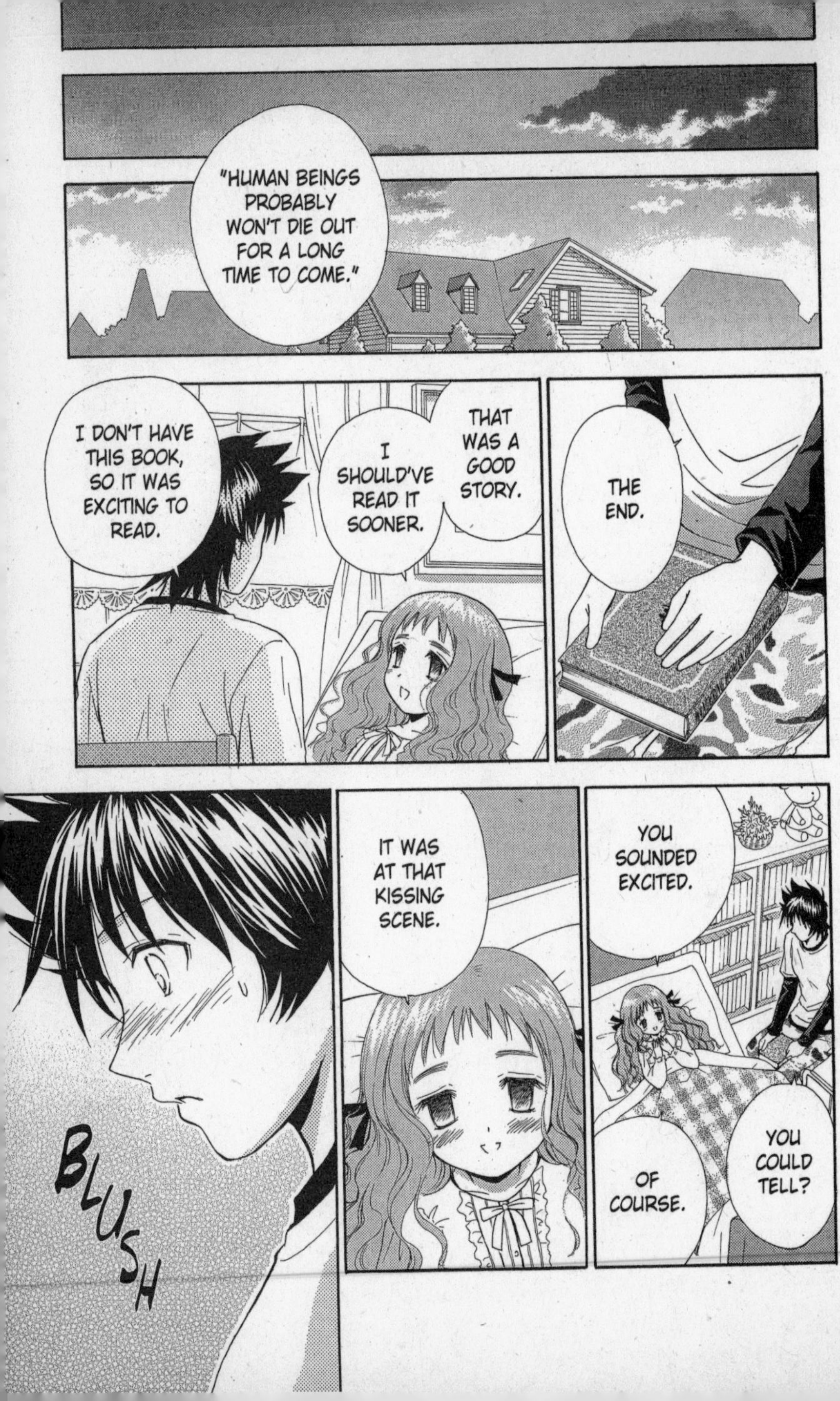
"HUMAN BEINGS PROBABLY WON'T DIE OUT FOR A LONG TIME TO COME."
THE END.
THAT WAS A GOOD STORY.
I SHOULD'VE READ IT SOONER.
I DON'T HAVE THIS BOOK, SO IT WAS EXCITING TO READ.
YOU SOUNDED EXCITED.
YOU COULD TELL?
OF COURSE.
IT WAS AT THAT KISSING SCENE.
BLUSH

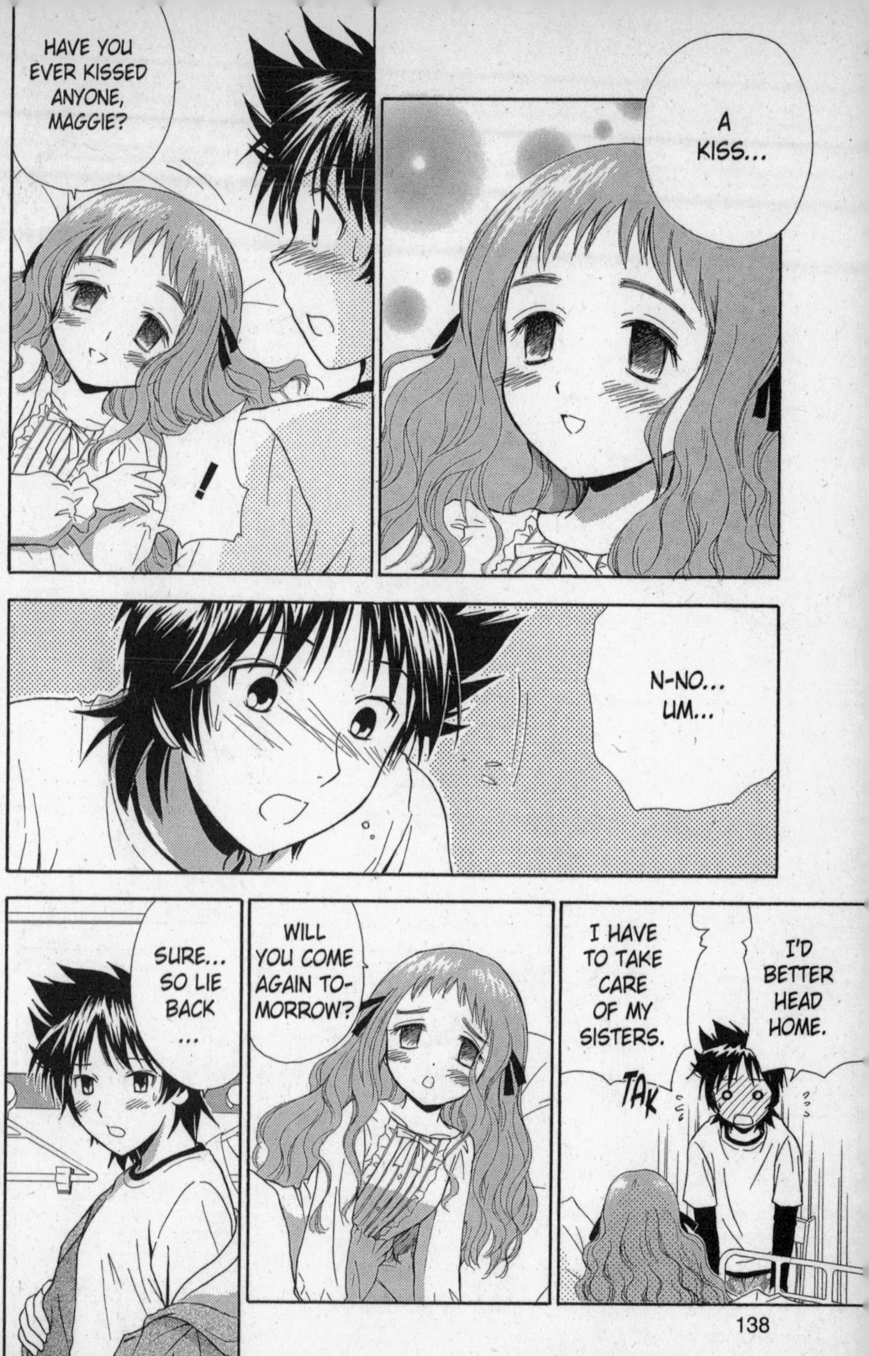
A KISS...
HAVE YOU EVER KISSED ANYONE, MAGGIE?
!
N-NO... UM...
I'D BETTER HEAD HOME.
I HAVE TO TAKE CARE OF MY SISTERS.
TAK
WILL YOU COME AGAIN TO-MORROW?
SURE... SO LIE BACK ...

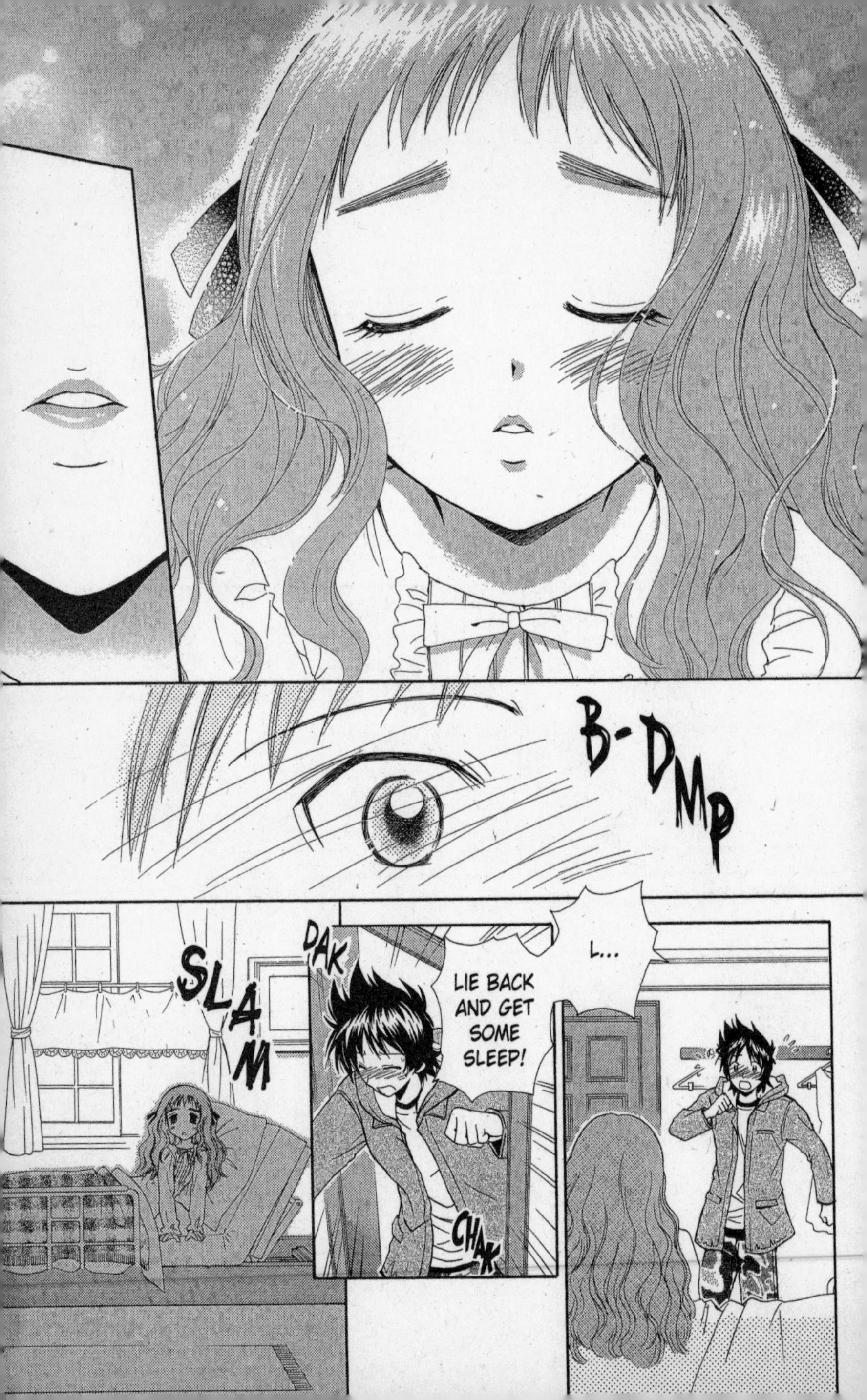
B-DMP
L...
DAK
LIE BACK AND GET SOME SLEEP!
CHAK
SLAM

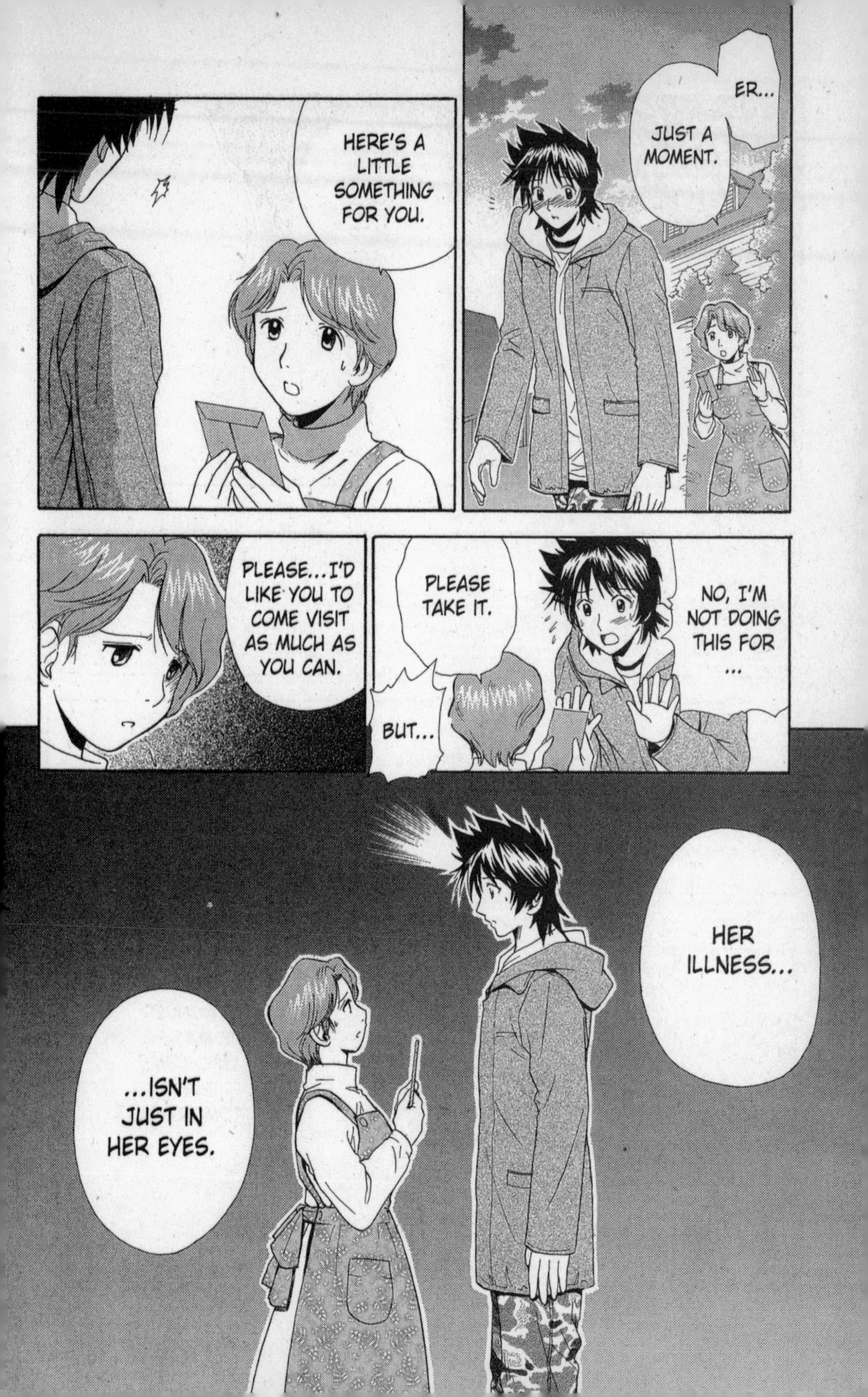
ER...
JUST A MOMENT.
HERE'S A LITTLE SOMETHING FOR YOU.
NO, I'M NOT DOING THIS FOR ...
PLEASE TAKE IT.
BUT...
PLEASE...I'D LIKE YOU TO COME VISIT AS MUCH AS YOU CAN.
HER ILLNESS...
...ISN'T JUST IN HER EYES.

IT WON'T STOP THERE.

THE TRUTH IS...

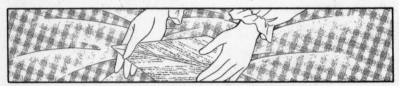

I WONDER IF MAGGIE WILL COME BACK TOMORROW...

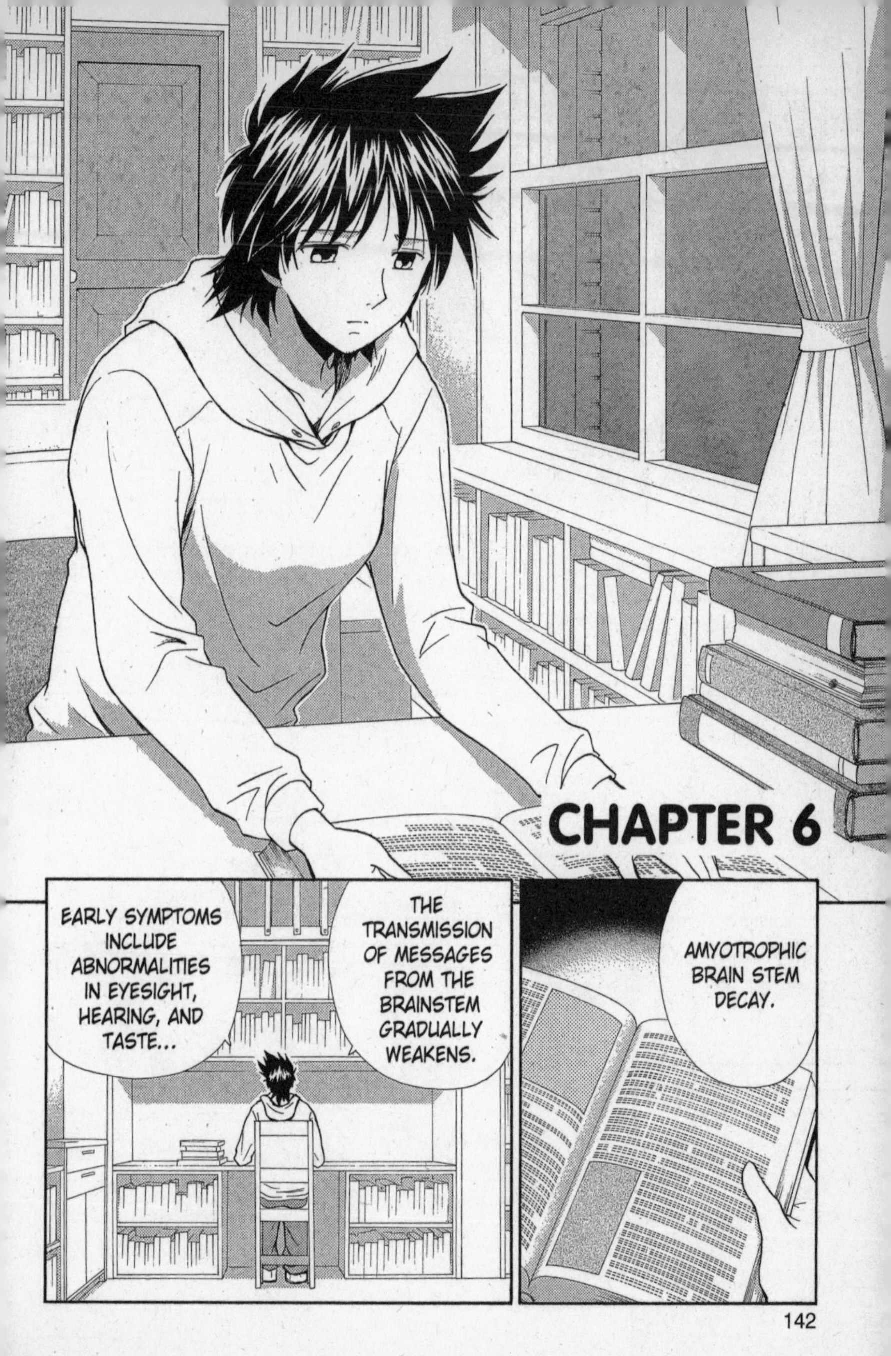
CHAPTER 6
AMYOTROPHIC BRAIN STEM DECAY.
THE TRANSMISSION OF MESSAGES FROM THE BRAINSTEM GRADUALLY WEAKENS.
EARLY SYMPTOMS INCLUDE ABNORMALITIES IN EYESIGHT, HEARING, AND TASTE...

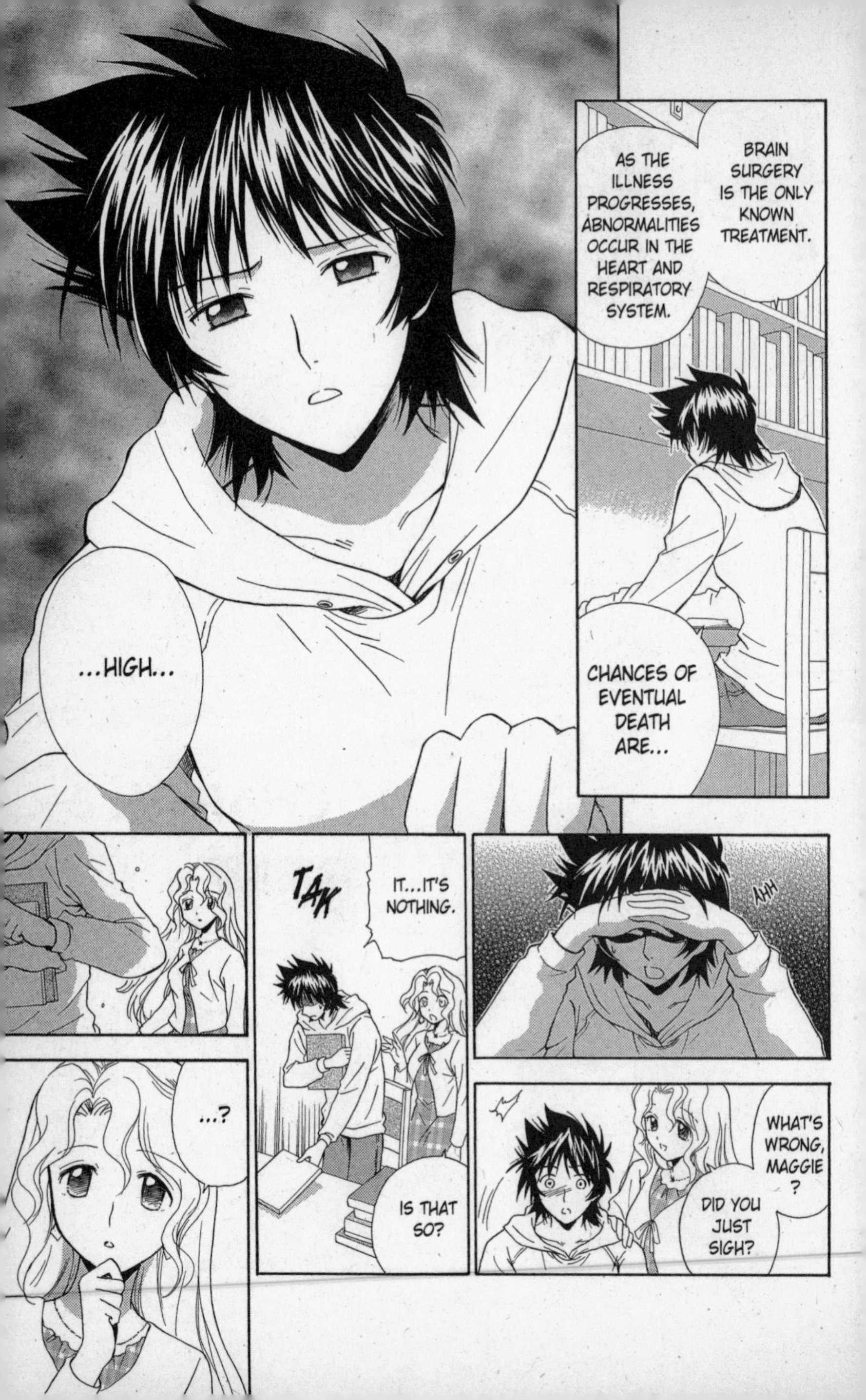
BRAIN SURGERY IS THE ONLY KNOWN TREATMENT.
AS THE ILLNESS PROGRESSES, ABNORMALITIES OCCUR IN THE HEART AND RESPIRATORY SYSTEM.
CHANCES OF EVENTUAL DEATH ARE...
...HIGH...
AHH
WHAT'S WRONG, MAGGIE?
DID YOU JUST SIGH?
TAK
IT...IT'S NOTHING.
IS THAT SO?
...?

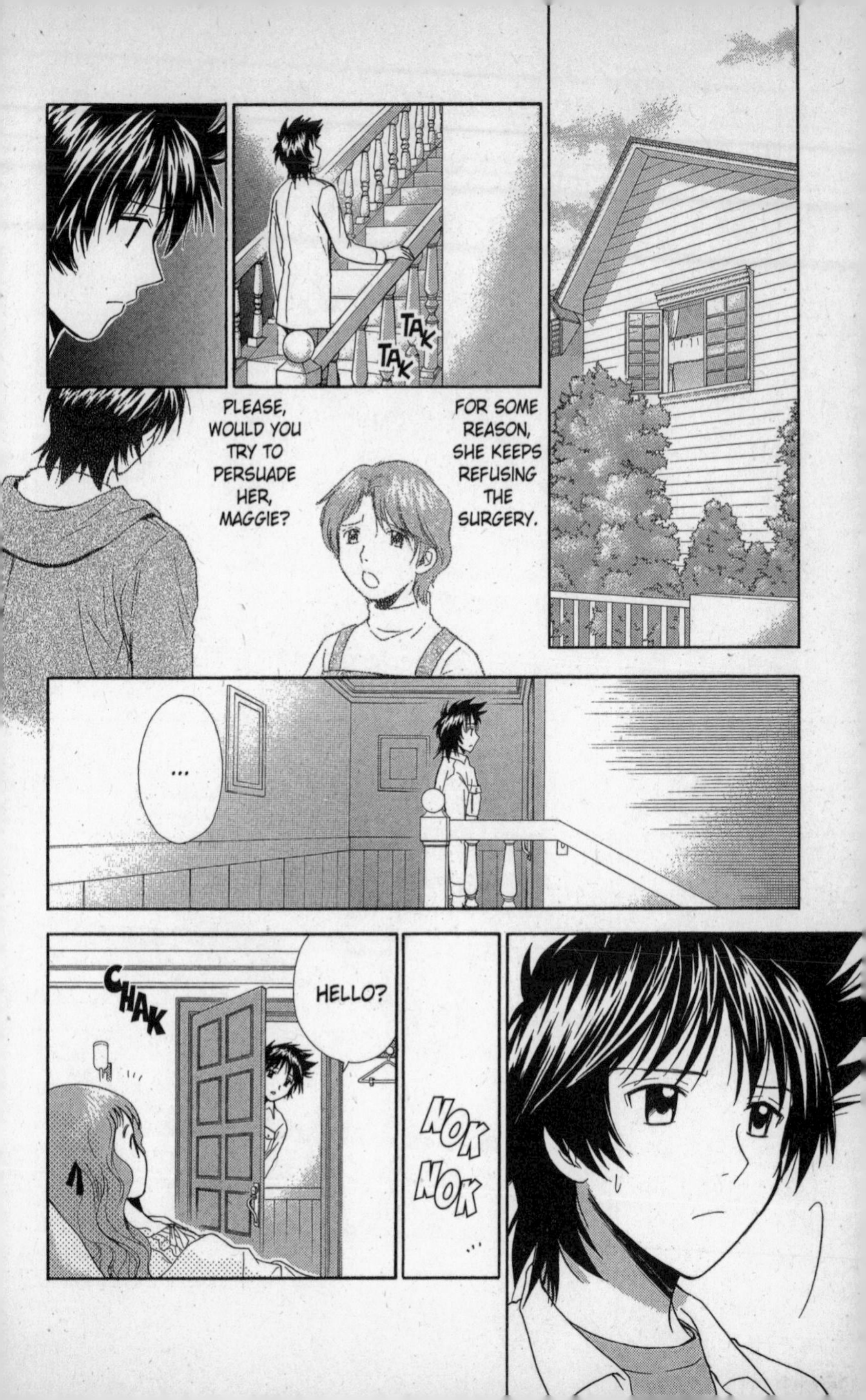
TAK
TAK
FOR SOME REASON, SHE KEEPS REFUSING THE SURGERY.
PLEASE, WOULD YOU TRY TO PERSUADE HER, MAGGIE?
...
NOK
NOK
...
HELLO?
CHAK

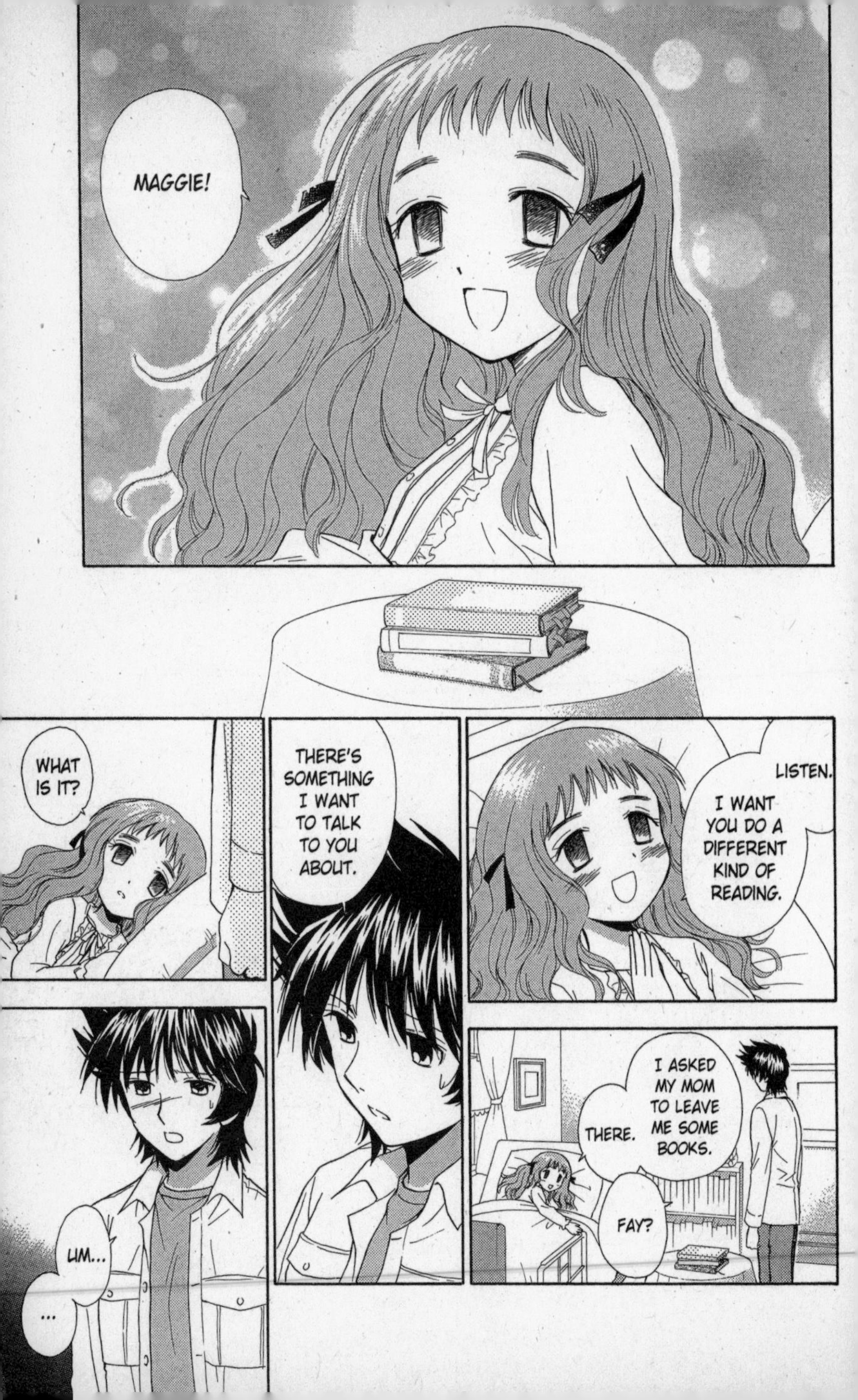
MAGGIE!
LISTEN.
I WANT YOU DO A DIFFERENT KIND OF READING.
I ASKED MY MOM TO LEAVE ME SOME BOOKS.
THERE.
FAY?
THERE'S SOMETHING I WANT TO TALK TO YOU ABOUT.
WHAT IS IT?
UM...
...

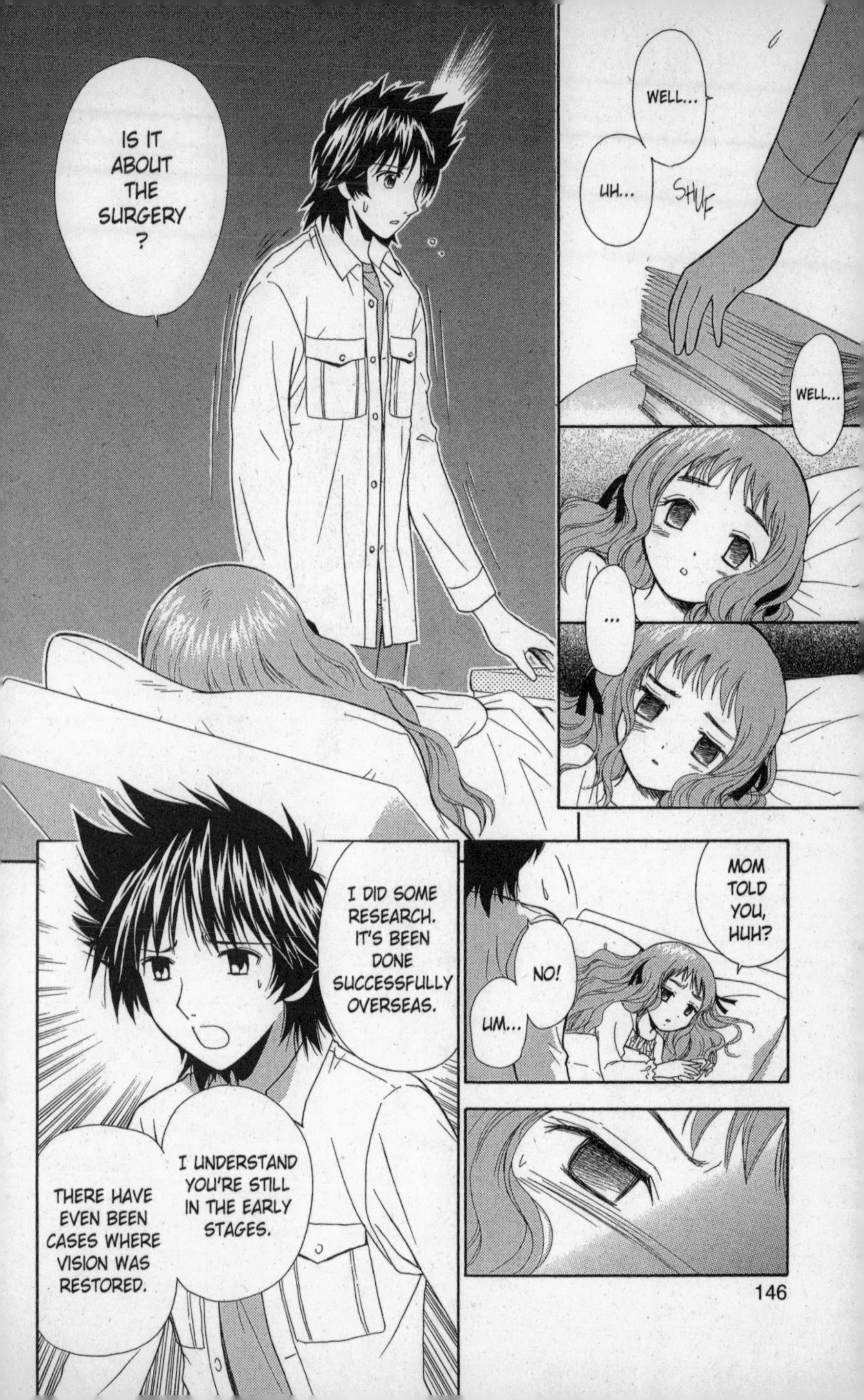
WELL...
UH...
SHUF
WELL...
...
IS IT ABOUT THE SURGERY ?
MOM TOLD YOU, HUH?
NO!
UM...
I DID SOME RESEARCH. IT'S BEEN DONE SUCCESSFULLY OVERSEAS.
I UNDERSTAND YOU'RE STILL IN THE EARLY STAGES.
THERE HAVE EVEN BEEN CASES WHERE VISION WAS RESTORED.

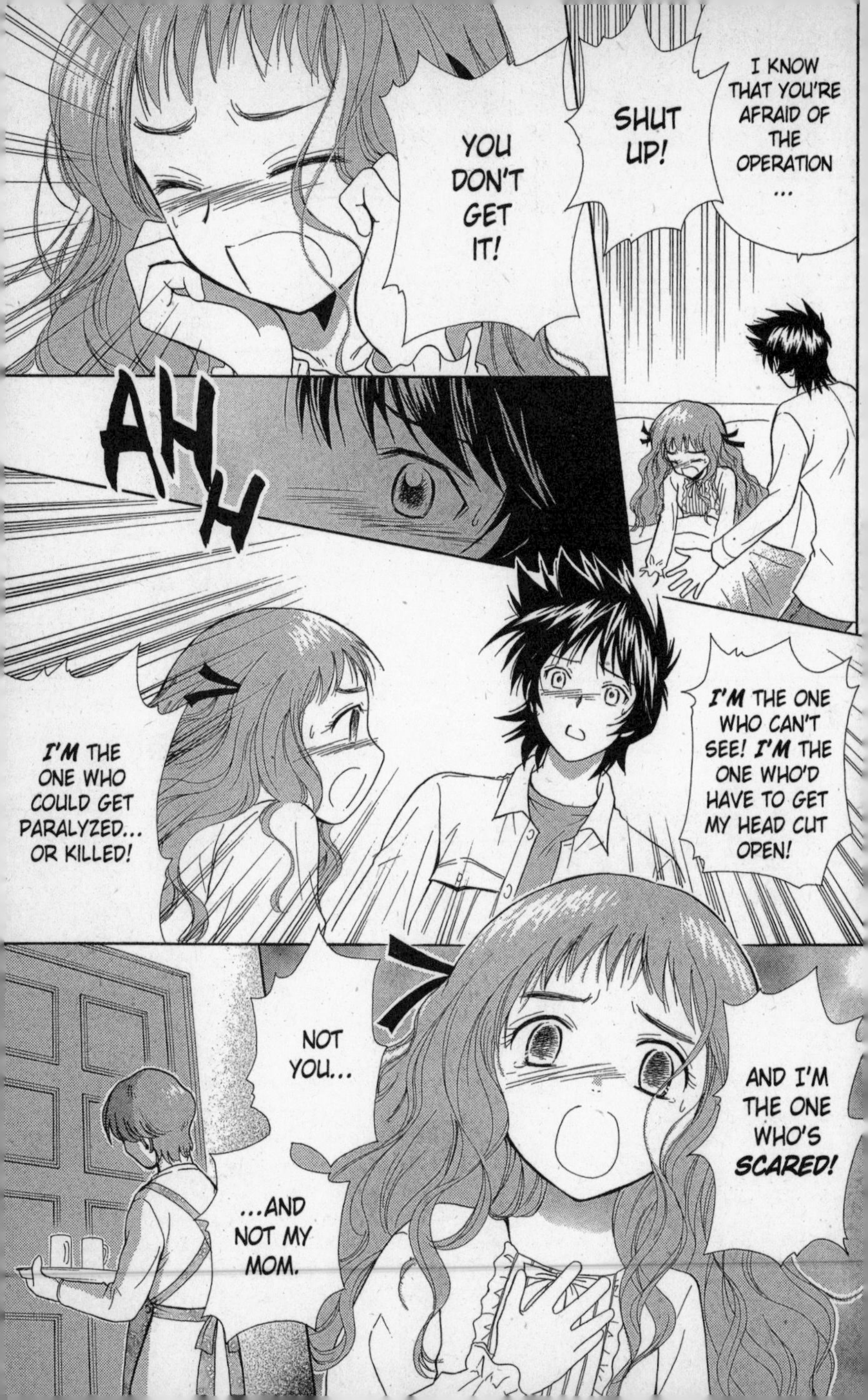
I KNOW THAT YOU'RE AFRAID OF THE OPERATION ...
SHUT UP!
YOU DON'T GET IT!
AHH
I'M THE ONE WHO CAN'T SEE! *I'M* THE ONE WHO'D HAVE TO GET MY HEAD CUT OPEN!
I'M THE ONE WHO COULD GET PARALYZED... OR KILLED!
AND I'M THE ONE WHO'S *SCARED!*
NOT YOU...
...AND NOT MY MOM.

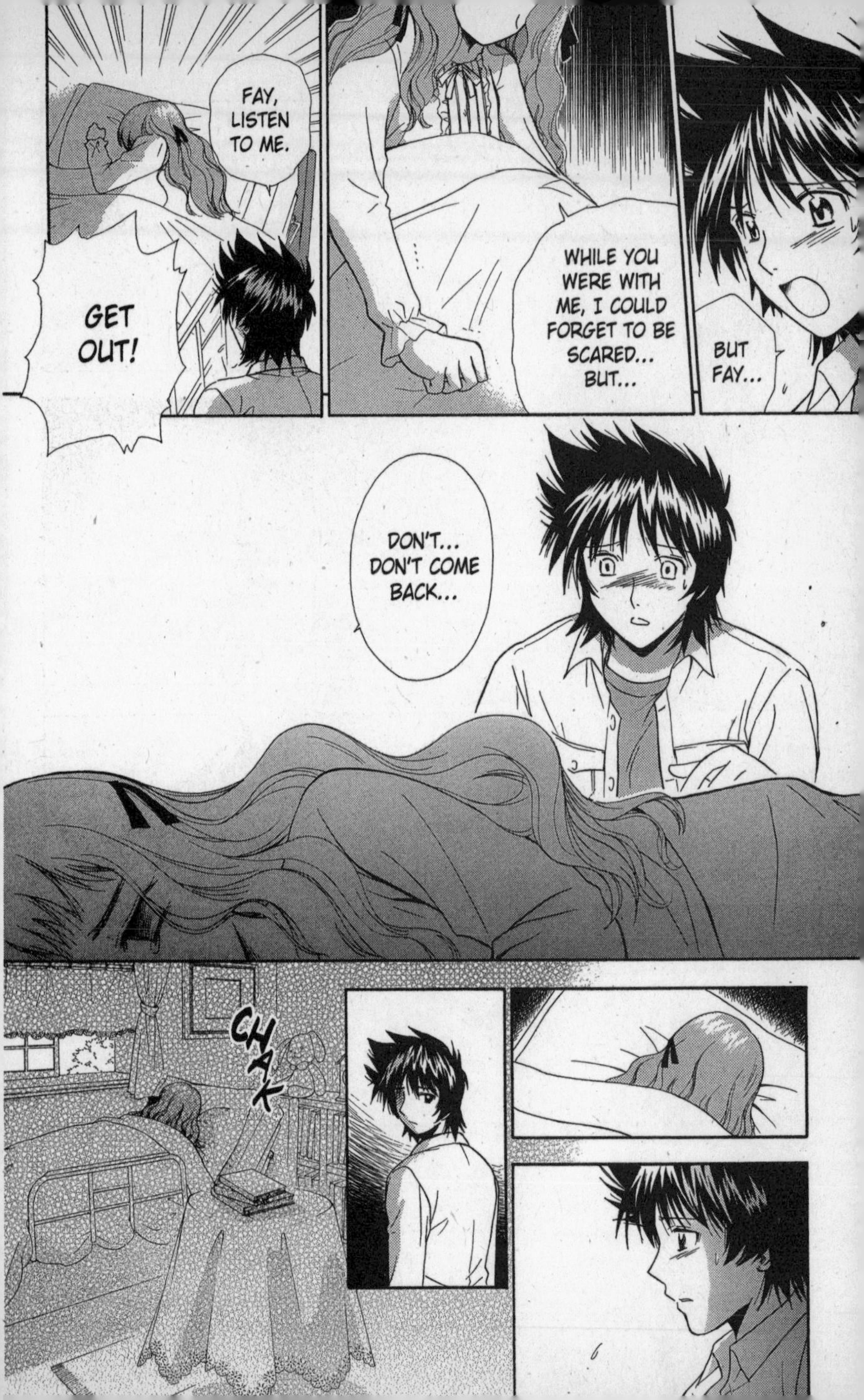
BUT FAY...
WHILE YOU WERE WITH ME, I COULD FORGET TO BE SCARED... BUT...
FAY, LISTEN TO ME.
GET OUT!
DON'T... DON'T COME BACK...
CHAK

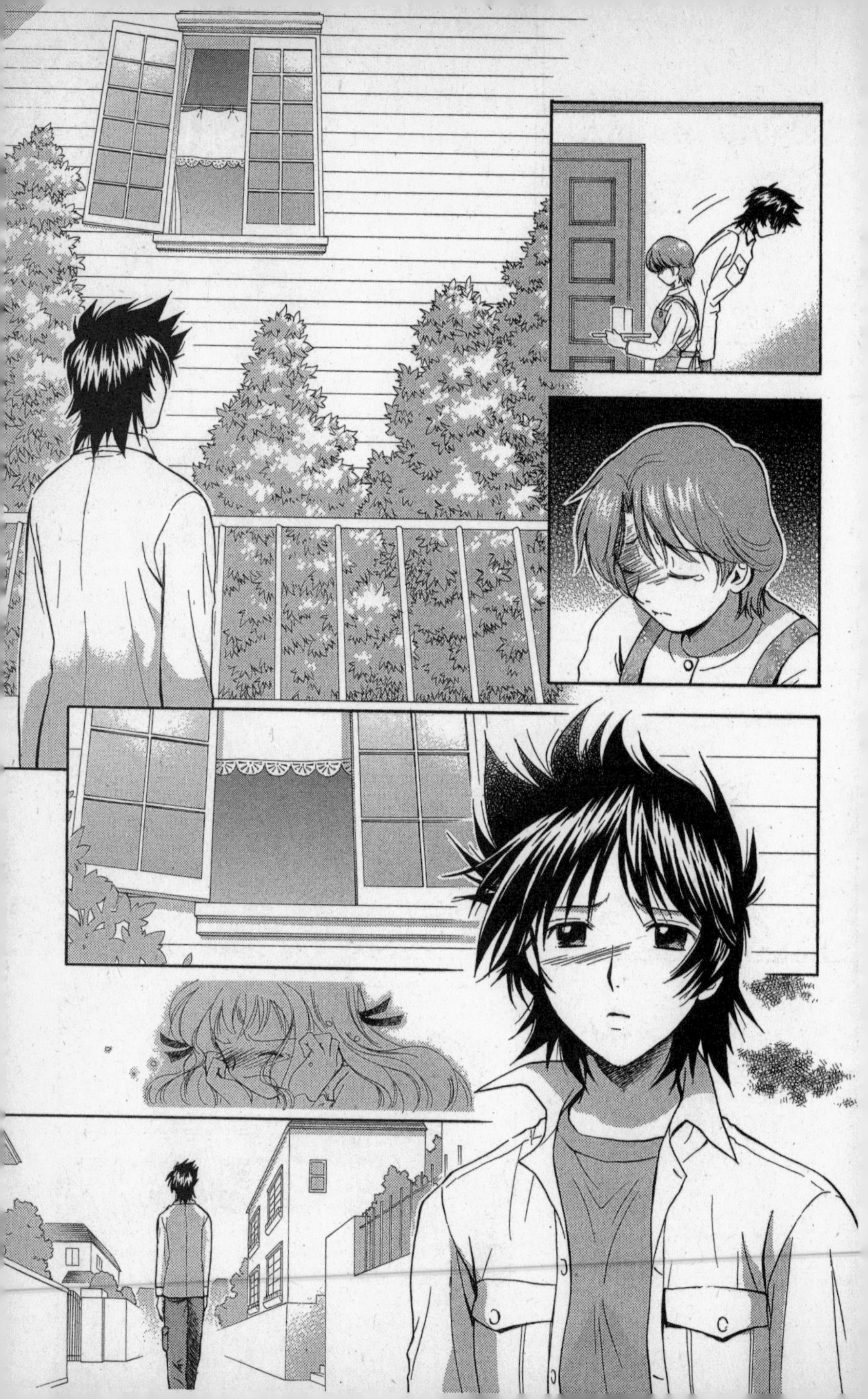

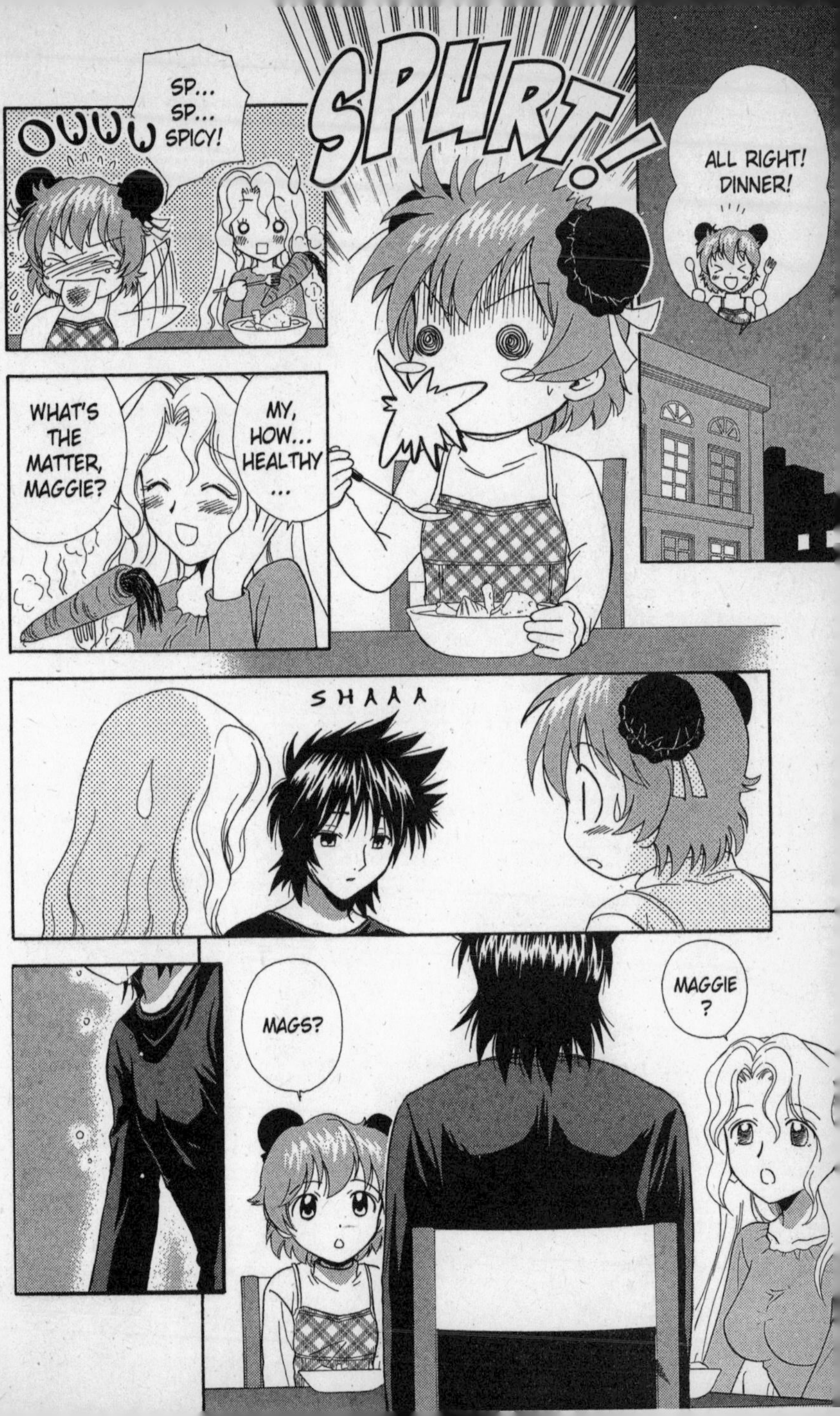
ALL RIGHT! DINNER!
SPURT!
OWWW
SP... SP... SPICY!
MY, HOW... HEALTHY ...
WHAT'S THE MATTER, MAGGIE?
SHAAA
MAGGIE ?
MAGS?

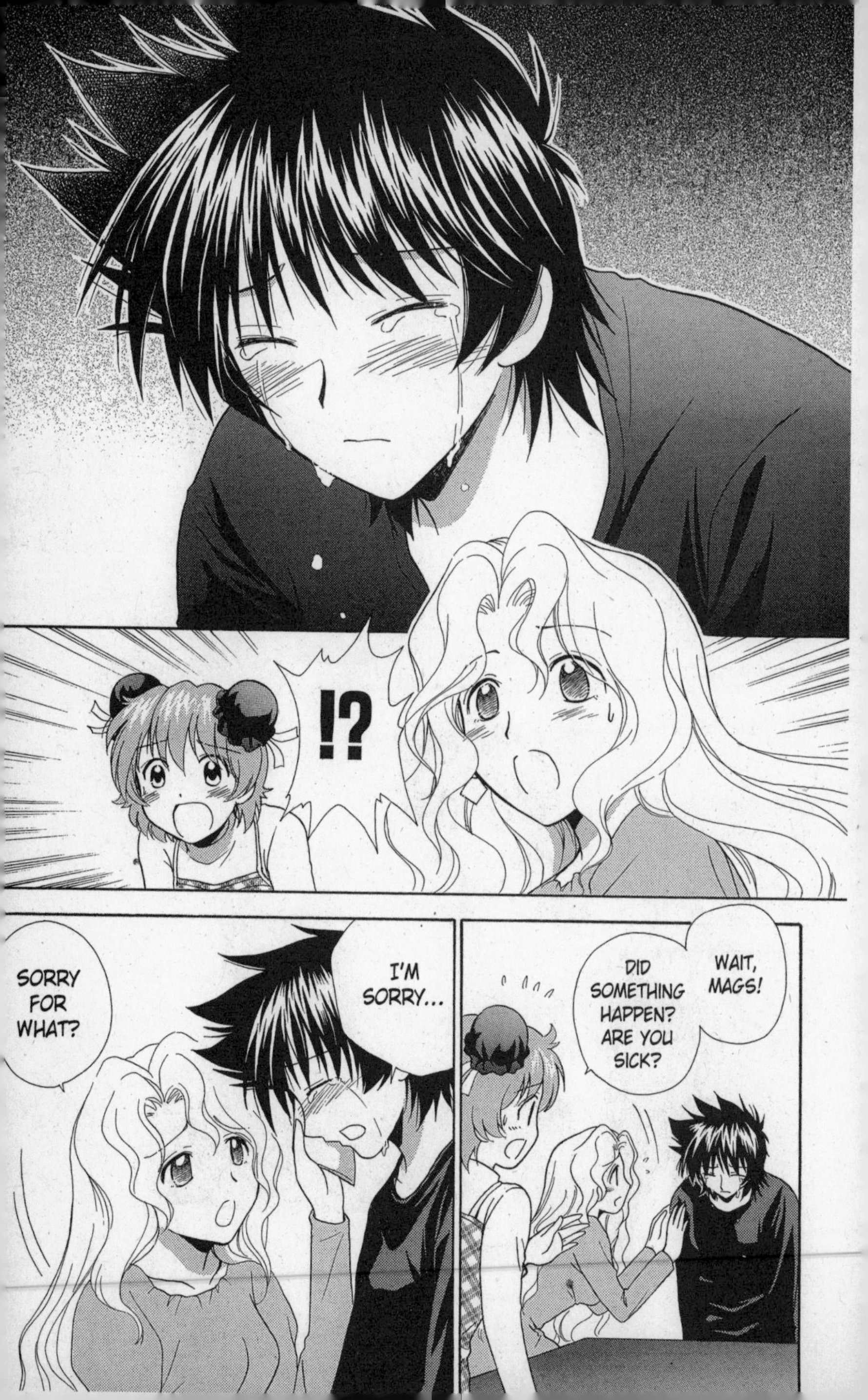
!?
WAIT, MAGS!
DID SOMETHING HAPPEN? ARE YOU SICK?
I'M SORRY...
SORRY FOR WHAT?

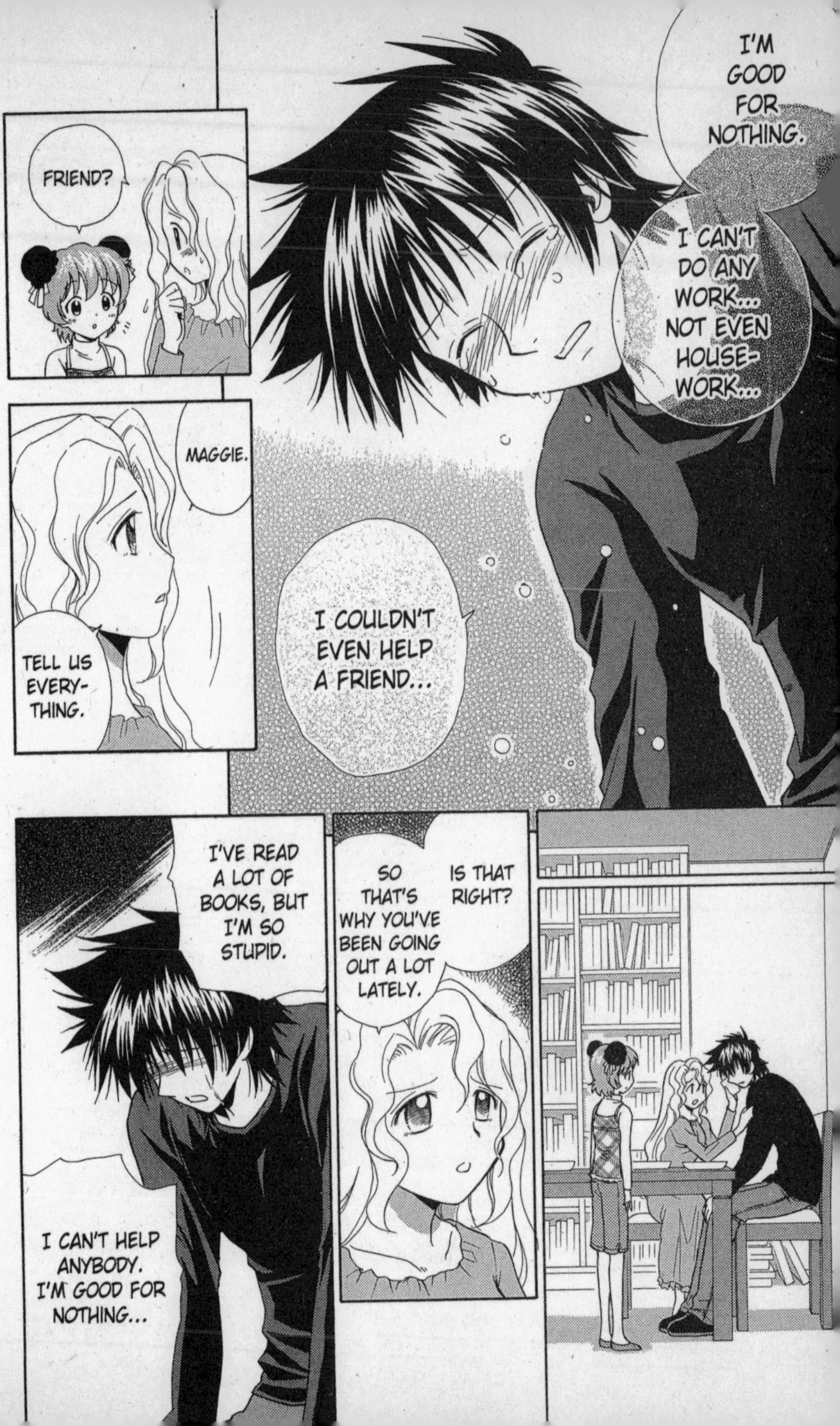
I'M GOOD FOR NOTHING.
I CAN'T DO ANY WORK... NOT EVEN HOUSE-WORK...
I COULDN'T EVEN HELP A FRIEND...
FRIEND?
MAGGIE.
TELL US EVERY-THING.
IS THAT RIGHT?
SO THAT'S WHY YOU'VE BEEN GOING OUT A LOT LATELY.
I'VE READ A LOT OF BOOKS, BUT I'M SO STUPID.
I CAN'T HELP ANYBODY. I'M GOOD FOR NOTHING...

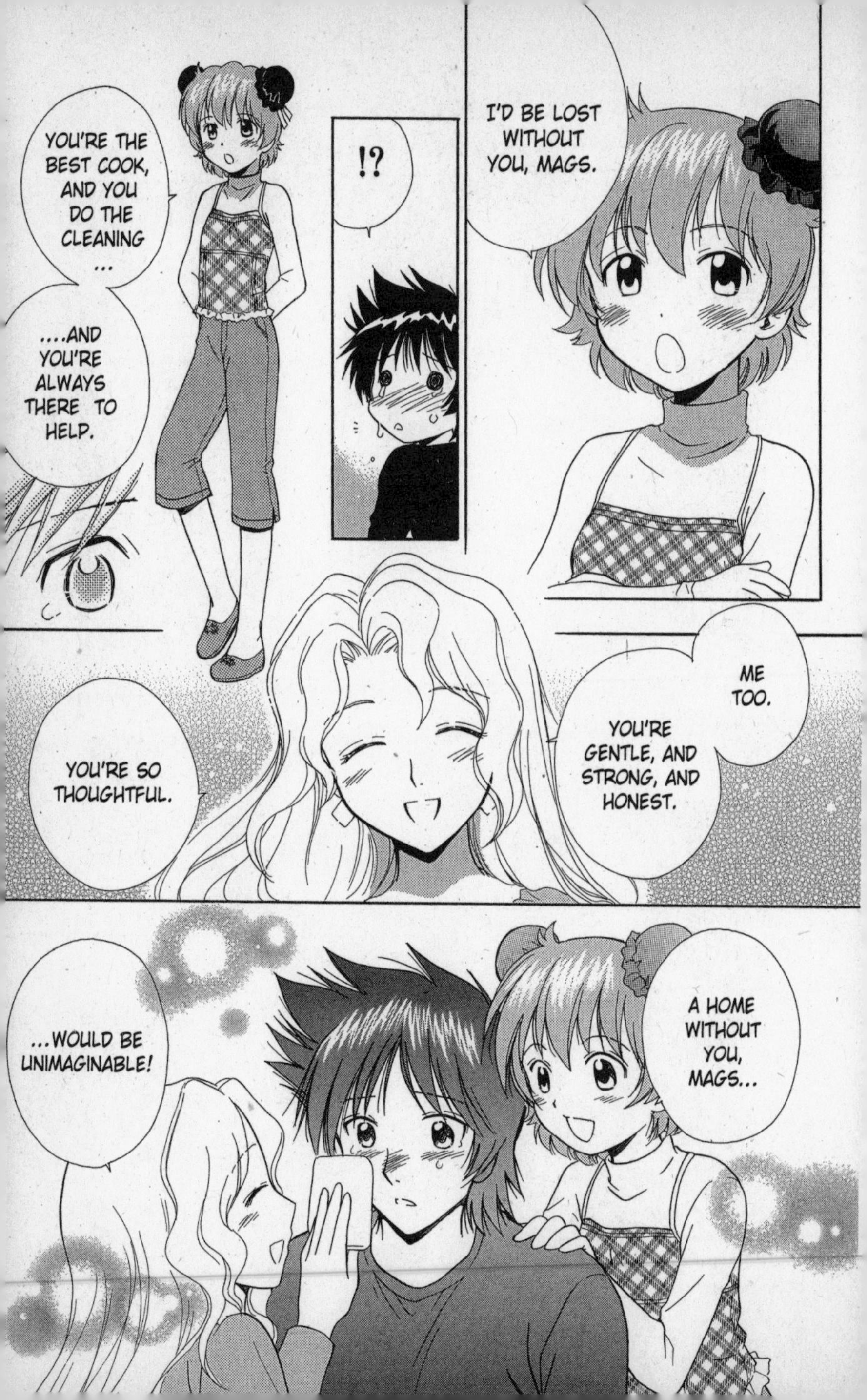
I'D BE LOST WITHOUT YOU, MAGS.
!?
YOU'RE THE BEST COOK, AND YOU DO THE CLEANING ...
....AND YOU'RE ALWAYS THERE TO HELP.
ME TOO.
YOU'RE GENTLE, AND STRONG, AND HONEST.
YOU'RE SO THOUGHTFUL.
A HOME WITHOUT YOU, MAGS...
...WOULD BE UNIMAGINABLE!

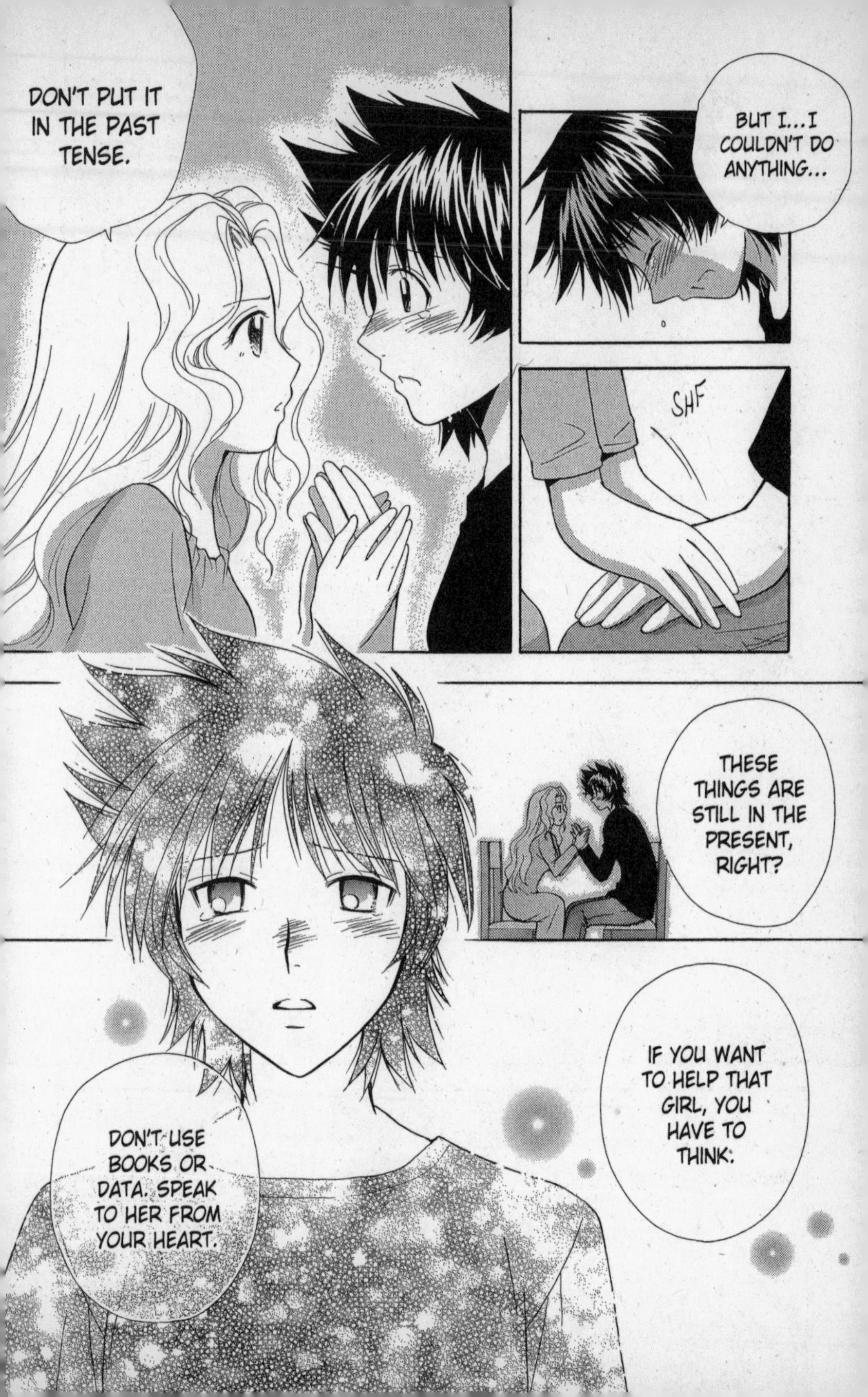
BUT I...I COULDN'T DO ANYTHING...
SHF
DON'T PUT IT IN THE PAST TENSE.
THESE THINGS ARE STILL IN THE PRESENT, RIGHT?
IF YOU WANT TO HELP THAT GIRL, YOU HAVE TO THINK.
DON'T USE BOOKS OR DATA. SPEAK TO HER FROM YOUR HEART.

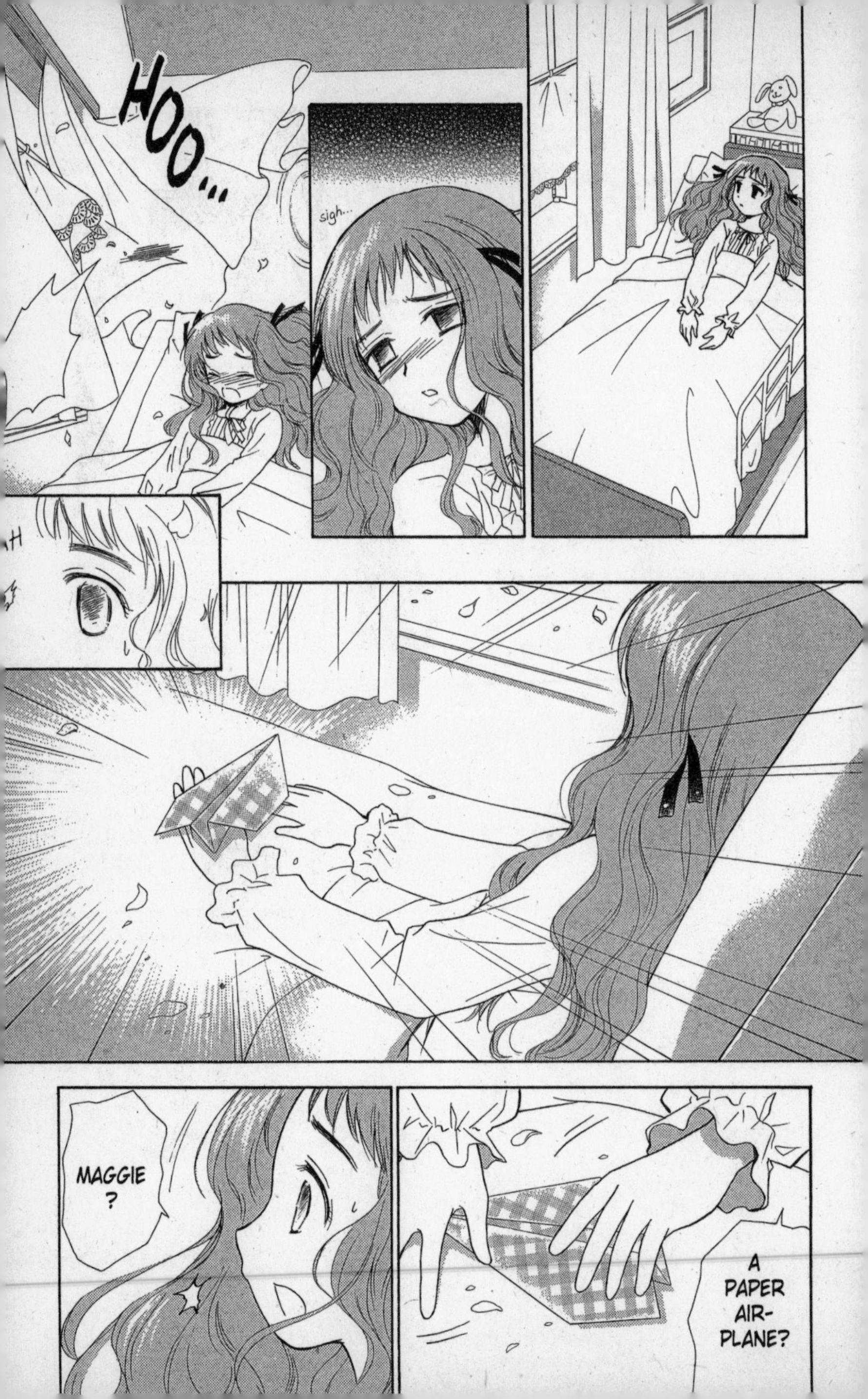
sigh...
HOO...
A PAPER AIR-PLANE?
MAGGIE ?

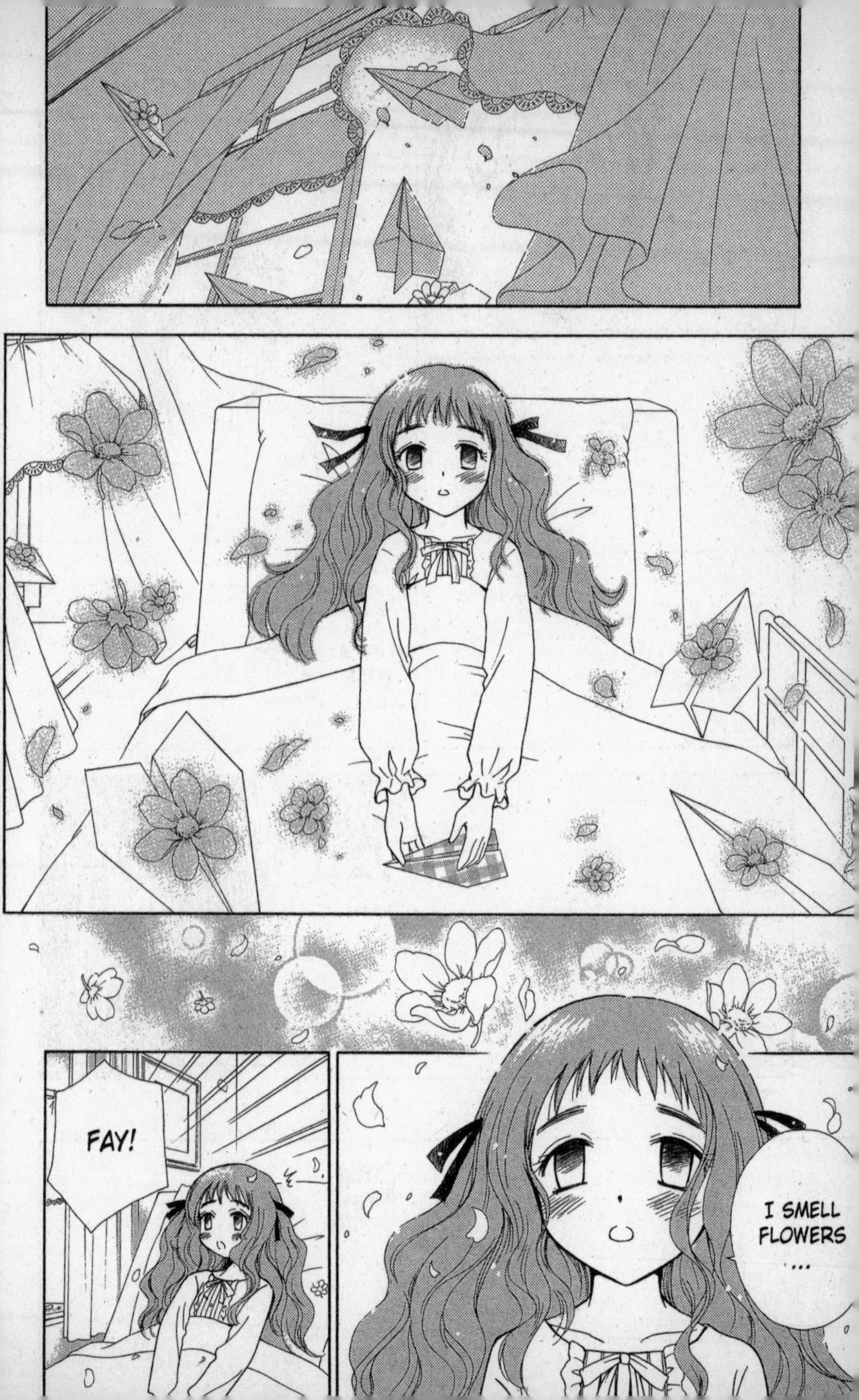
I SMELL FLOWERS ...
FAY!

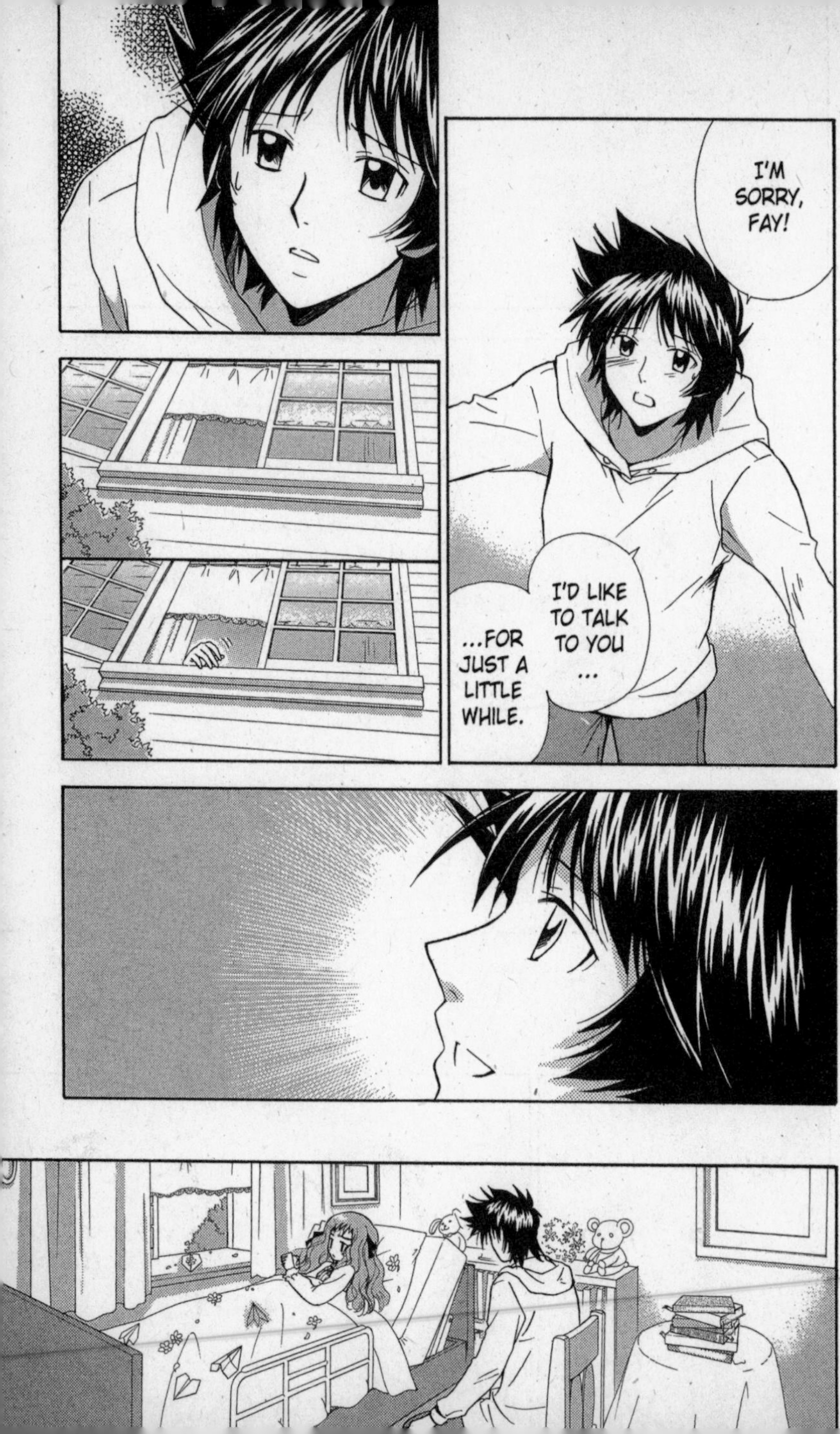
I'M SORRY, FAY!
I'D LIKE TO TALK TO YOU ...
...FOR JUST A LITTLE WHILE.

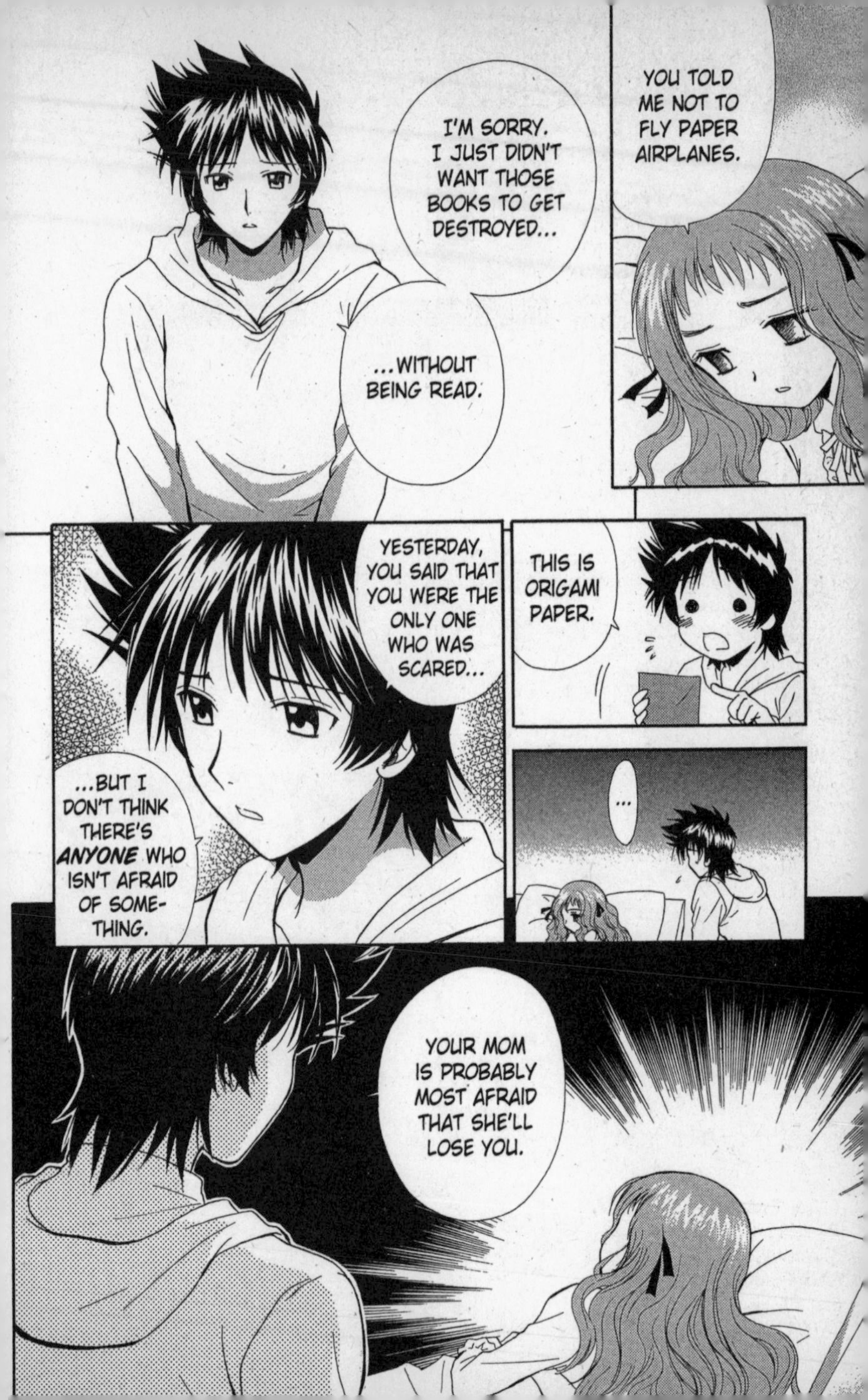
YOU TOLD ME NOT TO FLY PAPER AIRPLANES.
I'M SORRY. I JUST DIDN'T WANT THOSE BOOKS TO GET DESTROYED...
...WITHOUT BEING READ.
THIS IS ORIGAMI PAPER.
...
YESTERDAY, YOU SAID THAT YOU WERE THE ONLY ONE WHO WAS SCARED...
...BUT I DON'T THINK THERE'S ANYONE WHO ISN'T AFRAID OF SOME-THING.
YOUR MOM IS PROBABLY MOST AFRAID THAT SHE'LL LOSE YOU.

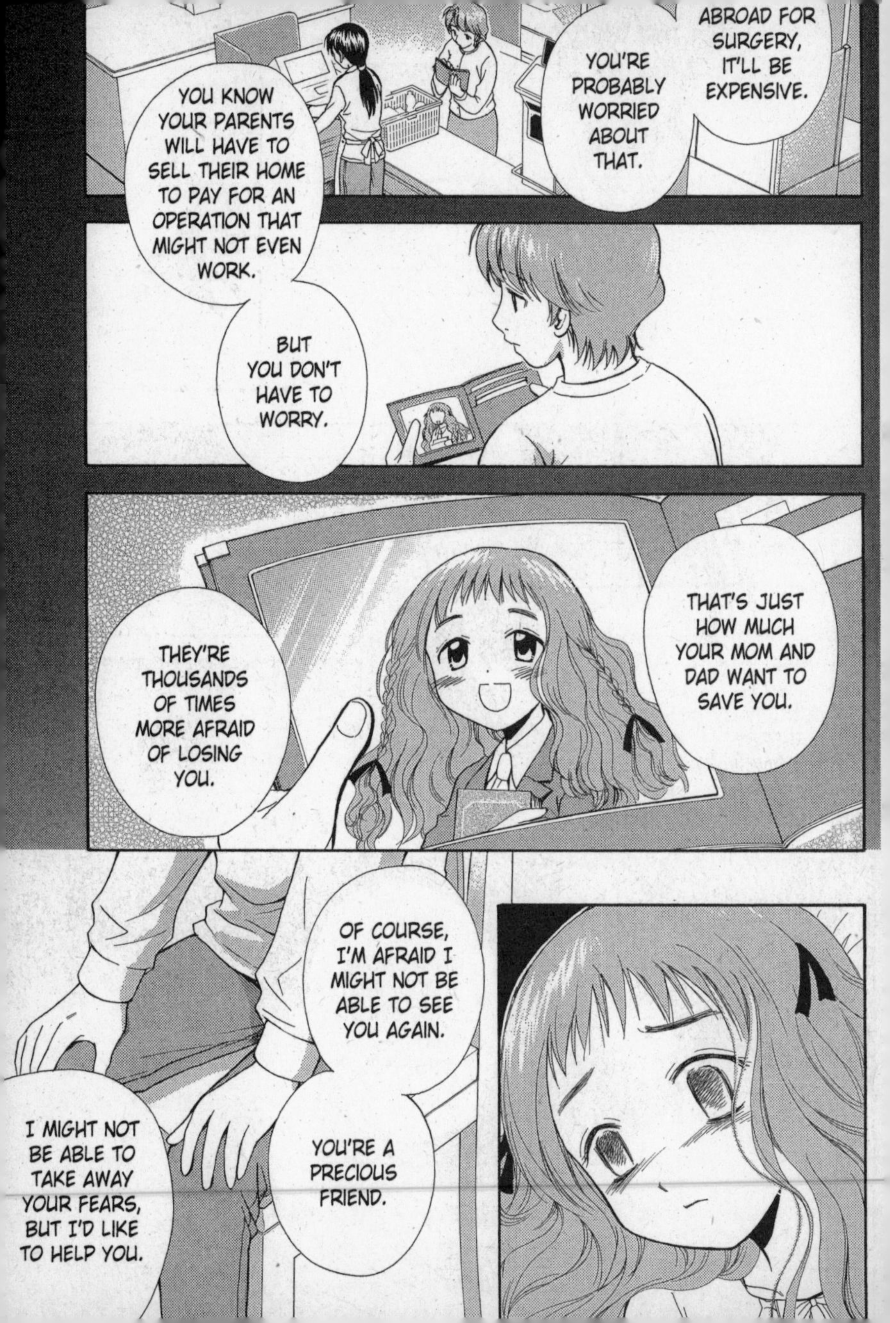
ABROAD FOR SURGERY, IT'LL BE EXPENSIVE.
YOU'RE PROBABLY WORRIED ABOUT THAT.
YOU KNOW YOUR PARENTS WILL HAVE TO SELL THEIR HOME TO PAY FOR AN OPERATION THAT MIGHT NOT EVEN WORK.
BUT YOU DON'T HAVE TO WORRY.
THAT'S JUST HOW MUCH YOUR MOM AND DAD WANT TO SAVE YOU.
THEY'RE THOUSANDS OF TIMES MORE AFRAID OF LOSING YOU.
OF COURSE, I'M AFRAID I MIGHT NOT BE ABLE TO SEE YOU AGAIN.
YOU'RE A PRECIOUS FRIEND.
I MIGHT NOT BE ABLE TO TAKE AWAY YOUR FEARS, BUT I'D LIKE TO HELP YOU.

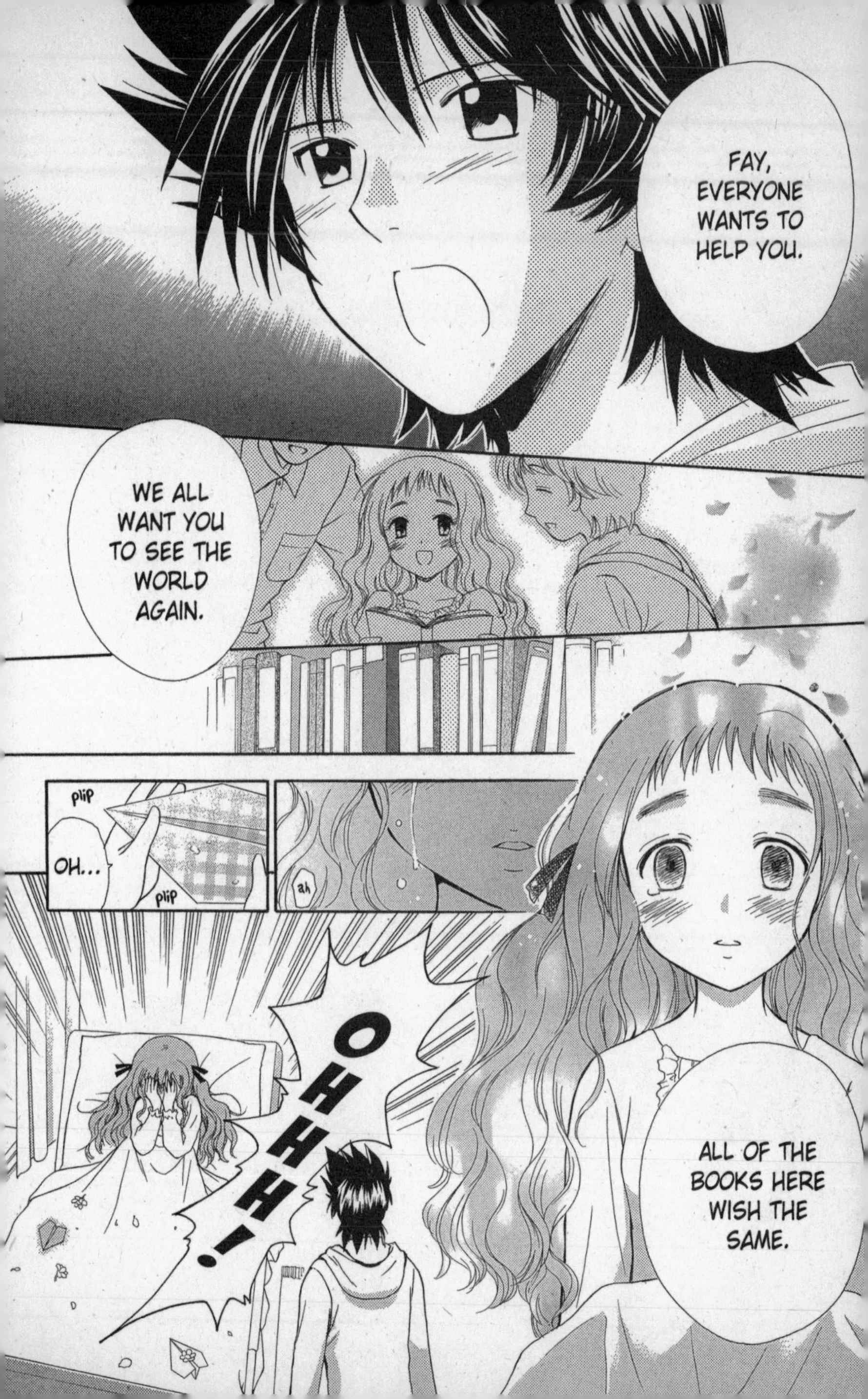
FAY, EVERYONE WANTS TO HELP YOU.
WE ALL WANT YOU TO SEE THE WORLD AGAIN.
ALL OF THE BOOKS HERE WISH THE SAME.
ah
plip
OH...
plip
OHHHH!

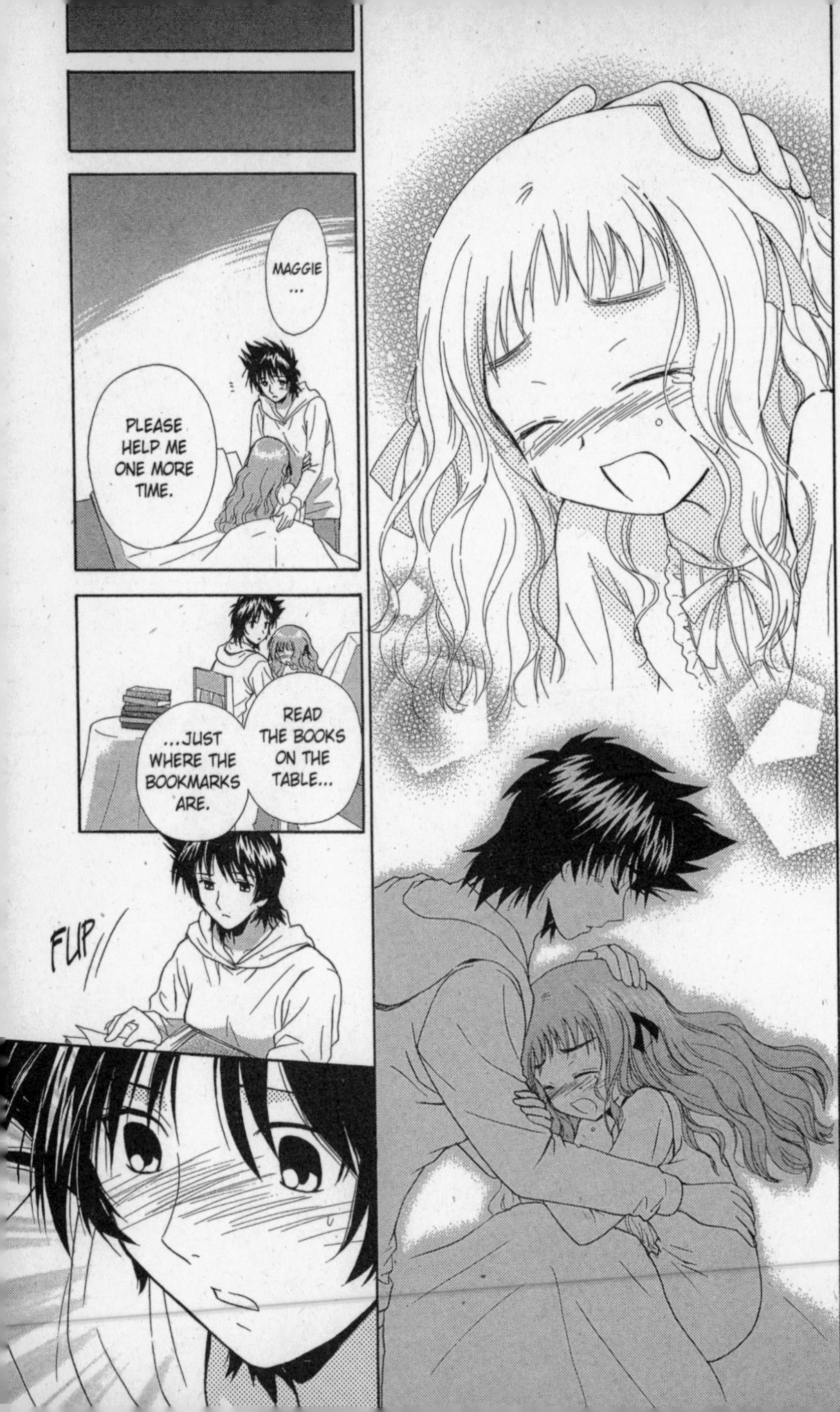
MAGGIE ...
PLEASE HELP ME ONE MORE TIME.
READ THE BOOKS ON THE TABLE...
...JUST WHERE THE BOOKMARKS ARE.
FLIP

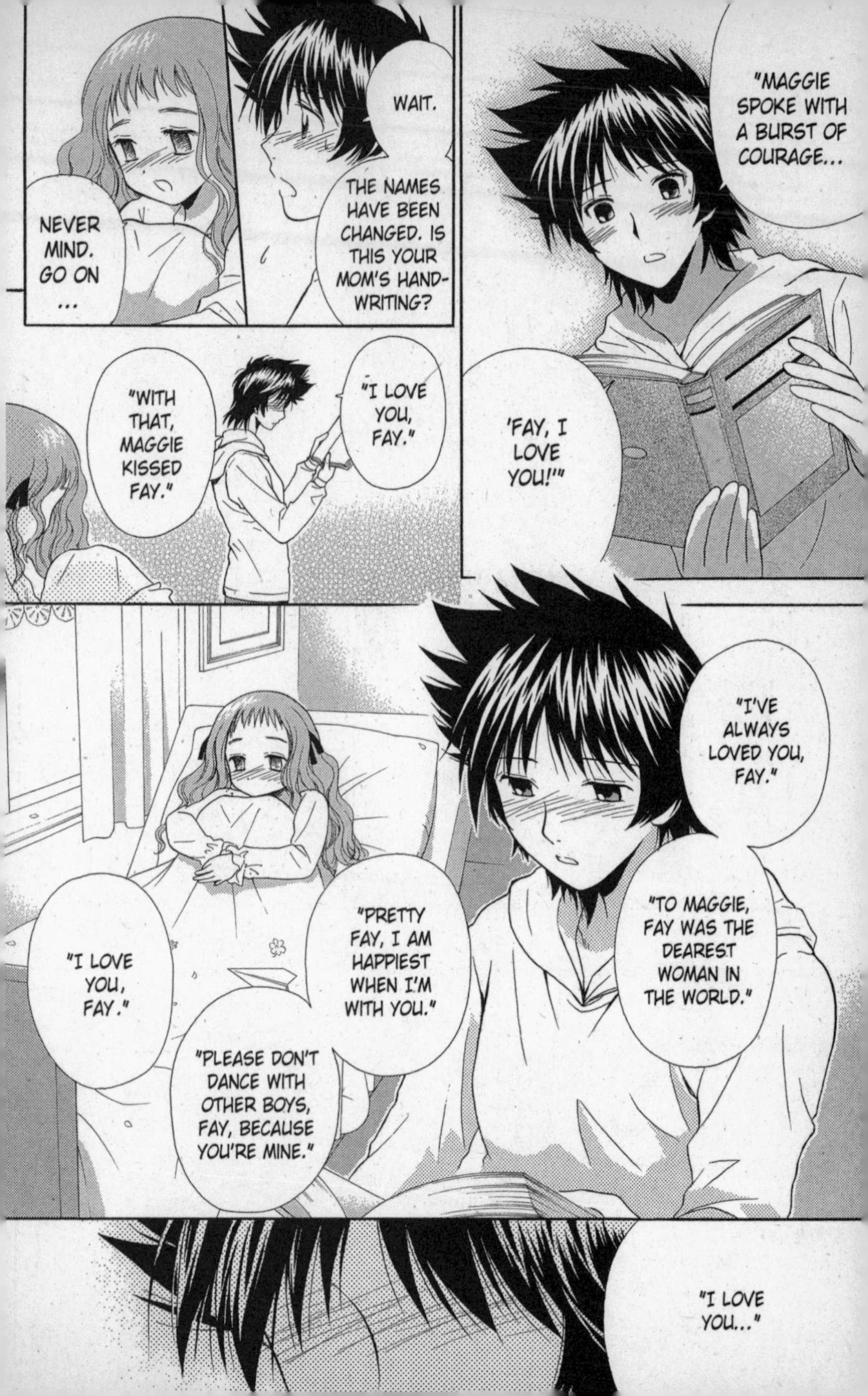
"MAGGIE SPOKE WITH A BURST OF COURAGE...
'FAY, I LOVE YOU!'"
WAIT.
THE NAMES HAVE BEEN CHANGED. IS THIS YOUR MOM'S HAND-WRITING?
NEVER MIND. GO ON ...
"I LOVE YOU, FAY."
"WITH THAT, MAGGIE KISSED FAY."
"I'VE ALWAYS LOVED YOU, FAY."
"TO MAGGIE, FAY WAS THE DEAREST WOMAN IN THE WORLD."
"PRETTY FAY, I AM HAPPIEST WHEN I'M WITH YOU."
"I LOVE YOU, FAY."
"PLEASE DON'T DANCE WITH OTHER BOYS, FAY, BECAUSE YOU'RE MINE."
"I LOVE YOU..."

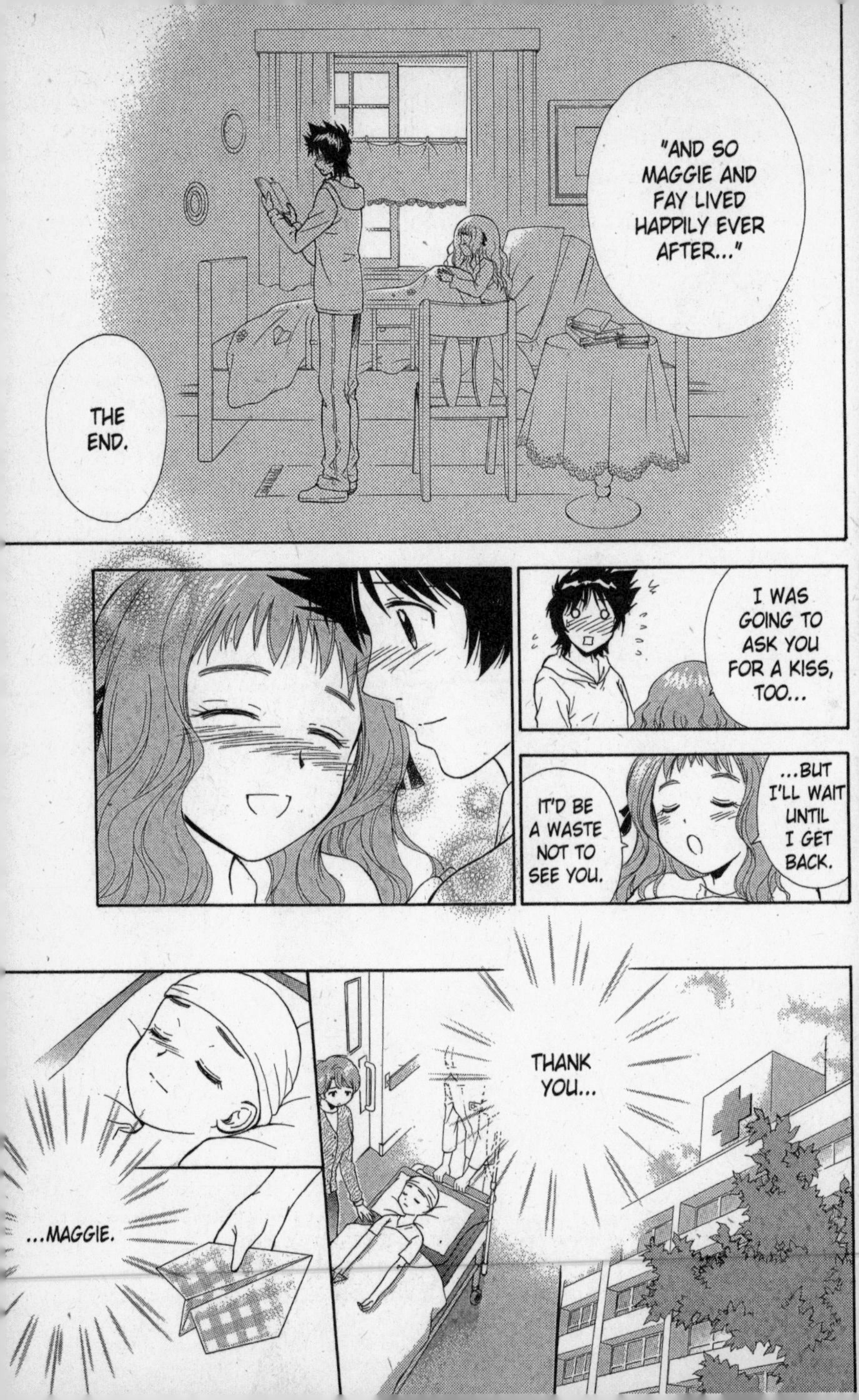
"AND SO MAGGIE AND FAY LIVED HAPPILY EVER AFTER..."
THE END.
I WAS GOING TO ASK YOU FOR A KISS, TOO...
...BUT I'LL WAIT UNTIL I GET BACK.
IT'D BE A WASTE NOT TO SEE YOU.
THANK YOU...
...MAGGIE.

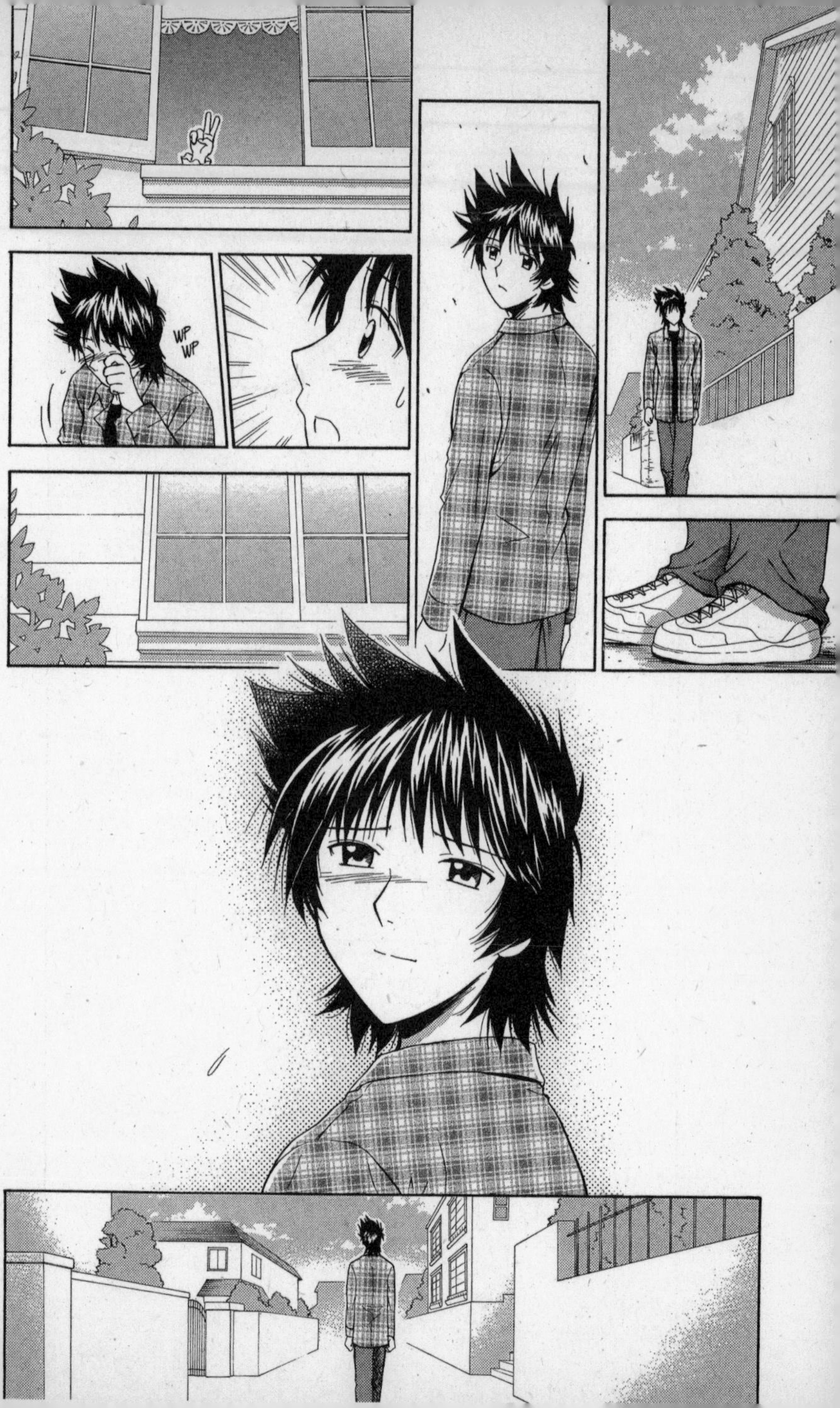
WP WP

CHAPTER 7

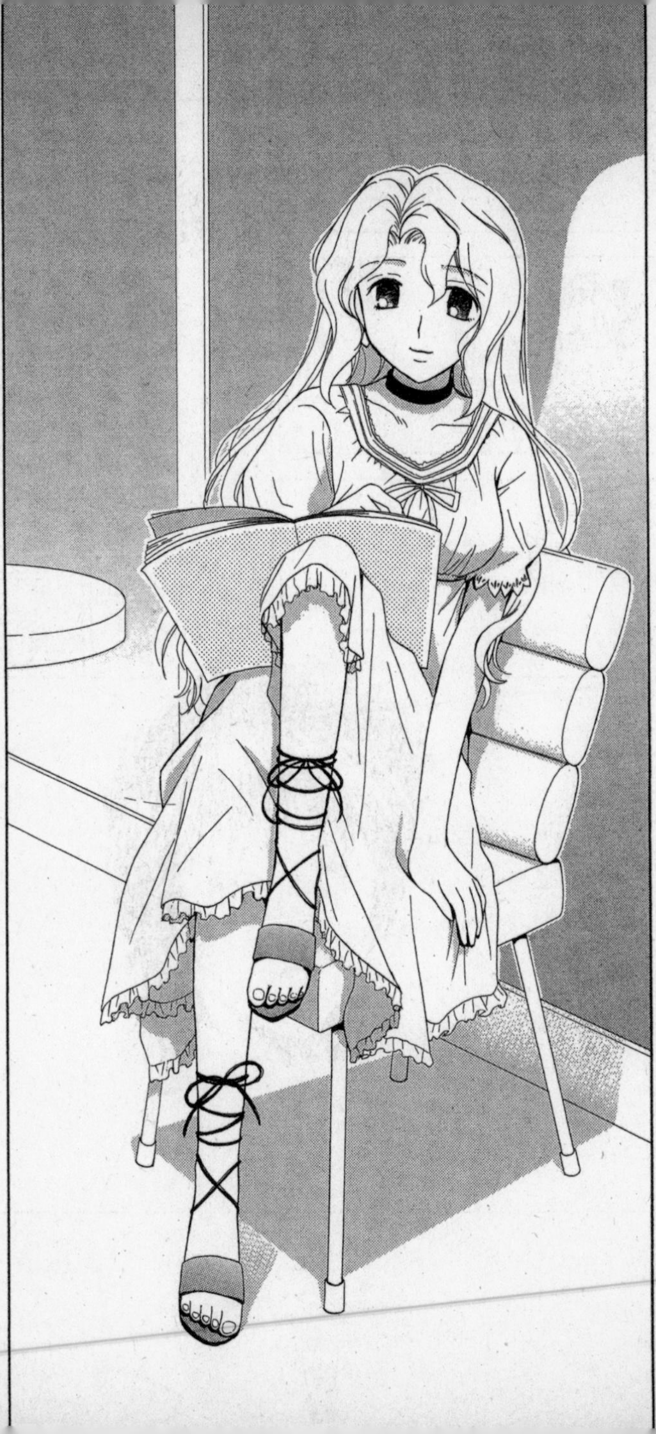

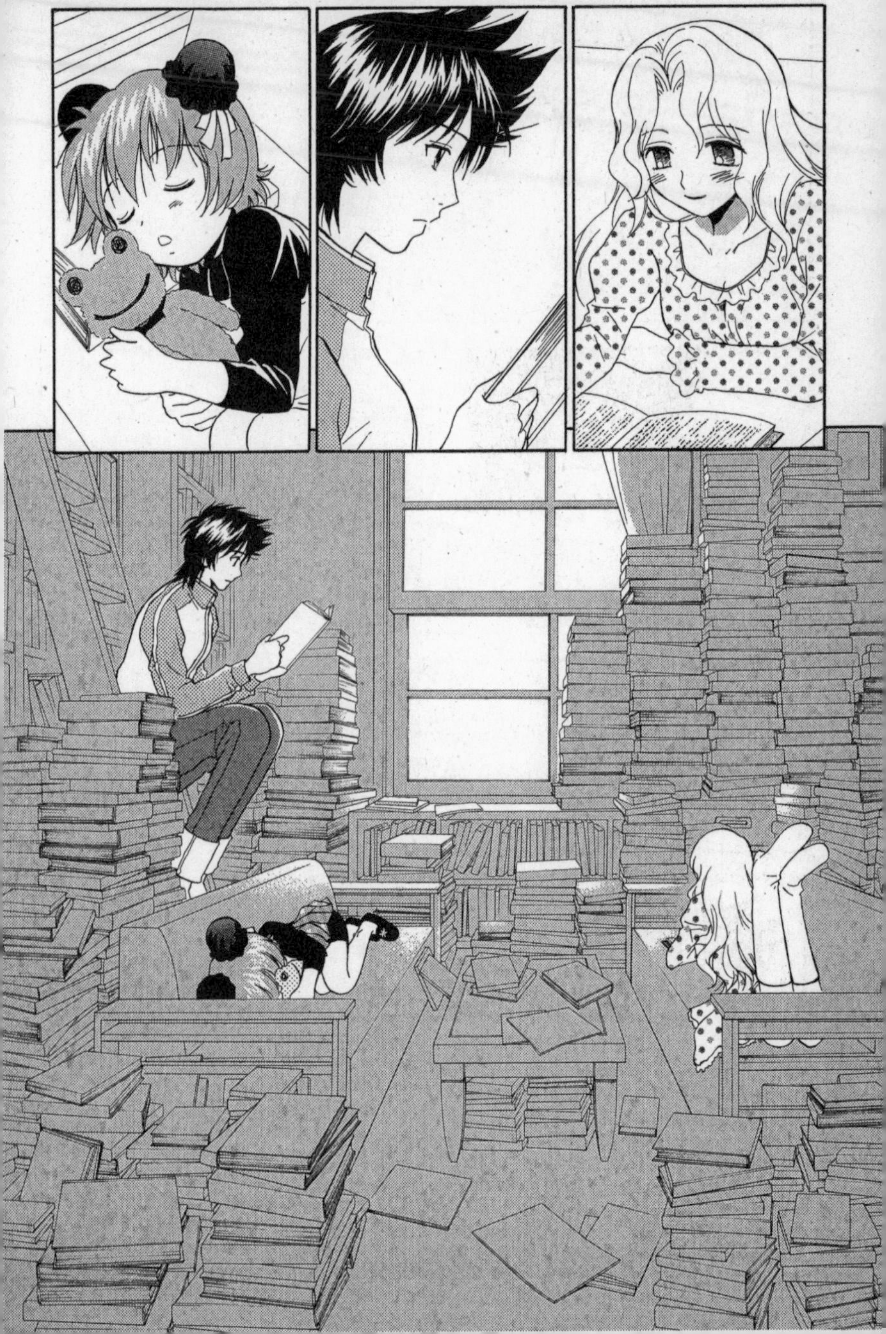

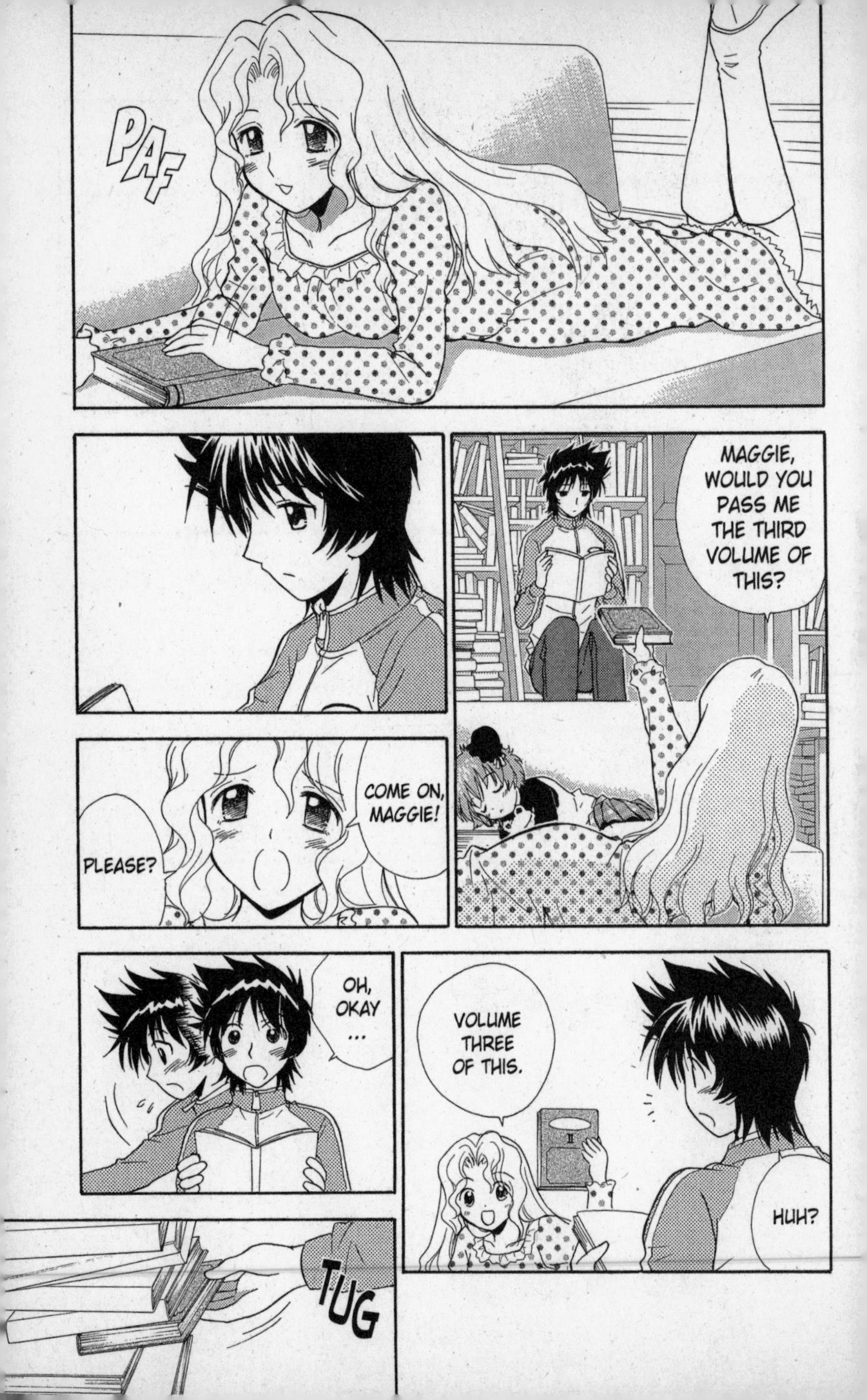
PAF
MAGGIE, WOULD YOU PASS ME THE THIRD VOLUME OF THIS?
COME ON, MAGGIE!
PLEASE?
VOLUME THREE OF THIS.
HUH?
OH, OKAY ...
TUG

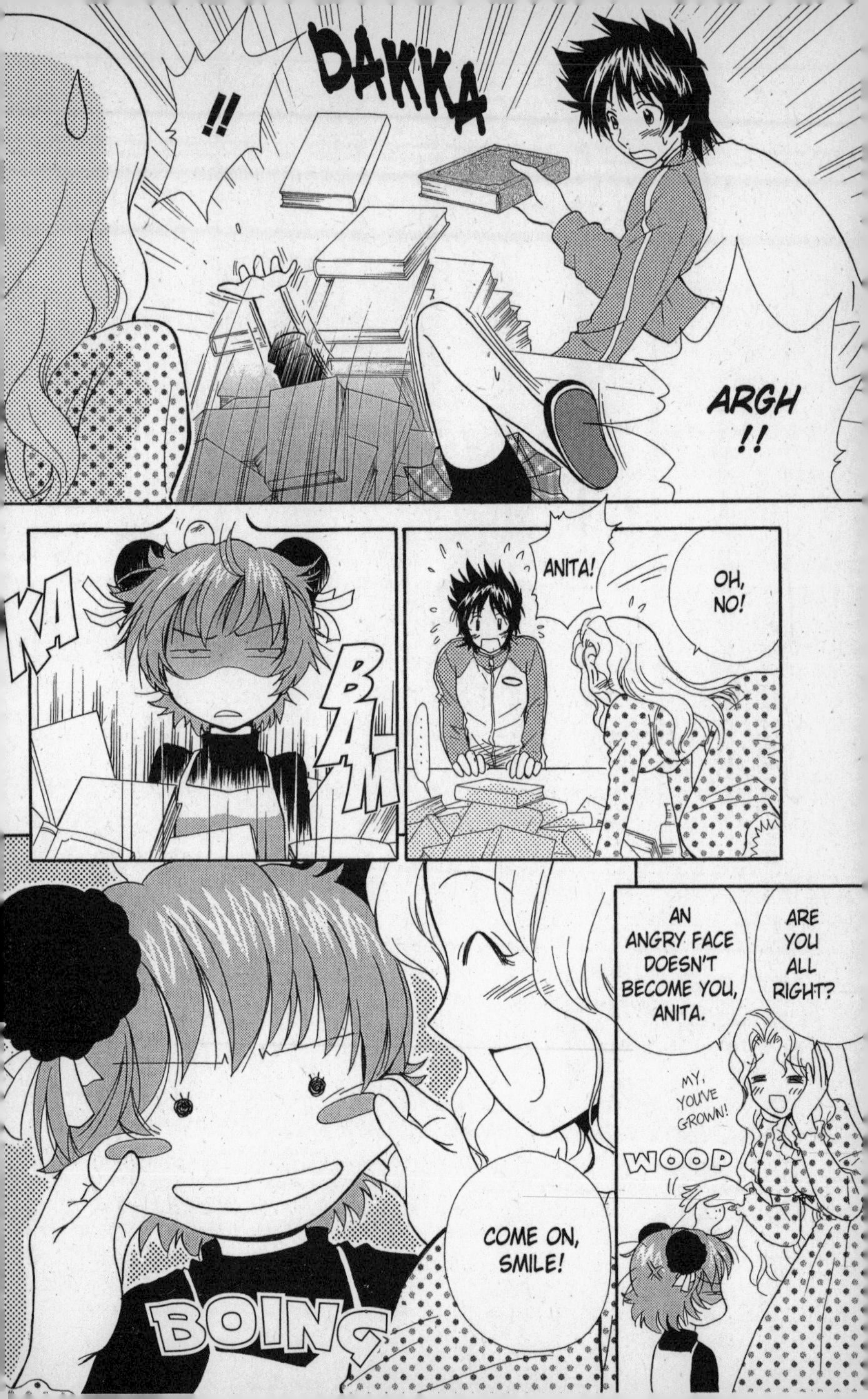
DAKKA
!!
ARGH !!
OH, NO!
ANITA!
BAM
KA
ARE YOU ALL RIGHT?
AN ANGRY FACE DOESN'T BECOME YOU, ANITA.
MY, YOU'VE GROWN!
WOOP
COME ON, SMILE!
BOING

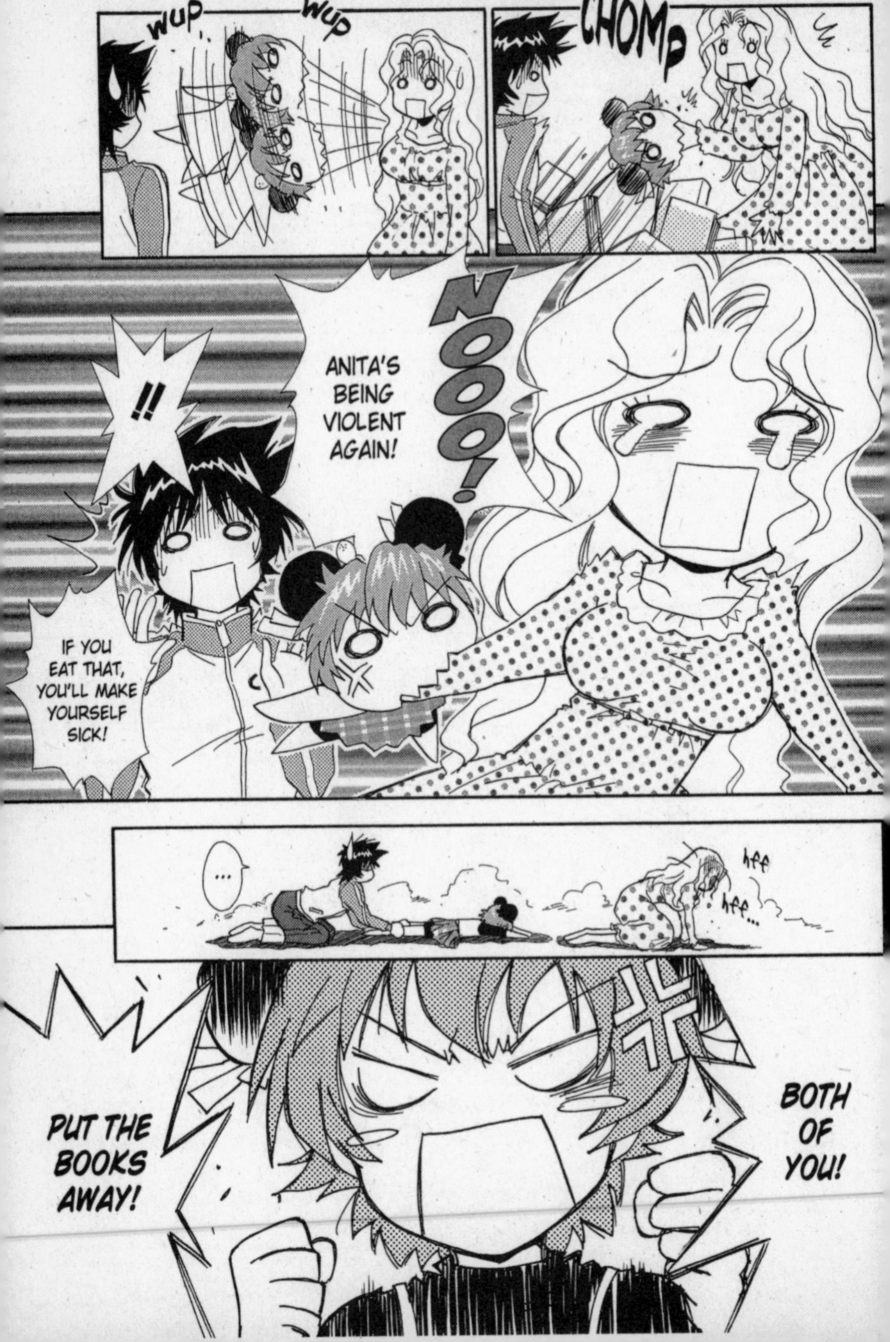
CHOMP
wup
wup
NOOO!
ANITA'S BEING VIOLENT AGAIN!
!!
IF YOU EAT THAT, YOU'LL MAKE YOURSELF SICK!
hff
hff...
...
BOTH OF YOU!
PUT THE BOOKS AWAY!

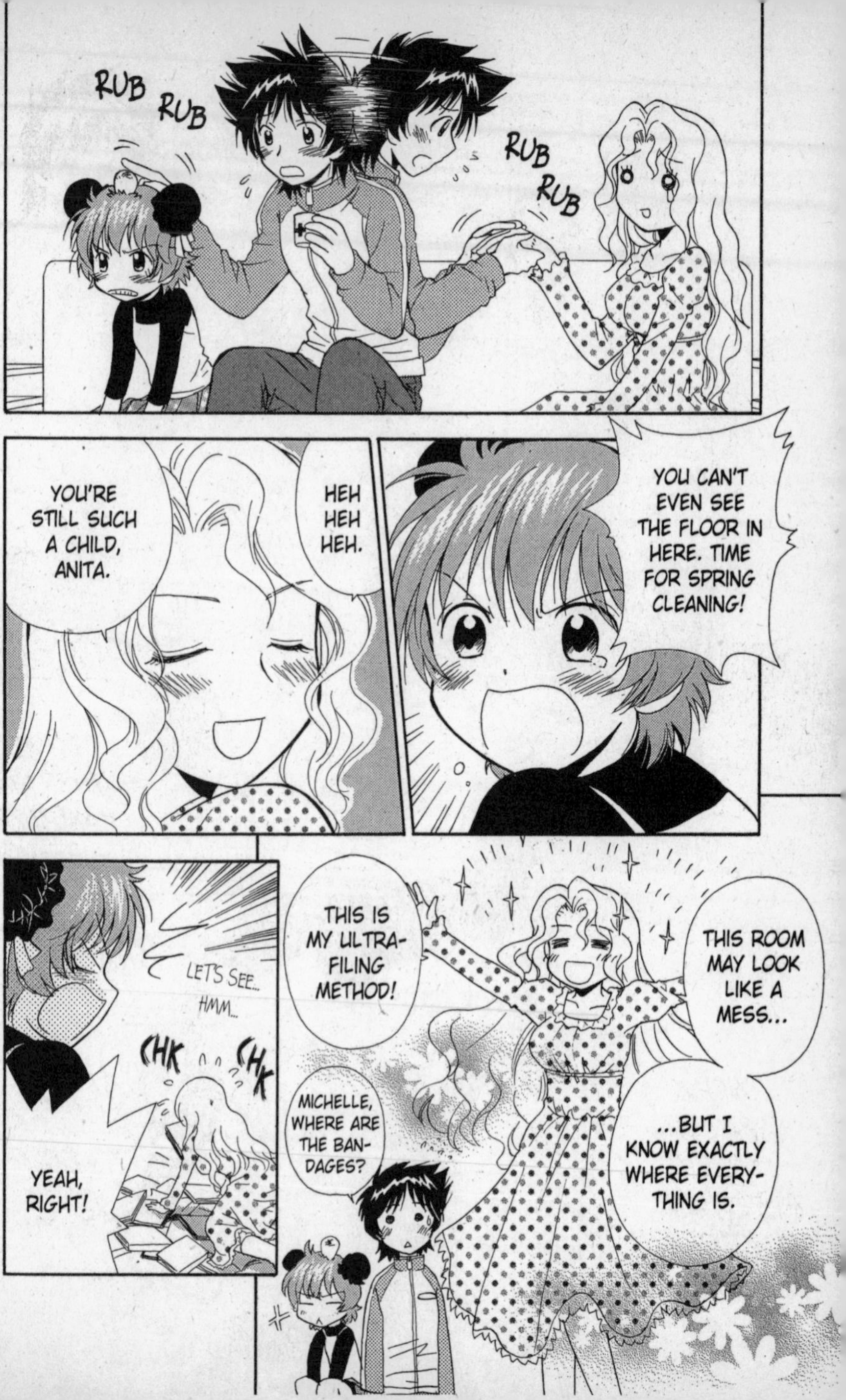
RUB RUB
RUB RUB
YOU CAN'T EVEN SEE THE FLOOR IN HERE. TIME FOR SPRING CLEANING!
HEH HEH HEH.
YOU'RE STILL SUCH A CHILD, ANITA.
THIS ROOM MAY LOOK LIKE A MESS...
THIS IS MY ULTRA-FILING METHOD!
...BUT I KNOW EXACTLY WHERE EVERY-THING IS.
MICHELLE, WHERE ARE THE BAN-DAGES?
LET'S SEE... HMM...
CHK CHK
YEAH, RIGHT!

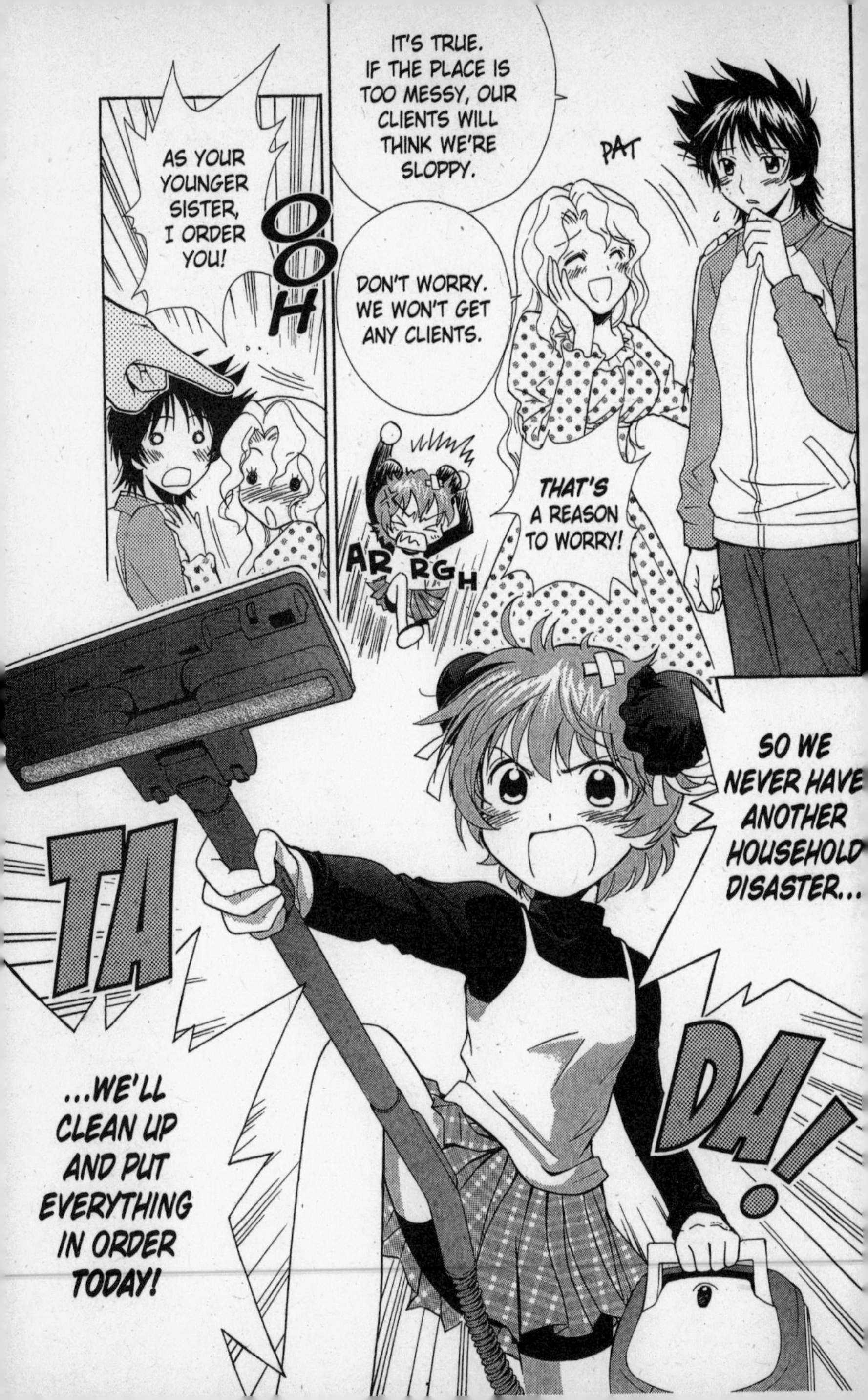
IT'S TRUE. IF THE PLACE IS TOO MESSY, OUR CLIENTS WILL THINK WE'RE SLOPPY.
PAT
DON'T WORRY. WE WON'T GET ANY CLIENTS.
THAT'S A REASON TO WORRY!
ARRGH
AS YOUR YOUNGER SISTER, I ORDER YOU!
OOH
SO WE NEVER HAVE ANOTHER HOUSEHOLD DISASTER...
TA
DA!
...WE'LL CLEAN UP AND PUT EVERYTHING IN ORDER TODAY!

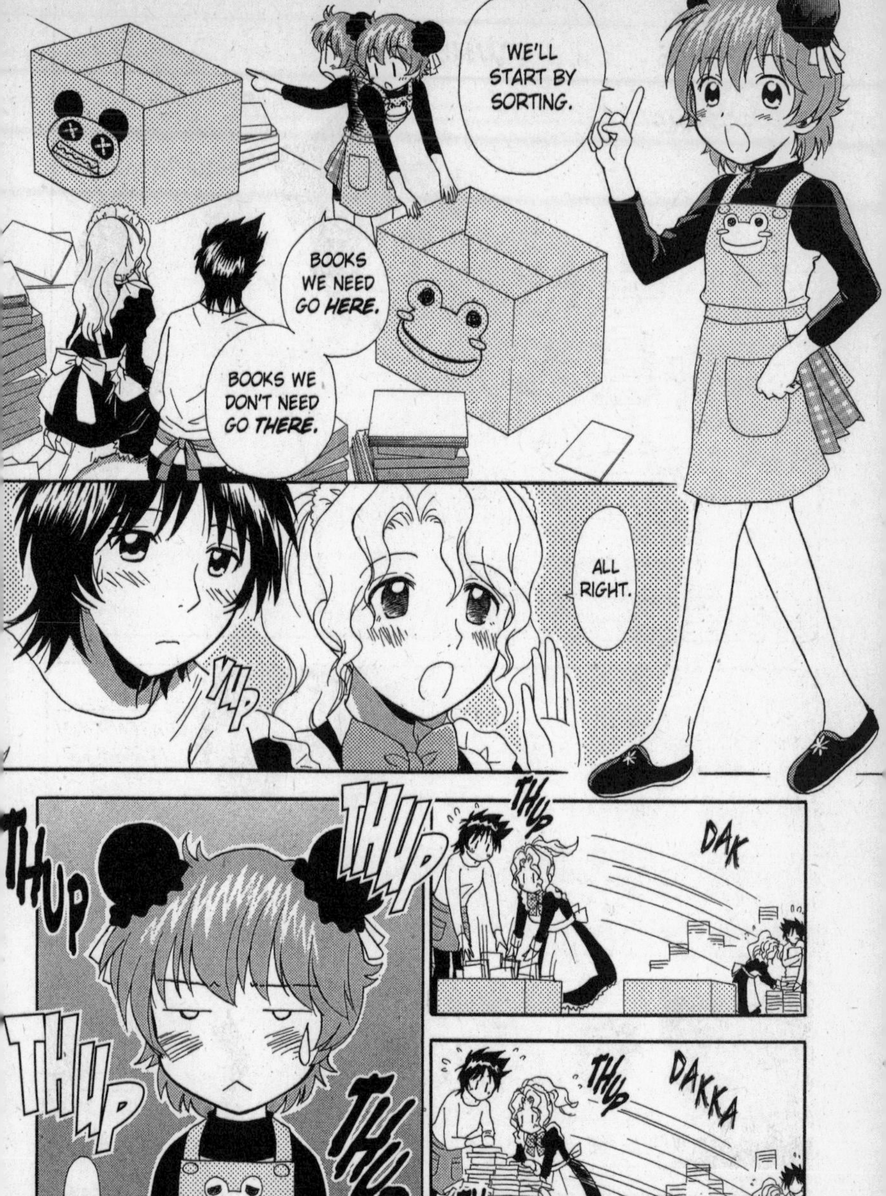

WE'LL START BY SORTING.
BOOKS WE NEED GO HERE.
BOOKS WE DON'T NEED GO THERE.
ALL RIGHT.
YUP
THUP
DAK
THUP
DAKKA
THUP
THUP
THUP
THUP
THUP
...

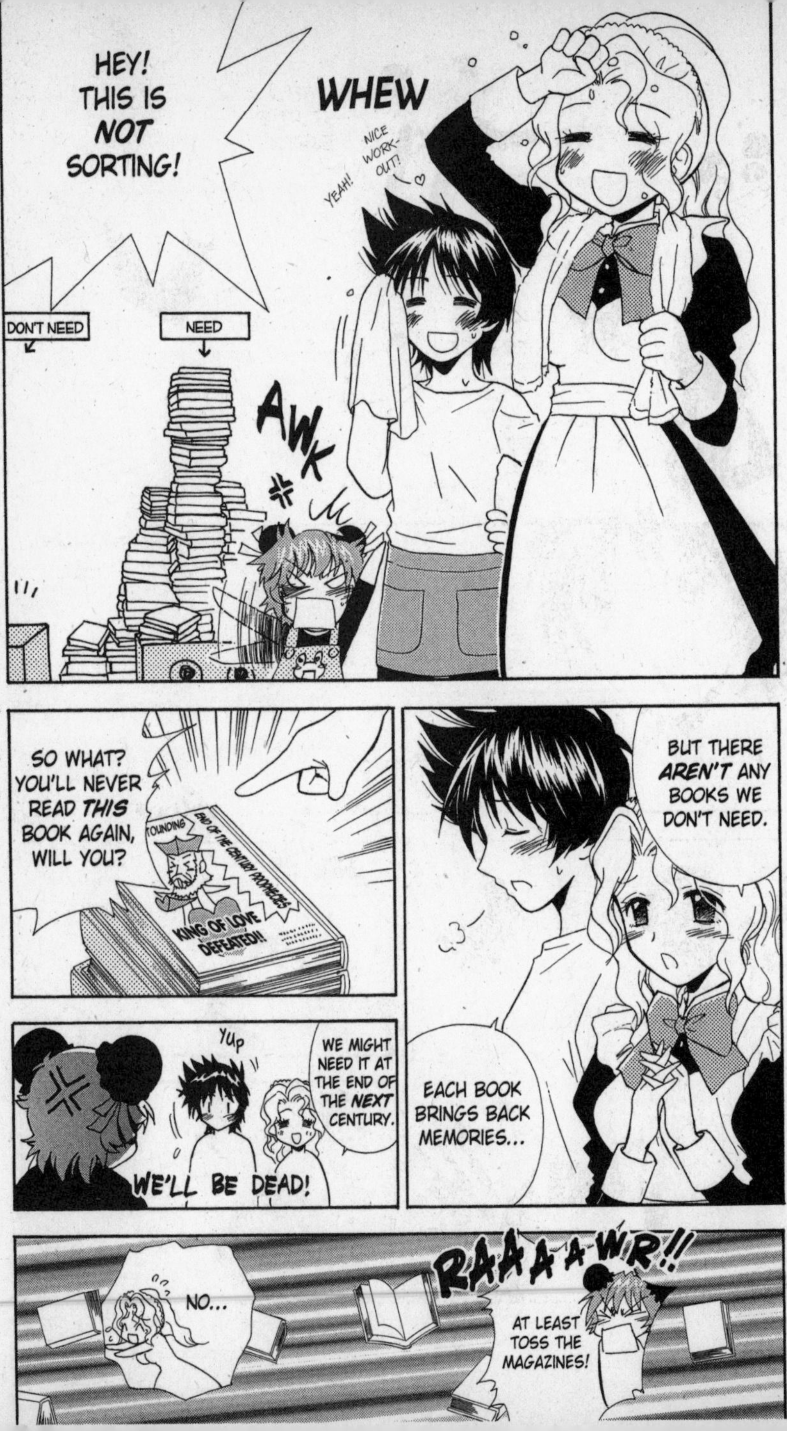
WHEW
NICE WORK-OUT!
YEAH!
HEY! THIS IS **NOT** SORTING!
AWK
NEED
DON'T NEED
BUT THERE **AREN'T** ANY BOOKS WE DON'T NEED.
EACH BOOK BRINGS BACK MEMORIES...
SO WHAT? YOU'LL NEVER READ **THIS** BOOK AGAIN, WILL YOU?
TOUNDING
END OF THE CENTURY PROPHECIES
KING OF LOVE DEFEATED!!
WE MIGHT NEED IT AT THE END OF THE **NEXT** CENTURY.
YUp
WE'LL BE DEAD!
RAAAAWR!!
AT LEAST TOSS THE MAGAZINES!
NO...

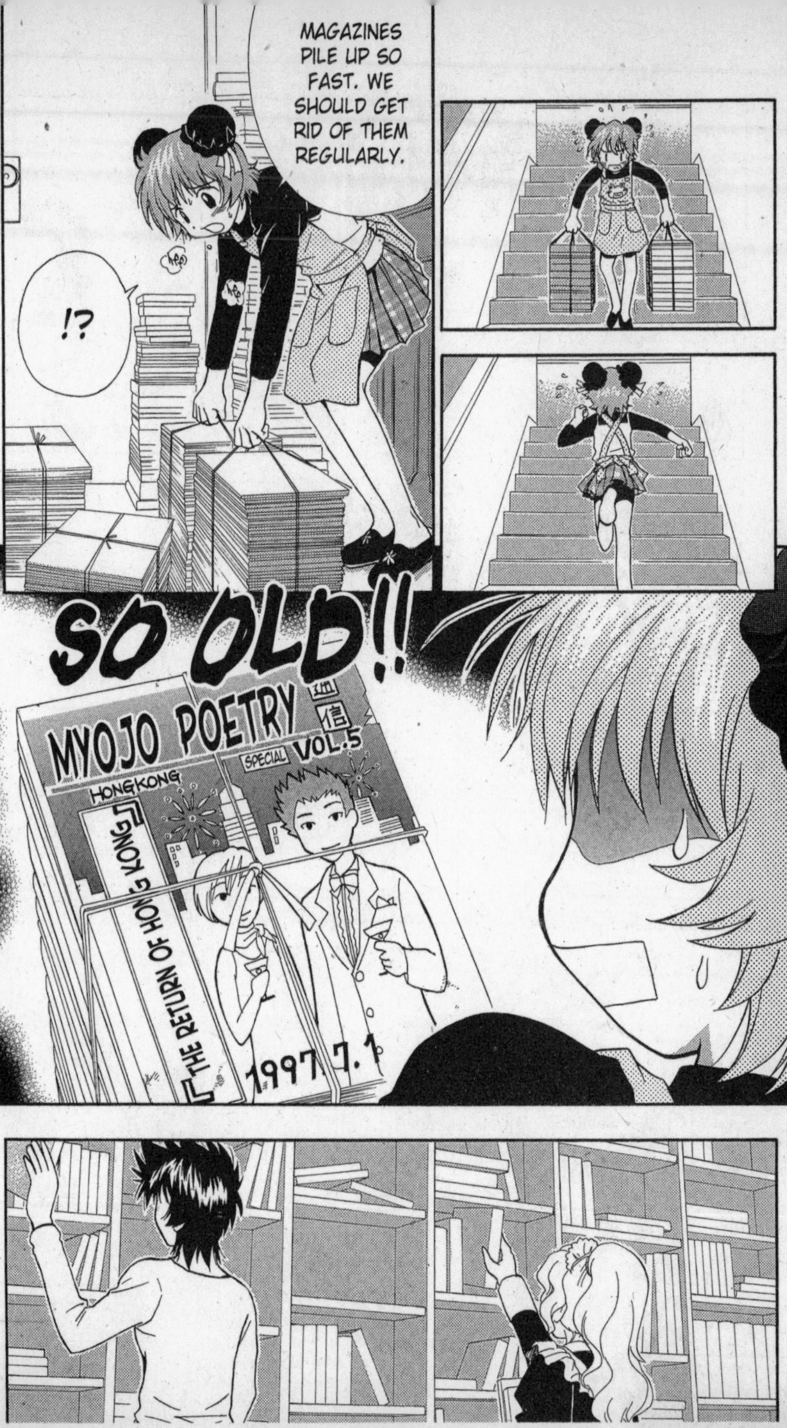
MAGAZINES PILE UP SO FAST. WE SHOULD GET RID OF THEM REGULARLY.
!?
SO OLD!!
MYOJO POETRY
通信
VOL.5
SPECIAL
HONGKONG
THE RETURN OF HONG KONG
1997.7.1

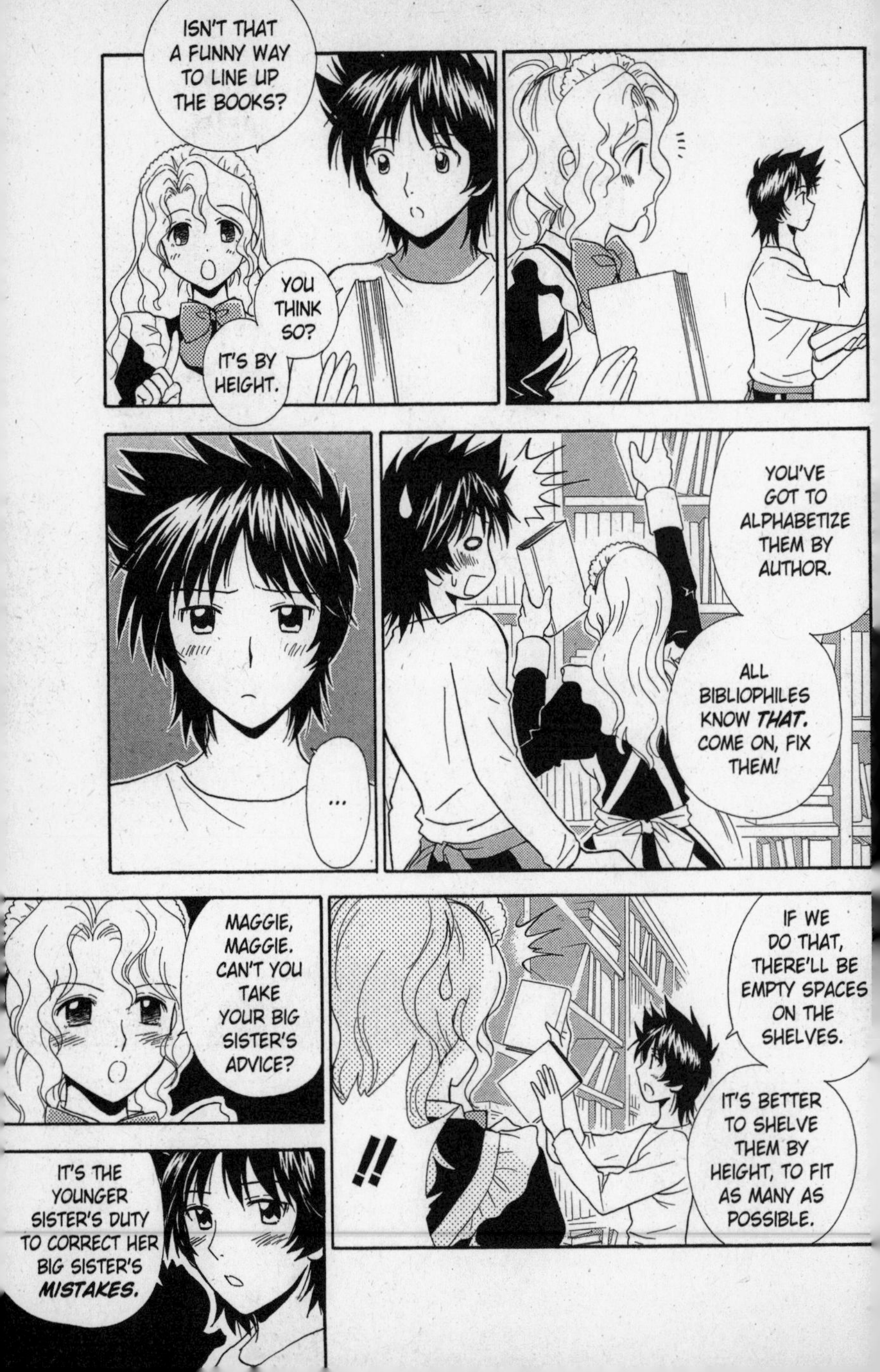
ISN'T THAT A FUNNY WAY TO LINE UP THE BOOKS?
YOU THINK SO?
IT'S BY HEIGHT.
YOU'VE GOT TO ALPHABETIZE THEM BY AUTHOR.
ALL BIBLIOPHILES KNOW *THAT.* COME ON, FIX THEM!
...
IF WE DO THAT, THERE'LL BE EMPTY SPACES ON THE SHELVES.
IT'S BETTER TO SHELVE THEM BY HEIGHT, TO FIT AS MANY AS POSSIBLE.
!!
MAGGIE, MAGGIE. CAN'T YOU TAKE YOUR BIG SISTER'S ADVICE?
IT'S THE YOUNGER SISTER'S DUTY TO CORRECT HER BIG SISTER'S *MISTAKES.*

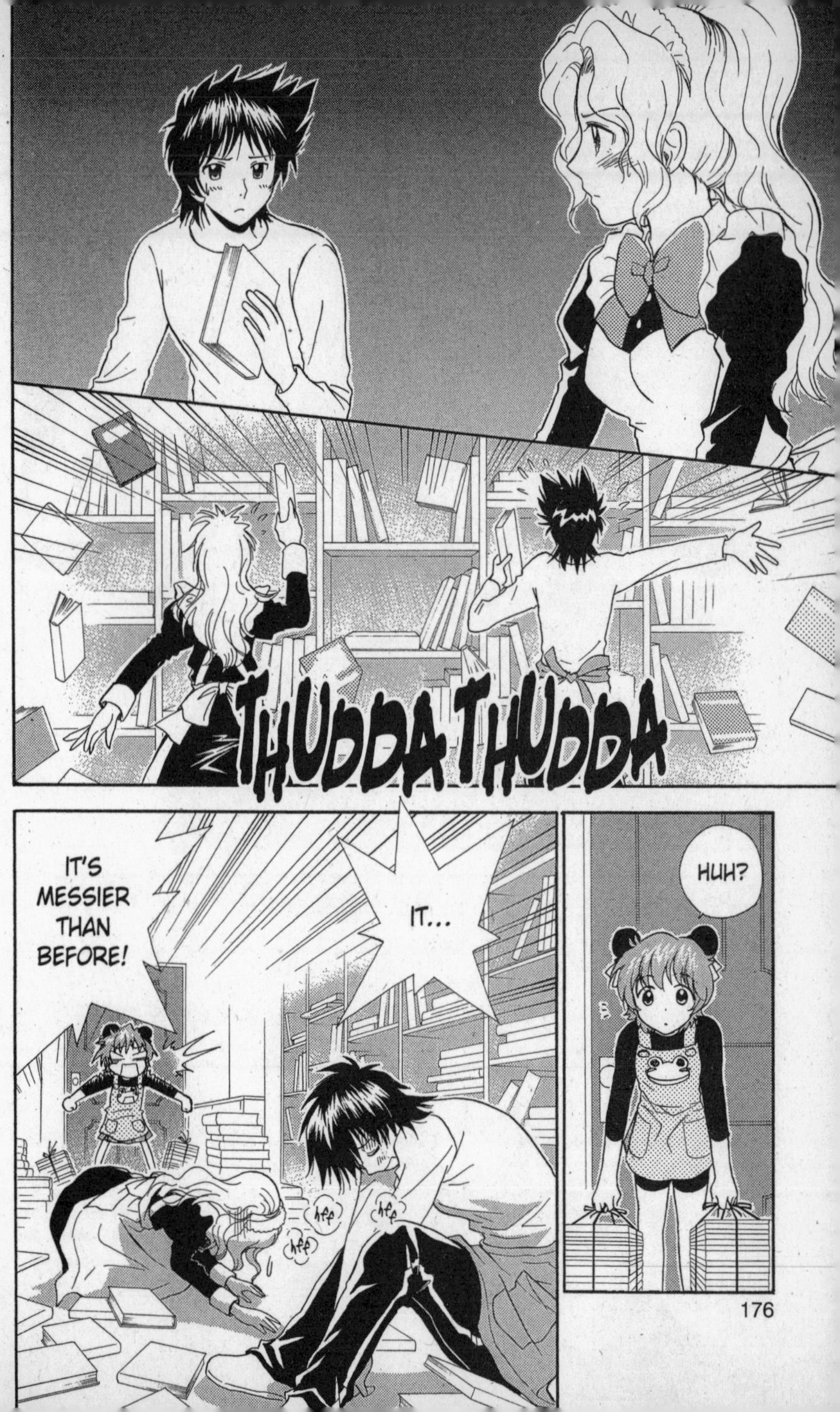
THUDDA THUDDA
HUH?
IT...
IT'S MESSIER THAN BEFORE!
hff
hff
hff

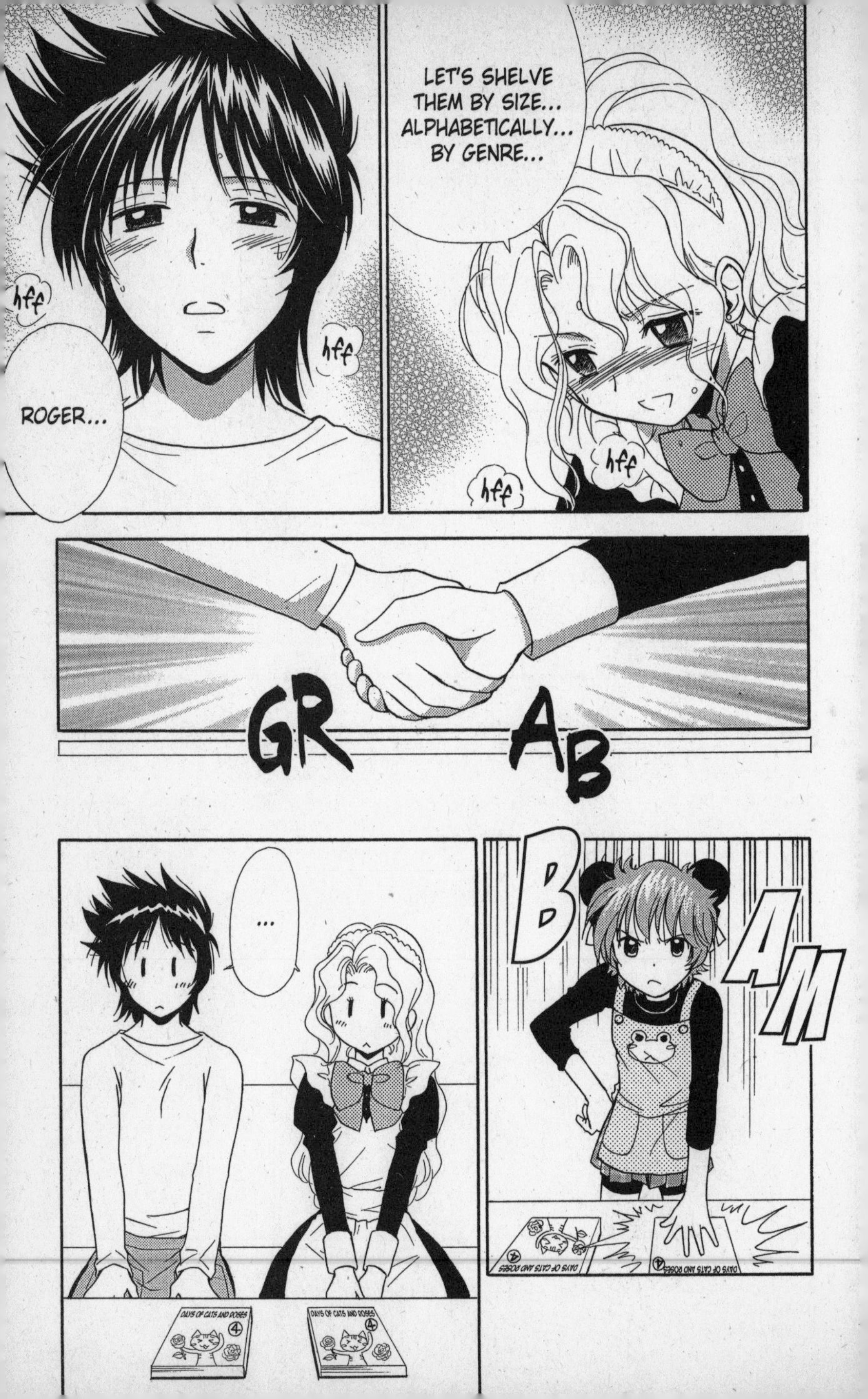
LET'S SHELVE THEM BY SIZE... ALPHABETICALLY... BY GENRE...
hff
hff
hff
hff
ROGER...
GRAB
BAM
DAYS OF CATS AND ROSES 4
DAYS OF CATS AND ROSES 4
...
DAYS OF CATS AND ROSES 4
DAYS OF CATS AND ROSES 4

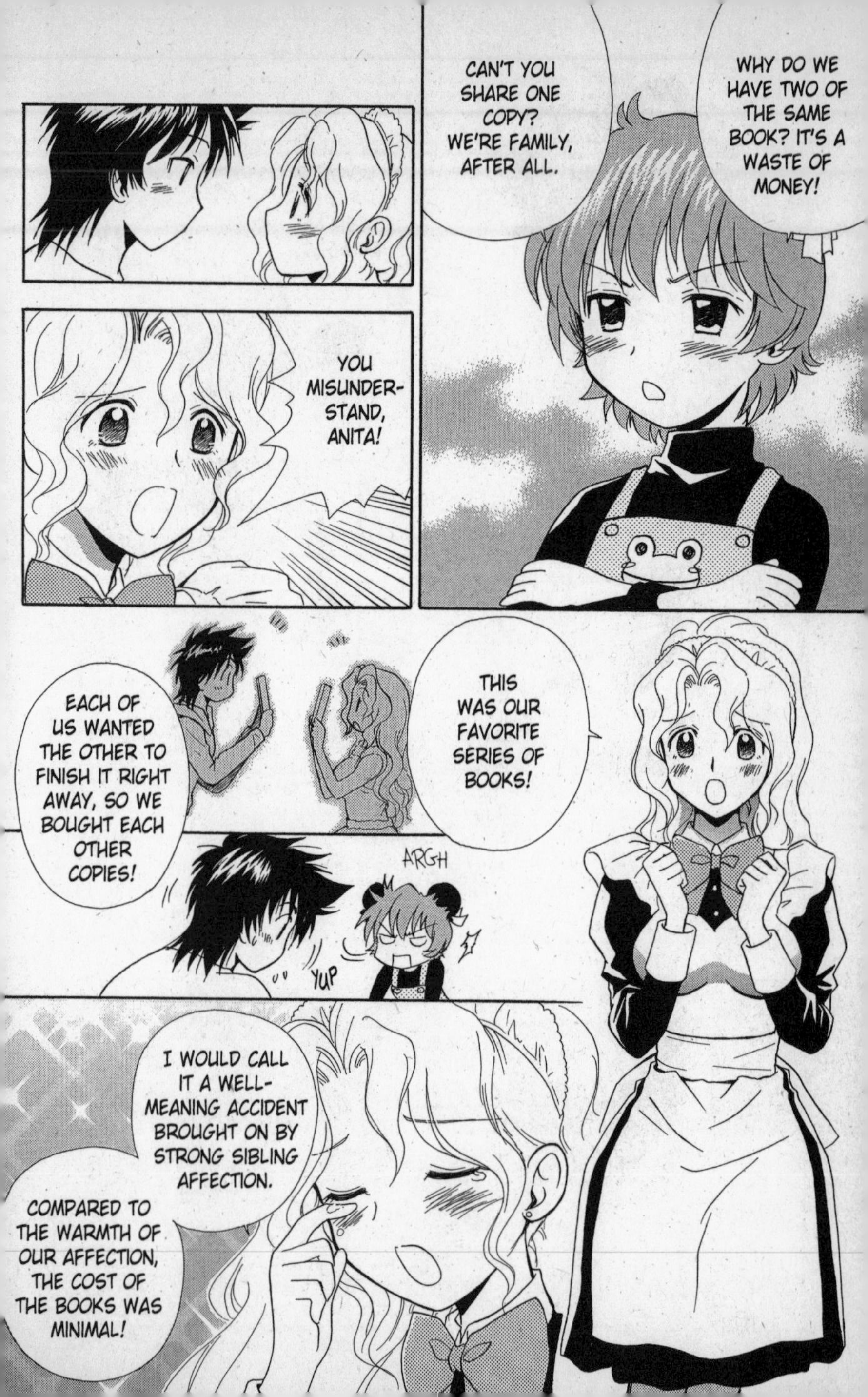
WHY DO WE HAVE TWO OF THE SAME BOOK? IT'S A WASTE OF MONEY!
CAN'T YOU SHARE ONE COPY? WE'RE FAMILY, AFTER ALL.
YOU MISUNDER-STAND, ANITA!
THIS WAS OUR FAVORITE SERIES OF BOOKS!
EACH OF US WANTED THE OTHER TO FINISH IT RIGHT AWAY, SO WE BOUGHT EACH OTHER COPIES!
ARGH
YUP
I WOULD CALL IT A WELL-MEANING ACCIDENT BROUGHT ON BY STRONG SIBLING AFFECTION.
COMPARED TO THE WARMTH OF OUR AFFECTION, THE COST OF THE BOOKS WAS MINIMAL!

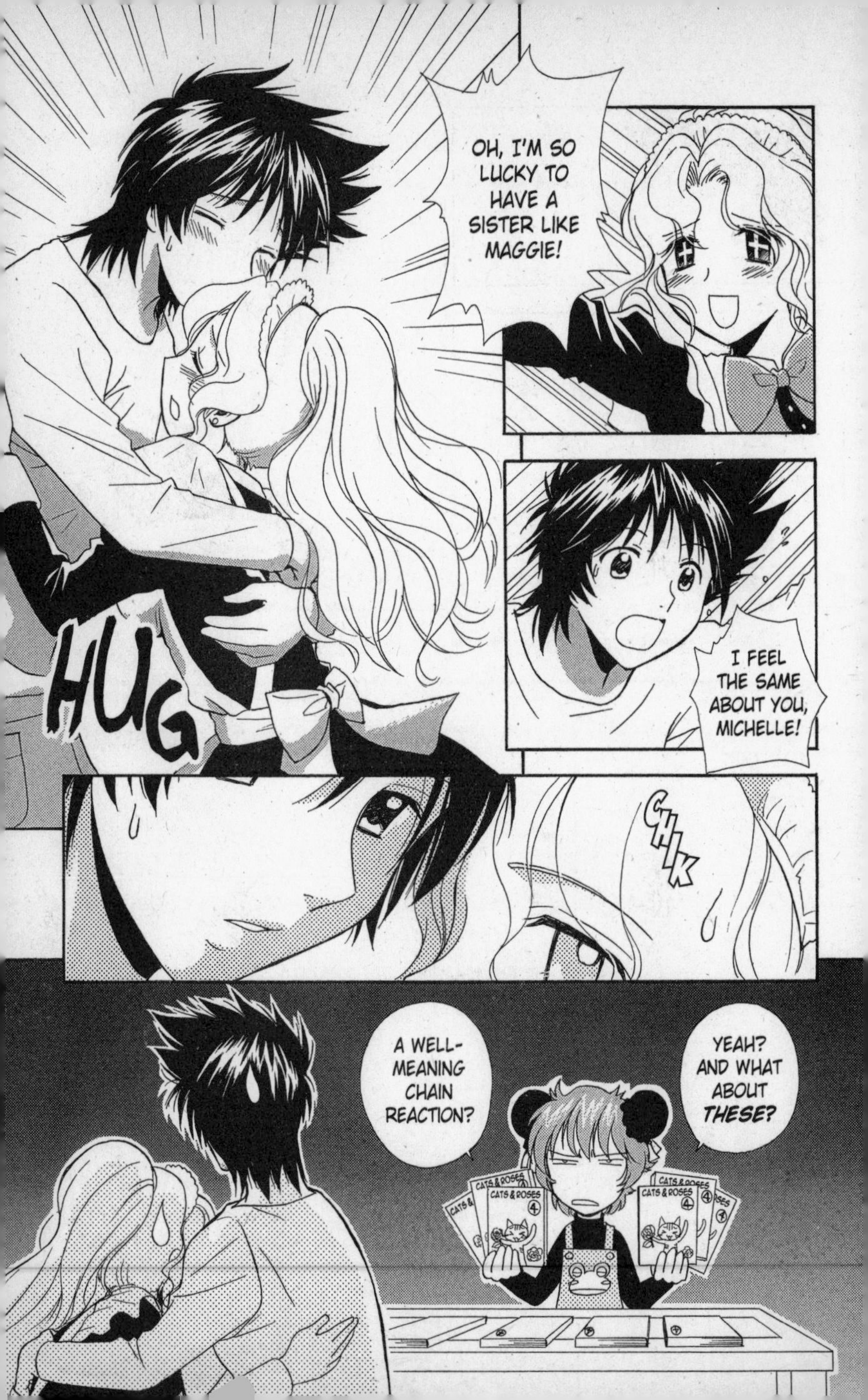
OH, I'M SO LUCKY TO HAVE A SISTER LIKE MAGGIE!
I FEEL THE SAME ABOUT YOU, MICHELLE!
HUG
CHIK
YEAH? AND WHAT ABOUT *THESE?*
A WELL-MEANING CHAIN REACTION?
CATS & ROSES 4

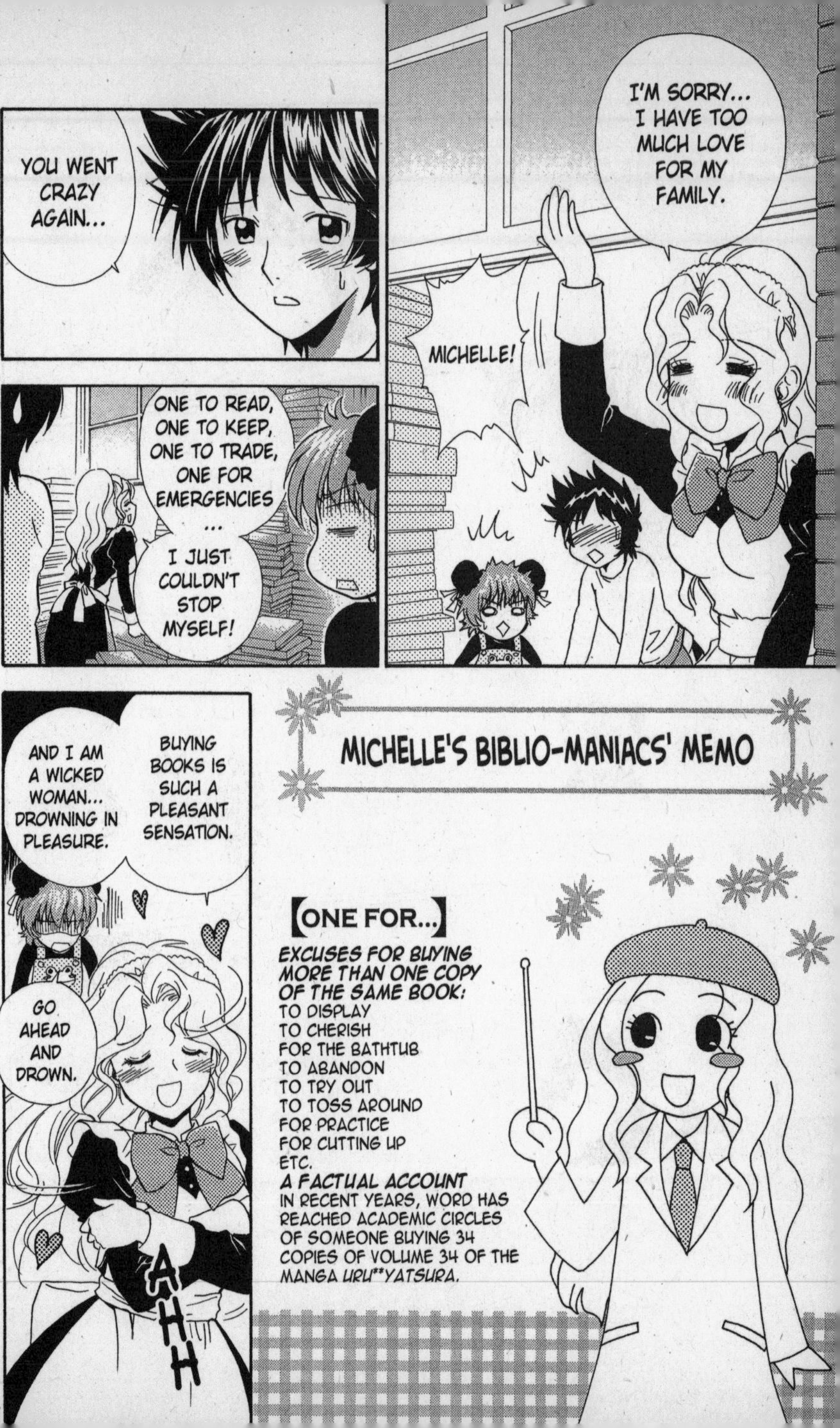
I'M SORRY... I HAVE TOO MUCH LOVE FOR MY FAMILY.
MICHELLE!
YOU WENT CRAZY AGAIN...
ONE TO READ, ONE TO KEEP, ONE TO TRADE, ONE FOR EMERGENCIES...
I JUST COULDN'T STOP MYSELF!
MICHELLE'S BIBLIO-MANIACS' MEMO
【ONE FOR...】
EXCUSES FOR BUYING MORE THAN ONE COPY OF THE SAME BOOK:
TO DISPLAY
TO CHERISH
FOR THE BATHTUB
TO ABANDON
TO TRY OUT
TO TOSS AROUND
FOR PRACTICE
FOR CUTTING UP
ETC.
A FACTUAL ACCOUNT
IN RECENT YEARS, WORD HAS REACHED ACADEMIC CIRCLES OF SOMEONE BUYING 34 COPIES OF VOLUME 34 OF THE MANGA URU**YATSURA.
BUYING BOOKS IS SUCH A PLEASANT SENSATION.
AND I AM A WICKED WOMAN... DROWNING IN PLEASURE.
GO AHEAD AND DROWN.
AHHH

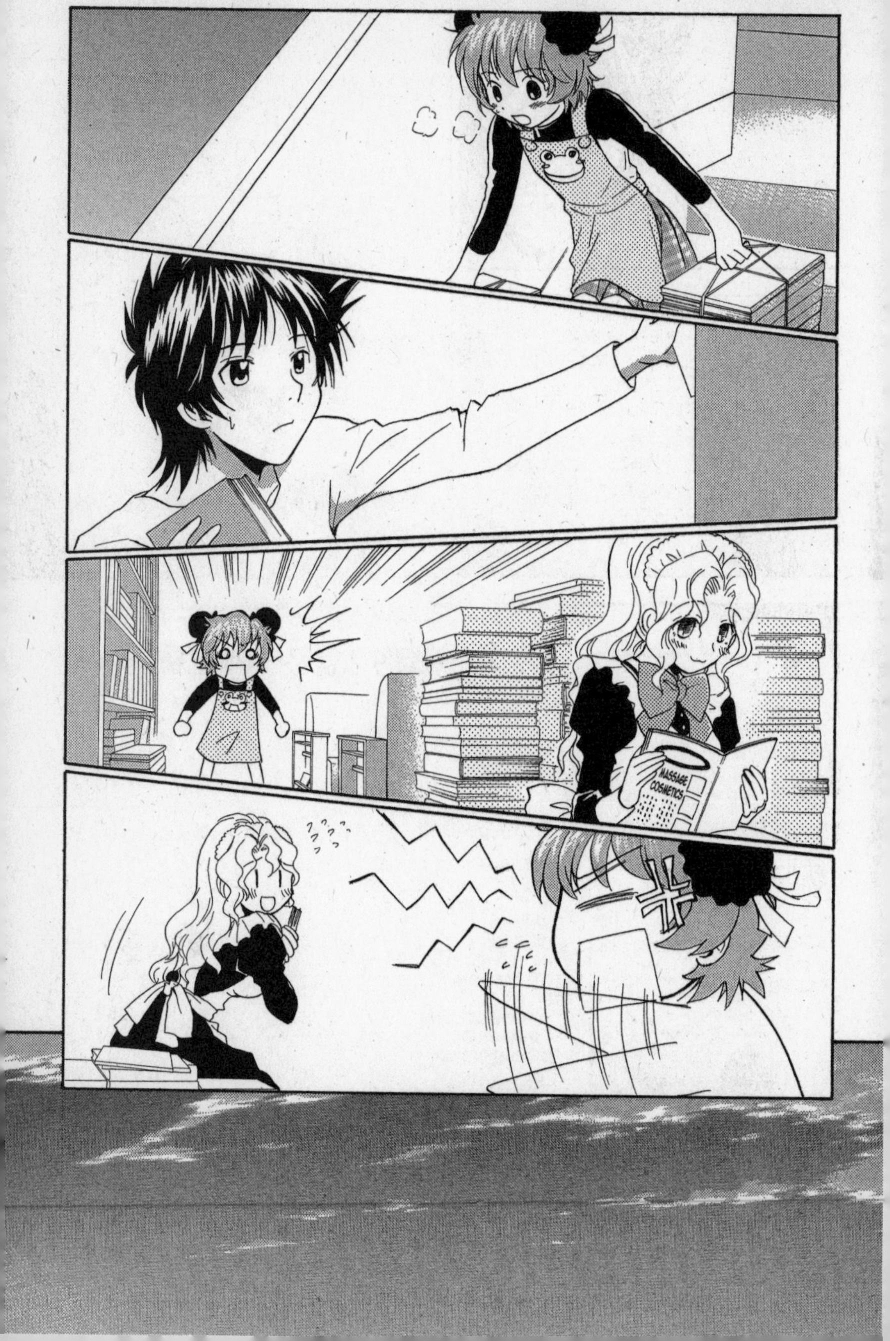
MASSAGE
COSMETICS

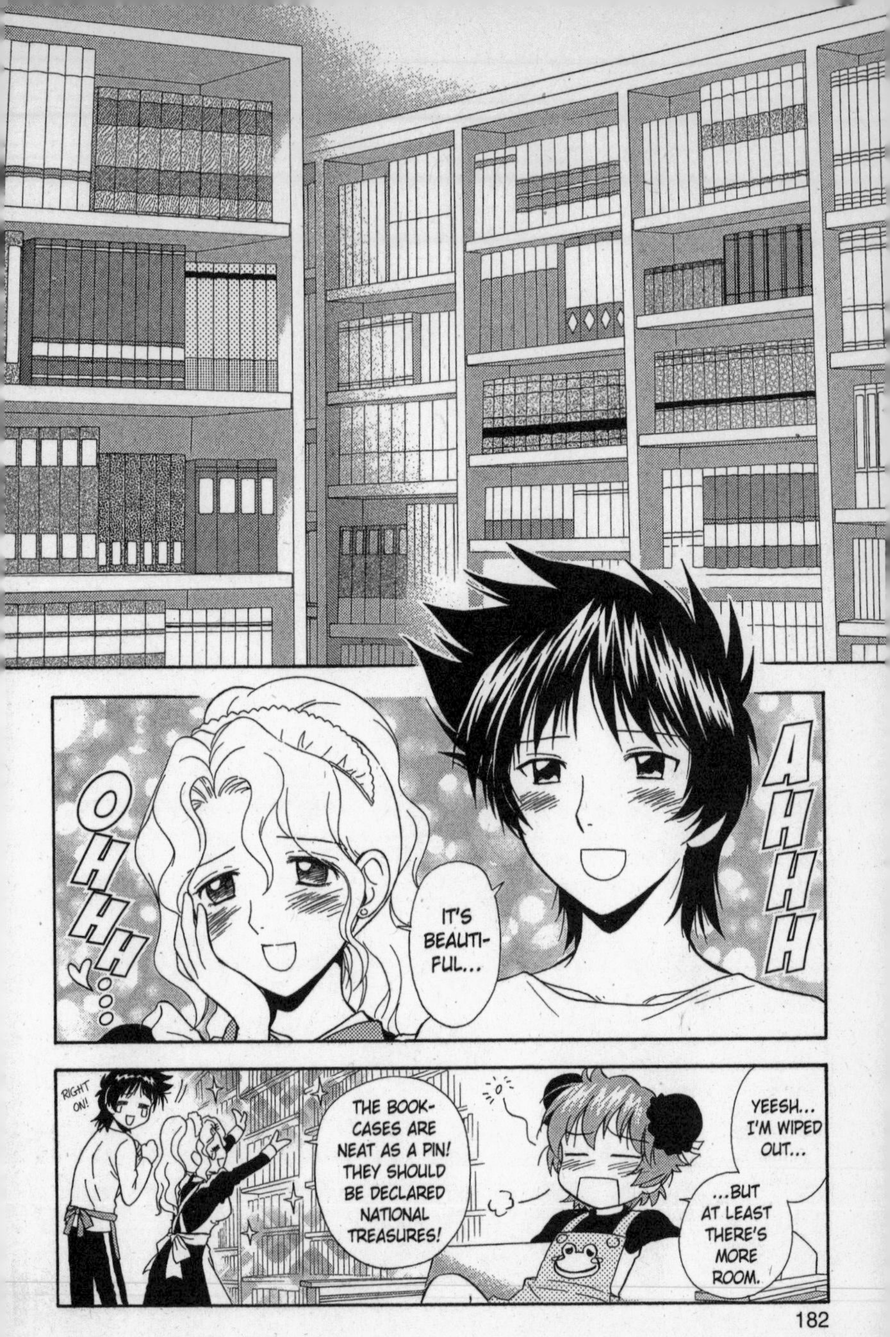
AHHHHH
IT'S BEAUTI-FUL...
OHHHH♡ooo
YEESH... I'M WIPED OUT...
...BUT AT LEAST THERE'S MORE ROOM.
THE BOOK-CASES ARE NEAT AS A PIN! THEY SHOULD BE DECLARED NATIONAL TREASURES!
RIGHT ON!

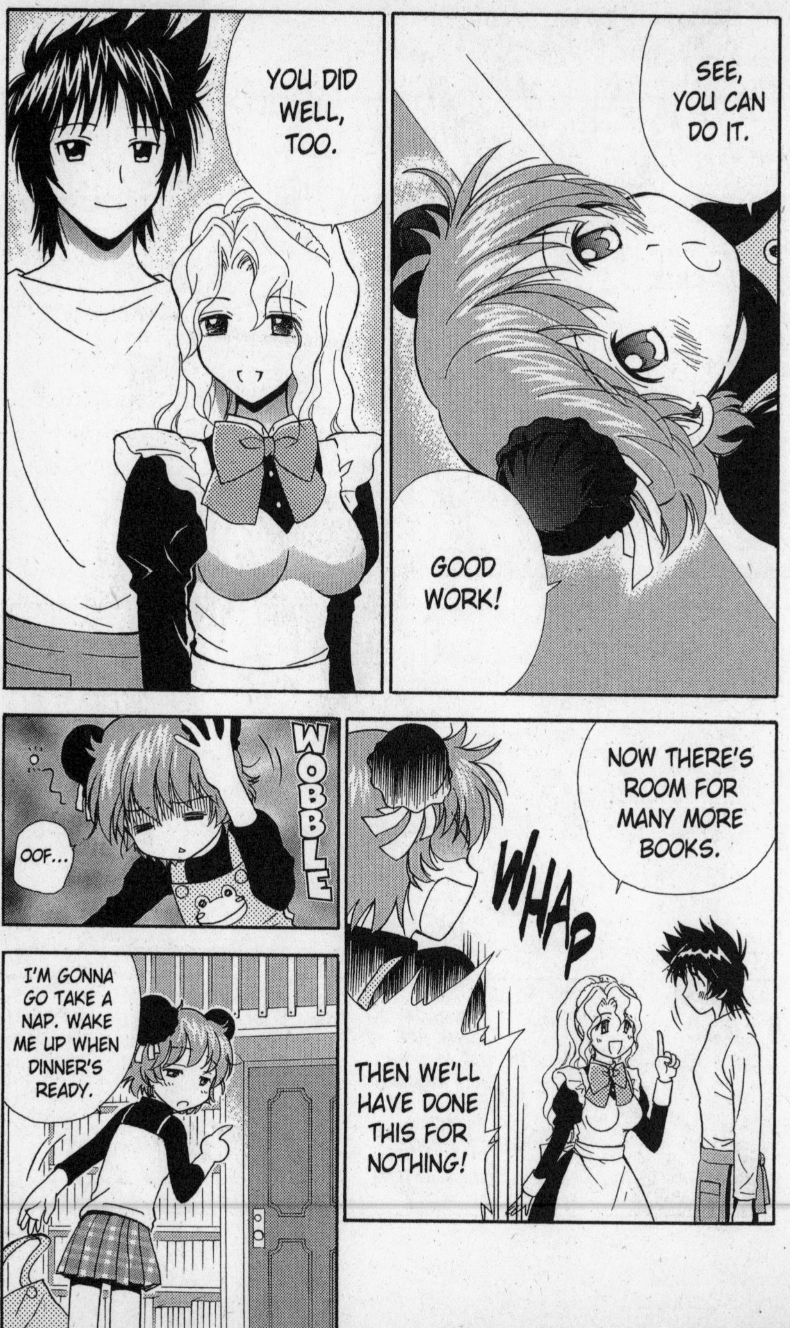
SEE, YOU CAN DO IT.
GOOD WORK!
YOU DID WELL, TOO.
NOW THERE'S ROOM FOR MANY MORE BOOKS.
WHAP
THEN WE'LL HAVE DONE THIS FOR NOTHING!
WOBBLE
OOF...
I'M GONNA GO TAKE A NAP. WAKE ME UP WHEN DINNER'S READY.

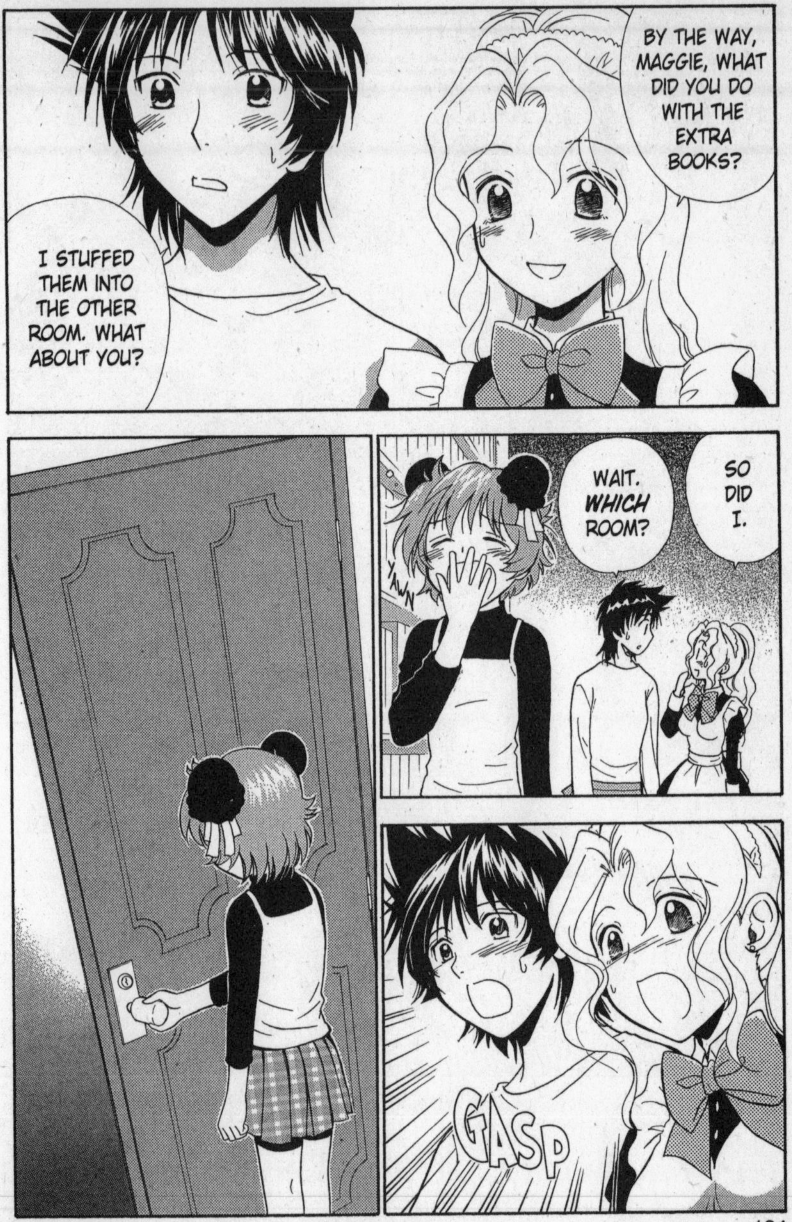
BY THE WAY, MAGGIE, WHAT DID YOU DO WITH THE EXTRA BOOKS?
I STUFFED THEM INTO THE OTHER ROOM. WHAT ABOUT YOU?
SO DID I.
WAIT. WHICH ROOM?
YAWN
GASP

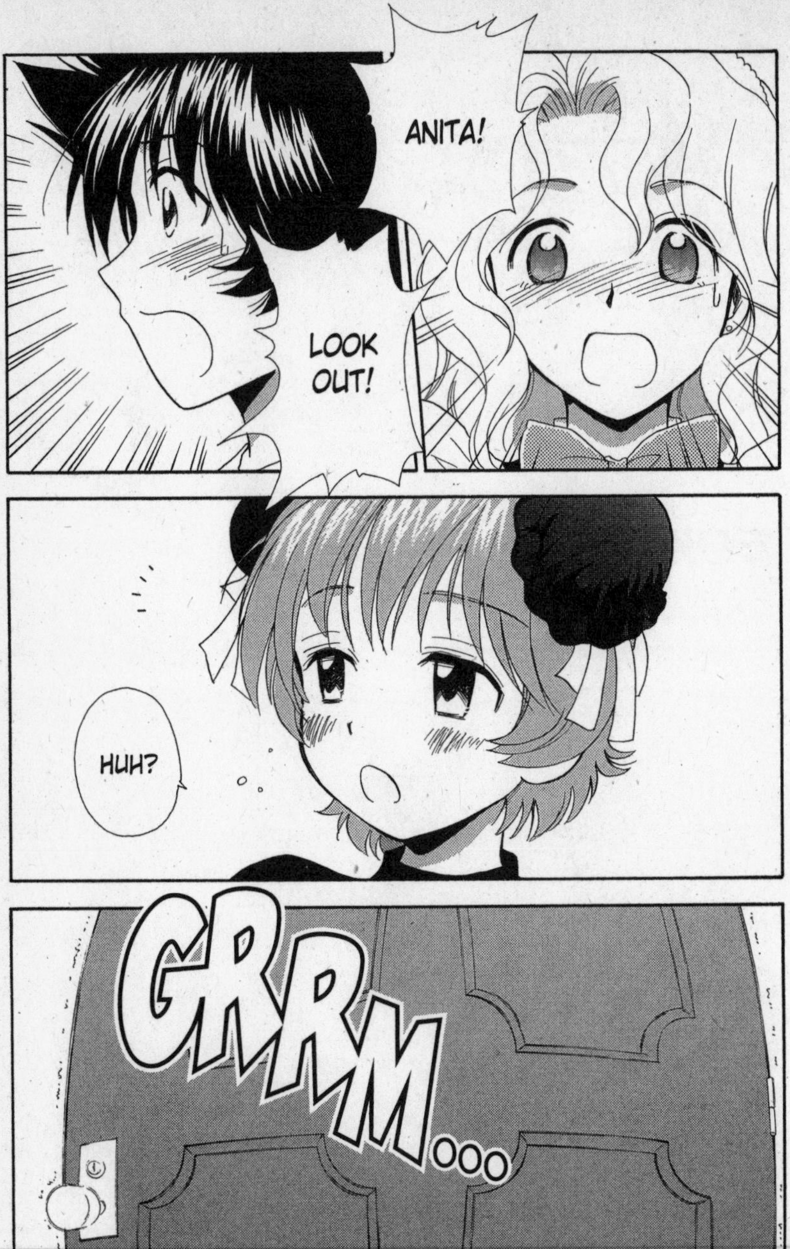
ANITA!
LOOK OUT!
HUH?
GRRM...

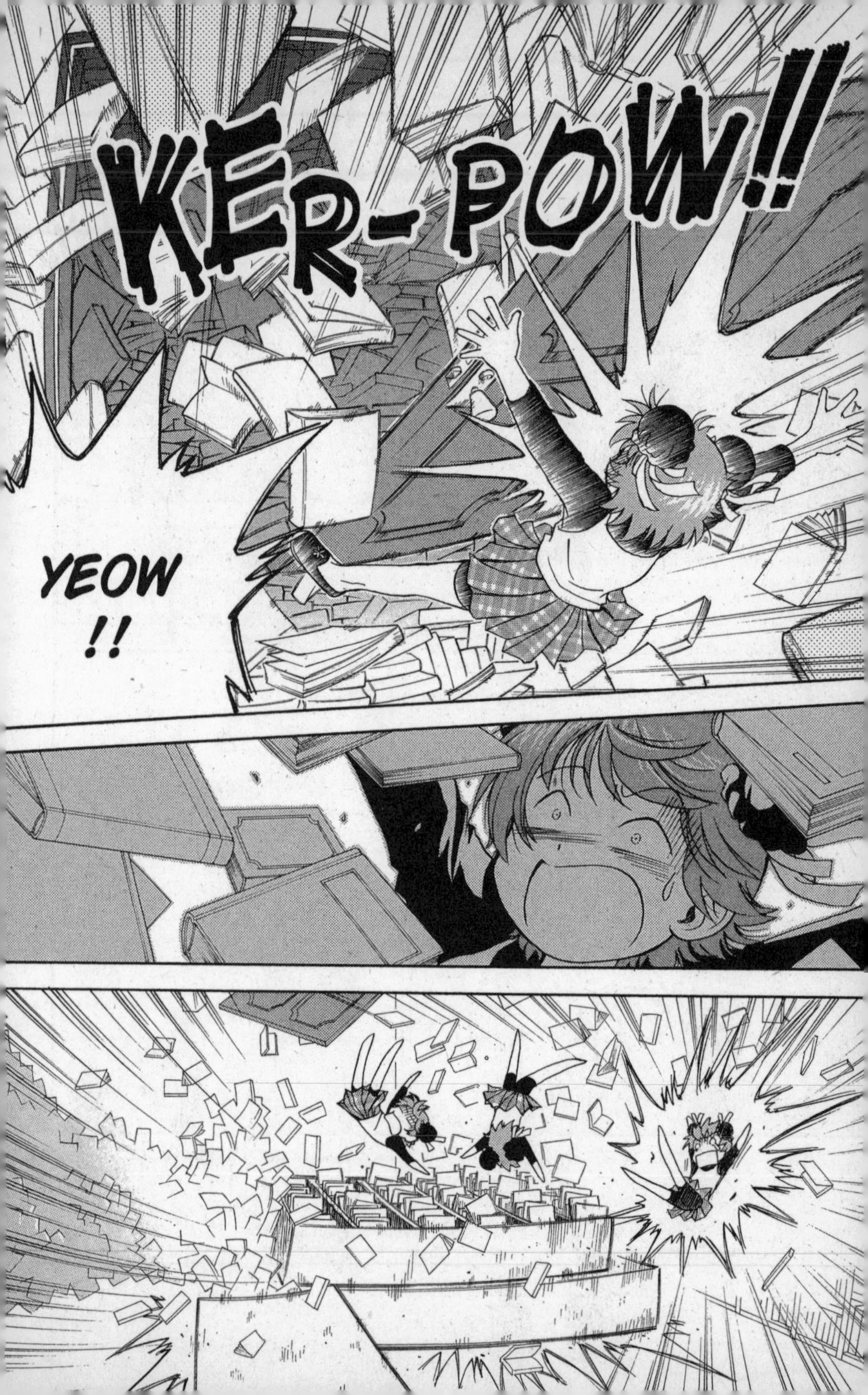
KER-POW!!
YEOW !!

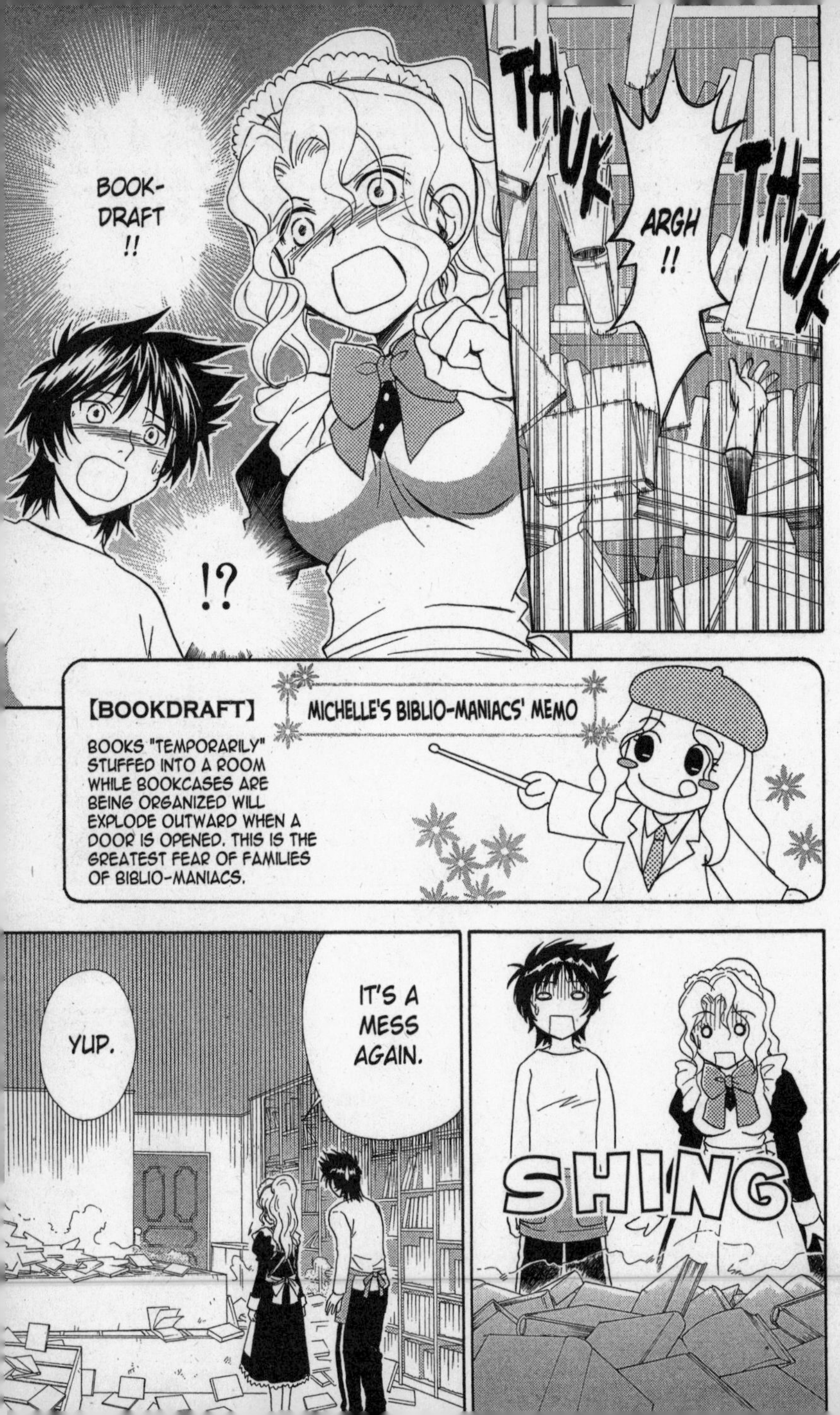
THUK
ARGH !!
THUK
BOOK-DRAFT !!
!?
【BOOKDRAFT】
MICHELLE'S BIBLIO-MANIACS' MEMO
BOOKS "TEMPORARILY" STUFFED INTO A ROOM WHILE BOOKCASES ARE BEING ORGANIZED WILL EXPLODE OUTWARD WHEN A DOOR IS OPENED. THIS IS THE GREATEST FEAR OF FAMILIES OF BIBLIO-MANIACS.
SHING
IT'S A MESS AGAIN.
YUP.

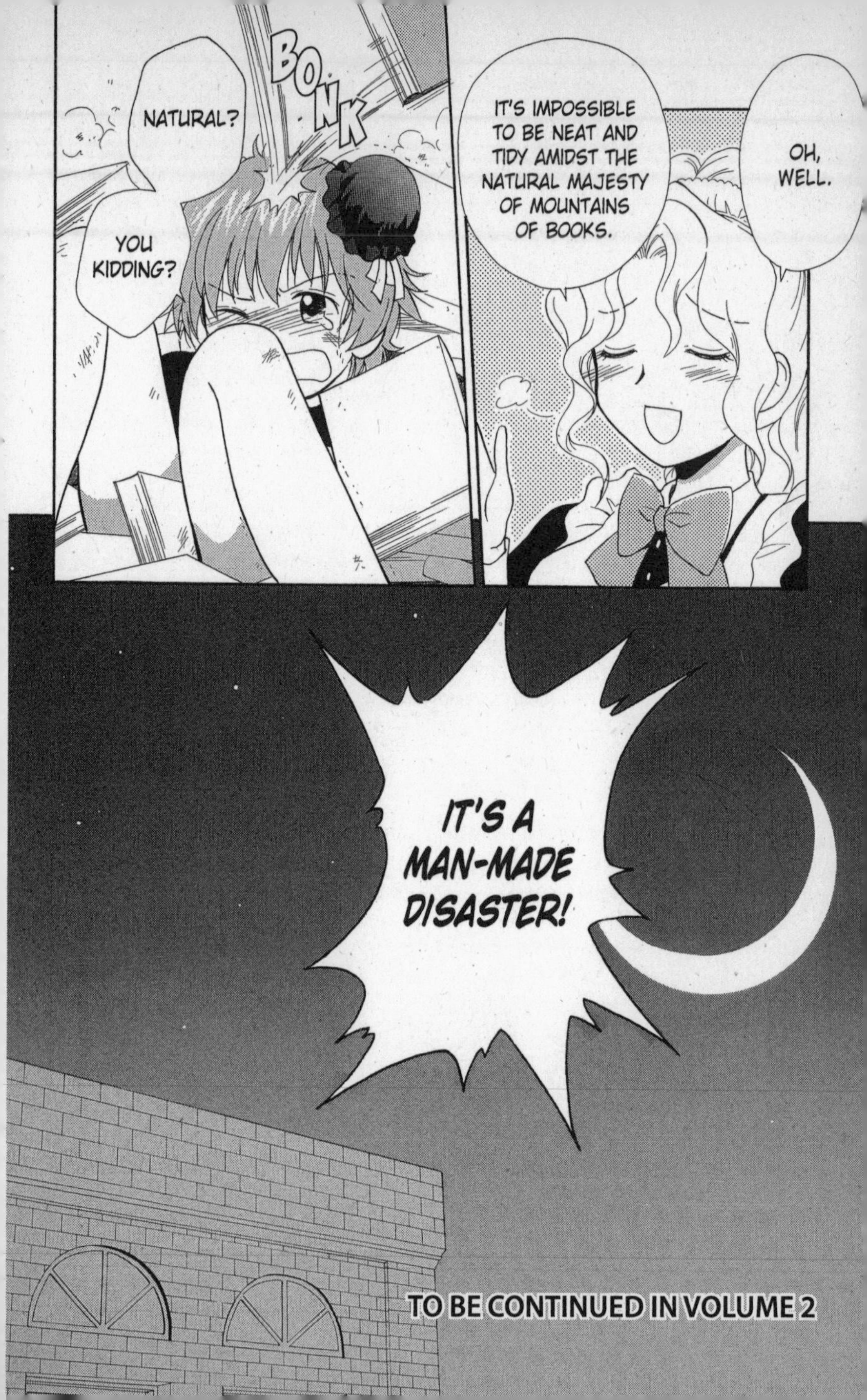
OH, WELL.
IT'S IMPOSSIBLE TO BE NEAT AND TIDY AMIDST THE NATURAL MAJESTY OF MOUNTAINS OF BOOKS.
BONK
NATURAL?
YOU KIDDING?
IT'S A MAN-MADE DISASTER!
TO BE CONTINUED IN VOLUME 2

STAFF

Manatee
Mikazu
Yasuyo Hirokane
Ai Udagawa

HELPING HANDS
Ichika Minami

EDITOR
Kunio Kondo

SPECIAL THANKS
MAGI

With gratitude and love to all
who read this, and to writer
Hideyuki Kurata for the
wonderful stories and the
encouragement you always
give me...

Ran Ayanaga

LOVELOVE CUE ♥

http://members.jcom.home.ne.jp/0724236901/

READER KING RETURNS!

HIDEYUKI KURATA × SHUTARO YAMADA × RAN AYANAGA + EDITOR-IN-CHIEF

THIS TIME, WE ALL HAVE SOME BOOZE IN US!

Volume One of Read or Dream is finally out! To mark this event, we've invited the artist of the original Read or Die manga, Shutaro Yamada, to a rap session with Read or Dream artist Ran Ayanaga and writer Hideyuki Kurata, along with their editor-in-chief. The torch passes from the old to the new R.O.D!

Editor: Nice work! Cheers!
All: Hic. Cheers...
Editor: Now, then... Please say something interesting.
Kurata: What's with the half-assed introduction?
Editor: We've been meeting for hours every month. You expect me to tell you what to say?
Kurata: Yeah, yeah, but Yamada and Miss Ayanaga barely know each other.
Yamada: I think we met once, when you started working on **Read or Dream.**
Ayanaga: That's right. I was very nervous that Mr. Yamada would be angry.
Kurata: Angry? Why?
Ayanaga: Mr. Yamada did such great work, and to bring my drawing style in...I worried that he'd think I'd destroyed his image of the series.
Kurata: Is that so, Yamada?
Yamada: That wasn't the case at all. In fact, I envied the warm and fuzzy atmosphere she created.
Ayanaga: Really?
Yamada: Yes.
Ayanaga: I can't believe it. I bet you're secretly upset!
Yamada: No. You have my word on it.
Editor: You've got to have more confidence, Miss Ayanaga!
Kurata: More importantly, Yamada, are you reading **Read or Dream?**
Yamada: Yes, of course...both the manga and Miss Ayanaga's website. (http://members.jcom.home.ne.jp/0724236901) I just read her blog entry from before her last deadline, and I thought she had a lot to learn if she was panicking when she had 10 days left.
Kurata: You check out the weirdest things.
Editor: Yes, well...don't tell her she doesn't have to worry with only 10 days to go. (The deadline's at the end of each month.)
Yamada: Come on...drink up!

The amount drunk thus far: Kurata -three bottles of beer; Ayanaga -one bottle of beer; Editor -three bottles of beer; Yamada -one bottle of beer and three glasses of oolong tea. Everyone's feeling good.

Kurata: Shall we begin the real interview?

Illustration : Shutaro Yamada

Editor: Shut up, you drunk!

Ayanaga: Ha ha ha ha...

Kurata: Eyeglasses are an encumbrance. I don't plan to use them needlessly. Keep an eye out.

Ayanaga: Ha ha ha…

The amount drunk thus far: Kurata, Editor -unknown; Yamada -one bottle of beer and about ten glasses of oolong tea. We don't know what's what.

Editor: Okay, let's tie it all up.

Ayanaga: What? Are we done? Let's keep drinking.

Kurata: I have another job after this.

Yamada: So? Why not go all the way? Just forget everything! Be a fool!

Kurata: Ignore that idiot. Please follow both the anime and manga versions of **Read or Dream**. I've got an ending in mind that will have you nodding your head. But I still don't know exactly how it will end…

Editor: That's it for now.

All: Please continue to give us your support.

The lesson for today:
 Yamada gets drunk on oolong tea.

1: **I Love Cats, After All** (Yappari Neko ga Suki) is a TV series that was adapted into a manga. **Aoichan Panic** is a shojo manga.

2: **Gwa2** was one of Ran Ayanaga's first manga. It appeared in **Ultra Jump**, the same magazine in which **Read or Dream** ran.

Yamada: Yes. I won't drink any more.

Editor: It's early. I don't have enough for an article yet, so please tell us something about **Read or Die**.

Yamada: It's already finished.

All: Is that all?

Kurata: Actually, the previous series was originally a one-shot that turned out to be very popular. I wanted to do something "heartwarming," but the main story ended up being too long. So it was decided that we'd do this series. This time, we decided to end each storyline in one chapter and give the whole thing a comic touch. I suppose you could say the previous piece was an action story, while this one is a fantasy. After all, the title is "Dream…"

Yamada: Good for you, Kurata. You explained it well.

Kurata: Listen…can you get drunk on oolong tea?

Ayanaga: But how did you decide on me? There are lots of other fine cartoonists.

Kurata: Well, we wanted something in the style of a cute manga like **I Love Cats, After All** or **Aoichan Panic**.¹ We looked for someone appropriate for that. The editor at the time showed us some pages from your manga **Gwa2**,² and we felt that this was the person we should go with.

Ayanaga: Then it didn't have to be me. Sob, sob.

Kurata: No one's saying that.

Ayanaga: Heh heh…

Kurata: You're starting to fall apart, Miss Ayanaga.

The amount drunk thus far: Kurata -six bottles of beer; Ayanaga -three bottles of beer; Editor -six bottles of beer; Yamada -one bottle of beer and five glasses of oolong tea. We're all quite drunk.

Editor: You were really into eyeglasses in **Read or Die**. Why aren't there any in this series? Aren't you interested in girls with glasses anymore?

Kurata: Huh? Let me ask you this. Will putting glasses on all girls make them prettier? That's rude to the girls and to the glasses. Only when glasses are worn by those who need them do they come alive!

Yamada: Glasses…Glasses…Glasses are great!!

Illustration : Ran Ayanaga

BONUS STORY:
CLEANING UP DEMONS
WITH ANITA THE CLEANER

ROTTINGHAM WAS A VERY LARGE CITY, BUSTLING WITH PEOPLE AND PRODUCTS FROM ALL OVER EUROPE. IN THIS TOWN, A GIRL COULD BE SEEN HOPPING FROM ROOFTOP TO ROOFTOP. SHE CARRIED A BROOM TO CLEAN CHIMNEYS. HER FACE WAS COVERED IN SOOT, AND BENEATH HER CAP YOU COULD SEE HER RED HAIR.

SHE WAS ANITA, THE TOWN'S BEST CHIMNEYSWEEP.

WHEN SHE WAS THROUGH CLEANING, THE CHIMNEYS SPARKLED INSIDE AND OUT. HER REPUTATION KEPT HER BUSY EVERY DAY FROM MORNING TO NIGHT.

ONE NIGHT, AS USUAL, ANITA WAS RESTING ON A ROOFTOP AFTER A LONG DAY OF WORK.

"OH, I'M SO TIRED..." AS SHE STRETCHED OUT, ANITA NOTICED A TINY, GLITTERING LIGHT FLYING TOWARD HER. "HUH? WHAT COULD THAT BE?"

STRAINING HER EYES, SHE SAW A LITTLE WINGED FAIRY. "WH-WHO ARE YOU?" STAMMERED ANITA.

THE FAIRY FLUTTERED HER WINGS. "MY NAME IS MICHELLE. I HAVE A FAVOR TO ASK OF YOU."

"WHO, ME?" ANITA SPOKE ROUGHLY. SHE HAD PICKED UP HER MANNERS FROM THE MALE CHIMNEYSWEEPS.

"LOOK, ANITA." MICHELLE POINTED TOWARD THE MANSION OF MAGGIE, THE TOWN'S WEALTHIEST RESIDENT. "I WANT YOU TO DO SOME CLEANING THERE."

"BUT THAT HOUSE DOESN'T HAVE CHIMNEYS."

MAGGIE WAS RICH, SO SHE USED GAS AND ELECTRICITY INSTEAD OF CHIMNEY FIRES.

"NO," SAID THE FAIRY. "WHAT I WANT YOU TO CLEAN IS MAGGIE'S HEART."

ACCORDING TO MICHELLE, MAGGIE HAD OPENED
A BOX LEFT TO HER BY HER GRANDFATHER, AND
WAS POSSESSED BY A DEMON THAT HAD BEEN
LOCKED INSIDE. MICHELLE, WHO HAD BEEN
WATCHING OVER MAGGIE'S HOME, HAD LEFT THE
MANSION TO LOOK FOR HELP. "IF WE DON'T DO
SOMETHING," SHE SAID, "MAGGIE WILL BE
OVERCOME BY EVIL!"

"BUT I CAN'T GET RID OF DEMONS," SAID ANITA.

"YES, YOU CAN, AS LONG AS YOUR HEART IS
PURE. AND I'LL ADD FAIRY POWER TO YOUR
BROOM."

AS SOON AS MICHELLE SPOKE, ANITA'S BROOM
STARTED TO SPARKLE.

"OH, IT'S SO BRIGHT!"

"NOW COME WITH ME!"

"WELL...OKAY!"

ANITA JUMPED UPON HER SPARKLING BROOM
AND HEADED FOR MAGGIE'S MANSION WITH
MICHELLE.

TO BE CONTINUED...

R.O.D

READ OR DREAM

We are Paper Sisters Detective Company

VIZ Media Edition
Vol. 1

STORY BY HIDEYUKI KURATA
ART BY RAN AYANAGA

Translation/JN Productions
Touch-up Art & Lettering/Mark McMurray
Design/Amy Martin
Editor/Shaenon K. Garrity

Managing Editor/Annette Roman
Editorial Director/Elizabeth Kawasaki
Editor in Chief/Alvin Lu
Sr. Director of Acquisitions/Rika Inouye
Sr. VP of Marketing/Liza Coppola
Exec. VP of Sales & Marketing/John Easum
Publisher/Hyoe Narita

R.O.D -READ OR DREAM- © 2002 by Hideyuki Kurata (Studio Orphee)·Aniplex, Ran Ayanaga. All rights reserved. First published in Japan in 2002 by SHUEISHA Inc., Tokyo. English translation rights in the United States of America and Canada arranged by SHUEISHA Inc. The stories, characters and incidents mentioned in this publication are entirely fictional.

Printed in the U.S.A.

Published by VIZ Media, LLC
P.O. Box 77010
San Francisco, CA 94107

10 9 8 7 6 5 4 3 2 1
First printing, November 2006

store.viz.com

www.viz.com

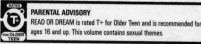

PARENTAL ADVISORY
READ OR DREAM is rated T+ for Older Teen and is recommended for ages 16 and up. This volume contains sexual themes.

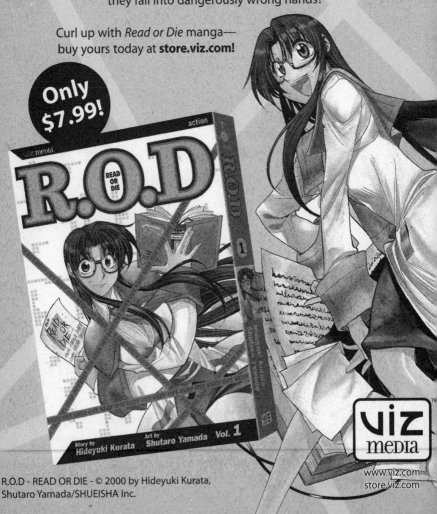

Fullmetal Alchemist Profiles

Get the background story and world history of the manga, plus:

- Character bios
- New, original artwork
- Interview with creator Hiromu Arakawa
- Bonus manga episode only available in this book

Fullmetal Alchemist Anime Profiles

Stay on top of your favorite episodes and characters with:

- Actual cel artwork from the TV series
- Summaries of all 51 TV episodes
- Definitive cast biographies
- Exclusive poster for your wall

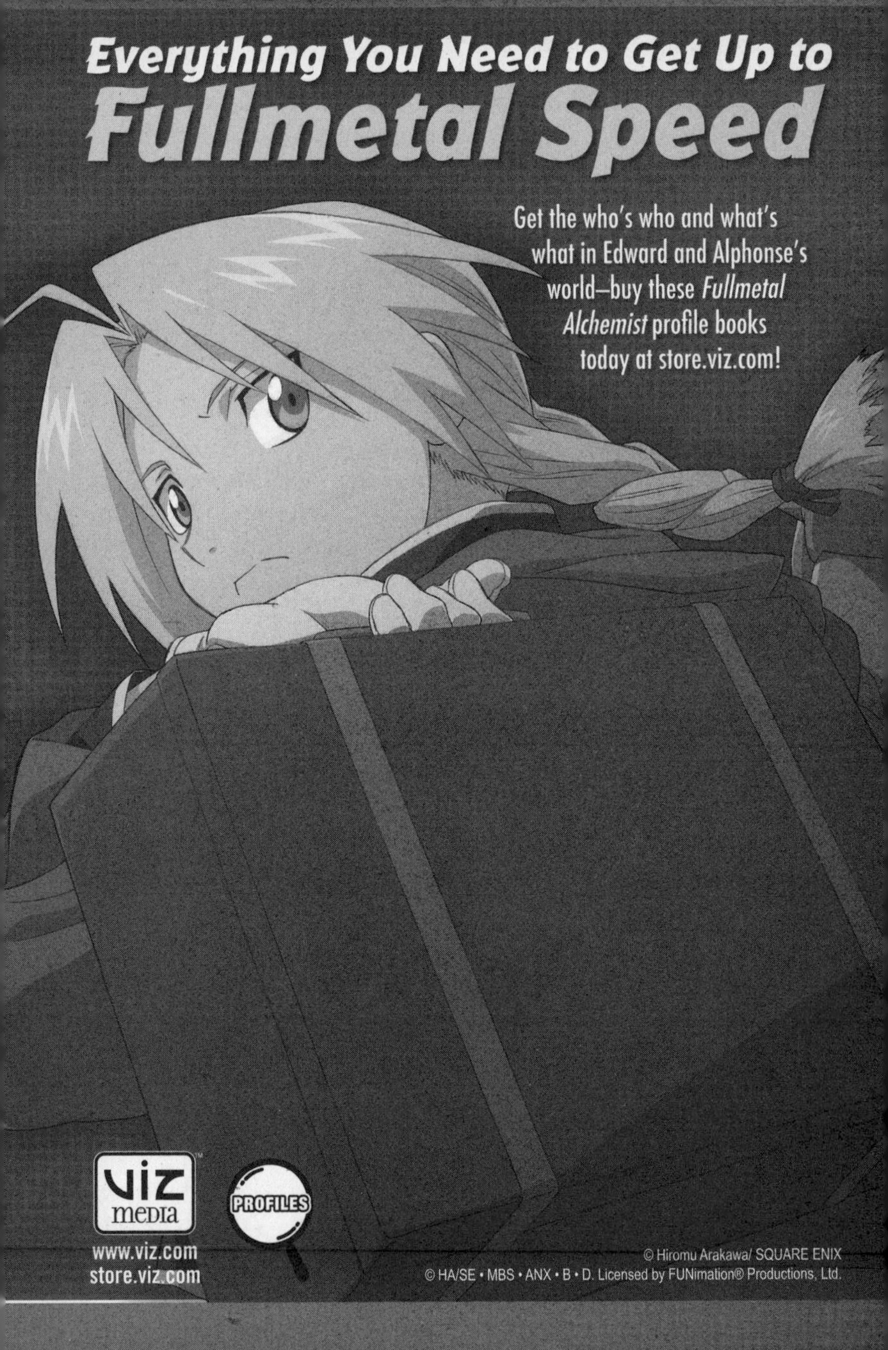
Everything You Need to Get Up to
Fullmetal Speed
Get the who's who and what's what in Edward and Alphonse's world—buy these *Fullmetal Alchemist* profile books today at store.viz.com!
VIZ media
PROFILES
www.viz.com
store.viz.com
© Hiromu Arakawa/ SQUARE ENIX
© HA/SE • MBS • ANX • B • D. Licensed by FUNimation® Productions, Ltd.

LOVE MANGA? LET US KNOW!

☐ Please do NOT send me information about VIZ Media products, news and events, special offers, or other information.

☐ Please do NOT send me information from VIZ Media's trusted business partners.

Name: _____

Address: _____

City: _____ **State:** _____ **Zip:** _____

E-mail: _____

☐ Male ☐ Female **Date of Birth (mm/dd/yyyy):** ___ / ___ / ___ (Under 13? Parental consent required)

What race/ethnicity do you consider yourself? (check all that apply)

☐ White/Caucasian ☐ Black/African American ☐ Hispanic/Latino

☐ Asian/Pacific Islander ☐ Native American/Alaskan Native ☐ Other: _____

What VIZ Media title(s) did you purchase? (indicate title(s) purchased) _____

_____

What other VIZ Media titles do you own? _____

_____

Reason for purchase: (check all that apply)

☐ Special offer ☐ Favorite title / author / artist / genre

☐ Gift ☐ Recommendation ☐ Collection

☐ Read excerpt in VIZ Media manga sampler ☐ Other _____

Where did you make your purchase? (please check one)

☐ Comic store ☐ Bookstore ☐ Grocery Store

☐ Convention ☐ Newsstand ☐ Video Game Store

☐ Online (site: _____) ☐ Other _____

How many manga titles have you purchased in the last year? How many were VIZ Media titles?
(please check one from each column)

MANGA	VIZ Media
☐ None	☐ None
☐ 1 – 4	☐ 1 – 4
☐ 5 – 10	☐ 5 – 10
☐ 11+	☐ 11+

How much influence do special promotions and gifts-with-purchase have on the titles you buy?
(please circle, with 5 being great influence and 1 being none)

1 2 3 4 5

Do you purchase every volume of your favorite series?

☐ Yes! Gotta have 'em as my own ☐ No. Please explain: ______________________

What kind of manga storylines do you most enjoy? **(check all that apply)**

☐ Action / Adventure	☐ Science Fiction	☐ Horror
☐ Comedy	☐ Romance (shojo)	☐ Fantasy (shojo)
☐ Fighting	☐ Sports	☐ Historical
☐ Artistic / Alternative	☐ Other ______________	

If you watch the anime or play a video or TCG game from a series, how likely are you to buy the manga? **(please circle, with 5 being very likely and 1 being unlikely)**

1 2 3 4 5

If unlikely, please explain: ______________________

Who are your favorite authors / artists? ______________________

____

What titles would like you translated and sold in English? ______________________

____

THANK YOU! Please send the completed form to:

NJW Research
42 Catharine Street
Poughkeepsie, NY 12601

Your privacy is very important to us. All information provided will be used for internal purposes only and will not be sold or otherwise divulged.